D1290114

BANNED

CONTROVERSIAL LITERATURE AND POLITICAL CONTROL IN BRITISH INDIA 1907–1947

UNIVERSITY OF MISSOURI STUDIES LXI

BANNED
CONTROVERSIAL LITERATURE AND POLITICAL CONTROL IN BRITISH INDIA
1907-1947

N. Gerald Barrier

University of Missouri Press

ISBN 0–8262–0159–8

Library of Congress Catalog Card Number 73–92241
Printed and bound in the United States of America
University of Missouri Press, Columbia, Missouri 65201

To Sourin Roy
Deputy Director
National Archives of India (Retired)
Archivist, Scholar, and Friend of Scholars

PREFACE

The relationship between government and the press lies at the heart of the political process. Perhaps inevitably, government Officials and journalists throughout the world often clash over the nature of information passed on to the public. Sometimes their struggles produce social or legal safeguards to freedom of expression; at other times, the consequences include censorship and banning of publications judged dangerous to the "national interest," "security," or "human decency."

Much has been written on specific episodes in the history of the press or about the evolution of publishers' freedom in countries such as England, the United States, and Nazi Germany. The extension of national attitudes and legal norms from the homeland to colonial areas, however, has received far less attention. British rule in India is a case in point. By the nineteenth century, law and public opinion in England created an atmosphere conducive to virtually free exchange of opinion and news. What happened when Englishmen in India or Indians themselves attempted to exercise a similar degree of printed expression? The existing accounts of press liberty in the Indian context do not present a satisfactory answer. Historians usually begin their studies in the late 1700s, focus on now well-known incidents of censorship and imprisonment during the next century, and conclude with a short sketch, if any, on post-1900 developments.[1] Lack of analysis of the latter period is particularly disturbing because the confrontation between ruler (the *raj*) and ruled after 1900 brought into focus the conflict between cherished British ideological traditions and the demands of control over a non-Western population. Censorship, banning, and other varieties of official interference with freedom of the press also constitute key but little-known elements in India's struggle for independence.

This examination of government–press interaction, 1907–1947, is intended primarily as a contribution to our understanding of political developments within the British Empire in India. Although the issues and details relate to one region, it is anticipated that the study will be useful for a broader audience. The dilemmas that confronted colonial bureaucrats and Indian pub-

1. Examples include the following: J. Natarajan, *History of Indian Journalism*; S. P. Sen, ed., *The Indian Press*; Sushila Agarawal, *Press, Public Opinion and Government in India*; Mohit Moitra, *A History of Indian Journalism*.

licists were not unique. How and why the British made certain decisions, and the results of those decisions, should have implications for anyone who is concerned with other dimensions of freedom of the press in any part of the world. The shifting rationale for interference with printed opinion and the mechanisms developed for exercising that control have universal implications.

Research on this topic has passed through several stages. In 1965, while exploring the politics of one region (Punjab), I continually came upon mystifying references in Government of India Home proceedings to proscription and banning. I had seen occasional references to banned works in the standard political surveys, but the extent of material startled me. As much as 10 per cent of an annual index would be devoted to listing individual titles seized by the British. Pursuit of the subject might have been postponed or neglected except for an accident: I purchased two sets of tracts in Lahore and London that, on examination, turned out to be essentially banned (proscribed) writings. Simultaneously, I discovered that the India Office and the British Museum had preserved more extensive collections. No one had utilized the publications because they had been locked away since 1947. The existence of a valuable, untapped resource on recent Indian history led me in two directions. I began handlisting the surviving material and then moved back into the records to piece together why and how works were seized.

My research has received support from various sources. Grants from the National Endowment for the Humanities, the American Institute of Indian Studies, the American Council of Learned Societies, the Social Science Research Council, and the Research Council of the University of Missouri–Columbia supported research and writing. My assistants, Ashok Mahindroo and Sukhwant Singh (Devinder), helped at the early stages. Satya Pal Nirash assisted in preparing descriptions of vernacular items and labored long in teaching me Panjabi. Prem Singh joined me in an intense foray into the London collections during the summer of 1971. The India Office Library and Records, the British Museum, and the National Archives of India extended permission to study in their collections. At the India Office, Miss E. M. Dimes, Mrs. Usha Tripathi, Miss Mary Lloyd, Miss J. R. Watson, Mrs. Valerie Weston, Dr. Anthony Domahiddy, and Mr. Martin Moir gave particular assistance and encouragement. Mr. J. H. Eisenegger, Dr. G. E. Marrison, and Mr. Peter Stocks contributed in many ways at the British Museum. The friendship and advice of Miss Dhan Keswani, Mr. R. C. Gupta, and Mr. Sourin Roy at the National Archives of India, New Delhi, made possible systematic research in British proceedings. Without the commitment of the Deputy Director of the Archives, Sourin Roy, to open access to records and his encouragement at critical points in my work, this book could not have been written. Every Western and Indian scholar working in the National Archives owes Sourin Roy a personal and professional debt for refusing to let red tape and fear of the unknown stand in the way of legitimate research. I dedicate this volume to him.

The book has benefited from discussion with scholars and friends. P. C. Joshi encouraged my study and gave helpful criticism. Seminars at the Jawaharlal Nehru University, the University of Chicago, and the University of Texas–Austin generated new approaches. Professors Emily Brown (University of Northern Iowa), Barbara Ramusack (University of Cincinnati), Bruce Graham (University of Sussex), Kenneth Jones (Kansas State University), Peter Reeves (University of Sussex), and Paul Wallace (University of Missouri–Columbia) read parts or all of earlier versions of the manuscript. Their comments have clarified my thinking and corrected grievous errors. Despite the generous contributions of many colleagues, however, I assume full responsibility for mistakes, omissions, and interpretations.

N. G. B.
Columbia, Missouri
December, 1973

CONTENTS

Abbreviations

BM— British Museum
C.C.— Chelmsford Collection
CRL— Center for Research Libraries, Chicago
The depository for the South Asia Microform Project
CRP— Crown Representative Papers
GI— Government of India
GIPOL— Government of India Home Political Proceedings
IOL— India Office Library Collection
IOR— India Office Records Collection
J&P— Judicial and Public Department Proceedings, IOL
M.C.— Minto Collection
NAI— National Archives of India Library Collection
PG— Punjab Government
PIB— Proscribed Indian Books, British Museum Collection
R.A.— Readily available in many libraries
R&L— Records and Library Department Proceedings (1884–1912), IOR
R&R— Registry and Record Department Proceedings (1913–1948), IOR
UP— United Provinces

Part One

THE POLITICS OF PROSCRIPTION

Chapter 1

GOVERNMENT, POLITICS, AND THE PRESS IN IMPERIAL BRITISH INDIA

The rationale for British Empire in India varied with time and personality, but a persistent theme runs through the period of colonial rule. Maintenance of order and with it survival of the bureaucracy rested on the government's ability to operate within a complex and expanding political system. The British stood at the apex of the system, periodically attempting to develop the means and tactics to implement political goals. High on the list of imperial priorities was retention of decisionmaking and policy functions. This control in turn necessitated satisfactory handling of pressures and expectations from numerous sources.

Decisions on allocation of resources had to be made in light of inputs from the publics of India and England, Parliament, political parties, and bureaucrats. These demands were met both in formal structures (particularly legislative councils) and in daily decisions at each administrative level. Under most circumstances, the Government of India infrequently used force to deal with demands or with direct challenges in the form of violence and revolutionary activity. The foreign-dominated bureaucracy learned to compromise and to manipulate patronage so as to maintain support groups and isolate opponents.

The functioning of government involved coordination within the bureaucratic chain stretching from Whitehall to the district office. In London, the Secretary of State and his advisory Indian Council exercised ultimate supervision of Indian affairs, but the Government of India (headed by the Governor General and Executive Council) formulated most all-India policies in cooperation with home authorities and had the primary responsibility for implementation of those policies. The central government's immediate subordinates, the "local governments" (presidency and provincial administrative units) dealt with issues directly affecting their domains. Similarly, the thousand or so Indian Civil Service officers in charge of districts made localized decisions. Secretariats tended to carry on the bulk of routine business at each of the three top administrative tiers.

This vast bureaucracy depended on an efficient system of communication and intelligence. Orders flowed downward through formal channels (dispatches and circulars), but the implementation of policy required further communication, often through less formal means such as "demi-official" correspondence and personal contact. Response from below was equally vital to the daily operation of government. Without detailed information on the attitudes and activities of Indians (or of Parliament for that matter), the colonial administrators lacked sufficient evidence on which to assess policy or to base new decisions.[1]

The emergence of an Indian publications industry complicated the political life of the British rulers. Books and journals could be valuable sources of information if channeled into an intelligence network; however, their appearance also raised questions of surveillance and control of mass media. During the nineteenth century, the government was ambivalent about whether and how to supervise the circulation of ideas within Indian society. Caught between a tradition that favored a free press and anxiety over all but the most innocuous criticism, the British swung back and forth from strict controls to virtual freedom of expression. Efforts at strict control usually resulted from specific episodes or from perennial concerns, such as threats of widespread violence and communal tension. In 1780, for example, Warren Hastings reacted to personal attacks in J. A. Hickey's *Bengal Gazette* by prosecuting the publisher and banning the paper from the mails. Select censorship and other restraints of the press accumulated until Charles Metcalfe's "liberation" of printed opinion in 1835. The 1857 Mutiny evoked a renewal of controls in the form of precensorship and jail sentences for recalcitrant editors, followed by a relaxing of those controls until 1878, when a new "gagging act" sought to limit vernacular papers' commentary on official policy. Governor General Ripon repealed the legislation three years later, however, in a gesture of liberality. The deterioration of Hindu–Muslim relations in the 1890s fostered fresh debate on the propriety of press restrictions, but before concrete steps could be taken, the immediate danger of massive religious conflict diminished. Although annoyed by the press and prepared to prosecute individuals for overstepping the bounds of acceptable

1. The standard references on the structure of government in post-Mutiny India include volumes of the *Cambridge History of India* and a recent study by B. B. Misra, *The Administrative History of British India, 1834–1947* (New York: Oxford Press, 1971). The overview of the process of governance illustrated throughout this study has been influenced by the work of David Easton, Gabriel A. Almond, and Lucian W. Pye.

criticism, the Government of India minimized overt interference with newspapers, books and tracts.[2]

A century of bureaucratic interest in the content of Indian publications left a legacy of laws and institutions designed to watch and, as necessary, to control the press. Act XXV of 1867, "for the regulation of printing presses and newspapers, for the preservation of copies of books printed in British India, and the registration of such books," became the legal basis for a surveillance system. The legislation facilitated identification of those responsible for a given work. From 1867 onward, books and newspapers were required to bear the names of authors, printers, and publishers. Moreover, the act set up mechanisms whereby Indian officials and the India Office could be informed about what was being printed. Copies of printed matter had to be delivered promptly to a designated representative of local government, who then prepared a quarterly catalogue of books and periodicals. The following information was included in the reports: title and content of the title page (with translation into English if vernacular), language, author, editor or translator, subject, names and place of printers and publishers, date, pagination, size, edition, number of copies, price, and copyright details. The government circulated the lists among officers and sent copies to the Secretary of State.[3]

The effort to construct a standardized registration system proved only partially successful. Reports eventually came to resemble each other because the central government instructed local authorities to follow a catalogue model suggested by Madras, but the apparatus for implementing the 1867 act differed widely. In some provinces, directors of public instruction registered books and prepared the catalogues, in others, special press officers. Regularity, accuracy, and comprehensiveness depended on the background of the registrars.[4]

A second channel for observation of the press grew up alongside the one relating to the registration act. Because of questions in the House of Commons and its own need for information on press opinion, the central secretariat decided that local governments should review the content of vernacular newspapers. The

2. Based on a précis relating to the history of British policy toward the Indian press, GIPOL July 1907, 178–180A. Useful surveys are in J. Natarajan, *History of Indian Journalism*, pp. 1–121; S. P. Sen, ed., *The Indian Press*, pp. 1–37.

3. Background in N. G. Barrier, "South Asia in Vernacular Publications," *The Journal of Asian Studies*, 27:4 (August 1969), 803–10. Also, for discussion and key cases, G. K. Roy, *Law Relating to Press and Sedition* (1922), pp. 70–87.

4. Notes and correspondence in GI Public, September 24, 1870, 23–30A. Also noting in GIPOL January 1912, 41–49A.

resulting confidential documents circulated among I.C.S. officers for intelligence purposes. Prepared annually, the reports consisted of analyses of the tone of the press and a statement with background on each paper. Moreover, provincial administrations regularly abstracted and translated articles from non-English journals. The confidential selections kept the government informed as to Indian opinion and at the same time supplied evidence for possible warnings or prosecution.[5]

Local governments had the primary function of investigating and collecting data on Indian literary trends. The Government of India served as a nerve center, monitoring reports, attempting to synthesize intelligence from information-gathering agencies, and circulating memoranda to subordinates and the India Office. A "Special Branch" of the Imperial Thagi and Dakaiti Department (the central police department) handled this intelligence operation in conjunction with local police units.[6]

Legislation affecting the content of publications accompanied the evolving report system. Several amendments to the Indian Penal Code extended bureaucratic authority over the press. In 1870, an apparent threat from Muslim fanatics led to the passage of Section 124A, a "sedition" clause aimed generally at actions which caused "disaffection." Except for judicial and executive discussion over what "disaffection" actually meant, the law concerned with sedition did not change until 1898, when once again responding to a crisis (disturbances in Bombay), the Government of India enacted a stronger measure. Act IV of 1898 attempted to amplify the nature of sedition, and in doing so, widened the scope for prosecution. Section 124A read as follows:

> Whoever by words, either spoken or written, or by signs, or by visible representation, or otherwise, brings or attempts to bring into hatred or contempt, or excites or attempts to excite disaffection towards Her Majesty, or the Government established by law in British India shall be punished. . . . Explanation 1. The expression "disaffection" includes disloyalty and all feelings of enmity.[7]

The act also introduced Section 153A, making punishable writings or speeches inciting "class hatred." A final amendment changed Section 505, which covered statements creating public mischief. Previously, the government had to prove that the author or editor printed rumors in the knowledge that they were false.

5. Background in N. G. Barrier and Paul Wallace, *The Punjab Press, 1880–1905*, pp. 3–5.

6. Secretariat noting in GIPOL May 1908, 1A.

7. Roy, *Law* (1922), p. 104. A discussion of the circumstances surrounding the various laws is in secretariat noting, GIPOL July 1907, 178–180A.

The revised section made this proof unnecessary, and in effect shifted the burden of demonstrating intent from prosecution to defense.[8]

These amendments focused on punishment as a deterrent to controversial writings. A simultaneous alteration of the Criminal Procedure Code equipped the British with extended preventive powers. Act V of 1898 permitted magistrates to execute bonds for good behavior in cases in which individuals disseminated seditious matter (124A), publications affecting class enmity (153A), or threats to the judiciary.[9]

The Indian government was invested with additional sanctions that were useful in checking circulation of printed matter. Modeled on English law, the 1889 Official Secrets Act prohibited unauthorized entry into government offices, divulgence of confidential information, and publication of such material. Section 26 of the Indian Post Office Act empowered the Governor General in Council to order interception of postal articles, and Section 19 of the 1878 Sea Customs Act extended similar authority to intercept items imported into India.[10]

The British experimented with techniques for influencing the press other than coercive or preventive legislation. Informal or formal warnings were employed occasionally.[11] Another approach involved official news releases and indirect management of the press. In 1864, for example, the Indian government established an editors' room where copies of correspondence and other documents were given to "friendly" press representatives. The scheme lapsed in 1870 because of disuse, to be succeeded in 1877 by appointment of a press officer (later a press commissioner) who served as an intermediary between officialdom and newspapermen. Suspicion among editors and alarm over interference in news reporting led to the demise of that office by 1880. The government did continue to send copies of gazettes and communiqués to editors known for their loyalty to the *raj*. Also considered were plans to subsidize newspapers through subscriptions, placement of government notifications, and advertisements. For example, the Punjab government purchased several hundred copies of an English paper in order to direct the Punjab press toward "safe" journalistic opinion. In Etawah, United Provinces, an official who later helped found the Indian National Congress, A. O. Hume, went so far as to edit a pro-British paper, the Urdu *Peoples*

8. Roy, *Law* (1922), pp. 106–8.
9. Roy, *Law* (1922), p. 129.
10. For information on the postal and customs law, documents in GIPOL June 1909, 132–134A.
11. Survey on experiments in a printed précis, GIPOL May 1911, 15D; Sen, *Indian Press*, pp. 1–37.

Friend.[12] The British, at the extreme of their efforts to control the press, discussed setting up papers to combat lies and to clear up misunderstandings but actually did little in the way of propaganda.

Throughout the nineteenth century, the Government of India preferred a low-key policy of informal influence over the press instead of direct subsidies and persistent application of penalties. The dreaded "gagging act" was never used, and only a handful of prosecutions under Sections 124A and 153A occurred between 1870 and 1900.[13] The bureaucracy remained concerned with what Indians printed, particularly in times of crisis such as the Mutiny or a disturbance on the frontier, but the limited scope of Indian journalism and the general reluctance of editors seriously to confront British authority did not seem to justify legislating punitive measures. By the end of 1905, however, the situation had changed dramatically.

The Viceroyalty of Lord Curzon, 1898–1905, brought to prominence political trends that had been developing since mid-century. One factor was the emergence of regional and communal political groupings that criticized and put pressure on the bureaucracy. At first working within accepted constitutional channels, a segment of these politicians became disillusioned with reliance on petitions and British good will. They accordingly explored new methods and strategies so as to inject themselves more fully into official decisionmaking. A natural offshoot of these concerns was a move toward mass politicizing, as exemplified by Bal Gangadhar Tilak's popular festivals in Maharashtra and later his labor campaign in Bombay. Another was a tendency to decry the Indian National Congress as an effective vehicle for political change. Indians looked to foreign countries for models of successful politics or back to their own cultural heritage for inspiration and legitimacy. Accumulated official injustice, the example of the Japanese and Italian peoples' efforts to build their nations, the imperial attitudes and policies personified by Lord Curzon—all reinforced a new militancy and sense of nationalist mission. The organizations reflecting these trends did little to disguise their

12. Précis, GIPOL May 1911, 15D. In the Punjab, the pro-British activities of *The Punjab Patriot* (subsidized by the government) created great tension. On such experiments, see GIPOL July 1909, 62A.

13. Statistics from Stuart note (March 9, 1907) and Adamson note (February 24, 1907), GIPOL July 1907, 178–180A. A few items judged dangerous on specific issues, such as Pan-Islam, were denied entry to India. Background on two Arabic works and a paper from Chandernagore is in *General Rules and Orders Made Under Enactments in Force in British India*, II, 72–74.

ultimate goals: The foreign bureaucracy must be watched, censored, and eventually forced to withdraw; colonial domination must give way to self-rule.[14]

Indian literature became a major vehicle for communicating and stimulating the new political ideology. Among other means, mass politics involved using printed matter to affect a widened audience. By 1905, the potential for developing this means existed throughout the subcontinent. Hundreds of printing presses regularly turned out books and pamphlets. An increasing number of these were polemic in tone and focused on politics. The relative cheapness of printing also reinforced a trend toward using publications as a means for political proselytization. At a cost of less than 25 Rupees, a propagandist could publish a 16-page tract for distribution to the literate or to be read aloud to villagers.[15]

Journalism provided an even more effective alternative for dissemination of appeal and ideology. The Indian periodical industry had increased markedly since its early beginnings in the eighteenth century. In 1905, for example, 1,359 newspapers and journals reached an estimated 2 million subscribers.[16] As indicated by the table on page 10, every region had a network of periodicals published both in English and the local languages.

The content of the press reflected the awakening mood of Indian politics. Although newspapers previously had launched sporadic attacks on the British, the first substantial signs of the new militancy among journalists surfaced just prior to 1900. Tilak's *Kesari* lambasted the government; for that he was prosecuted, as were the editorial staffs of the *Bangabasi* and later, the *Bande Mataram* and *Yugantar*. By 1905, over 200 newspapers commented on political issues. Most of these, according to British

14. Elements in this process are analyzed in J. R. McLane, "The Development of Nationalist Ideas and Tactics and the Policies of the Government of India, 1897–1907" (Ph.D. diss., University of London, 1961); Richard Ian Cashman, "The Politics of Mass Recruitment" (Ph.D. diss., Duke University, 1969). Lajpat Rai presents an interesting contemporary history in *Young India*, 2d ed., rev.

15. Discussed in Kenneth W. Jones, "Sources for Arya Samaj History," *The Indian Archives*, 18 (1969), 20–36; N. G. Barrier, "The Sikh Resurgence, 1849–1947," *The Indian Archives*, 18 (1969), 46–63. Printing costs based on discussion in Chief Khalsa Diwan proceedings at the C.K.D. headquarters, Amritsar, and comments in Munsha Singh Dukhi, *Jivan Bhai Sahib Bhai Mohan Singh Vaidji* (Amritsar: n.d.).

16. Statistics from *Statements of English, Foreign, Anglo-Vernacular and Vernacular Newspapers Published in India and Burma During the Year 1905*, a confidential police report (Simla: Indian Home Department, 1907). 210 periodicals had circulations between 1 and 200; 911, 201–1,000; 204, 1,001–; unknown, 34. Several newspapers, such as the *Bengalee*, *Kesari*, and *Hitavadi*, reached very large audiences.

Background on the Indian Press, 1905[17]

Distribution

Baluchistan, 1	Central Indian States, 7
East Bengal, Bengal, 179	Central Provinces, 18
Bombay, 320	Madras, Madras Princely States, 304
Portuguese India, 9	Punjab, N.W.F.P., 263
Burma, 54	United Provinces, 197
Ajmer-Merwara, 9	

Language

English, 285	Tamil, 79	Sindhi, 11
English and a vernacular, 82	Hindi, 78	Oriya, 7
Other European, 16	Bengali, 74	Khasi, 5
Two or more Indian vernaculars, 28	Malayalam, 54	Sanskrit, 3
Urdu, 338	Kanarese, 30	Persian, 2
Gujarati, 97	Telegu, 29	Assamese, 1
Marathi, 93	Burmese, 20	Nagra, 1
	Panjabi, 12	Unknown, 14

observers, tended to be disloyal or pursued dangerous editorial policies.[18] Undaunted by the threat of British reprisal, the new breed of patriot wrote unequivocably about political necessity and the use of force:

> War or a revolution is an infinitely better thing than the peace under which mortality is fast rising in India. . . . If you cannot prove yourself a man in life, play the man in death. . . . The laws of the English are based on their brute force. If we want to liberate ourselves from those laws, it is brute force that is necessary for us to accumulate.[19]

17. Statistics drawn from *Statements*. A detailed study of publication trends in one province is in Barrier and Wallace, *The Punjab Press*.

18. Based on British commentary in *Statements*. Also, review of press influence in secretariat notes, GIPOL July 1907, 178–180A; Prem Narain, *Press and Politics in India, 1885–1905*; first nine chapters of James Campbell Ker, *Political Troubles in India, 1907–1917*, confidential C.I.D. handbook.

19. Press comment extracted from Ker, *Political Troubles*, pp. 72–73.

Emergent Problems of British Administration

Built into the nature of British rule in India were at least three weaknesses that potentially affected attempts to confront these political challenges. First, the government did not consist of a unified bureaucracy, with clear-cut chains of command and implementation. Second, the British lacked a tested system of surveillance and control specifically designed to meet organized resistance. Finally, the bureaucracy had not resolved the inherent ideological tension between theoretical adherence to democratic ideas and ultimate recourse to repression as a means of political survival.

Internal problems plagued the Indian government—difficulties that were usually not apparent until crises demanded rapid, unified action. Red tape clogged administrative channels, and coordination constantly threatened to break down.[20] Besides this normal state of affairs, Curzon's attempts at centralization brought to the surface the latent suspicions and conflict of authority that existed between the Government of India and the provinces. When Curzon tried to eliminate what he judged were unwarranted prerogatives of decisionmaking among his subordinates, the resulting clamor left the bureaucracy divided and jealous of its power. With Curzon's resignation (1905), heads of local governments preferred to return to the earlier pattern of compromise and, on some matters, open negotiation with the center.[21] Certainly they were sensitive to any efforts by the central government to resume powers that had been tacitly reserved for men on the spot. It was a major task to bring into agreement discordant members of government and to unify and coordinate an effective all-India campaign even in the face of impending danger.

Center–provincial relations also affected a second trouble spot of administration: the paucity of institutions and strategies calculated to combat widespread threats. The government had an assortment of press and sedition laws, but these had been applied infrequently, and their effectiveness was untested. Similarly, the rudimentary system for investigating political crime, which like legislation had developed in response to particular episodes rather than on a planned basis, had sustained no major test. Local police

20. The best over-all study on the inner operations of the bureaucracy is in Bradford Spangenburg, "Status and Policy," (Ph.D. diss., Duke University, 1967).

21. Administrative reforms discussed in David Dilks, *Curzon in India*, I, 221–48. The intricate negotiations and compromises affecting one piece of legislation are described in N. G. Barrier, *The Punjab Alienation of Land Bill of 1900*.

handled immediate problems, but the central organization to coordinate and supervise provincial activities tended to be inoperative. The Imperial Thagi Department, as Curzon noted in 1902, seemed to be a "holiday billet" that lacked meaningful functions.[22]

Curzon's drive to create an imperial police force with extensive power to investigate political crime aroused firm opposition from the provinces. Although the Viceroy skirted the resistance and revamped the Thagi Department in 1904, the three years of negotiation had chipped away at his design for centralization to the extent that provincial governments still retained primary investigative powers. Each province had a Criminal Investigation Department supervised by a Deputy Inspector General of Police. These departments were concerned with special crimes against the state and were responsible to the provincial administration, not to a central agency. The local C.I.D. also assumed surveillance of publications. The Central Intelligence Department in Calcutta, which replaced the Thagi Department there and was headed by a Director of Criminal Intelligence, could not use its small staff of detectives to initiate special investigations without prior provincial approval, nor could it interfere in local matters. By 1905, therefore, the Government of India had only begun to shore up its intelligence system with changes designed in part to handle political developments. The details as to who made decisions within the C.I.D. network and how provincial operations were to be coordinated had yet to be formulated.[23]

Uncertainty over motives and the goals of colonial government, not structural problems, probably constituted the most troublesome element affecting British political response. In the post-Mutiny period, the government's commitment to preserve the *raj* at any cost was implemented as ambivalently and partially as was its bureaucratic relationship with the press. Sporadic repression had created only minor ideological anxiety among the rulers. Summary action against a militant sect in Punjab (the Kukas), or random press prosecution admittedly raised questions in England, but on the whole, Parliament exhibited more alarm over pro-Indian measures such as the Ilbert Bill, which gave Indian judges authority over Englishmen, and the extension of legislative councils than over coercion of the Indian press.[24]

22. Curzon note (May 25, 1902), GI Public, June 1904, 136–155A.

23. Evolution of the C.I.D. is documented in the following: GI Police, August 1910, 83–87A; GI Police, June 1904, 136–155A; J&P 1904, 494. "Interference" and center–province relations were the key issues underlying the discussion.

24. Parliament, and the evolution of a pro-Indian lobby in England, are discussed in Harish Kaushik, *The Indian National Congress in England*

That too had changed by 1905. The British Congress Committee, drawing support from the Liberal Parliamentary party, lobbied in the House of Commons on specific issues. Freedom of the press was especially dear to these men, many of whom had fought coercion in Ireland.[25] Although parliamentary debate rarely had a direct effect on Indian policies, the question hour in the House of Commons high-lighted issues and helped reinforce broad limits on how the bureaucracy conducted business.

The allies of the Indian sympathizers in England, the moderates who controlled the Indian National Congress, also stood ready to criticize any repressive tendencies of government. Increasingly bitter over bureaucratic refusal to share power and under fire from extremists as ineffective leaders, Congressmen were more sensitive than in the past to highly visible acts that were inconsistent with what they believed to be the essence of English democratic tradition. Interference in the expression of opinion was such an issue.

The Organization of This Study

How to juggle these pressures and at the same time moderate or stamp out seemingly dangerous publications became a knotty political problem for the Government of India. The stage had been set for a dramatic encounter between bureaucracy and Indian publicists that was to endure for the last forty years of British rule. In the course of the struggle, the British banned thousands of books, tracts, and newspapers, adopted fresh methods of political control, and vied with the Congress and revolutionaries for influence among the Indian public.

This interaction between ruler and ruled has never been studied. At least two factors account for the inattention. First, historians have been interested in other facets of politics. A few have examined constitutional development, others key incidents. Organizations and individuals often become the pegs on which the historical narrative hangs—most notable among them, the Congress, Muslim League, Gandhi, Nehru, Jinnah, and a succession of viceroys. Although histories of Indian journalism refer to British repression, they tend to accept the image the govern-

1885–1920. However, as the following quotation from Governor General Lansdowne to Secretary of State for India Lord Cross indicates, the Indian government did keep an eye on possible parliamentary response: "The question of the Press is, as you know, a very delicate one with a democratic House of Commons." Lansdowne to Cross, October 1, 1891, Lansdowne Papers, Eur. Mss. D 558, IOL.

25. Notes on "Parliamentary uproar" in Morley to Minto, May 16, 1907, M.C.; Hirtzel diaries (IOL, Home Misc. 864), July 20, 1906; debates in Great Britain, *4 Parliamentary Debates*, 174 (1907), 611–19.

ment attempted to sustain in public, that of a monolithic foreign bureaucracy with policies made at the highest levels on the basis of fixed principles and implemented relentlessly by subordinate administrators.[26]

Inaccessibility of official documents has reinforced the historiographic trends. Students of history could not see many twentieth-century proceedings prior to the recent shift from a fifty- to a thirty-year rule governing use of records in Great Britain. Similar circumstances pertained in the secretariat and departmental records of the Indian government, housed in the National Archives of India at New Delhi. With a few exceptions, both major sets of proceedings and private papers now are open through the Second World War. The notes, demi-official correspondence, and other government records documenting day-to-day decisions await scrutiny.

This study utilizes the records to examine British handling of controversial literature. It explores several related questions: What was the changing context in which the government had to operate? How did the bureaucracy respond to crises, and how were its programs implemented? What patterns of banning and other controls emerge from the period? The discussion has been placed in a chronological framework because institutions and personalities involved in encounters altered with time. My primary concern is the political process, however, not the reconstruction of a comprehensive history of the period. What do British initiative and response reveal about the nature of colonial government in India and the intricate exchange between bureaucrat and Indian politician?

The British were but one component of Indian politics. Originally, part of this book was to have been devoted to their antagonists and to the literature itself. Chapters were to survey how and why the banned works were produced, their format, the content of representative material, the effects of control, and translations of significant pieces. As writing progressed, however, it became obvious that the subjects required detailed and separate treatment. Another volume along the lines indicated above is in preparation.

The next chapter of this study traces the evolution of press restrictions, 1907–1913, and how they operated. Chapter 3 deals with the experience of the First World War and consequent

26. In addition to the studies by Prem Narain, S. P. Sen, and J. Natarajan, the following survey the post-1900 period: Sushila Agrawal, *Press, Public Opinion and Government in India*; Hemendra Prased Ghose, *Press and Press Laws in India*; N. Krishnamurthy, *Indian Journalism*; Mohit Moitra, *A History of Indian Journalism.*

British efforts to develop additional methods of supervision and propaganda. The startling shift in policy, from tight controls to repeal of the major press act in 1922, also receives attention, as do the problems faced by the British when they tried to rule without special press provisions. The peculiarities of records caused by decentralization present special difficulties in reconstructing events between 1936 and 1947, and therefore the fourth chapter, on developments from 1929 until independence, should be considered a suggestive rather than an exhaustive treatment. The concluding chapter draws together themes and patterns suggested by the research and examines the legacy of government–press relations for the Indian and Pakistan governments.

While it destroyed the bulk of a segment of Indian literary production for almost half a century, the Government of India preserved copies for intelligence or antiquarian purposes. The second part of the book reviews why and how banned works were preserved and provides an annotated guide to sections (Hindi, Panjabi, and English) of the three largest collections. This discussion on banning and banned literature, I hope, will contribute to fresh interest in a largely forgotten aspect of Indian political and literary development.

Chapter 2

THE EMERGENCE OF PRESS CONTROLS AND THEIR IMPLEMENTATION, 1907–1913

"We are overwhelmed with a mass of heterogeneous material, some of it misguided, some of it frankly seditious, the mere bulk of which to say nothing of its chaotic character, renders it unmanageable. . . . This mass of matter has already got beyond our control."[1] Thus a high-ranking officer assessed the Government of India's relationship with the press in 1906. The rapid increase of books and newspapers hostile to British rule coincided with overt challenges to authority. Aware that publications were both a symptom and a cause of unrest, the government coupled checks on extremist literature with enlarged executive and judicial powers to combat sedition in all forms.

The ensuing experiments with press restrictions took into consideration the maintenance of alliances with Indian groups and the development of new political support. The Morley–Minto reforms of 1909, which liberalized the constitution by introducing elections and curtailing direct British control over the legislatures, afforded opportunity for closer Indian association with government. The goal of keeping at least some Indian politicians on the British side conflicted with authoritarian impulse and forced the Government of India to balance coercion with conciliatory gestures and cooperation.

Divergence of administrative opinion also affected decisions on Indian publications. Representations of men on the spot, most notably provincial governments, had to be heard and evaluated. The issues relating to Indian politics evoked differing responses from administrative heads, with similar splits occurring within the central secretariat and the Governor General's Council. Moreover, a contest of wills appeared at the uppermost rung of administration. Many of the decisions of Secretary of State John Morley and the Viceroy Lord Minto reflected a consensus of opinion, but

1. H. H. Risley note (February 7, 1907), GIPOL July 1907, 178–180A.

their individual differences indelibly characterized the arguments over freedom of the press.

The complexity of political considerations worked against the formulation of a comprehensive policy toward polemic literature. As a result, official action tended to be responses to immediate crises rather than products of careful planning. A series of incidents propelled the British haltingly toward a system of press surveillance and control.

Frustrated Attempts at Coercion

The years 1905 and 1906 were uneasy for British administrators. Curzon had gone, but his successor, Lord Minto, found morale in the Indian Civil Service at a low level. Another Curzonian legacy was a menacing burst of political agitation that exceeded earlier demonstrations in quantity and fervor. Much of the unrest had its origin in the decision to partition Bengal despite the protests of well-organized Bengali politicians. There followed numerous confrontations and violence, the form and spirit of which soon spread to other parts of India. In discussing the unrest, the Government of India considered whether accelerated prosecution might help contain radical writings. The secretariat's study dragged on throughout 1906, when suddenly the emergence of anti-British sentiment in Punjab, a province noted for its quiescence and a major recruitment center for the Indian army, brought the issue to a head.[2] The resulting deliberations reflected the seriousness of the problem and the varied opinions as to how it should be handled.

A member of the Governor General's Council, Erle Richards, sounded the alarm after reviewing a C.I.D. report on the Punjab press. Sedition, he claimed, had reached such proportions that the government, unknowing, stood on the brink of disaster.[3] Most of his colleagues agreed, and in typical bureaucratic fashion, reacted by writing long minutes on the subject. A dominant theme in these notes was the multifaceted threat posed by Indian publicists. Papers could influence Parliament with "calculated lies" or terrorize moderate politicians. In addition, the councilors saw the role of books and newspapers in demoralizing a generation of Indian students as a basic danger, summarized by this secretarial comment: "A Press which deliberately perverts history and

2. A detailed survey of politics, 1905–1907, is in a new book by Arun Chandra Guha, *First Spark of Revolution*, pp. 1–133. On the Punjab situation, N. G. Barrier, "The Punjab Disturbances of 1907" (Ph.D. diss., Duke University, 1966); Sri Ram Sharma, *Punjab in Ferment*.

3. E. Richards note (December 23, 1906), and subsequent notes, GIPOL July 1907, 178–180A.

which lays itself out to turn thousands of students into malcontents and seeks to employ them in spreading treasonable notions all over the country deserved to be severely dealt with."[4]

The press file also covered legal and bureaucratic difficulties in dealing with printed matter. All discussants agreed that local governments could not be relied upon to supply adequate intelligence on provincial and district developments. Even when such information was accessible, local authorities did not in many cases prosecute unless prodded by the center. The head of the Imperial C.I.D., Harold Stuart, insisted that at least mild administrative anarchy prevailed, with the provinces going their way without appropriate supervision from the Governor General's Council. Because the Government of India had not given strong leadership in putting down sedition, he argued, "impotence and indecision" reigned within the bureaucratic system.[5]

Unanimity within the Council dissolved when it turned from analyzing the problem to finding solutions. Secretaries and Council members agreed that surveillance of the press must be improved, but they tended to shy away from overruling the decisions of local officers. Some members favored wholesale attacks on extremist wings of the press, others advised issuance of warnings and new efforts to conciliate opponents. Richards was particularly concerned with the government's role in molding public opinion. He suggested that the secretariat prepare an annual press report in popular form for distribution in Parliament, which would illustrate the tone of the press and establish a case for stronger steps against offenders. Such reports also were to cultivate support for governmental measures among moderates in London and India.[6]

Although a majority favored a firmer press policy—one that would result in more prosecutions—two reasons influenced the decision not to pursue that course. First, experience indicated that prosecutions generally were ineffective as deterrents and, further, potentially dangerous; in some circumstances, such as the *Panjabee* case, they could backfire. The *Panjabee*, a nationalist newspaper in Lahore, had published harsh criticism of government since its inception in 1904. The most controversial article was an alleged exposé of an English officer's murder of a Muslim peon. The Punjab government had been awaiting an opportunity

4. Risley note (December 23, 1906), GIPOL July 1907, 178–180A.

5. H. A. Stuart note (March 9, 1907), GIPOL July 1907, 178–180A.

6. Richards note (December 29, 1906). Risley commented that the Indian government had to educate itself and the public: "We must render that knowledge readily accessible to the tribunal which will in the last resort pronounce upon our proposals—the English Parliament" (February 7, 1907). Several Council members and secretaries questioned this call for a report. Discussion drawn from GIPOL July 1907, 178–180A.

to crush the paper, so it asked the Indian government for sanction to initiate proceedings under the sedition section of the penal code (124A). The center balked and instead suggested prosecution for inciting racial hatred (153A). This change was intended to prevent unrest because the conviction on 153A carried a lighter sentence than on 124A, but to the consternation of the British, the racial overtones of the trial polarized Hindu–Muslim opposition to the government. Moving slowly through the appeal system (October 1906–March 1907), the drawn-out proceedings evoked sharp public criticism. Other papers portrayed the convicted printer and editor as martyrs who attempted to defend hapless Indians against bigoted autocrats, and with each successive appeal, anti-British feeling escalated. The Punjab's reluctance to prosecute an English-owned paper, the *Civil and Military Gazette*, which churned out imperialist and racist articles as inciting as those in the *Panjabee*, heightened the outcry. When the final appeals sparked a demonstration in Lahore, the Indian government belatedly admitted that the entire handling of the case had been disastrous.[7]

Prosecutions of the press also raised the possibility of home authorities intervening in Indian decisionmaking. The Liberals had just gained control of Parliament and could be expected to be sensitive to repression. More importantly, the Liberal victory at the polls had brought John Morley to the India Office.

The two new policymakers, Morley in England and Minto in India, had much in common. Both saw the wisdom of associating Indians more closely with government, and they worked together to increase nonofficial participation in legislative councils.[8] In addition, each lacked experience with India and therefore had to rely initially on the advice of their respective councils. Early exchanges of letters reflect their efforts to sort out policies and to forge a bond of understanding between London and Calcutta. As they learned to operate in their respective spheres, however, differences in personality and political perspective began to emerge. Minto was sensitive to the demands of the bureaucracy and Indian problems, while Morley was responsible to Parliament and had a broader, philosophically based overview. Although

7. Minutes on the prosecution by Adamson and other members, GIPOL July 1907, 178–180A. Discussion of the *Panjabee* case in Barrier, "Disturbances," pp. 170–71, 193–94, 208–10; Sharma, *Punjab*, pp. 47, 55.

8. The 1909 Government of India Act fixed the maximum number of nominated and elected members at 60 for the Imperial Legislative Council, 50 in the larger provinces, and 30 for the Punjab and Burma. Total membership rose from 124 to 331, and elected members from 39 to 135, with majorities of nonofficials (including nominees) in all but the central council. Detailed treatment in Syed Razi Wasti, *Lord Minto and the Indian Nationalist Movement, 1905–1910.*

Morley and Minto cooperated in the intricate maneuvers underlying the 1909 reforms, questions of law and order increasingly impinged on London–India relations.

John Morley's political liberalism signaled trouble for advocates of coercion in India. His personal experiences as Irish Secretary had reinforced his dissatisfaction with force as a political instrument and, particularly, his distrust of executive controls as a means of influencing the press.[9] Morley linked to this orientation a conviction that major issues should be resolved in London. The representative of Parliament, the India Office, must have ultimate power over the Governor General, who was the "agent of His Majesty's government."[10] As for the vaunted I.C.S., Morley labeled its members petty bureaucrats who were politically unaware and out of step with England's democratic traditions.[11]

The pressures of the office of Secretary of State intensified Morley's inclination to question decisions made in India. Personally vain and autocratic, the Secretary resented any effort by Minto and his own Council to modify his views.[12] A small but vocal pro-India lobby in Parliament created additional strains. Morley dreaded question periods, in which Henry Cotton and other critics posed queries and remarked pointedly on the contradictions between Morley's philosophical outlook and his defense of Indian autocracy. That the "donkey" Cotton usually had more facts on incidents than the India Office did little to assuage Morley's anxiety. Irritated by parliamentary slings and infuriated by Indian demands to back the man on the spot, Morley sometimes rattled off impetuous telegrams to his "subordinate" Minto.[13]

Minto disagreed with Morley on administration and what had to be done to preserve the *raj*. The Governor General quickly accepted many assumptions of the I.C.S., exemplified by his assessment of the British situation: "We are here a small British garrison surrounded by millions composed of factors of an inflam-

9. Aside from the viceregal correspondence, the best source on Morley's daily activity is the diary of his secretary, Arthur Hirtzel (IOL, Home Mis. 864). The relationship between the two men and background on their respective viewpoints are covered in the following: Wasti, *Lord Minto*; Stephen E. Koss, *John Morley at the India Office, 1905–1910*; Stanley A. Wolpert, *Morley and India, 1906–1910*; Martin Gilbert, *Servant of India*.

10. Morley to Minto, September 18, 1908, M.C. Also, Morley to Minto, May 7, 1908.

11. Morley to Minto, July 13, 1906; June 21, 1907. Morley's favorite caricature of the I.C.S. was "tchinovnik," a reference to Russian minor bureaucrats who symbolized red tape and dim-witted activity.

12. Hirtzel diary, May 13, 23, 1907. Also, comments by Dunlop Smith in Gilbert, *Servant*, p. 158.

13. Morley to Minto, May 18, 1906, M.C. Hirtzel diary, January 17, May 10, 1907.

mability unknown to the Western world, unsuited to Western forms of government, and we must be physically strong or go to the wall."[14] Such strength required support from London. The House of Commons, which Morley virtually worshiped, must be excluded from interfering in Indian affairs: "The modern House of Commons is absolutely incapable of understanding Indian humanity and the influence of many creeds and traditions," Minto asserted, "and is to my mind perhaps the great danger to the continuance of our rule in this country."[15] With regard to political control, Minto personally disliked reliance on force, but the former Governor General of Canada tempered this attitude with the belief that seeming weakness would undermine the loyalty of Indians, many of whom supposedly were undecided on the best course and were watching every British move.[16] Collision with Morley therefore was a matter of time. Although he resented the Secretary's pompous political diatribes and his insistence on always being dominant, Minto frequently acquiesced in all but the most vital issues in order to avoid incessant fights with Morley.

Mindful of Morley's attitude toward the press and divided over solutions to the deteriorating tone of political writings, the Government of India might have delayed a decision on controls except for the occurrence of disturbances in the Punjab during April and May of 1907. Rural agitation over colonization and canal bills in Punjab coincided with district-level agitations on a variety of issues. Overreacting to the unrest and riots in Lahore and Rawalpindi, the Punjab government on May 3 asked Minto for extensive executive powers to combat a conspiracy that turned out to be largely imaginary. The Indian government lacked firsthand intelligence and therefore backed the local authorities in their misjudgment of the situation. Two alleged leaders, Lajpat Rai and Ajit Singh, were deported, and an ordinance banning public meetings soon followed.[17]

The explosive situation in the North-West accelerated discussion on Indian newspapers. Subsequent minuting reflected a growing division over policy. Minto's Council members initially supported summary action in the Punjab, but as the crisis subsided, a few had second thoughts about the long-range implications of repression. When Richard swayed the Council with arguments for the revival of the 1878 "gagging act," for example, the Home Department's chief, Harvey Adamson, objected strenuously.[18] Minto also hesitated, commenting that he would need

14. Minto to Morley, May 28, 1906, M.C.
15. Minto to Morley, May 19, 1908, M.C.
16. Minto to Morley, July 14, 1908, M.C.
17. Background in Barrier, "Disturbances," and Sharma, *Punjab.*
18. Noting in GIPOL July 1907, 178–180A.

to justify future decisions to the India Office. Morley had grudgingly gone along with the handling of the Punjab, but meetings ordinances and deportation made him uneasy. He informed Minto on May 9 that he would require "real evidence" of sedition before he would approve direct action and warned that the British public would be suspicious of any efforts to restrict the press.[19]

The Council therefore moved in two directions. While gathering data to convince Morley of the need for a revision in press laws, it attempted through a press resolution to deal with immediate demonstrations of seditious writing. To achieve agreement on the wording of the half-page document required eight days. The Home Department wrote the first draft—a panicky note that was highly critical of Indian newspapers. Minto allied with the Commander-in-chief, Lord Kitchener, and E. N. Baker, a Council member known for democratic views, to tone down the draft, on the grounds that it would set England and India "ablaze."[20] Although the resolution concluded with the hope that a warning would "avert the necessity of numerous prosecutions," the British signaled their intentions to get tough. Traditionally, all proceedings under Sections 153A and 124A had to be sanctioned by the Governor General, thus delaying prosecutions. The resolution announced that, henceforth, local governments could institute cases without prior consultations.[21] When Minto telegraphed the proposed draft to London, Morley balked. He argued that the government should undertake preventive measures, such as increased demands of security under Section 108, rather than accelerate press prosecutions. Under no conditions should Minto relinquish authority to local administrators, whom Morley judged incompetent. Morley nevertheless withdrew his objections when Minto insisted that security proceedings required too much time and spread the notoriety of guilty papers. The resolution was published on June 3, 1907.[22]

The brief exchange over the resolution foreshadowed the examination of press controls. Despite the opposition of Adamson and Baker to greater restrictions, the alleged danger of sedition among troops influenced the drafting of new emergency legislation. The first half of the bill made permanent the power to ban meetings after the expiring of the six-month ordinance on November 10; the second half permitted the demand of security bonds from presses that published literature which affected the

19. Morley to Minto, May 9, 1907, M.C. Minto note, June 1, 1907, GIPOL July 1907, 178–180A.

20. Minto to Morley, June 5, 1907. Background in Minto to Lady Minto, June 5, 1907, M.C.

21. Resolution in GI *Gazette*, pt. 1, June 8, 1907, p. 443.

22. Telegrams in GIPOL July 1907, 178–180A.

loyalty of the Indian army. The bonds and the printing presses themselves would be forfeit if warnings were not heeded. At the insistence of Baker, the Council agreed to ask local officials for opinions on the measure. They also requested speedy approval from Morley.[23]

John Morley was in no mood for an omnibus press and meetings bill. Attacks in Parliament had multiplied during the summer, and Morley had been warned informally that had he not built an impeccable reputation for defense of civil liberties, the challenges would have been merciless.[24] The Secretary also realized to his chagrin that Minto had panicked and had misled him on the Punjab situation. Embattled at home and distrustful of news from India, Morley drew the line at restrictions of the press. He admitted the need for extending supervision of meetings, but he refused to be rushed into a press law on the "very thin" evidence marshaled by the army and Minto.[25]

Consultation with colleagues and India specialists in London supported Morley's skepticism. A prominent member of the India Council, William Lee-Warner, questioned the need for new laws. Another member, Theodore Morison, was more antagonistic. The Government of India seemed intent on suppressing legitimate public opinion, according to Morison, as well as having failed to build public confidence through a minimal program of propaganda.[26] Morley also took the matter to the Cabinet, where the press provisions drew negative comments.[27] Finally, because a few of his Council members urged that the men on the spot be backed at all costs, Morley formed a special press committee to study the issues. The reading was unanimous. No legislation would be permitted unless the Government of India could present a strong case for press controls.[28]

Despite uneasiness in London, Minto and the Executive Council maintained that danger in India justified additional powers. All replies to the circular sent to the provincial governments pointed to widespread political turmoil. Some governments, such as Punjab and Burma, suggested modification of the press sections, but a majority went along with the draft bill.[29] With the

23. Based on noting, GIPOL July 1907, 178–180A. The circular was 1842–51, July 22, 1907, and the dispatch to the India Office containing papers on the issue, Public 13, July 11, 1907.
24. Hirtzel diary, July 1, 1907.
25. Hirtzel diary, June 17, July 24, 1907. Morley to Minto, August 2, 1907.
26. Notes by Lee-Warner (August 14, 1907) and Morison (August 12, 1907), J&P 1907, 4060.
27. Hirtzel diary, August 9–17, 1907.
28. Hirtzel diary, August 9–17, 1907. Also, notes in J&P 1907, 4060.
29. Replies in GI Public 25, September 26, 1907, J&P 1907, 4060.

replies in hand, Minto again requested that prompt legislation be permitted. His appeal produced a telegram from Morley in which he ordered that discussion be suspended and warned of "precipitancy."[30] Morley's private note to Minto was more direct: "It startles me that even hard Tchinovniks (petty Russian bureaucrats) . . . should so far forget that they are the servants and agents of Parliament in a free country, and should dream that a Secretary of State should live one hour after the assembling of Parliament, who should have assented to those new provisions."[31]

The Indian government was blocked. Either it had to forgo legislation or remove the controversial press provisions. Following the latter course, the Legislative Department prepared a new version that did not mention newspapers. Morley telegraphed approval of the meetings measure.[32]

Minto had a bill, but how and when to introduce it involved delicate considerations. The Government of India and the Imperial Legislative Council were about to make their annual shift from the summer capital at Simla to Calcutta. If Minto postponed introduction until the reconvening of the legislature in late 1907, private talks with moderate politicians such as Gokhale in the interim might minimize the public response to bans on meetings. The potential danger that could arise if the ordinance should lapse overweighed the argument for postponement, however, and eventually Minto rushed the measure to the legislature just before its exodus.[33] The Indian protest came as feared. Newspapers denounced the move as despotic, and while the bill passed the official-dominated legislature on the first of November, three nonofficial members spoke and voted against the British.[34]

Legislation was not the sole response to Indian unrest. When discussing the press bill, the government tried other ways to limit the spread of dangerous ideas. Prosecution of newspapers, such as *India* and *Yugantar* (*Mutiny*), offered one channel of action. Successful proceedings nevertheless did not stop papers from changing hands and reappearing as hostile critics.[35] In in-

30. Morley telegram, September 19, and noting, GIPOL July 1907, 178–180A.

31. Morley to Minto, September 19, 1907, M.C.

32. Noting in GIPOL December 1907, 64–84A; July 1907, 178–180A.

33. Noting in GIPOL December 1907, 64–84A; Minto to Morley, September 26, 1907, M.C. Minto also preferred the relative isolation of Simla to the "vituperation" and hostile press to which he was subjected in Calcutta.

34. Proceedings in J&P 1907, 4060; GIPOL December 1907, 64–84A. The latter also contains press excerpts. Voting against the bill were G. K. Gokhale, the Maharaja of Nabha, and Rashbehari Ghose.

35. *India* prosecution discussed in GIPOL July 1907, 3–5A; *Yugantar* in James Campbell Ker, *Political Troubles in India, 1907–1917*, pp. 72–78. General discussion in Guha, *Spark*, pp. 101–15.

stances in which publicists could not be identified or were inaccessible, the government resorted to interception of materials in the mails. Under Section 26 of the Postal Act, the Governor General could direct postmasters to seize and examine specific items or categories of material. In July of 1907, for example, the Burmese government warned the Indian authorities of leaflets addressed to Punjabi troops in Rangoon and received permission to intercept them.[36] Indian authorities took particular care to monitor articles from England. Customs officials initially confiscated only pamphlets by Socialist leaders such as Max Hyndman, but gradually the net extended to trap newspapers and journals. On May 14, 1907, Minto ordered Bombay customs to hand over to special police officers any items thought to contain sedition.[37]

Interference with mail from England brought Minto into collision with Morley. The Secretary read in a September edition of the *Daily Telegraph* that the importation and sale of the Socialist journal *Justice* had been prohibited in India. Although personally antagonistic to the editor, Hyndman, Morley feared the repercussions in Parliament and demanded information.[38] On confirmation of the *Telegraph* story, he ordered an end to the confiscation and asked why he had not been consulted. Morley's telegrams surprised the Imperial secretariat. No reference had been made to London because the Indian government had the legal power to restrict circulation of any imported item. The Council debated the matter and then asked Morley to reconsider. This he did because of Minto's plea that a cancellation of the ban would reflect negatively on the Government of India. Nevertheless, Morley recorded his displeasure at the handling of the case and insisted on consultation before any future repressive action was undertaken.[39]

Morley returned to the warpath within a month, this time investigating a charge that the Indian government had tampered with the private correspondence of an M.P., William Wedderburn. The officials at Calcutta apologized after heated exchanges; they maintained that Wedderburn's mail probably had been opened inadvertently by officials who were searching for seditious matter.[40]

36. Discussed in GIPOL August 1907, 101–105A.

37. Background in GIPOL August 1907, 243–250A; April 1908, 40–41A.

38. Morley telegram September 19, 1907, M.C. On Morley's attitude toward Hyndman, Hirtzel diary, July 2, 1907.

39. Correspondence and telegrams in GIPOL January 1908, 38–42A. One reason for the ban had been the India Office's earlier suggestion that Hyndman's *The Ruin of India by British Rule* be intercepted. Background in J&P 1907, 2198.

40. Noting and documents in J&P 1908, 382; GIPOL April 1908,

Such incidents strengthened Morley's distrust and left Minto frustrated and angry. Since May of 1907, the Government of India had attempted to deal with materials that appeared to presage a rising tide of revolution. Its actions precipitated struggles with the India Office, which placed limits on possible remedies. Morley continued to declare throughout the discussions that he would permit all necessary powers if proof of danger could be demonstrated. Unable to provide evidence that met the Secretary's exacting criteria, Minto and his colleagues were thrown back on existing regulations and occasional interference in the circulation of printed matter. Events soon permitted the authorities at Calcutta, however, to regain the initiative in charting official policy toward the press. The rapid surfacing of terrorism in 1908 supplied abundant evidence of threats to the *raj* and thereby paved the way for new political controls.

A Varied Response to Revolution

The bullet and the bomb became prominent factors in Indian politics after December of 1907. The first major episodes included an attempt to derail a train in which the Lieutenant Governor of Bengal was traveling (December 6), and the shooting of Magistrate B. C. Allen in Dacca seventeen days later. In surveying the violence, Minto wrote Morley that he hoped the events originated from individual ruffianism and not organized assassination.[41] That hope was not fulfilled. The revolutionaries struck again and again, in some attacks killing Indian officers and informers, in others aiming at personnel of the I.C.S. and robbing armories. In May of 1908, an especially notorious assassination occurred in Muzaffarpur, where conspirators killed two Englishwomen by mistake rather than their intended target, a controversial judge. Although sometimes the spontaneous acts of individuals, most often the outrages were the results of plots by a network of revolutionary groups. The Anusilan Committee of Dacca, for example, recruited young men and instructed them in weaponry. The committee also had a lending library of bomb manuals and nationalist tracts, literature that tended to reinforce the members' spirit of sacrifice. Bomb factories were operating in at least three Indian cities by the end of 1908.[42]

40–41A. As Risley noted in the GIPOL file (January 9, 1908), the Indian government was confused as to what happened.

41. Minto to Morley, December 26, 1907, M.C.

42. Background in trial proceedings, GIPOL August 1912, 2–23A. For detailed treatment of the revolutionary groups, the following: Ker, *Political Troubles*, pp. 136–69; K. C. Ghosh, *The Roll of Honour*, pp. 149–97; Guha, *Spark*, pp. 101–70.

Revolutionary activity generated a secondary wave of patriotism among more conventional politicians. While usually careful to guard their praise of extremism, newspaper editors extolled the bravery and self-sacrifice of men who were willing to die for Mother India.[43] On the other hand, the bombings widened and intensified repression by the British. The Indian government struck quickly. Police round-ups resulted in several conspiracy trials, in which ringleaders were sentenced either to death or to transportation for life. In addition, the Legislative Council enacted two bills specifically aimed at terrorism. The first outlawed possession of explosives, and the second, a bill "for the speedy trial of certain offenses, and for the prohibition of associations dangerous to the public peace," provided for special tribunals and for declaring organizations illegal.[44]

The political outburst of 1908 marked a decisive shift in the Government of India's relationship with the India Office. Minto and his Council took advantage of the terrorist attacks to reassert their authority over issues of law and order. Morley reminded them that "excess of severity is not the path to order . . . it is the path to the bomb," but he agreed with the policy of coercion.[45] Morley's policy did not give Minto and the Indian government free rein in making decisions. Assumption of greater initiative meant, to the contrary, that the British needed to be more careful in weighing the political consequences of their actions. References to Morley and Parliament now appeared more frequently in the Home–Political files of the central secretariat. Moreover, enlarged responsibility necessitated closer coordination with provincial governments. The trend since 1907 had been a shift of discretionary power to men on the spot, but as the repressive laws accumulated, supervision of how they were to be used became imperative. Consequently, the center and the provinces corresponded actively about the application of legislation in local situations.[46]

Coercion brought with it an intensified effort to explain official decisions to educated Indians in order that at least some of this class would associate themselves with British policy. Unless the government could justify its actions, the good will and political advantage gained by the proposed constitutional reforms would

43. Evidence in letters from local governments, and noting, GIPOL June 1908, 57–86A. Examples also in Ker, *Political Troubles*, pp. 72–98.

44. Bills reproduced in G. K. Roy, *Law Relating to Press and Sedition* (1915), pp. 29–34, 39–44. Also, see Minto to Morley, December 10, 1908, M.C. According to Ker (p. 365), the trials resulted in 36 death sentences, 77 life imprisonments or transportations, and 15 shorter terms.

45. Morley to Minto, July 30, 1908, M.C.

46. See, for example, the consideration of Bengal's request to deport several politicians. Documents, GIPOL May 1908, 103–111A.

be nullified. The maneuvering behind the unlawful association bill illustrated how these considerations affected strategy. Minto rushed the measure through the legislature so it would be law prior to the announcement of imminent reforms. Supposedly, the timing would dampen criticism of repression: "We must give the medicine first and then do all we can to take the taste away."[47] The Governor General also worked hard to ensure that Indians on the legislative council supported the bill. Private conversations won over all except Rashbehari Ghose, but even his opposition was moderate, subsequent to extensive talks with Minto. Ghose had been "most reasonable," Minto wrote Morley; Ghose had suggested that if he did not oppose the bill, "he would lose support of moderates, and that on public grounds, it was important not to injure his control. I told him I quite recognized tactical requirements of his position, and that it was desirable from my point of view also that he should retain it."[48]

New directions in press control reflected the assertiveness of the Indian government and, in turn, its evaluation of political variables. As late as March 1908, Calcutta shied from mentioning press laws because of probable veto from London. Responding to Morley's speech on the freedom of expression and the "great experiment" of transferring democratic institutions to India, a Council member noted that "Mr. Morley's Arbroath speech prohibits us from legislature in many ways that would be really useful. I have no wish to stir up the mud at present."[49] Bombings and the discovery of a conspiracy in the capital nevertheless reopened the issue shortly thereafter. Minto caustically minuted that Morley would have to change his ideas on democratic norms and India: "Under present conditions, I think we need not take for granted Mr. Morley will adhere to his experiment. . . . Perhaps now it may be brought home to him that conditions affecting the press at home do not exist in India."[50]

The Government of India did not need to spend time eliciting information from subordinates when it reconsidered the press laws. Evidence and proposals had been flooding into the Calcutta secretariat for months. According to the provincial reports, many newspapers supported violence and systematically stimulated anti-British feeling. How did Indians feel about the tone of the press and possible intervention by the government? The following com-

47. Minto to Morley, November 30, 1908, M.C.
48. Minto to Morley, December 10, 11, 1908, M.C.
49. Adamson note (March 13, 1908), GIPOL June 1908, 57–86A.
50. Minto note (May 11, 1908), GIPOL June 1908, 57–68A. Minto correctly judged Morley's attitude, but he did not realize at the time that the Secretary of State probably would have permitted a comprehensive act. Fraser to Minto, July 23, 1908, M.C.

ment from a district officer's memorandum typified the over-all assessment of public opinion:

> I have often discussed this question with Indians, including moderate men of the advanced school. I have been surprised at the unanimity of feeling among them that some action on the part of Government is required. Country people, and men of the old school, are amazed at our apathy, and if encouraged to speak freely, do not hesitate to condemn it. Even among men of the new school . . . there is practical unanimity that some action is required. . . . In fact, as editors of moderate papers put it, people like spice and flavour in what they read, and the existence and prosperity of seditious newspapers constitute a strong temptation to others to follow their lead.[51]

The same document suggested that, while prosecution should remain a deterrent, its wide use might magnify seditious thought. A few editors allegedly were tempting British prosecution, "thinking that the advertisement, which such a prosecution would give, with the opportunities for publishing inflammatory speeches of the counsel for defence and comments on the case, and so of stirring up excitement, will more than compensate for the danger of a conviction." Provincial governments generally agreed on a remedy—executive, extrajudicial control of printed matter.

Minto telegraphed Morley on May 26 that the Council was considering either an ordinance or a bill with provisions for forfeiture of printing presses. Morley yielded, specifying only that the action be in the form of regular law and permit appeals to high courts. Prior to his assent, the Secretary had defended the principle of seizure combined with judicial review in a Cabinet session.[52] Some Council members resisted appeals, but Adamson and Baker swayed them with the argument that reliance on executive decision without review would alienate public opinion. Although accepting the final authority of the courts, the Council divided over the scope of the bill. The government should utilize the chance, one faction urged, to resolve a range of press problems: "If we throw away this opportunity, it may be a very long time before another presents itself."[53] Another group favored a narrow measure that would relate only to the most violent papers. "Public opinion," wrote the spokesman of this group, Home Member Adamson, prevented "hurried and irregular legislation that goes beyond the actual scope of the bomb emergency." The

51. Younghusband letter, May 18, 1908, GIPOL June 1908, 57–86A.
52. Telegrams in GIPOL June 1908, 57–86A; Morley to Minto, May 28, 1908, M.C.
53. Baker note (June 2, 1908), GIPOL June 1908, 57–86A.

British could not "afford to alienate native opinion in this country by making the bomb outrages an excuse for passing repressive measures against people in no wise sympathizing with these outrages."[54] That position prevailed. In reviewing the June 3 decision for a limited bill, Minto informed Morley that, while he accepted the verdict, circumstances might necessitate a broader approach in the future.[55]

Adamson presented the "Newspapers (Incitement to Offences) Bill" to an astonished Legislative Council on June 6. Minto purposely had not circulated a draft earlier so as to curtail public discussion.[56] Adamson defended the legislation with the argument that prosecutions had failed to deter incitements to violence. *Yugantar*, for example, continued to print hostile editorials despite several prosecutions. The bill consequently had three features. First, its provisions were limited to incitements to murder, to offenses under the Explosives Substances Act, and to acts of violence. Second, local officials would be empowered to request a magistrate to forfeit presses that produced such material, with an appeal to the high court permissible within fifteen days. Following forfeiture, the government annulled the declaration made under the 1867 Registration Act; thereafter, neither the newspaper nor any related journal could be published. The Council enacted the bill two days later over the bitter objection of Indian members.[57]

Morley tried to reaffirm his ultimate authority over press affairs almost before the ink on the act had dried. On June 9, he rebuked Minto for stating in public debate that further control of newspapers would be necessary. Minto apologetically replied that, at such a critical juncture, he felt public nervousness demanded a firm commitment to control violence. Morley dropped the subject, but the significance of the interchange was clear. The Secretary intended to watch every utterance and decision relating to newspapers. Within a month, he asked Minto to supply him with information on each prosecution because "there is an uneasy susceptibility just now in the House of Commons about their voice, and their public duty in respect to India."[58]

Morley's concern accounts partially for the limited applica-

54. Adamson note (May 31, 1908) and Richards note (May 31, 1908), GIPOL June 1908, 57–68A.

55. Minto to Morley, June 4, 1908, M.C. The file contains a report on the council proceedings.

56. Minto to Morley, June 4, 1908, M.C.

57. Copy of the act in Roy, *Law* (1915), pp. 35–38.

58. Morley to Minto, June 28, 1908, M.C. The relevant telegrams include Morley to Minto, June 9, 11, and Minto to Morley, June 10, M.C.

tion of the new act. The British seized just a few presses in 1908 and 1909. In at least one instance, the bureaucracy defended, not itself but a sometime political opponent. Two numbers of the Bombay *Hindu Punch* (March and August 1909) called for revenge against moderates who collaborated with officials. Gokhale, the articles commented, should be a prime target because he sat on the Legislative Council while young nationalists were giving up their lives. The secretariat's notes on the proposed prosecution of the paper expressed delight at the opportunity to perhaps cultivate moderate support: "An excellent case to take action in. We have often been charged with deserting our friends; here we shall come forward in defence of our most effective critic."[59]

The Government of India combined stringent penalties for incitement with doubled efforts to punish less dangerous forms of writing. In 1908 the staffs of over twenty journals were convicted under 124A. One prosecution especially drew attention, the trial of the extremist Tilak for defending the conspirators in Muzaffarpur and suggesting that the murders demonstrated a link between religious duty and violence.[60]

Difficulties in initiating proceedings against offenders occasionally derived from local governments and not the India Office. The Punjab, for example, hesitated at prosecuting newspapers thought seditious by the Imperial C.I.D. Stung by the *Panjabee* riots, the provincial authorities responded to repeated warnings with a policy of inaction. The Punjab supposedly was quiet, and therefore press trials should be avoided: "It would be a pity to give the editors of such petty prints as *Jhang Sial* and *Hitkari*, both of which are reported to be in a poor way, the benefit of a press prosecution for sedition which might tend to disturb matters generally in the Province."[61] In addition, the government resisted pressure to break up the Bharat Mata Agency, a publishing firm that specialized in political literature. Prodding from the Indian government finally prevailed, but according to a secretariat note, the Punjab remained "the only province in India where sedition is allowed to flourish with impunity."[62]

On the whole, however, the Government of India believed that

59. Risley note (September 28, 1909), in GIPOL January 1910, 154–164A; background in GIPOL July 1909, 124–125A. On another controversial case, *Bande Mataram*, see GIPOL January 1909, 75–93A.

60. Summaries of the trial in *The Trial of Bal Gangadhar Tilak*.

61. PG to GI, 1044SB, July 30, 1908, GIPOL October 1908, 32–34A.

62. Adamson note (May 18, 1909); Stuart note (May 18, 1909), GIPOL October 1909, 145–153A. Final prosecutions discussed in GIPOL May 1910, 115–117A.

the threat of confiscation of presses and a generally tougher policy had proven to be a successful deterrent. Minto and his Council confidently agreed that "the present condition of sedition as far as newspapers are concerned is that by steady prosecution and the recent Newspaper Act, sedition, as defined by the Penal Code, has been almost driven out of India."[63] It seemed that a general press law would not be required in the near future.

The lull in the battle to combat printed sedition permitted the Indian government to focus on other problems relating to political literature. This attention led to increased cooperation with princely states, improvement of intelligence apparatus, and systematic interference in the mails. The Governor General also permitted experimentation with subsidies to loyal newspapers so as to counter false information emitting from a hostile press.

The princes of India traditionally sided with the British in troubled times such as the Afghan wars and the 1857 Mutiny. The government responded to the recent revolutionary activities by once again mobilizing their support. Minto had several objectives in sending a circular letter to the princes in 1908. First, he and colleagues in the Political Department hoped to gain better information on legal and police arrangements within the states. Once the weaknesses and strengths of the various regimes had been analyzed, the Police Department could suggest possible changes and areas of cooperation between the states and British agents. The over-all intent of the circular was to sensitize the semiautonomous rulers to the immediate dangers that were not only confronting the Government of India but were also potentially affecting all those in power. With these motivations, Minto invited the princes to correspond freely with him on issues of mutual interest.[64]

The circular had the desired effect. Most princes replied promptly that they were tightening controls on political activism within their domains. Bhopal, for example, initiated precensorship of printed matter and legislation on sedition. Mysore went further by extending to the police unrestricted control over publications. On receiving the Mysore letter, Minto sighed, "I only wish we could do likewise. Fortunately for him, he has not a House of Commons to deal with."[65] Each prince agreed to ensure

63. Adamson note (April 5, 1909), GIPOL July 1909, 124–125A. Minto agreed; note of April 23, in the same file.

64. Background in C.R. 1/19/400. Correspondence also reprinted in *Selections from the Government of India Records*, 443 (Calcutta: Government of India, 1910).

65. Minto note (November 21, 1909), C.R. 1/19/400. On Baroda and Mysore press regulations, see GIPOL February 1910, 33B.

that no revolutionaries or anti-British publicists operated from their domains, and as planned, representatives from the states began to regularize exchange of information with British agents.[66]

Supply of reports from the princely areas constituted only one aspect of the larger intelligence issue that faced the Indian government. Conspiracies had high-lighted the difficulties within its bureaucratic mechanism for discovering and tracing political activists. The Government of India often did not know what political activity was in progress or being fomented. On some occasions, such as the Punjab disturbances, the supply of inaccurate information from subordinates fostered miscalculations. The inexperience of the C.I.D. and the unresolved tensions that surrounded center–province relations further complicated matters, exemplified by the Indian government's attempt in the summer of 1907 to prevent publication of a book supposedly written by Ajit Singh. A C.I.D. report mentioned the work, but Punjab authorities could not confirm its existence because the Imperial C.I.D.'s special agent, Aziz-ud-Din, declined to have his file transferred to the Punjab Special Branch. Upset by this partial knowledge, yet unable to supply full information, the central secretariat was forced to withdraw from the case and to hope that the Punjab police would uncover sufficient evidence for prosecution. They never did.[67]

Minto's Council knew that a problem existed concerning intelligence, but as frequently happened, the members split over how to proceed. Stevenson-Moore, the officiating director of the C.I.D., urged that the current crises necessitated tighter centralization. The prevailing system, he noted, consisted of a patchwork of conflicting ideologies and structures. No single police officer had total administrative control over political affairs in Bengal and Bombay, for example, because the Inspectors General of Police heading the local C.I.D.'s did not have jurisdiction in presidency capitals. The central government therefore should develop a small secret service, manned by qualified officers who might be attracted by good pay, travel opportunities, and above all, anonymity.[68] Minto agreed with Adamson's opposing view that the calling of the Royal Decentralization Commission made such revision inopportune.[69] Fear of local reaction was based on no fantasy.

66. One of the first examples was the famous Patiala sedition case in which the state prosecuted members of one sect, the Arya Samaj, as "fomentors of sedition."

67. Notes and documents in GIPOL July 1907, 38D.

68. Stevenson-Moore note (May 13, 1908), GIPOL May 1908, 1A.

69. Notes by Adamson (December 28, 1907) and Minto (January 13, 1907), GIPOL May 1908, 1A.

The Government of India and the United Provinces currently were embroiled in a dispute over whether central C.I.D. officers could work directly with local police or must go through regular channels. The provincial establishment denounced direct contact as "snooping."[70] The Council gathered opinion for several months and then decided that the basic structure of the investigation /intelligence system could not be altered. It did take steps, however, to ensure more efficient functioning of the decentralized operations.

First, the Indian government supplied extra funds, which permitted expansion of local police cadres specializing in political work. The following table illustrates the C.I.D. build-up:

C.I.D. Inspectors, Constables: 1907–1910

	Madras	U.P.	Bengal	C.P.	Punjab	Bombay	Total
1907	27	74	57	44	34	48	284
1908	56	88	64	47	39	57	351
1909	64	89	165	57	46	64	485
1910	63	134	165	58	54	77	525

The Imperial Intelligence Department made a similar increase in its own detective staff but avoided open conflict with provincial departments.[71]

At the same time, the central secretariat tried to improve coverage of press content. A 1908 survey revealed considerable variation in the examination of vernacular newspapers. The United Provinces, for example, instructed a full-time inspector and staff to send translations to the Chief Secretary, who then prepared annual reports for submission to the Indian government. District magistrates cooperated by discussing the attitude of new papers with district policemen. Madras, on the other hand, delegated authority to an officer on temporary duty (usually a former military man) who worked with translators for each of four languages (Kanarese, Tamil, Telegu, and Malayalam).[72] Two patterns emerged from the survey: persistent understaffing and inadequate reviews. At best, the meager staff in charge of scruti-

70. UP to GI, 1321C, September 23, 1907, GIPOL January 1908, 3D.
71. Table based on statistics and background documents in GI Police, October 1911, 69–81A.
72. UP to GI, 127, February 1, 1908; Madras to GI, 414, May 16, 1908, GIPOL January 1909, 64–74A.

nizing papers could survey only a selection of the total output. Some improvement in the survey resulted when the Government of India made possible the assembling of a permanent staff by supplying more funds.[73]

Political intelligence increasingly involved more than events in India. The importing of controversial publications from Europe and North America necessitated the expansion of police supervision. In London, Shyamji Krishnavarma and his associates formed in 1905 the "India House," which specialized in propaganda and indoctrination of young students. Soon after its inception in the same year, Krishnavarma's magazine, *The Indian Sociologist*, acquired a reputation for publishing articles in violent opposition to British rule.[74] Across the Channel in Paris, a revolutionary Parsi, Madama Cama, published pamphlets and a controversial journal, *Bande Mataram*.[75] In New York, the Irish League, the Pan-Aryan Society, and the Indian Home Rule League cooperated in sponsoring anti-British demonstrations and sending tracts to India. On the West Coast, Punjabi immigrants published two radical newspapers, *The Aryan* and the *Swadesh Sewak*. In addition, Vancouver associations joined with Indian students in the Berkeley area to form the Ghadar (Mutiny) Association in San Francisco.[76]

Most of the British information on developments in North America came through a long and faulty pipeline. William Hopkinson, a retired Indian officer who had become an employee of the Canada immigration service, supplied firsthand reports on Indians in British Columbia. His material then sifted through the Canadian government, the Foreign Office, and the India Office, where it was analyzed and passed to India. The Governor General of Canada also sent occasional reports to Minto.[77]

Securing accurate news and assistance from other Western countries proved more difficult. Hopkinson toured California and

73. Noting in GIPOL January 1909, 64–74A. A similar change was made in the collection and presentation of police abstracts. GIPOL December 1909, 77A.

74. Background in Indulal Yajnik, *Shyamaji Krishnavarma*. A general survey of Indian revolutionary activity outside the subcontinent is Arun Coomer Bose, *Indian Revolutionaries Abroad, 1905–1922*.

75. Yajnik, *Krishnavarma*, pp. 222–75; Dharmavira, *Lala Har Dayal and Revolutionary Movement of His Times*, pp. 115–34. The publication site of *Bande Mataram* shifted constantly.

76. Documents on these movements in J&P 1907, 2824. Also, published accounts in Dharmavira; L. P. Mathur, *Indian Revolutionary Movements in the United States*; N. S. Hardikar, *Lala Lajpat Rai in America*; Khushwant Singh, *Ghadar, 1915*.

77. Intelligence problems discussed in J&P 1909, 1309. Also, Governor General of Canada to Minto, November 20, 1907, M.C.

wrote up synopses of conversations with Indians.[78] Because Canada and America had similar problems with migration from India, their immigration departments also shared information on a regular basis, some of which fed into the British intelligence network.[79] The U.S. Department of State consistently refused to aid the British ambassador in collecting information, however, and with the exception of prosecuting the founder and first editor of the *Ghadar*, Har Dayal, in 1914, it permitted Indian political activists to operate in relative freedom prior to the First World War.[80] Although the Indian government disliked relying on such sources, it did not pursue another suggestion that appeared sporadically in secretariat minutes—the dispatch of special agents to work in Canada and America.[81]

While European countries were more cooperative in helping contain revolutionary activity, they also provided sanctuary for nationalists who maintained a low visibility and did not interfere in local politics. The nature of relations between the French and Indian governments fluctuated through periods of tension and cordiality. The escape of a revolutionary, V. D. Savarkar, who was being returned to India for trial, particularly upset British hopes of eliminating Paris as a haven for Indian propagandists. When Savarkar jumped ship at Marseilles on July 8, 1910, police officers followed and arrested him on French soil despite his pleas for asylum. The French Chamber demanded that he be repatriated to France, and the resulting diplomatic struggle ended in the International Court at The Hague.[82] Bad feelings that had been caused by the Savarkar incident gradually diminished until, by 1913, French officials regularly confiscated revolutionary materials, fined Indians who used Paris as a distribution center for Ghadar publications, and reported news to London and India. In March of 1914, for example, a box of addressed envelopes that contained copies of a very inflammatory pamphlet, *Shabash*, fell into the hands of French customs. Ghadarites had sent the literature to Madama Cama for transshipment to India.

78. Hopkinson reports in U.S. Immigration Department file 52903/110A, 1911–1913 (U.S. National Archives). Also, J&P 1912, 275.

79. Correspondence between Commissioner General to Acting Commissioner, Ellis Island, April–May 1914, file 52903/110D, 1914, Immigration Department.

80. U.S. policies examined in Diwakar Prasad Singh, "American Official Attitudes Toward the Indian Nationalist Movement, 1905–1929" (Ph.D. diss., University of Hawaii, 1964). Comments of C. R. Cleveland (May 9, 1914), GIPOL June 1914, 75–77A.

81. Suggested by police officials and several Council members in files on the Ghadar activities in America.

82. Several voluminous J&P collections relate to the controversy. A succinct coverage is in Dharmavira, *Har Dayal*, pp. 135–37.

The French warned the Imperial C.I.D., which had the tract notified under the Sea Customs Act so as to capture additional copies that were being shipped directly from San Francisco.[83]

The India Office soon became the nerve center for disseminating intelligence on Indians abroad. As early as 1907, Scotland Yard began shadowing radicals in London at the request of the India Council, and detectives followed John Morley for a time to protect him from imagined harm. Morley generally did not involve himself in surveillance, leaving such matters to the Permanent Under Secretary, Arthur Godley, the head of the Judicial and Public Committee, Lee-Warner, and Morley's political aide-de-camp, Curzon Wylie.[84] The J&P Committee studied issues of *The Indian Sociologist* and notified India of particularly dangerous articles. Despite this help, the Indian government felt that the India Office cared little about controlling sedition in London or for sending useful intelligence. Morley did not see the India Office in the role of policeman or prosecutor, although he admitted to Minto that the Home Office and Scotland Yard were ill-equipped to handle Indian conspirators:

> They have no sort of agency to distinguish Hindu from Muslim, or Verma from Varna. They are entirely unfitted to obtain information about secret Indian societies, or traffic in arms, or the circulation of certain pamphlets. . . . Both you and I can easily understand that the ordinary square-toed English constable, even in the detective branch, would be rather clumsy in tracing your wily Asiatics. Meanwhile, the only proposal seems to be, by way of experiment, the engagement of an Indian police officer (retired) who is to work under the direction of somebody in this office. On the whole, I doubt whether this office should in any way make its own connections here and in foreign capitals, with us as persons whom they may consult when they like, and who, in turn, may tell them anything we may think useful.[85]

When Scotland Yard did bring in examples of seditious writings, Morley avoided prosecution because a case might publicize the

83. The pamphlet and proceedings are in GIPOL June 1914, 75–77A. I am obliged to Professor Emily Brown, University of Northern Iowa, for this and other references relating to Har Dayal. Japan also forced closure of especially virulent publications, most notably Barkatullah's *Islamic Fraternity* (published in Tokyo), due to pressure from the British Foreign Office. Bose, *Revolutionaries*, p. 69.

84. Hirtzel diary, May 21, 1907; notes in P&S files 1907, 2573 and 3313.

85. Morley to Minto, June 4, 1908, M.C. Other correspondence relating to the situation includes Kitchener to Minto, January 22, 1908; Stuart to Pinhey, June 19, 1908; Coldstream to D. Smith, Jan. 2, 1909, all M.C. Ironically, the first British inclination, when confronted with revolutionaries in 1907, was to import European detectives to track down "seditionists."

nationalist cause and raise questions in the public's mind by its discussion in the English press.[86]

Minto and his Council became so disturbed with Morley's attitude that they dispatched a strong request in March of 1909 for improved cooperation in "checking the manufacture of sedition in England."[87] The dispatch brought no improvements, but a murder did.

On July 1, 1909, a young revolutionary, Madan Lal Dhingra, assassinated Curzon Wylie at a meeting of the National Indian Association in London. Minto immediately appreciated the murder's impact on opinion in England:

> It seems a somewhat terrible thing to say, but together with the grief here, there is the universal expression of a belief that good will come from what has happened—that people at home will at least realize the dangers of allowing the hatching of sedition in their midst—not only for themselves but for us in India. . . . I am afraid the exaggerated worship of so-called freedom has led the British public to ignore hard facts—and horrible as the lesson has been, I hope it will not be useless.[88]

A noticeable shift in attitudes in the India Office toward dissent came a few days later. Minto had pressed Morley for some time to permit a ban of Hyndman's *Justice*. On June 15, Morley noted on the file that *Justice* had best be left alone, but Wylie's assassination apparently changed his mind.[89] The India Office also reversed the decision not to prosecute the staff of *The Indian Sociologist*, and despite Krishnavarma's escape to Paris, two successive printers of the paper received jail sentences.[90] Within a year of Wylie's murder, almost all Indian revolutionaries in England had been imprisoned, driven abroad, or silenced. Aware of danger on its doorstep, the India Office now paid more attention to the collection and dispatch of intelligence relating to Indian politics.

That intelligence permitted closer checks on publications mailed to India. Authorities in London sent out background on specific items, and then Customs attempted interception, a procedure illustrated by the "Khalsa pamphlets" incident. Scotland Yard wired India in 1909 that members of the India House had

86. Morley note (September 15, 1908), J&P 1908, 3430.
87. Home–Political Despatch, 3, March 4, 1909, and notes, GIPOL March 1909, 148–150A.
88. Minto to Morley, July 7, 1909, and Morley's response, July 8, 1909, M.C.
89. Morley note (June 15, 1909), J&P 1909, 2174; in same file, telegram of July 19, 1909.
90. Morley to Minto, August 26, 1909, M.C. Yajnik, *Krishnavarma*, p. 272.

posted a series of tracts aimed at Sikhs and particularly Jat Sikh soldiers. The Government of India banned entry under the Customs Act without seeing the tracts and ordered their seizure at the Aden Post Office. On receiving specimens from Aden, the Imperial C.I.D. notified postal officials to watch for similar material that might possibly slip through the sea cordon.[91]

Confiscations bred greater wariness, however, among revolutionaries abroad. In 1907 tracts generally entered India in easily identifiable, open packets; by 1908 they usually were shipped in sealed covers or wrapped in magazines, stuffed in self-improvement manuals, and even sewn into innocuous books such as *Oliver Twist*.[92] The leakage in the system forced the Indian Home Department and C.I.D. to find additional means of identifying political writings and coordinating bans. Those efforts ran afoul of the same problems that affected earlier control of material in the mails.

Several experiments focused on postal articles sent to specific categories of Indians. During December of 1908, special officers sorted through mail being transported from Aden to Bombay. Armed with lists of revolutionary contacts, these watchdogs examined items directed to suspicious addresses. Nervousness over the uproar if such interference became public led to the cessation of the "travelling censors" after examination of a few mails. In any event, as a C.I.D. official noted, "the haul" was a "poor one."[93] During the same period, the British tried to intercept political documents addressed to students. One early effort was made when Indians in London sent tracts to the Dayanand Anglo-Vedic and Islamia Colleges in Lahore. Acting without full legal authority, the Punjab government confidentially ordered that mail addressed to students generally and not by name, or obviously addressed in a mass fashion, be delivered to the school's principal. The Indian government applauded the Punjab's action but decided to abandon the project on two grounds. First, the Home Department warned, principals should not be obliged to differentiate between harmless and dangerous matter. Also, the illegality of confiscation without an appropriate notification could generate criticism and thereby cause more trouble than it prevented.[94]

A year later the Indian government attempted a broadened

91. Background in GIPOL February 1909, 204A.

92. For example, C.I.D. note by Stevenson-Moore (January 19, 1909), GIPOL October 1909, 14–48A. Considerable attention will be paid to such devices in my forthcoming study of political literature.

93. Note by Stuart (June 2, 1909), GIPOL June 1909, 132–134A.

94. Notes by Risley (January 7, February 11, 1908), and GI to PG, 1933, February 21, 1908, GIPOL May 1908, 22–25A.

version of the Punjab plan. Postal officers intercepted articles generally addressed to students or to hostels and handed them to the C.I.D. Specialists then read the material and returned mail that they judged was devoid of political impact. The system rapidly got out of hand, incurring considerable delays and destruction of innocent documents. The Home Department's efforts to adjust the procedure in May of 1910 created new problems as well as a breakdown in communication at the highest echelons of the bureaucracy. The C.I.D. Director was not consulted on a key circular and he angrily attacked the Home Department for proceeding without his advice. Soon afterward, the government suspended the interceptions before getting "deeper in the mire."[95]

Legal uncertainty caused much of the confusion over postal interceptions. Officials occasionally acted without authority and had to retreat from their position, and others hesitated to search for and seize material because of the vagueness of orders. A revision of the Postal Act in 1912 somewhat clarified the situation. The new legislation delineated procedures and made possible closer coordination between Customs and the Post Office. Moreover, postal employees received enlarged powers to seize packets and unsealed material, but not correspondence in closed covers.[96]

The deliberations on the sanctity of first-class mail mirrored the British balancing of priorities. The Government of India did not view the examination of packets as controversial because this was accepted practice in England. Also, packets were easy to rewrap. Opening sealed mail was another matter. The privacy of first-class mail rested on a century of tradition, and resealing envelopes usually left marks of tampering. The disturbance caused by the opening of M. P. Wedderburn's correspondence had underscored the certainty of the recriminations that would result from indiscriminate interference with mail. Since 1907, therefore, the Home Department opposed suggestions by local governments to seize letters that were thought to contain political matter. When the United Provinces prepared to search all mail items, for example, the center intervened and limited the activities primarily to parcels and sample packets. In commenting on the incident, even the C.I.D. Director felt that established tradition forbade tampering with closed covers: "I would sooner risk the delivery of envelopes containing seditious matter than the appearance or reality of a police supervision of the post. . . . We must accept

95. Note by C. R. Cleveland (July 5, 1910), GIPOL September 1910, 93–97A; in the same file, comments by Cleveland (June 8, 1910) and H. Woodman (June 10, 1910).

96. Legislation discussed in J&P 1911, 2431.

the immunity of closed letters as a small sacrifice to the sacred character of the post."[97] Although the expense of first-class international postage probably minimized the chances of literature being mass mailed to India, the Government of India was willing to let such articles get through rather than to break a traditional privacy. It still could direct the opening of specific items, but those powers were exercised with care.[98]

A barrage of criticism from nationalists persisted despite postal and intelligence restraint toward the circulation of the most dangerous varieties of anti-British writings. Unless the bureaucracy somehow neutralized those attacks, according to the Home Department secretariat, the inevitable result would be public opinion "on entirely the wrong lines."[99] This concern led to discussion of a fresh strategy—assisting newspapers loyal to the *raj*.

During 1908 and early 1909, the Governor General's Council sifted through various schemes on how to cultivate a friendly press. Two ideas were rejected quickly: publication of an official newspaper and creation of a semiofficial news agency.[100] A third suggestion, from the editor of a Marathi weekly, *Jagat Vrita*, received more favorable comment. The editor, F. F. Gordon, argued that subsidies to loyal papers would ensure fair coverage of British policies and counter false reports. A related letter from Alfred Nundy, former editor of the Lahore *Tribune*, emphasized that select government support alone would ensure the survival of pro-British journals. Moderate editors supposedly did not feel called upon to give the government side of the question, especially if that meant financial loss.[101] Two members of the Council, Fleetwood Wilson and S. P. Sinha, questioned involvement in propaganda, but a majority felt that the responses of local governments should be gathered. The resulting circular asked for detailed alternate means of influencing the press. If half a dozen papers could be "brought to the doors of the people in parts of India where they are most wanted," the circular concluded, "an im-

97. Note by Cleveland (August 23, December 23, 1910), GIPOL February 1911, 60–65A. Policy and law receive detailed treatment in this file and also in GIPOL February 1913, 10D.

98. Particular care was taken to intercept letters of leading revolutionaries like Har Dayal. Background in GIPOL January 1914, 5A.

99. Notes by Minto (May 1909) and earlier Council minuting, GIPOL July 1909, 62A.

100. Correspondence and summary note by Stuart (June 30, 1908), GIPOL July 1909, 62A. On later efforts to form a press agency, GIPOL July 1910, 96–98A.

101. Nundy correspondence (September 28, 1910), GIPOL July 1909, 62A.

portant step would have been taken towards checking the spread of disloyal views founded on ignorance of the true facts of the administration of the country."[102]

Provincial heads generally favored support of pro-British journals on two conditions. First, the Imperial exchequer was to cover the costs, either directly or through expanded provincial budgets. Second, respondents agreed, funds should go to papers published in vernacular languages rather than to those published in English. English periodicals, they suggested, reached only an elite group, and anyway, they seemed to be more loyal in tone than their vernacular counterparts. The Government of India reviewed the replies and then decided that circumstances dictated a new effort at influence of the press. In May of 1910, Minto initiated subsidies to journals for a year, at the end of which time the approach would be evaluated.[103]

The sole negative response came from the Punjab. The provincial government opposed ties to papers involved in political discourse and countered with a suggestion that a Lahore educational journal be enlarged to present "correct views" of British policy. When the Indian government refused, the Punjab authorities attempted to show why subsidies would be unwise. Parts of the document merit being reproduced at length because they demonstrate how one segment of the bureaucracy evaluated the variables involved in manipulation of press opinion:

> In the Punjab religion plays a very important part in politics, and official discretion has ever to be on the alert to hold the balance in the rivalries of the three principal sects. A newspaper, to secure circulation, readers, and influence, must either be an organ frankly hostile to the Government or be the champion of the interests of the Muhammadan, Hindu or Sikh community. The state-subsidized paper would of course be debarred from resort to the matter and methods which lend zest and relish to the journals which cultivate sedition. If religious controversy and sectarian politics also were to be banned, there would be nothing to commend the subsidized journal to the ordinary Punjab reader. . . . Experience has shown that the championing of religious interests in the vernacular press in four cases out of five resolves itself into an indictment either of Government or of some local departmental official for exhibiting partiality to the rival sect. But if this feature in Provincial journalism thus constitutes an obstacle to the Government of India scheme, it is not without its compensating advantages. The situation which the Government of India scheme is designed to ameliorate is one in which the masses are contemplated as being fed with a stream

102. Circular 972–80, July 1, 1909, GIPOL July 1909, 62A.
103. Replies, and Circular 538–42, May 12, 1910, in GIPOL June 1910, 65–78A.

of misrepresentations and insidious and malevolent deductions uncounteracted by any presentation of the questions at issue from the point of view of truth and accuracy, or of the aims and intentions of Government. Now in a society such as we have in the Punjab in which public questions are customarily viewed and discussed from a party point of view, and where party cleavage is on religious than on pro- and anti-Government lines, there is much more frequent emergence in journalistic controversy of true and just views of public questions than in those provinces in which almost all the persons who concern themselves with politics do so as opponents of Government.[104]

The argument was convincing, and the Indian government agreed that, for the time being, the Punjab could postpone supporting a particular journal.

Six provincial governments proceeded with subsidies. Bombay purchased 10,000 weekly copies of the *Jagat Vrita* (annual cost, Rs. 15,000) and distributed them among villagers.[105] Rai Narendra Nath Sen received Rs. 62,500 annually from the Bengal government in payment for 25,000 copies of the weekly *Sulabh Samachar*, sent to villages, *panchayats* (village councils), and educational institutions. Similarly, the United Provinces subscribed to 300 copies of the Urdu *Independent*, and the East Bengal government paid Rs. 32,000 annually for 10,000 copies of the *Biswa Barta*. Smaller subsidies were made in the North-West Frontier Province to the Urdu *Afghan* (Rs. 1,200) and in the Central Provinces, to a Hindi monthly, *Hitkarini*.

The public outcry and the expense argued against continuation of the subsidies when the Indian government subsequently reviewed the situation. The subsidies had evoked sharp criticism from the press and members of the Imperial Legislative Council. The M.L.A.s kept asking for statistics and background on British affiliation with journalists, and in March 1911 they tried to alter the Bengal budget to prevent further payments. Criticism also came from London. A delegation of M.P.s met with Morley and challenged the effectiveness and the principles involved in the support of periodicals. Negotiations on the issue lasted for a year, leading finally to a dispatch from the Indian Office questioning subsidies.[106]

The Government of India perhaps could have maintained at least a portion of the subsidies had they proven successful. Re-

104. PG to GI, 3043, October 21, 1909, GIPOL June 1910, 65–78A.

105. Background on these subsidies based on notes and a précis, GIPOL May 1911; 15D; J&P 1911, 902.

106. Public Despatch 77, May 3, 1912, and reply, GI Despatch Political 13, November 28, 1912, J&P 1911, 902. On M.L.A.s and subsidies, see GIPOL April 1911, 129–149A.

ports from local authorities indicated otherwise. The Central Provinces doubted the value of continued payments, as did East Bengal. Support for the *Afghan* already had ceased because the frontier paper took a pro-Muslim, controversial direction. The United Province's *Independent* had been prosecuted for obscenity and lost money steadily. When its editor demanded a doubled subsidy, the government stopped all payment. Although lukewarm toward the *Sulabh Samachar*, the Bengal government continued to cover most of its costs. The subsidy terminated, however, when the son of the former proprietor, who died in 1911, tried to renegotiate monetary arrangements. Only in Bombay did district officers note success in influencing public opinion. Otherwise, the Indian government admitted the failure of the experiment by canceling extant subsidies except for the *Jagat Vrita*, and that too lapsed after 1912.[107]

In the meantime, correspondence on the tone of the press had begun to reflect an old theme. Warning that temporary moderation had given way by the fall of 1909 to a crescendo of anti-British writing, local governments again raised a question of extended controls. Concern with the growing bravado of publicists coincided with the emergence of defects in existing regulations. Registration details on newspapers frequently were inaccurate; some of them, for example, indicated dummy proprietors and printers instead of those who were actually responsible for the contents.[108] Locating and prosecuting authors of tracts or books became more difficult because they increasingly tended to remain anonymous. Individual items could be notified as seditious, but the law prevented the British from summarily removing them from circulation without judicial process. Often, material had spread widely by the time the trial was completed. Finally, seizure of printing presses threatened only a small sector of Indian journalists. Provincial officials requested new measures, such as broad demands for security, which would affect many papers able to avoid the stringent incitement to violence act.[109]

Minto's Council accordingly examined the options open to the bureaucracy. Several members called for a comprehensive bill,

107. Reports and future policy discussed in GIPOL December 1912, 1–10A.

108. Notes by Adamson (July 26, 1908), GIPOL July 1909, 124–125A; Stuart (December 31, 1909), GIPOL July 1910, 5–32A. Sometimes the British discovered they were prepared to prosecute a small boy instead of a hardened editor. See, for example, the *Matri Puja* case, J&P 1910, 3420.

109. H. Woodman note (December 8, 1909), GIPOL July 1910, 65–78A, and opinions of local government in the same file.

but the two adamant opponents of the move, Wilson and Sinha, helped postpone serious debate with the argument that violent language alone did not justify granting wider powers to the government. Neither Indian politicians nor London would agree.[110] Only a political turn for the worse, a new outbreak or outrage, could create the circumstances favorable to an extension of press controls.

The 1910 Press Act and Its Operation

On November 18, 1909, a bomb bounced harmlessly off the carriage in which Lord and Lady Minto were touring Ahmedabad. Magistrate A. M. T. Jackson of Nasik (Maharashtra) was not so fortunate. Members of the Abhinav Bharat, a terrorist organization, riddled him with bullets on December 21, 1909. A week later, the police discovered bombs in front of the District Commissioner's home in Ambala, Punjab. Indian revolutionaries obviously had moved into an accelerated phase of violent protest.

The recrudescence of terrorism opened another chapter of British repression in India. Minto tended to make light of the attempt on his own life, but he viewed differently the well-planned shooting of Jackson and the Ambala bombs. Conspiracy and plots, he wrote Morley, seemed to be everywhere.[111] Consequently, force met force, as the government attempted to destroy revolutionary groups and reassert its authority. Trials, expansion of police activities, and greater protection for informers followed. Panicked and unclear as to the enormity of revolutionary threats, Minto suggested, to Morley's horror, that martial law might be required.[112]

The prevailing atmosphere of fear and insecurity among the Governor General and his Council produced new legislation on the press. The Home Department revived the earlier files and gathered opinion on the press situation. The key assumption during the resulting debate was that tracts and newspapers created a political ethos conducive to revolution, a view summed up in this statement by the new Home Member, Herbert Risley:

> If it is good for India that British rule should continue, it is equally essential that the relations between Government and the educated community should be cordial and intimate, and that cannot long

110. Noting in GIPOL July 1910, 5–32A; earlier discussion in July 1909, 124–125A. A good description of the various groups within the Council is in Wolpert, *Morley*, p. 65.

111. Minto to Morley, November 19, December 23, 1909, M.C.

112. Minto to Morley, January 13, 1910, M.C. Background on the various trials and attacks is in Guha, *Spark*, pp. 125–78.

> continue to be the case if organs of the educated community lay themselves out to embitter those relations in every sort of way, and to create a permanent atmosphere of latent and often open hostility.[113]

The opponents of controls in the Council rallied, but Minto joined other members in overriding their protests. While the Legislative Department drafted a bill, Minto intimated in a speech to the newly elected Imperial Legislature that the government would be intervening decisively to handle the revolutionary press. He also wired Morley about the pending legislation.[114]

The Judicial and Public Committee of the India Council quickly examined the telegraphed proposals and generally accepted the argument that prosecutions would not suffice in a crisis. One member, Theodore Morison, dissented. Questioning the wisdom of interference with Indian opinion, he said that the bureaucracy could not arrest a popular movement by coercive tactics. Since most Indians supported the *raj*, their assistance in isolating extremists should be solicited rather than to rely on acts that could alienate broad-based support. The committee majority nevertheless prevailed, Morley approved, and Minto received permission to present the measure to the legislature.[115]

Risley introduced the Indian Press bill on February 4 with a speech designed to maximize support and to meet anticipated criticism. Rehearsing the history of revolution in India, he argued that mythology, reverence for foreign radicals such as Mazzini, and particularly, dissemination of hate literature had led unsophisticated youths on the path of murder and treason. Stopping the drift demanded severe action. Minto then called for a suspension of legislative rules so the bill could go to a select committee without the usual delays. His tactic of placing Gopal Krishna Gokhale, S. P. Sinha, and three other Indians on the review body tended to minimize Indian protest at the acceleration of proceedings.[116]

The bill had three major objectives. First, it would increase the government's control over printing presses and publishers. All press proprietors who made a declaration under the 1867 Press Act for the first time would be required to deposit security unless it was dispensed with by a local magistrate. Owners of

113. Risley note (January 16, 1910); notes by Stuart (December 31, 1909), GIPOL July 1910, 5–32A.

114. Based on noting in GIPOL July 1910, 5–32A; Minto to Morley, January 27, 1910; Lady Minto, *India, Minto and Morley, 1905–1910*, p. 372.

115. India Council notes, J&P 1910, 608 and 989.

116. Proceedings in GIPOL July 1910, 5–32A.

existing presses would make the deposit only if they printed "objectionable matter" (incitement to murder, tampering with the loyalty of the army, exciting racial or religious animosity, expressing hatred of government, criminal intimidation). Once the security had been deposited, local governments could declare the amount (up to Rs. 5,000) forfeit if objectionable matter were printed. The press would either cease to function or the owner would be required to put up a larger deposit (Rs. 1,000–10,000). If thereafter the printer published similar material, the security and the press could be seized. Newspaper proprietors also had to make deposits and were liable to forfeiture. Second, the bill extended bureaucratic control over the importation and transmission of political literature. Customs and postal authorities could detain and search suspicious mail without specific orders from the Government of India. Newspapers for which a security had not been deposited, as required by a magistrate, also could be seized summarily. Finally, the legislation authorized local governments to declare forfeit (banned) any newspaper, book, or other printed document containing matter of the prohibited description, and, on such public declaration, police could search for and seize the material. The press bill therefore provided for new deterrents (securities) and executive action to remove publications from circulation. It barred recourse to judicial review except through appeal to a special bench of high court judges, who could decide whether the matter objected to was or was not of the kind defined in the act.[117]

The select committee presented a slightly modified draft after four days of excited deliberation. The revisions included reducing the initial maximum security from Rs. 5,000 to Rs. 2,000 and limiting confiscation by postal and customs officials to mail other than closed packets and letters. Three Indians—Gokhale, R. N. Mudholkar, and M. M. Malaviya—appended minutes of dissent. While admitting the need to end assassinations and other political crimes, the legislators questioned whether the measures should become permanent in the statute book. They attempted in vain to alter the bill so its provisions would lapse after three years. Noting that the bureaucracy already had substantial powers, Malaviya took a firmer stand and denounced official haste in enacting the bill. He suggested that one principle be reversed, namely, that the judiciary rather than the executive branch deal with matters related to the press. A magistrate thus would call on the owner of a press or on a publisher to show

117. Draft bill in GIPOL July 1910, 5–32A. Final act in Roy, *Law* (1915), pp. 50–58.

cause why security should not be deposited, and later, the magistrate would initiate the proceedings for declaring the security forfeit.[118]

Indian opposition would have been more vocal except for Minto's efforts to cultivate legislative support. In talks and at private dinners, Minto tried to convince critics that the government would not misuse the new powers. Moreover, he promised Gokhale that leniency would be exercised in dealing with already operating presses.[119] These tactics were important because the recent constitutional reforms had expanded the over-all size, function, and Indian representation of the Imperial Legislative Council. The British still had a comfortable bloc of official and nominated members, but Minto wished to avoid antagonism and consequent polarization on key issues.

Minto's lobbying contributed to a relatively peaceful passage of the bill on February 8. Gokhale presented amendments to limit the securities and executive discretion, but most Indians joined with the government to negate his proposals by a heavy majority. In reviewing the proceedings, Minto told Morley that he was proud of the legislature's "responsible" debate. Characteristically, the Governor General salved the feelings of moderate politicians (and Morley) by releasing Bengali deportees the day after enactment of the press bill.[120]

Maneuvering a controversial measure through legislative shoals was relatively simple compared with putting it into operation. The initial step involved instructions on procedure. A March 1 circular contained the Indian government's views as to the task facing the bureaucracy. First, each local unit would be expected to assume responsibility for enforcing security obligations. The circular did not establish guidelines on which new papers should give security, but it did mention dispensing with deposits in case of hardship (as with small presses). In order to make security provisions effective, governments must reexamine and strengthen arrangements for the surveillance of publications. The instructions also stressed the need for communication within the bureaucracy. Local governments could initiate forfeitures after consultation with legal personnel, but they must keep the Government of India informed.[121]

Two other circulars supplemented the initial statement. The

118. Committee report and notes in J&P 1910, 989. Also, Roy, *Law* (1915), pp. 46–50.

119. Council noting on negotiations, GIPOL July 1910, 5–32A; Minto's comments, Minto to Morley, February 9, 1910, M.C.

120. Minto to Morley, February 9, 1910, M.C.

121. Circular 324–333, March 1, 1910 and notes, GIPOL July 1910, 5–32A.

first called on all I.C.S. officers to cooperate in stamping out sedition. Education officials, for example, were expected to monitor history tests and classroom instruction to prevent "crude teachings" on the negative aspects of British rule.[122] The government urged officers to check disloyalty through personal influence and by passing on information to judges and the local secretariat. They also should warn religious leaders of the harm "done to young men by the perversion of sacred writings for seditious purposes," and express official disapproval toward further publication of such material. In short, all officials were to be associated intimately with a campaign to eliminate political threats. The second circular was written in a more conciliatory tone. Soon after the dispatch of the first instructions, Gokhale learned of their content and told Minto privately that the government had reneged on its promise to moderate security demands. The Governor General publicly did not accept Gokhale's interpretation, but the secretariat issued a new circular that pointed out the wisdom of lenient exemptions from the security requirement.[123]

The three documents contained references to the major problems affecting implementation of the press act. Despite repeated efforts to improve reporting on newspapers, the system required constant adjustment if the government were to exercise closer supervision of literary output. In addition, coordinated action depended on flow of information and cooperation among bureaucrats. The circulars left to local authorities the tricky question of what matters constituted grounds for security and forfeiture. They did mention, however, that decisions should take into account legal restraints, local circumstances, and the government's persistent need to defend itself against London and Indian critics.

A self-study by the C.I.D. in early 1910 indicated that changes in police operations would aid enforcement of the new restrictions. The touring head of the Imperial C.I.D., C. R. Cleveland, found that police efficiency and arrangements continued to vary from province to province. Some departments, he charged, had been negligent in uncovering dangerous printed matter: "I do not think that in Bengal, Bombay, and the Punjab books, pamphlets, dramas, songs, etc. have been examined in the past with sufficient care or knowledge, and I receive evidence from time to time of the existence of publications which a more careful system would have branded."[124] Newspapers tended to

122. Circular 344–353, March 4, 1910, GIPOL July 1910, 5–32A.

123. Circular 403–412, March 31, 1910, and notes, GIPOL July 1910, 5–32A.

124. C. R. Cleveland note (July 6, 1910), GIPOL January 1912, 41–49A.

be more carefully scrutinized than tracts, which appeared suddenly and spread before police shut "the stable door too late."[125] Cleveland's criticism focused attention on three defects within the administrative system—inadequate machinery for surveillance, inaccurate and belated reporting to the Indian government, and lack of coordination.

The Government of India turned first to surveillance. In July of 1910, local governments were instructed to reevaluate their supervision of books and tracts. Noting that items kept slipping through the official net, the circular also asked for reports on how books were examined and how the procedure might be improved.[126] Answers dribbled in over a two-year period. The slowness in response probably resulted from resistance to interference in local affairs. Provincial heads agreed to place a closer watch on printed matter, but uniformly opposed extensive modification of existing arrangements. Bengal, for example, wanted to continue relying on district magistrates to warn of potentially dangerous publications. The United Provinces instructed its Director of Public Instruction to assign officers to examine publications at random and prepare reports. Leaving the initial screening to departments of education or to libraries that received books through copyright was a common practice. The Punjab questioned the need for additional machinery. Arguing that a majority of Indians sided with the government, the Punjab Lieutenant Governor also offered this interesting rationale for not expanding supervision facilities: "The factional feeling so strongly prevalent in the Punjab affords further safeguard against any prolonged dissemination of objectionable books. The vigilance of the Vernacular Press and its contributors may be trusted to draw attention to anything from which one side can hope to make capital at the expense of its opponents."[127]

Although the Indian government could not overcome all aspects of traditional decentralization, its persistent pressure did effect change. Provincial police reinforced their control of translating facilities and attempted to expedite discovery of illicit publications.[128] Another area of success in administrative reform was the standardization of reports. The center depended on local

125. Cleveland note.

126. Circular 734–741, July 26, 1910, GIPOL January 1912, 41–49A.

127. PG to GI, 13C, February 25, 1914, GIPOL March 1914, 108–116A. The file contains the replies, in addition to notes on major issues.

128. For example, the Bengal correspondence and notes, in GI Police, September 1914, 177–178A. A detailed commentary on internal operations of the C.I.D. is extremely difficult because many police records remain closed to scholars.

officials for annual press statements and quarterly reviews of nonperiodical literature. These surveys were in some instances incomplete and in others misleading, since they reflected the orientation of the reviewer. Hindu reporters exaggerated the negative aspects of Muslim books and vice versa; interpretations by Englishmen tended to be alarmist. The C.I.D. Director correctly summarized the reporting system as an "Augean stable," emitting material "strongly tinged with the individuality and race of the officers who write them."[129] The Home Department therefore prepared model forms to be followed by reporters and warned them to be punctual and not to stray from the established facts.[130] The secretariat tried to ensure at the same time that local authorities supplied up-to-date information on forfeitures, deposits, and, most importantly, individual proscribed works. Occasionally, men involved in provincial administration were too preoccupied to report on banned tracts and books. The center devoted endless days to gathering such information because it permitted an overview of Indian literary and political trends. Moreover, Indian councils and Parliament increasingly expected accurate details on press actions.[131]

The analysis of provincial reports was related to the Government of India's function as a vital link within an imperial bureaucratic network. In addition to distributing reports up and down the system, officials at the capital attempted to coordinate press proceedings throughout the subcontinent. Except for a few newspapers with limited all-India circulation, Indian periodicals typically reached only local subscribers, and therefore action against them required little governmental cooperation across provincial lines. Proscription of tract literature, however, created confusion and potential conflict. A work might be proscribed in one province and circulate freely in a neighboring one. The Government of India hoped to prevent this irregularity by distributing the opinion of a legal adviser that notifications proscribing titles affected all provinces no matter which administrative unit initiated the ban. When some officials questioned the ruling, the secretariat instructed governments to communicate directly with each other.[132] Exchange of notifications supposedly would provide

129. Cleveland note (July 2, 1910), GIPOL September 1910, 104–106A. The general problem of bias receives attention in Barrier and Wallace, *Punjab Press*.

130. Circular 856–864, September 5, 1910, GIPOL September 1910, 104–106A. Circular 795–801, August 22, 1910, GIPOL August 1910, 151–152A.

131. Wheeler note (January 9, 1914), GIPOL February 1914, 67–68A.

132. Circular 763–770, August 10, 1910, and noting, GIPOL August 1910, 135–137A. An earlier discussion is in August 1910, 104–105A.

warnings and eliminate inconsistencies. Despite the 1910 circulars, the local governments still continued to make their own decisions on banning procedures. Burma decided, for example, that books could not be proscribed unless they had been examined by Burmese magistrates.[133] The provinces' independence produced controversy over specific works such as the jurisdictional squabble between the governments of Punjab and the North-West Frontier Province. A politician in Peshawar (N.W.F.P.) published a controversial book in Amritsar, but because copies did not circulate outside the Punjab, the N.W.F.P. government ruled that it was unable to ban the item or arrest the culprit. The Punjab refused to ban the book, and the affair ended with no arrests and no proscription.[134] To avoid such differences, the Indian government finally empowered secretariats to proscribe publications without prior examination. The Indian Home Department also compiled a reasonably accurate master list of banned literature for the information of provincial police departments.[135] Apparently these corrective acts functioned effectively, because the issue received little comment in subsequent Home–Political files.

The basic mechanisms implementing the 1910 Press Act had been routinized by 1914. Although mistakes and disparities persisted, press proceedings tended to go so smoothly that the Governor General and his Council permitted the central and provincial secretariats to handle all but the most controversial cases.[136] Proceedings concerning newspapers went through three phases —investigation, seizure of security, and demand for enhanced security—a pattern illustrated by the forfeiture of the *Punjab Advocate*'s deposit. In June 1912, the paper charged the bureaucracy with "personal rule," which disregarded Indian interests. The C.I.D. had been watching the paper for months and decided that an article it published provided ample grounds for prosecution. After correspondence within the Punjab and with the Imperial Home Department, a magistrate confiscated the paper's Rs. 300 deposit. The publisher deposited fresh security and moderated his editorial policy.[137] Proscription of books and

133. Burma to GI, and consequent exchange of letters, GIPOL October 1914, 241–256A.

134. Correspondence (particularly NWFP to GI, 2102, December 10, 1913), GIPOL October 1914, 241–256A.

135. Circular 377–386, July 11, 1914, GIPOL October 1914, 241–256A; on the lists, February 1914, 67–68A; April 1914, 41–64A.

136. Based primarily on a survey of files, 1910–1914. Minto had little firsthand acquaintance with the internal administration of the C.I.D. Minto note (March 22, 1910), GIPOL April 1910, 59–62A.

137. Proceedings and correspondence in GIPOL August 1912, 93–98A.

tracts followed similar lines. Depending on the site of publication, the India Office, central secretariat, or local officers raised the alarm about an item. On receiving a copy (or occasionally, mere background information on content), the government ordered a magistrate to ban the publication. Seizure of copies quickly followed notification of the ban in the local gazette. Authors and publishers sometimes simplified the process by submitting books for scrutiny. When Gandhi discovered that his Gujarati study, *Indian Home Rule*, had been confiscated, for example, he sent the Government of India an English version to demonstrate that the pamphlet was not seditious. Unimpressed by Gandhi's protestations against violence, the police noted that nonviolence could be dangerous and therefore banned the new edition.[138]

British Experiments in Perspective

Although this study of British experiments traces the evolution of laws and institutions between 1906 and 1913, it has yet to deal with several broad issues that relate to control of publications. What were the criteria and elements involved in decisions to ban? What patterns emerged from the period? and What were their implications for future political encounter? An assessment of the initial experience with extensive press controls should provide useful answers to these questions.

The Government of India's views on the success of restrictions of the press varied sharply with circumstance. The first special C.I.D. report on the 1910 press act claimed improvement in the tone of Indian literature.[139] The same analyses could be found at each level of administration in 1912. While supplying background on Indian measures to the Netherlands' colonial office, for example, the India Office boasted that the press legislation had moderated opinion and had stunted the growth of anti-British writings.[140] The tide of revolution had supposedly turned. This self-confidence did not last beyond 1912, however, because of yet another surge of revolutionary activity, symbolized by a bombing in Delhi that injured Viceroy Lord Hardinge on December 23 of that year. A bedside communication from Hardinge prevented massive British reprisals, but his Council felt

138. Notified under the Customs Act, July 30, 1910. Background in J&P 1910, 1468.

139. *Report on the Indian Press, 1911* (C.I.D. note), in GIPOL September 1912, 9D.

140. Correspondence between the Under Secretary of State for India and the Under Secretary of State for Foreign Affairs, J&P 1913, 885. Also, comments of the PG, UP in GIPOL January 1912, 41–49A.

that this incident required executive control of the press. A confidential circular ordered officers to increase banning and security demands. "Indulgent toleration" supposedly had permitted the reemergence of sedition, and to prevent its continuation, more repression was in order.[141]

British ambivalence toward increased coercion derived largely from inadequate information on the extremists' activities. The secretariat did not have a clear picture of what was happening and thus tended to treat symptoms, such as bombings or lulls between outrages, as hard evidence of the effects of policy. The decentralized nature of administration intensified their problem. Files of the Home Department referred often to local governments (and other Imperial departments) as drawing different conclusions from events or as being lax with intelligence. Informers or special agents such as Hopkinson also injected bias or false evidence into the information system. Always operating under stress, the C.I.D. pieced together bits of news in an effort to discover trends and political guideposts. Not surprisingly, the resulting picture could be inconsistent and unreal.

Fluctuations in assessments of the press's nature and influence underline the difficulty in reaching conclusions about what the bureaucracy was doing and why. There was not one but many policies and strategies relating to printed matter, and caution is required in generalizing on trends. Nevertheless, distinct patterns emerge from the shifts in policy discussion and from the aura of uncertainty that colors official documents.

First, seven years of experimentation produced lasting institutions and techniques of control. Police, customs, and postal arrangements tightened with time and became more efficient. Those mechanisms—and the laws underpinning them—continued to operate until the departure of the British from India. Except for a temporary cessation of security demands in the 1920s, the Indian Press Act or its derivatives served as the basis for intervention in circulation of printed matter. The annual and quarterly reports flowing through the system also continued, gradually improving in detail and usefulness. Defects in the C.I.D. became apparent, but with less frequency and less resultant alarm.[142] The early efforts to confront problems of intelli-

141. Circular 89–100, April 8, 1913, GIPOL May 1913, 5–9A. The dynamics behind the resurgence are discussed in Guha, *Spark*, pp. 179–93.

142. Although details on the evolving C.I.D. network are not readily available, one indication of improvement was the predominant feeling among revolutionaries from approximately 1910–1912 onward that the police had them under constant surveillance. See, for example, the references in Jogesh Chandra Chatterji, *In Search of Freedom*.

gence and coordination equipped the British with tested, well-oiled machinery that came into use in later battles with their opponents in India.

Statistics on press action indicate that the *raj* utilized that machinery selectively. Ten papers were prosecuted under the Incitements Act, all prior to 1911. Between January 1909 and December 1910, the British initiated 57 proceedings against publicists under the penal code, the next two years, only 20. Instead of resorting to punitive measures, the government generally preferred invoking the preventive sections of the 1910 Press Act. A total of 272 securities were demanded from proprietors of printing presses (1910–1913) and 158 deposits from owners of newspapers. During the same time, local governments proscribed approximately 200 tracts, books, handbills, and posters, and about 100 individual issues of newspapers.[143] Given the excitement and haste surrounding the press bill's enactment, such wide use of power would seem logical. There were signs, however, of British restraint. Most securities were minimal (Rs. 200–500), and of the 1,341 presses and 1,068 newspapers begun (1910–1913), less than 15 per cent were required to deposit any amount.[144] Moreover, the government forfeited a total of 15 deposits and did not seize a single press.

Indian authorities undoubtedly would have gone further except for the political variables that affected their decisions. Although the rationality of bureaucratic decisionmaking can be exaggerated, four factors appeared constantly in proceedings on Indian publications. First, assumptions concerning colonial administration supplied both impetus for and checks on extensive controls. Maintaining the legitimacy of British rule was a paramount concern of officialdom. Among other factors this meant a defense of the ruler's *izzat*—"face" or honor. Indians theoretically respected the *raj* because of its image of strength, its unquestioned authority; as secretaries repeatedly noted in the files, they expected swift reaction to seditious literature. If the bureaucracy instead pursued a policy of toleration, those whose attitudes were not firm would question whether the British had the courage or

143. Statistics collected from J&P 1910, 1221; GIPOL July 1910, 198–199A; May 1913, 9–13A. British compilations have been adjusted with data from files on specific works. Although the records are useful, great caution must be exercised in using them because the central secretariat (and the India Office) never had full information from local departments.

144. These approximate figures are based on tables in GIPOL February 1914, 67–68A, adjusted slightly with data from other files. The government prepared lists of tracts, but compilations varied.

the right to rule. The periodic checking of critics therefore had a dual purpose—to prevent the spread of ideas that might affect especially vulnerable portions of the population and to demonstrate the strength of government.[145]

Concern with perpetuating the image of a politically superior, virtually omniscient ruler, on the other hand, deterred summary action. Unsuccessful prosecutions or judicial challenge had necessarily to be avoided because these failures might indicate weakness in the executive. Because officials in the two branches tended to see issues, such as defining *objectionable material*, from the same vantage point, conflicts over the legality of proceedings were minimal. The Government of India took pride in its virtually unblemished record for successful prosecutions. Nevertheless, legal remembrancers (advisers) worked overtime to ensure that all acts would be legal, as defined by the penal code. Sometimes deliberations within the secretariat took a humorous turn, such as the issue of whether *dhotis* (long pieces of cloth worn by males) stamped with patriotic poems could be considered printed matter under the Press Act (they finally were banned); at other times, bureaucrats wrote pages of opinion on which subsection or regulation could be employed to greatest advantage.[146] The government became committed to the review process because the alternative—launching a questionable prosecution—could undermine prestige and, with it, power.

The self-image of the British also became significant in center–local government relations, the second element to affect press maneuvers. Supporting the man on the spot was more than romantic verbiage. The Government of India saw the principle as an integral part of its attempt to portray the I.C.S. as a confident group of administrators who acted with a commonly shared will. An image of the united bureaucracy supposedly signified strength, while cracks in the "steel frame," internal commotion, and divergence of policy publicized weakness and disunity to opponents. In addition, refusal to back men on the spot would undercut their effectiveness. The ultimate result could be deteri-

145. This viewpoint is reflected in notes by Risley (GIPOL July 1910, 5–32A) and GI circular 344–353, March 4, 1910, GIPOL March 1910, 42–46A. Many of the same images also are found in two documents on political and social relations with Indians in N. G. Barrier, "How to Rule India," *Panjab Past and Present*, 5 (1971), 276–97.

146. For such detailed debate, see the file on the Mackarness tract and notes in J&P 1910, 1714. Discussion of the issues on the *dhoti* in GIPOL April 1910, 36–39A. The clothing in question consisted of five yards of cloth, with its border covered by these lines: "Mother farewell. I shall go to the gallows with a smile. The people of India will see this. One bomb can kill a man." The remainder eulogizes revolutionaries like Khudhi Ram Bose.

oration of morale and further strains on the command/intelligence system.[147]

Thus, when formulating press policies and legislation, the government took every opportunity to weigh local opinion so as to ensure close cooperation from all levels of administration. The constant flow of circulars slowed decisions but permitted evaluation of issues that might become troublesome at a later stage. A second implication was that the Governor General permitted subordinates to devise their own press tactics in light of how they interpreted local conditions. The following table suggests the variety of approaches subsumed under "Indian policy":

Actions Against Indian Publications, 1910–1913[148]

	Banned Items	Prosecution	Forfeiture	Warnings
Madras	31	8	8	—
Bombay	204	32	1	1
Bengal	119	43	4	25
Punjab	45	18	2	11
U.P.	54	7	—	—
Burma	247	1	—	1
N.W.F.P.	118	—	—	2
Delhi	6	—	—	—
C.P.	295	11	—	—
Assam	2	—	—	—

According to the statistics and supplemental observations by C.I.D. officers, Madras preferred the extreme step of forfeiture as a demonstration of strength over other methods. Bengal used all powers, as did Bombay. The Punjab relied heavily on warnings and security demands, while the North-West Frontier Province, Burma, and the Central Provinces regarded proscription as a means of clamping down on controversial material.

Although it encouraged flexibility and generally backed its subordinates, the Government of India superintended local decisions. The Imperial Home Department intervened when those decisions seemed to conflict with the "all-India" strategy. The

147. For example, the Butler argument in GIPOL May 1913, 9–13A, and earlier correspondence between Denzil Ibbetson and Minto over the resignation of a lieutenant governor, Fuller (Ibbetson to Minto, June 25, 1906; July 21, 1906; Minto to Ibbetson, July 21, 23, 1906, M.C.).

148. Tables based on data extracted from GIPOL May 1913, 9–13A; GIPOL February 1914, 67–68A; April 1914, 41–46A. The reservations mentioned earlier also pertain to these statistics.

frustrating campaign to increase prosecutions in the Punjab illustrated the process. As noted earlier, the lieutenant governor of the Punjab, Louis Dane (1908–1914), chose a conciliatory press policy instead of prosecutions on a wide scale. Fearing a recurrence of earlier disturbances, he successfully ignored demands for action from the center to forestall the explosion of political "dry powder."[149] More frequently, however, the Indian government had to prevent precipitate use of measures instead of prodding underlings. Besides suspending prosecutions or opposing deportations, the Governor General took an increasingly hard look at interception of publications from Great Britain. Ire in Parliament over such incidents as the seizure of books written by a prominent Englishman, Wilfred Blunt, resulted in a circular requesting all governments to check with the center before they interfered with English works.[150] Sensitivity extended to books published in London but written by controversial Indians. When the Bombay authorities wanted to ban B. C. Pal's *The Spirit of Indian Nationalism*, for example, the matter was referred to the Secretary of State, who vetoed the move.[151]

The India Office's role in the Pal affair symbolized its constant interference with decisions on the Indian press. The Governor General opposed injection of home opinion, on the grounds that it undercut the authority of the *raj* and removed discretionary power from men on the spot. London rarely accepted this argument except in crises. Morley continued to be a keen observer of repressive tendencies, and frequently found that prosecutions, such as that of a Calcutta journal *Karmayogin*, placed him in embarrassing situations. He had initially defended the *Karmayogin* case against charges of impropriety on the part of the government only to find, on receipt of full information, that the prosecution was indeed suspect. Labeling the proceedings a gross "mispolicy," Morley commented that "if I did not happen to be Secretary of State and were in the House of Commons, I would harry the Lieutenant Governor of Bengal to death in this case."[152] Unfortunately for Morley's image, the assessment proved accurate. The Calcutta High Court overturned the earlier conviction.

149. Cleveland note (August 28, 1914), GI Police, September 1914, 177–178A; comments by H. Wheeler (January 1913) and S. H. Butler (January 8, 1913), GIPOL May 1913, 9–13A.

150. Telegrams and notes in J&P 1913, 2957; circulars in GIPOL February 1911, 90–91A. The government confiscated—and later released—copies of *Parliaments of Justice under British Rule in Egypt* and *Secret History of English Occupation in Egypt*.

151. Correspondence and telegram (April 25, 1911), SS to GI, GIPOL February 1911, 90–91A.

152. Morley note (July 6, 1910), J&P 1910, 1051.

The Indian government received no breathing spell after Morley's retirement in 1910. If anything, the tendency to scrutinize press issues increased, as exemplified by the *Jhang Sial* incident in 1913. The Punjab declared forfeit the paper's Rs. 2,000 security for articles on bomb attacks. On reviewing the file, the new Secretary of State, Lord Crewe, and his colleagues in the India Council were shaken to find that, while commending the bravery of young patriots, the editor clearly advised them to participate in constitutional programs rather than throw their lives away. Edwin Montagu, the under secretary, drafted a dispatch to India urging that the forfeiture be set aside. The aim of the Press Act, Montagu stressed, was not to crush criticism but to direct it into constructive channels. After declaring that the article seemed an example of the latter objective, Montagu warned that the India Office could defend only wise measures, not misuse of power. His draft proved too strong for the Judicial and Public Committee, which passed a copy of the essay, without comment, to a retired lieutenant governor, J. P. Hewett. Hewett said that, on the whole, the author should be congratulated for his common sense. The committee eventually dropped the issue because it could not work out a compromise dispatch, but obviously specialists in London and India viewed political opinion from different perspectives.[153] Some men on the spot, a secretary in the India Office wrote, would "cheerfully confiscate the whole of European literature" if given a free hand.[154]

That judgment glossed over a fourth aspect of the tempering of repressive measures. The Government of India pictured itself as an element, albeit a dominant one, in a multidimensional political process. The British appreciated the effects of decisions on supporters and potential allies. A show of strength might ensure help from indecisive observers, but indiscriminate prosecution also could alienate influential Indians who, in crises, sided with government. Too, cultivating ties with a widened constituency became more essential as India advanced constitutionally. Officials recognized that British political life would be very difficult unless they devised fresh approaches to operating in the institutional milieu introduced by the Morley–Minto reforms. Minto's efforts to cultivate Gokhale symbolized such a concern. Other directions included a province-by-province appraisal of political alignments.[155]

In addition to building alliances and coming to terms with

153. Based on Council noting, J&P 1913, 1806.
154. S. N. Brown note (September 23, 1913), J&P 1913, 2957.
155. Exemplified by a Butler note on Indian politics (April 20, 1910), enclosed in Minto to Morley, April 28, 1910, M.C.

transplanted democratic institutions, the British faced a spreading threat to public order occasioned by religious controversy. Communal differences had been accumulating since the nineteenth century, but except for scattered riots and a flurry of activity on cow protection in the 1890s, the attention of religious leaders had been directed to self-strengthening rather than confrontation with other communities. Revivalism had progressed to a new stage by 1913, one characterized by a more militant, formalized version of religious politics. Muslims, Hindus, and Sikhs organized to defend themselves, to attack enemies, and to force concessions from the rulers. Tracts and newspapers became favorite techniques for accomplishing those goals.[156]

Discussion of a Sikh history book and literature on cow protection illustrate official concern with communal writings. In 1913, a London firm announced plans to publish a new edition of J. D. Cunningham's *History of the Sikhs*. The original (1847) had been so sympathetic toward the Sikhs and so critical of British policy that its circulation ruined Cunningham's career as a political agent. News of the pending republication coincided with the C.I.D.'s alarm at the appearance of anti-British militancy in Sikh schools. The question then was raised whether the India Office should request postponement of the publication because of the dangerous ideas in the book. After the issue received study by numerous officials, the Punjab government decided that while it might inflate "Sikh vanity," the book was sound and did not justify intervention. Its circulation was judged to be less dangerous than the notoriety if Sikhs became aware of British interest.[157]

Another variety of literature, on the sanctity and value of the cow, potentially affected Hindu-Muslim relations. Cow societies had increased markedly by 1908 and had launched a propaganda campaign complete with songs, tracts, and posters. The commotion placed the British in a dilemma. If officials tried to limit the movement and, especially, the circulation of printed matter, Hindus might consider the *raj* pro-Muslim. Conversely, inflammatory tracts could (and occasionally did) heighten ten-

156. Discussed in Kenneth Jones, "Sources," and N. G. Barrier, "Sikh Resurgence." Also see the essays on local politics in John Gallagher, Gordon Johnson, and Anil Seal eds., *Locality, Province and Nation: Essays on Indian Politics, 1870–1940*. In 1905, 295 of the 1,359 periodicals in India dealt primarily with religion, and many of those were openly sectarian. Based on *Statements of English, Foreign, Anglo-Vernacular and Vernacular Newspapers Published in India and Burma During the Year 1905*.

157. PG to GI, August 6, 1914, and noting in J&P 1914, 378A.

sion and produce riots. The India secretariat typically adopted the middle path: it banned only virulent works. The government almost proscribed a broadside entitled "The Cow Containing 84 Gods," for example, but finally backed away because the item had circulated for almost a year and was not overtly antagonistic to Muslims. The concluding note in the file accurately summarized how the British viewed such literature and cow protection in general:

> The whole anti-kine-killing movement is, of course, antagonistic to Europeans and Muhammadans. That is inevitable. Therefore it may be said that the picture reflects upon these races, which is true; but we tolerate the agitation as long as it does not become too violent, and I should not describe the picture as a particularly violent manifestation of it.[158]

Action against publications resulted, therefore, not from a single calculated policy, but from a complex range of factors that issued from the initiative of local officers to on-going evaluations of political assumptions and consequences. Prosecution and proscription were not entirely random, however; study of banned literature suggests to the contrary that method underlay the fluctuations in British maneuvers. The bureaucracy tightened control of newspapers and tracts in times of crisis. The government initiated 86 cases (warnings, security demands, prosecutions) against printing presses during 1910. This number dropped to 75 in 1911 and 68 in 1912, then shot upward to 126 in 1914 in response to an increase of terrorism.[159] Another trend involved the languages in which banned works were written. Although it continued to seize English tracts and periodicals (primarily from abroad), the government concentrated on vernacular material because of its broader appeal. Between 1910 and 1914, the British proscribed 50 works in English and 272 in vernacular languages, including 114 in Marathi, 52 in Urdu, and 51 in Bengali.[160]

An analysis of the content and types of banned material points to a final generalization. Despite decentralization and varied opinion within the I.C.S., the bureaucracy held to a loose but shared set of priorities that influenced which publications were to be labeled *objectionable*. The table below contains a partial breakdown of the themes and the manner of presentation in proscribed items:

158. Wheeler note (November 27, 1913), GIPOL December 1913, 9D.

159. Statistics drawn from correspondence in J&P 1919, 4468, and GIPOL April 1914, 41–46A.

160. Lists, slightly amended, in GIPOL February 1914, 67–68A.

Select Statistics on the Content and Types of Banned Literature, 1908–1914[161]

Category	Number	Category	Number
General Commentaries on Politics	13	Commentaries, Histories of Nationalism (India, including Mutiny)	27
Calls for Violence, Revolution	32	Histories of Revolution Outside India	3
Addressed to Army	5	Irish, Russian Politics	4
Addressed to Sikhs	5	Bomb Manuals	2
Appeals to Students	4	Speeches, Trial Reports	19
Anti-Hindu Themes	3	Biographies	9
Anti-Muslim Themes	4	Works on Tilak	18
Cow Protection	2	Songs, poems	33
Plays	26	Works by Non-Indians	12

This table is suggestive rather than comprehensive because insufficient information prevented inclusion of many titles. The statistics and supporting data from departmental files nevertheless permit brief comments on criteria that led to the ban on this assortment of literary works.

The British automatically banned printed matter that incited violence and disruption of order. This category included calls to revolution (Har Dayal's *Shabash*), eulogic biographies of extremists (V. D. Savarkar, Daniel Breen, Madan Lal Dhingra), histories of revolution, and poetry or drama referring to the assassination of the British.[162] The mounting number of works on the 1857 Mutiny as a freedom struggle (for example, Savarkar's classic, *The First Indian War of Independence*) received special attention.[163] So did publications of organizations outside India (Hindustan Ghadar party, Free Hindustan party), banned individually or by general notifications. Although the vast majority of these works aimed at the British, the bureaucracy felt that communal material posed equally dangerous threats and consequently proscribed obnoxious examples.[164]

161. Categories are not inclusive, that is, some poems and songs also are included under their subject content, such as "anti-Hindu" or "addressed to Sikhs."

162. Several proscribed works are discussed in Guha, *Sparks*, while Dharam Paul Sarin, *Influence of Political Movements on Hindi Literature, 1906–1947*, analyzes themes in controversial political poetry.

163. Background in GIPOL May 1910, 1D. The British banned the book without seeing a copy, knowing only that "it is a big book and that its tone is highly inflammatory" (comment by J. H. DuBoulay, July 21, 1909).

164. The publications of the Arya Samaj, Ahmadiya sect, and Sanatan

Distinctions between open calls for revolution and sophisticated attempts to erode support for the *raj* often were blurred. Appreciating the significance of Indian patriots rewriting history, the British carefully examined the content of new or reprinted studies on their rule. Books and dramas that described alleged British atrocities or portrayed officials as Simon Legree-type exploiters became targets for proscription.[165] Concern with interpretations of British motives related to other patterns. First, the government banned titles strongly critical of Western civilization or Christianity.[166] The underlying assumption seems to have been that indictment of the ruler's cultural tradition questioned his claim to be superior, benevolent, and legitimate. A similar danger arose from books attacking the Empire or British imperialism. Hence, the government tried unsuccessfully to stop the importation of Wilfred Blunt's studies on the British in Egypt and later blocked the circulation of a two-page melodrama on Gandhi and Indians in the Transvaal, poignantly titled *South African Horrors*.[167]

British strategy accounted for bans on additional types of literature. Indian allies, whether rulers of states or moderate politicians, were to be protected. One instance was the confiscation of *Choose, Oh Indian Princes*, a warning of impending doom to princes unless they quit cooperating with imperialism.[168] Moreover, the Foreign Department considered a comprehensive bill to protect rulers against blackmail and insults. Although eventually judged unnecessary, the discussion of a bill signified official resolve to maintain princely power if circumstances changed.[169] Another tactic was to keep controversial matter from reaching groups or classes who were believed to be susceptible to propaganda. The government accordingly tried to prevent contact between revolutionaries and students, the military, and Sikhs.[170]

Dharm particularly fell in this category. See appropriate sections in Part Two of this volume.

165. Dramas discussed in files on the Bharat Mata Agency, GIPOL October 1909, 145–153A; *Bombay History of the Freedom Movement* (Bombay: Maharashtra, 1964), II, 678–80.

166. For example, Walter Strickland, *Pagans and Christians or the Black Spot in the East* (discussed in GIPOL February 1911, 36–40A). The C.I.D. considered Strickland, who wrote for the *Indian Sociologist* and flaunted his anti-Christian views, "of doubtful sanity." Ker, *Political Troubles*, p. 263.

167. A copy and discussion in J&P 1914, 1302. The work originally had been printed in a Telegu journal and was not banned until republication in English.

168. Published in England, c. 1909 (discussion in GIPOL July 1915, 56–72A).

169. Notes by A. B. Minchin (July 26, 1909) and H. Risley (September 7, 1909), plus reports from residents, C. R. 1/19/396.

170. There are approximately 100 files, c. 1907–1914, in this category.

Denunciation of British rule by Western observers probably aggravated the bureaucracy more abrasively than any other publications except those which called for violent action against the *raj*. Revolutionaries outside India cultivated the sympathy of editors and public leaders and then used them as means to distribute their literary products. In 1912, for example, a columnist for the San Francisco *Bulletin* (John Barry) published a collection of articles on the conquest of India, Indian education and "starvation," and the extravagance of *durbars* (large public meetings). The tract, *Sidelights of India*, resulted from exchanges between Barry and a leading Ghadarite, Har Dayal.[171] The British banned this and similar works because they tended to authenticate the nationalists' charges. The opinions of Westerners—or so the secretariat believed—were more influential than those of Indians and consequently more dangerous. The interception of some publications, such as the Social Democratic party's *The Infamies of Liberal Rule*, presented no problems, but as outlined earlier, other titles stimulated questions in Parliament and debate on freedom of the press.[172] Two cases were significant in that regard. Indian nationalists influenced the U.S. Secretary of State, William Jennings Bryan, to dash off, in typically crusading fashion, adverse comments on British administration. The appearance of the tract (*British Rule in India*) understandably upset the Indian government, but it postponed a ban for several months, at which time it learned that an Indian editor had taken many of Bryan's quotations out of context. Even then, the specter of negative reaction among Americans haunted the government.[173] The publisher of the Bryan tract, the Ghadar party, also brought out an essay, *The Methods of the Indian Police in the 20th Century*, supposedly written by an M.P., Frederic Mackarness. After an interchange of telegrams with London, Indian authorities proceeded to ban the work, knowing full well that an uproar in Parliament lay ahead.[174]

See, for example, the secretariat review of *To the Men of the British Army* (GIPOL July 1907, 305A).

171. *Sidelights on India* (San Francisco: 1912). Background in Dharmavira, *Har Dayal*, pp. 153, 172.

172. Background in GIPOL April 1911, 68–75A.

173. Discussion in GIPOL May 1910, 127–131A. Bryan visited India and saw the plight of Indians as one of his causes. The essay originally was printed in *India* (a publication of the British Congress Committee), July 20, 1906. The Ghadar group reprinted the essay in several languages during the First World War, and the Bharat Mata Agency, Lahore, published another version. For a short discussion of Bryan and India, see Singh, "American Attitudes," pp. 113–14.

174. Documents in J&P 1910, 1714.

In conclusion, the initial British experience with press restraints produced laws and mechanisms to implement those laws which were to remain key elements in governance until 1947. Conflicts within the bureaucracy's assumptions and self-image, the central government's relations with local and London authorities, and increasing tendencies for British involvement in political maneuvering determined to a large extent decisions on how and when the laws should be employed. Several trends run through the period. Crises created the momentum for passage of repressive bills and also accounted for the periodic acceleration of repression. A survey of proscribed literature suggests further that the British developed strategies and a set of criteria as to what printed matter should be banned.

The government evaluated its relationship with the press in light of changing circumstance. Riots and outrages had marked the end of an era of acquiescence, shattering the relative calm of the previous five decades. Following successive periods of violence and repressive response, the British temporarily felt secure, only to have their confidence disturbed by new incidents. On June 28, 1914, pistol shots in far-away Sarajevo introduced another phase of challenge and response. An unstable but potentially serious alliance between Indian nationalists and Germany accompanied the First World War. The demands for Home Rule and Pan-Islam flared up, and at the end of the tunnel, there loomed the first confrontations with Mahatma Gandhi. These were to test the capability of the Government of India to develop alternate approaches to politics, to change in order to survive.

Chapter 3

COERCION AND CONCILIATION, 1914–1929

Events during the First World War and its aftermath brought into relief conflicting principles of government inherent in British rule—coercion and conciliation. The Government of India responded to wartime crises and the non-cooperation challenge of the Congress by strengthening traditional reliance on repressive methods for maintaining political control. Banning, security demands, censorship, and imprisonment remained at a high level for most of the period. During the same time, however, the government attempted to cultivate allies and conciliate Indian politicians. While applying rigorous sanctions under the Defence of India Act, for example, the British had been preparing a scheme for shifting responsible government to India. Similarly, although crushing political dissent in 1919 with a ferocity reminiscent of the 1857 anti-Mutiny campaign, the government began easing press controls. From the British point of view, the two approaches to politics reinforced each other. Restrictions of extremist activity sustained order and British authority, both judged crucial to constitutional advance. Conciliation in turn would broaden support for the *raj*, moderate criticism, and lessen the need for harsh restraints. To further an atmosphere of cooperation and reform, in 1922 the government relinquished many repressive and controversial powers, including most features of the 1910 Press Act. Only Indians had different concerns and another script. By 1929, communal unrest and militant nationalism threatened to end the British efforts at balancing force with conciliation and, with it, brought to a conclusion a brief interlude of relaxed press controls.

Wartime Controls and Propaganda

The First World War multiplied British administrative problems in India. Depletion of the I.C.S. ranks, a drive to send economic aid to the Allies, and extensive demand for Indian recruits disrupted the routine of governance. Wartime conditions also helped spread disorder within the Indian Empire. In addition to labor unrest and riots in recruiting areas, international relations produced two new sources of danger. An alliance between Germans and Indian revolutionaries living abroad threatened India, as did the hostility of Indian Muslims, who were concerned with the fate of Turkey (the center for traditional Muslim political institutions, the *khilafate*).

A marriage of convenience joined the interests of Indian exiles and the German Foreign Office. Germany hoped that a sudden burst of unrest within India would divert the Indian government's attention from the war to domestic problems. Caring little about the war itself, the Indian patriots needed German funds and international contacts to pursue their goal of weakening the British hold on their homeland. The San Francisco-based Ghadar (mutiny) party accordingly accepted thousands of dollars from German agents. Extremely disorganized, at times dishonest, the Ghadar propagandists succeeded primarily in increasing their barrage of anti-British literature, some of which was smuggled into India through German networks. Attempts to send men and arms to India met with less success. Faulty communication with Germans frustrated several projects, although one dramatic influx of Ghadarites occurred in late 1914 when a ship *Komagata Maru* loaded with Sikh immigrants who had been expelled from Canada and a sprinkling of Ghadar sympathizers arrived at Budge Budge harbor near Calcutta. Following a shoot-out with police, a few revolutionaries escaped and spread havoc through western India.[1]

A second Indian organization operated directly from Berlin. Headed by Taraknath Das, Har Dayal, and Dr. C. Chakravarty, the Indian National Party specialized in propaganda. They also sent representatives to the United States (New York), Sweden, and Mexico to set up corresponding committees, which would reprint or write similar material. The "Oriental Propaganda Bureau," an agency closely connected with the German Foreign Office, funded these activities.[2]

1. Background on Ghadar activities in Don K. Dignan, "The Hindu Conspiracy in Anglo-American Relations During World War I," *Pacific Historical Review*, 40: 1 (February 1971), 57–76. F. C. Isemonger and J. Slattery, *An Account of the Ghadar Conspiracy, 1913–15*; L. P. Mathur, *Indian Revolutionary Movements in the United States*, pp. 34–53; Arun Coomer Bose, *Indian Revolutionaries Abroad, 1905–1922*, pp. 34–53. Details on activities, from U.S. perspective, in Justice Department Records, Group 60, 193424.

2. Notes and catalogues of "hostile propaganda" in Eur. Mss. E. 288, IOL. Mathur, *Indian Revolutionary Movements*, pp. 72–106; Dharmavir, *Lala Har Dayal and Revolutionary Movement of His Times*, pp. 220–38. Intercepted German propaganda, preserved in the IOL, includes the fol-

The Ghadar group and the National Party aimed their publications at several audiences. *Why India Is in Revolt Against British Rule*, for example, attempted to influence neutralist attitudes toward the Government of India. England supposedly entered the war to capture German colonies and to extend her control over other Asiatics; a concomitant message was that Germany alone sympathized with Asian aspirations.[3] In addition, the Berlin party prepared brochures in Urdu and Panjabi for distribution among Indian soldiers. Dropped from German aircraft, the material played up poor pay, racism, and British attacks on Indian religions.[4] Similar themes appeared in books and tracts directed toward India. British atrocities and pro-Turkish rhetoric were prominent in at least twenty items.[5]

International politics also affected the attitude of Indian Muslims toward the *raj*. Emerging from a phase of intense self-examination and revitalization, Muslims were particularly sensitive to issues that affected their interests. Some Muslim politicians, for example, interpreted the 1911 decision to reverse the partition of Bengal as a move hostile to their community, and they raised the cry, "Islam in danger!" An incident that centered on a mosque in Cawnpur, United Province, evoked a similar response.[6] The question of Turkey's future and the related fate of the Muslim political institution, the *khilafate*, became especially important because of this growing concern with self-interest and cultural heritage. According to one section of Muslim leadership, Britain's support of Turkey's enemies indicated yet another foreign effort to subvert Islam. Two newspapers led the pro-*khilafate* campaign. The *Comrade*, edited by Muhammad Ali, reprinted caustic essays on British policy and the Balkan situation,

---

lowing: Thierry Preyer, *Aegypten und Indien* (Berlin: Ullstein, 1916); Ganga Rao Grahmputra, *Indien: Seine Stellung zum Weltkrieg und zu Seiner zu Kunft* (Tublingen: 1916); A. K. Viator, *Deutschlands Anteilan Indiens Schicksal* (Leipzig: 1918); Hermann Von Staden, *Indien in Weltkriege* (Stuttgart: 1915).

3. *Why India Is in Revolt Against British Rule* (London, Berlin: Indian Nationalist Party, 1916). The tract went through at least ten editions, with approximately 1,000 copies each edition.

4. A listing is in Eur. Mss. E 288. Also, see description in Section 2 of this volume.

5. Background on "the state of Muslim feeling" in GIPOL March 1913, 45–55A; on the Cawnpur Mosque incident, GIPOL October 1913, 100–118A. *Cawnpur Ki Khuni Dastan* (*The Bloody Massacre of Cawnpur*) was typical of Muslim rage over the incident. GIPOL October 1913, 49A.

6. The following GIPOL files cover the Pan-Islamic agitation: August 1913, 40–41A; January 1915, 76–97A, 108–182A; also, J&P 1913, 1475, 3873; discussion in Muhammad Ali, *My Life: A Fragment*, 2d rev. ed., pp. 34–69. The most analytic treatment is in Gail Minault Graham, "The Khilafat Movement" (Ph.D. diss., University of Pennsylvania, 1972).

and Zafar Ali Khan's *Zamindar* championed the Muslim cause. Turkey's transition from involvement in the Balkan War to alliance with Germany increased the possibility of encounter between Pan-Islamists and the British. *Khilafate* sentiment spread rapidly, and a groundswell of public interest seemed likely to erode the allegiance of a community long considered most loyal to the government.

The Government of India met such threats in part through enactment of special wartime legislation. The Defence of India Act authorized for certain crimes summary trial without jury, simplified prohibition of public meetings, and internment. It also added censorship to the growing armory of emergency controls. After experimenting with various arrangements, the British created provincial press committees to act as channels of communication between newspapermen and censors. The censors issued guidelines on controversial material (such as comments on military operations, religion, enemy reports, and Middle Eastern affairs) and generally supervised the press.[7]

The bureaucracy employed the widened powers as well as those already in hand to crush revolutionary activity. Special tribunals conducted conspiracy trials across North India. In the Lahore cases, for example, the British imprisoned or condemned to death dozens of activists. When specific crimes could not be proven, politicians were interned and held either in their home villages or at a central location.[8] Appreciating the danger from abroad, the C.I.D. seized actual or suspected agents as they tried to enter India. Shipments of weapons and "seditious" printed matter from abroad continued to be a problem, but postal officials used almost unlimited authority to block delivery. Sanctity of the mails became a peacetime principle that was not to be taken seriously during the crisis of war.[9]

Pan-Islamic leaders proved more difficult to control. Home Department officials had become alarmed at the implications of *khilafate* agitation as early as 1913, but shied away from suppression of the movement because of possible Muslim reaction. When a year of private conversations and warnings failed to moderate the position of prominent Muslims such as Muhammad

7. On preparation of the Defence of India Act, IV of 1915, see GIPOL April 1914, 385–411A; June 1915, 112–114A; February 1916, 143–163A. On censorship, J&P 1915, 2700. Full discussion of the bill and debate in G. K. Roy, *Law Relating to Press and Sedition* (1915), pp. 71–92.

8. Trials surveyed in GIPOL October 1915, 91A; Michael O'Dwyer, *India As I Knew It*, 2d rev. ed., pp. 190–209.

9. The following GIPOL files contain information on interceptions: August 1914, 43–44A; January 1915, 65–87A; March 1915, 407–412A. A list of customs notifications is in *General Rules and Orders*, pp. 76–101.

Ali, the government began to forfeit securities. The *Zamindar* lost a Rs. 2,000 security, but it immediately put up Rs. 10,000 to continue publication. The proprietor could sustain the loss because his paper's notoriety increased subscriptions to 15,000. Similarly, the *Comrade* refused to mute its criticism and lost securities of Rs. 2,000 and 10,000. Not only did the sanctions fail to affect publicists, but to the embarrassment of the British, the publishers fought a running court battle, which challenged application of the Press Act and broadcast the Pan-Islamic message. Ultimately, the Government of India resorted to pre-censorship and, fearing the reaction to public prosecution of leaders, interned them for the duration of the war.[10]

Although application of controls fluctuated with time and region, several generalizations on this aspect of wartime experience appear warranted. First, a total statistical account of British repression is impossible because of confusion and breakdowns in the police/information system. The central bureaucracy at times did not know what was being banned, or it learned about prosecutions secondhand.[11]

Intensified reliance on the 1910 Press Act constituted another pattern. The British banned over a thousand individual titles between 1914 and 1918 and, as the following table indicates, demanded substantial securities:

Security Actions, 1914–1918

	Demanded	Enhanced	Forfeited
Newspapers			
1914–15	182	11	5
1916	41		1
1917	36		1
1918	30	1	4
Presses			
1914–15	178	10	9
1916	84	14	12
1917	75	11	8
1918	52	n.a.	4

10. In addition to the files listed in note 6, background in S.M.A. Feroze, *Press in Pakistan*, rev. ed., pp. 74–76.

11. Background in GIPOL August 1914, 241–256A; also, the frantic effort to assemble data, note by Craddock (November 23, 1916), GIPOL November 1916, 373–388A.

The securities placed approximately 10 per cent of Indian newspapers and printing presses under fiscal restraint. The British tendency to demand deposits from new publishers also had the further effect of curtailing the establishment of more newspapers and presses. In 1914 and 1915, for example, approximately 150 printing presses and 100 papers were not started because of the government's demands.[12] Even when magistrates or officers did not require deposits, they used the threat of such action to modify press opinion. During the war, approximately three hundred editors or publishers received warnings.[13]

Despite the general tendency toward repression, however, no over-all "India" policy on how the Press and Defence of India acts should be applied seems to have been operative. The Indian government continued the practice of granting subordinates discretionary power, and if anything, the stresses of wartime conditions necessitated wider latitude for local decisionmaking. Provincial governments therefore developed their own strategies for dealing with political trouble. Bengal relied heavily on security demands, for example, while the Punjab apparently preferred warnings, prosecution, and frequent proscription.[14]

The criteria on which proscription or security were based tended to follow the pattern that had been current prior to 1914. Large numbers of works on terrorism, religious controversy, and British rule fell into the police net. The only major exception was a sharp increase in proscribed titles related to Islam. Determined to prevent the distribution of *khilafate* documents, the Government of India systematically banned those judged inflammatory —at least twenty security-bound journals and sixty banned titles dealt with Muslim theology, politics, or Islam in its world setting.[15] Sensitivity to issues relating to Muslims had implications even for seemingly innocuous books written by Europeans.

12. Data from the following files: GIPOL January 1917, 374A; November 1916, 373–388A; March 1921, 97–120A; J&P 1919, 4468, 4496. Notes by the Indian Press Association, mentioned in J. Natarajan, *History of Indian Journalism*, pp. 158–59, and K. B. Menon, *The Press Laws of India*, p. 10, suggest a wider use, but inadequate documentation makes this difficult to verify.

13. Natarajan, *Indian Journalism*, p. 158. The exact total is unverifiable because information on warnings tend to be buried within provincial records. Some details are provided, however, in GIPOL January 1917, 374A.

14. Drawn from data in GIPOL March 1921, 97–120A; also important are comments from local governments appended to reports on actions under the Press and Defence acts.

15. Based on cumulative lists drawn from GIPOL files, 1915–1918. Postal and sea customs procedure discussed in GIPOL December 1914, 4–8A; October 1918, 170–190A, 201–215B. For an interesting discussion of rationale, GIPOL March 1921, 97–120B.

When, in 1918, for example, G. K. Chesterton included the phrase, "Mosleems denied even souls to women," in a new history of England, British Intelligence discovered the passage and prevailed on Chesterton to eliminate the passage, out of a "sense of patriotism."[16]

The press advisory/censorship system probably prevented more widespread application of the 1910 Press Act. Arrangements and reliance on censors tended to take on a provincial complexion. Madras, Bengal, and Bombay reported their newspapers as being generally cooperative and the relationship between censors and newspapermen satisfactory. The Punjab government, on the other hand, apparently adopted an aggressive policy toward the press. Punjab statistics for 1915 indicate a continual pattern of intervention. Censors passed 169 items without amendment, changed 633, and rejected 238.[17]

During the first years of the war, the British were responding more to fear of potential danger than to actual emergencies. Little evidence pointed to the need for the type of controls employed on domestic publications and Indian politicians. To the contrary, Indians rallied dramatically to the Allied cause and contributed greatly to the war effort. Under stress and a cloud of uncertainty, however, the British preferred to take no chances. The same attitude underlay the development of propaganda. The war reinforced official awareness that the successful operation of the *raj* depended largely on support from its subjects. From one perspective, the British were pitted against German and Indian opponents in a struggle for the minds of the population. Force could reduce overt acts of violence, and a postal cordon could cut down the circulation of inciting material, but only counterargument would neutralize the substantial propaganda attack of the enemy. The Government of India had experimented in the past with presenting its case to the Indian people, but the pressures of war made propaganda a permanent tool of British administration.

Preparation of propaganda involved at least four issues. In search of the most effective media, the British initially relied on newspaper accounts and communiqués, then shifted toward public lectures, mass mailings, and new techniques like slide shows. Decisions on the topic or direction of propaganda varied, and they frequently depended (as did the choice of media) on the public the British hoped to influence. From the beginning, some propaganda was designed for particular groups, but enough un-

16. Noting and correspondence in J&P 1918, 188.

17. Correspondence in GIPOL February 1916, 143–163A. On bureaucratic difficulties in censorship coordination, see the file on *Young India* (GIPOL December 1918, 36–54A).

certainty remained to keep the issue of audience a source of debate and potential conflict within the bureaucracy. Who was to plan and carry out propaganda constituted a final question. The Government of India had gained control of all operations in India by the end of the war, but only after several bouts with London officials.

The first propaganda effort grew out of the concern with German publications. In 1914, Valentine Chirol, an English journalist with some background in Indian affairs, offered to prepare a series of essays and public letters for inclusion in the London *Times*. The Foreign Office agreed. Although Chirol's writings were meant to counterbalance German propaganda in general, he particularly hoped to neutralize claims about the *khilafate* and to convince the public, both Indian and British, of official good intentions toward Muslims. Less than enthusiastic about the proposal, the Indian government nevertheless supplied Chirol with reports and confidential C.I.D. material for a year. The informal pipeline into the *Times* forum ended in January 1915, when Chirol came to India as a correspondent.[18]

The next experiments related to two strategically important elements, Indian soldiers and the Sikhs from whom a large proportion of the army was recruited. In 1916, the Indian government gave Punjab authorities permission to publish a newspaper for distribution among the troops. A similar proposal had been rejected earlier, but growing fear of revolutionary material influencing the army helped change the Home Department's mind. The local government published the *Fauji Akhbar*, a small paper that featured stories on the war, service problems, and recruitment, at the cost of approximately Rs. 50,000 a year. The *Akhbar* hammered home the dual themes of benefits under British rule and the need for loyalty. The publication of a similar journal in English, Urdu, and Panjabi, *Hak*, began soon afterward.[19]

The newspaper venture coincided with a request from the Maharaja of Patiala, a prominent Sikh leader, to sponsor a deputation to America for the purpose of winning back the loyalties of disaffected Sikhs living on the West Coast. Patiala planned to visit Sikh centers and improve the British image. Although concerned that such a deputation might be overwhelmed by articulate, anti-British forces in America, the Government of India

18. Discussed in GIPOL November 1914, 33–38A; January 1915, 275–276A. Propaganda during the First World War includes the following: James Morgan Read, *Atrocity Propaganda 1914–19 in the World War;* Harold Dwight Lasswell, *Propaganda Technique;* and George Sylvester Viereck, *Spreading Germs of Hate.*

19. Financial Despatch 67, April 5, 1918, and noting, J&P 1918, 1929. *Publicity Campaign in India*, p. 15.

sanctioned the project. The India and Colonial officers thought otherwise and stopped the deputation because it would appear "too got up." No Indian group visited America, but the Indian government subsequently did assist in a tour by a knowledgeable Punjab officer, Popham Young. Young attempted to explain official policy and investigated rumors and attitudes in America.[20]

During 1916, the India Office staff also had been discussing the value of effective propaganda. One of its programs involved films. The British government had prepared two reels, "Britain Prepared" and "The Battle of the Somme," for circulation among allies and neutrals, but the India Office decided that they might be appropriate for Western-educated Indians. The Government of India supervised distribution and worked closely with local authorities to arouse interest in the material. The Punjab government, for example, accorded the films a gala opening, complete with pictures and lavish Urdu descriptions in appropriate newspapers.[21] In addition, officials in London felt the need for a "short popular pamphlet (written preferably by an Indian) cracking up British rule in India."[22] The India Office investigated potential candidates living in England and finally "hooked" Sir Mancherjee Bhownaggree, K.C.I.E., an M.P. from Bethnal Green. Hodder and Stoughton published his *Verdict of India*, a syrupy tract openly dedicated to combating "the propaganda literature of the enemy." The India Office apparently had not decided prior to publication to whom the message should be addressed, and therefore the essay served little purpose. A few copies went to neutrals through British consulates, but the Indian government blocked a move to reprint the item in vernacular languages on the grounds that it was so naive as to be ineffective against the arguments of sophisticated nationalists.[23] Better no propaganda than poor propaganda.

Undaunted, the India Office embarked on a larger project to bolster the British image and generate Indian loyalty. The French sparked the plan by publishing a book of testimonials secured from Muslim leaders and chiefs in their colonial territories. The India Council hoped to duplicate the French volume but got bogged down over how to obtain "representative views."

20. Background in GIPOL November 1916, 301A; May 1917, 24–28A; J&P 1917, 362. Bose, *Indian Revolutionaries*, p. 57, mentions that Sikh *granthis* (priests) and other Indians were used to split the Ghadar group, but this statement could not be confirmed. On Young, GIPOL March 1919, 21D.

21. Discussed in J&P 1916, 240.

22. Note by E. Gowers, J&P 1916, 240.

23. Correspondence between London and Delhi, J&P 1916, 2322.

Indian authorities shied away from one suggestion—that Delhi issue reply postcards to important Muslims. Leaving aside the touchy question of communal favoritism, the Government of India argued, selection of Muslim leaders would be difficult, and those who were not asked their views would inevitably harbor bad feelings. Moreover, an appeal to Muslims would indicate that the government distrusted them.[24] Still fascinated with utilizing the mails, the India Office then proceeded with a scheme to sell "Loyalty" postcards. The front of the card was to show pictures of a fluttering British flag and the following verse underneath: "Symbol of Freedom, Truth and Right, Proud Neath Thy Folds Our Soldiers Fight, Each with His Life Thy Cause Defends, and Heaven to Each Its Blessing Sends." Indians supposedly would buy cards and mail them to associates, thus proving their commitment to the British and publicizing the Allied cause. The India Office initially printed 414,400 cards in Indian languages (approximately 60,000 each in Hindi, Urdu, Tamil, Marathi, Gurmukhi, Gujarati, and Bengali) and sold them through booksellers in major Indian towns. Apparently the cards met British expectations because London quickly advanced to a grandiose scheme of 36 different cards (a million copies each) with a variety of messages. Virtually bypassed in the earlier card project, the Indian government vetoed the new move. In a sharply worded note, the Governor General stated that officers in Delhi were quite capable of producing propaganda, and in any event, they should control all material circulating in India. The dispatch also suggested that the original card and those proposed were not suited to Indian needs.[25]

The "loyalty cards" episode reinforced the Government of India's determination to elaborate its own system of propaganda. By 1918, the Home Department had arranged for visits of friendly Indian editors to the European front, and it held both Imperial and provincial "war conferences."[26] The meetings, at which British officials sought to mobilize public opinion and funds, preluded the creation of provincial publicity boards. Each province had publicity units to counter rumor and enemy claims. Although a central agency coordinated activities and handled publications destined for other countries like America, the provincial boards tailored programs to local needs. A common function was circulation of English and Indian-language tracts on current topics

24. GI telegram to IO, August 5, 1916, J&P 1918, 2720.

25. Copies and background in J&P 1918, 2720.

26. On the visits, J&P 1918, 2288; war conferences, J&P 1918, 2325. Also discussed in *Report of the Administration of Lord Chelmsford.*

such as "Germany's Eastern Dream," "Why America Made War," and "Teja Singh Khalsa Joins the Army."[27] Indian members of the boards also toured troop installations and lectured in schools and colleges. Appreciating that most Indians could not read printed matter, the agencies devised alternate methods of communication. Publicity teams presented films in towns with electricity and magic-lantern shows in outlying areas. The Punjab board, for example, prepared fourteen different slide lectures on topics ranging from recruitment to "Heroes of the War."[28]

In summary, the government reinforced wartime press controls with propaganda intended to maximize public support. The institutionalization of Indian–British cooperation in the 1918 publicity campaign was only one aspect of a broader policy to integrate Indians more fully into the war effort. Local leaders cooperated in recruitment and fund-raising drives. The results generally surprised and pleased the British rulers. Some officers in fact suggested that extension of propaganda and the spirit of cooperation might eventually undercut widespread criticism of the government and perhaps obviate formal press controls.[29] The determination of that issue, however, had to be weighed against the backdrop of the discussion of India's political future after the war.

To Repeal an Act

On August 20, 1917, Edwin Montagu, the new Secretary of State for India told the House of Commons that the Government of India had adopted a policy "of increasing association of Indians in every branch of the administration, and the gradual development of self-governing institutions, with a view to progressive realization of responsible government in India as an integral part of the British Empire."[30] Montagu and his reform partner, Governor General Frederick Chelmsford, followed the declaration with constitutional proposals. Indians were to be associated closely with the British at every level of decisionmaking, including widened legislative power and a larger share of bureaucratic posts. The resulting 1919 Government of India Act transformed the relationship between ruler and ruled. Ministers of provincial governments were to be chosen by and responsible to popularly

27. *Publicity Campaign*, p. 6; data in J&P 1917, 4032; 1918, 2829.
28. *Publicity Campaign*, p. 71.
29. Discussed in J&P 1919, 2078; GIPOL July 1920, 265–266A.
30. Speech quoted in S. R. Mehrotra, "The Politics Behind the Montagu Declaration of 1917," in C. H. Philips ed., *Politics and Society in India*, p. 71. The article surveys the maneuvers behind the declaration.

elected legislatures. In an arrangement labeled *dyarchy*, responsibility for administration would be divided between the ministers and a British-appointed governor. Ministers would determine some matters, ranging from education to agriculture, but ultimate decisions on others would be made by the Governor, who was responsible to Parliament. Elected Indian majorities controlled the provincial and central legislatures, the latter being divided into two houses—the Council of State and the much larger Legislative Assembly. Because the Governor General would remain responsible to Parliament, and not to the central legislature, he had reserve power to certify bills and issue ordinances in cases of emergency.[31] The reforms also had provisions affecting princely India. Montagu and Chelmsford initiated a Chamber of Princes in February 1921. The Chamber advised government and served as a forum through which princes could articulate criticism or demands.[32]

The constitutional changes had grown out of India's wartime experiences. The rally of princes and the Indian public to the Empire had impressed the government. As early as 1915, high-ranking British administrators observed privately that, once the war ended, the show of citizenship should be matched by significant concessions.[33] Indians certainly expected such a move. "A change," as a confidential survey of Chelmsford's viceroyalty summarized, "had come over the spirit of India."[34] Moderate nationalists warned that without strides toward self-government, their calls for continued patience among Indians would be drowned out, a claim high-lighted by an extremist direction among Congressmen and the appearance of Home Rule leagues.[35]

The Government of India recognized the validity of the warnings. Official handling of the agitation for Home Rule, which had begun in 1914 and received support from Congress two

31. Documents and analysis in Maurice Gwyer, ed., *Speeches and Documents on the Indian Constitution, 1921–47*, I, xxix–xxxii, 14–153.

32. Summary statement in Urmila Phadnis, *Towards the Integration of Indian States*, pp. 25–34. For a full treatment of the princes and politics, see Barbara Neil Ramusack, "Indian Princes As Imperial Politicians, 1914–1939" (Ph.D. diss., University of Michigan, 1969).

33. For example, the memorandum of Lord Hardinge on reforms after the war. Copies available in several sets of private papers, including those of Hardinge, Hailey. Summarized in Mehrotra, "Politics," p. 83. For background on shifts in orientation toward India, see Dewitt Ellinwood, "The Round Table Movement and India, 1909–1920," *Journal of Commonwealth Political Studies*, 9 (1971), 183–209.

34. *Report of Chelmsford Administration*, p. 1.

35. For example, speeches in *Report of the 30th Indian National Congress* (n.p.: Indian National Congress, 1916), pp. 21–30; comments in *Report of Chelmsford Administration*, pp. 58–73.

years later, reflected British appreciation that the *raj* stood at a critical juncture. The government watched the leagues carefully but postponed precipitate action liable to arouse sympathy for their leaders, Tilak and Annie Besant. Eventually the bureaucracy struck, seizing the deposit on Besant's newspaper, *New India*, interning her, and banning some Home Rule literature.[36] At the same time, however, the Governor General and his Council tried to couple the crackdown with an announcement of pending reforms. News of the policy would "arrest the future defection of moderate opinion [and] set against a visionary Home Rule Scheme, our sane and practical proposals."[37] The reforms therefore grew out of how the British read Indian expectations and out of changing political pressures.

If Indians gradually gained control of the legislatures, how could the government ensure political stability and its own authority? The answer already had become an accepted part of administrative routine. First, bureaucrats were becoming politicians. Earlier tendencies to evaluate political alternatives, build alliances with Indians, and develop a viable communication system had to be further elaborated if government were to manage the new legislatures and the party politics that necessarily arose from broadened electorates. Second, the government continued to keep safeguards for emergencies. If Indians were not cooperative or pursued a course that seemingly led to disorder, the British could rely on force. Keeping this fact in mind, the government decided to maintain sections of the Defence of India Act in the postwar period, especially preventive detention and arrangements for speedy trials without jury.[38]

The British dilemma was how to preserve and use elements of force without jeopardizing reform and political maneuvering. How could coercive powers and conciliatory action be balanced in a fashion acceptable both to ruler and ruled? The issue of continued press controls quickly became a focal point in discussions of policy among high-ranking officials. On the one hand, many provincial governments had become accustomed to extensive supervision of Indian writings and preferred continuation of that power into the reform period. At least one province, Punjab, in-

36. For British policy, GIPOL July 1917, 299–313A; J&P 1916, 1397. Background on the organization in Pattabhai Sitaramayya, *The History of the Indian National Congress*, I, 201–19; Hugh Owen, "Towards Nation-Wide Agitation and Organization: The Home Rule Leagues, 1915–1918," in D.A. Low, ed., *Soundings in Modern South Asian History*, pp. 159–95.

37. Quotations from Chelmsford note (February 1, 1917) and telegram to IO, May 19, 1917, GIPOL July 1917, 299–313A.

38. Background in K.W. to GIPOL July 1917, 299–313A.

sisted that without these checks, the pent-up forces of extremism might break forth and endanger the *raj.*[39] Equally compelling considerations, however, recommended the wisdom of relaxed press restrictions.

The overt challenges to British rule had at least temporarily stabilized by 1918. The most extreme Indian journalists were imprisoned or muzzled, and external danger also appeared to be subsiding. The improvement of an Imperial intelligence system during the war meant that Indian authorities kept closer surveillance of revolutionaries outside India. Even when the information did not lead to direct controls, it facilitated interception of literature and personnel coming from the Far East, Europe, and North America.[40] The entry of the United States into the war also had put an immediate damper on revolutionary activity in that country. The U.S. government had been reluctant to interfere with Indians prior to 1917. "The ordinary American has a strong distaste for an Indian as a human being," one British officer noted, "but sentimental regard for anyone . . . who claims to be a champion of Liberty."[41] These attitudes changed as America drifted toward war. The U.S. Justice and Immigration departments put pressure on nationalists, culminating in the San Francisco–Chicago trials directed against Indian and German conspirators and in confiscation of political literature in the mail.[42] Although stray pamphlets from America continued to reach India, the altered situation drove revolutionaries underground or forced moderation of public statements.[43]

Growing opposition to the Press Act further contributed to an atmosphere conducive to its repeal. Once an initial round of enthusiasm for the Allies subsided, Indian publicists began to chafe under the restrictions. As early as 1915, a delegation of press representatives met with government over application of security provisions. A more formidable group, representing the

39. Punjab attitude discussed in G. Gwynne note (April 12, 1920), GIPOL 1921, 4–I; also, O'Dwyer attitudes reflected in *India.*

40. On intelligence arrangement, Don K. Dignan, *New Perspectives on British Far East Policy, 1913–1919*, University of Queensland Papers, I: 5; Petrie involvement in GIPOL February 1916, 496–514A; April 1916, 89–91A; June 1916, 285–297A.

41. M. C. Seton to Wheeler, July 31, 1913, in GIPOL December 1914, 96–98A. On English–U.S. negotiations, Dignan, "Hindu."

42. In addition to summaries in Dignan, Mathur, and U.S. Justice files (Record Group 60, 193424), a short book by a police officer, Thomas J. Tunney, describes what happened: *Throttled.* Lajpat Rai's banned works are discussed in J&P 1917, 5122.

43. On propaganda, see J&P 1919; GIPOL November 1916, 301A. During the 1920s, the dispersed Ghadar group realigned with communism and used California as a base from which to send Socialist literature to India. Subsequent red scares put their operation out of business.

Indian Press Association, met again with the Governor General on March 5, 1917. Headed by Pandit Malaviya, C. Y. Chintamani, and B. G. Horniman, the deputation presented a detailed analysis of repression and urged more lenience. Official denial that the Press Act made life perilous for honest journalists did nothing to stem the tide of criticism.[44] The Indian Legislative Council provided another arena for debate on press controls. Members frequently asked pointed questions on policy or incidents.[45] In September of 1918, legislators went so far as to demand a committee to study the legal and other ramifications of the Press Act. The Council negated the proposal after a heated exchange, but a cleavage along racial lines had emerged. Except for three Indians who backed the British, all other Indian legislators voted for the investigative body.[46]

The weightiest questioning of the regulations came from within government itself. An internal review of how restrictions affected journalism revealed that the Press Act had been effective until 1914, but afterward extremist papers printed what they chose despite penalties; most of the press assumed a loyalist stance.[47] The incongruity of maintaining controls while attempting reform also bothered some bureaucrats, illustrated by the following appraisal:

> We have the Press Act, the Seditious Meetings Act and so forth; but the trouble is that they are all rather a denial of our own principles; we use them too intermittently, and they are weapons too big and clumsy to deal with nine-tenths of the actual mischief . . . if after reforms a dangerous situation continued, means must be found for stopping it. But inasmuch as reforms are themselves a halfway measure . . . agitation there is bound to be: and yet under reforms repression will be harder than ever.[48]

The Secretary of State seconded this line of reasoning. Although Montagu thought India not "fit" for freedom of the press, he kept urging that restrictions be reexamined and perhaps altered.[49] Several instances of miscarriage of the law intensified London's uneasiness about press controls. In 1915, for example, seizure of the *Comrade*'s security brought charges that harassment of the paper was "unjust and inexpedient." Permitting hon-

44. Newspaper cutting on the meeting in J&P 1919, 4468. Background in GIPOL January 1917, 374A, K.W.; March 1917, 374–375A.

45. Questions appeared almost every session, for example, questions in GIPOL March 1921, 97–120A.

46. Notes in J&P 1919, 4468.

47. Reviewed and noted in GIPOL March 1917, 374–375A.

48. Marris note (June13, 1919), GIPOL August 1917, 452–453A.

49. Montagu to Chelmsford, January 1918, in C.P. An account of Montagu's ideas is in S. D. Waley, *Edwin Montagu.*

est criticism appeared preferable, an India Council minute suggested, to stumbling around, handicapped by a misunderstanding of Muslim sentiment.[50] Two subsequent incidents revived the issue. When the *Observer*, a Muslim paper edited by Barkat Ali, criticized Punjab authorities for not appointing Fazal-i-Husain to the Lahore High Court in 1918, the Lieutenant Governor responded irrationally and forfeited the paper's Rs. 1,000 security. Extremely upset, Montagu ordered an overturning of the decision because he felt that such "misguided" acts only weakened legitimate rationale for newspaper laws.[51] The *Observer* incident coincided with the Government of India's decision not to prosecute an English-owned paper sympathetic to the *raj*, the *Indian Daily News*, for its publication of an inciting article on Islam. Montagu sarcastically noted that, had the paper been Indian, the bureaucracy would not have been so lenient.[52]

Such cases finally led Montagu to suggest amendment of the Press Act. His proposals centered on a transfer of power from executive hands to the judiciary. The Government of India agreed to discuss the matter and circulated a note to local officials. The response was mixed. While requesting safeguards, the Madras, Bombay, and United Provinces governments generally leaned toward Montagu's position; other respondents, notably the Punjab, opposed change for the reason that the press act was a vital weapon against present and anticipated danger.[53] Overworked with preparation of reform measures and hesitant to ignore resistance from men on the spot, the Government of India kept postponing discussion of possible amendment.

The sudden deterioration of the political situation in the spring of 1919 caused further delay. The Indian government emerged from the European war to find itself confronted by two domestic threats to public order. First, Gandhi and the Congress responded to passage of the Rowlatt bill, which continued wartime controls, with massive agitation throughout India. The Rowlatt *satyagraha* (a Gandhian political agitation characterized by nonviolence and discipline) evolved into a non-cooperation campaign in 1920 and 1921—two years of incessant fighting between nationalists and bureaucrats. This disturbance coincided with the dismemberment

50. T. Morrison note (April 2, 1915), J&P 1915, 935.

51. Montagu notes and dispatch, August 31, 1918, J&P 1918, 4629.

52. Montagu to Chelmsford, December 23, 1918, and Chelmsford to Montagu, November 6, 11, 1918, C.P. Background in P. C. Bamford, *Histories of the Non-Co-operation and Khilafat Movements* (Delhi: Government of India, 1925), p. 131; John Broomfield, "The Bengal Muslims and September 1918," in Low, *Soundings*, pp. 209–11.

53. Summarized in Gwynne note (April 12, 1920), GIPOL 1921, 4–I. Background in GIPOL March 1917, 274–275A; GIPOL 1923, 203.

of Turkish territories and a resurgence of *khilafate* and Pan-Islamic fervor. Muslims held large meetings, and their propaganda agencies, including an Islamic Information Bureau in London, produced numerous anti-British tracts. Congress and *khilafate* leaders joined forces and moved into the countryside to mobilize mass support.[54]

The British had never faced such concerted opposition to government fiat. Not only were the disturbances widespread, but the techniques employed, such as nonpayment of taxes, resignations from posts, work stoppages, and above all, passive resistance, also proved disconcerting. Unsure of itself, the government characteristically fell back on repressive measures. The results are almost too well known to recount. Martial law went into effect in Punjab, followed by censorship, mass arrests, aerial attacks, and the shooting of over 400 unarmed Punjabis at Jallianwala Bagh in Amritsar.[55] Determined to crush what seemed at the moment open rebellion, the British unleased a reign of terror. Banning increased, as did demands for security. Actions against presses and newspapers had numbered approximately 80 in 1918; there were 170 in 1919. Most restrictions pertained to the Congress or to *khilafate* material; approximately 50 banned items dealt with the Punjab disturbances and Jallianwala Bagh.[56]

As the immediate crises subsided, the Government of India paused for a moment of introspection. The soul searching led to inquiries on the April disturbances of 1919, amnesty for most Indians tried summarily, and a reaffirmation of commitment to constitutional reforms. After making gestures of conciliation, the government then sat back to play a game of political cat and mouse with their opponents. In the succeeding two years, the Governor General and his colleagues maneuvered, compromised, bluffed, and, when backed into a corner, resorted to a resumption of repression. Such a situation occurred in late 1921, and the British hit hard again with prosecutions and bans.[57] In addition

54. The Bamford survey and Sitaramayya (*The Indian National Congress*, I, 270–427) cover the basic developments of the period. An excellent series of essays on the 1919 disturbance is in Ravindar Kumar, ed., *Essays on Gandhian Politics: The Rowlatt Satyagraha of 1919*; also Graham, "The Khilafat Movement."

55. Two different perspectives are in O'Dwyer, *India*, and V. N. Datta, *Jallianwala Bagh*.

56. Statistics and background based on J&P 4496 and study of files on specific newspapers and banned items, GIPOL. The bitterness of the literature is illustrated by this quotation from *Panjab Ka Khun* (*The Blood of Punjab*, Cawnpur, 1920): "Punjab is weeping with the doings of coward Dyer. The soil of Jallianwala Bagh is still wet with the blood of our babies."

57. Treatment of the Indian government's strategy is in D. A. Low, "The Government of India and the First Non-Cooperation Movement—1920–1922," *The Journal of Asian Studies*, 25:2 (February 1966), 241–

to all-India patterns, the use of coercion frequently resulted from local issues that may or may not have had any connection with the Congress and *khilafate* movements. Each provincial government dealt with immediate problems as they arose. Punjab officials, for example, spent much of their time in battle with militant Sikhs who were determined to seize control of their community's temples (*gurdwaras*).[58]

The violence and excesses in 1919 reinforced Montagu's conviction that coercion in India would only lead to wider unrest and more repression. In addition to working hard on details relating to implementation of the constitutional reforms, he suggested a conciliatory attitude toward Indian politicians. Press restrictions became a special concern. Although Montagu's effort to include remission of press securities within the amnesty agreement was blocked by Delhi, he kept pushing on the matter. By January of 1920, the Secretary of State felt that changes in press regulations could be postponed no longer. In a dispatch he argued that repressive laws, and particularly press actions, would receive embarrassing scrutiny in the new legislatures controlled by Indians. If the British could modify the law prior to the creation of the new assemblies, that action might generate good will and prevent nasty confrontations. Montagu's assessment also rested on the belief that the press had matured and should be given opportunity to act responsibly. The reform package he suggested included amendment of the Indian Penal Code and the 1867 Registration Act to provide minimal protection. The revised law would provide for security demands by executives but would give courts the power to forfeit. Once these provisions were made, the controversial Press Act could be repealed.[59]

In the meantime, Chelmsford called a special meeting of administrative heads to discuss political strategy. William Vincent, the Home Member, informed the assemblage that the Delhi government had successfully opposed Montagu's request for a general remission of securities. The Governor of Madras, Lord Willingdon, said he also favored conciliation. Lord Ronaldshay of Bengal responded that Willingdon's plans to remit all securities might seem reasonable in the Madras context, but he preferred holding

69. The official version is in *Report of Chelmsford Administration*, pp. 241–69, and *The History of Freedom Movement in Madya Pradesh*. Approximate totals for proscriptions: 1920, 42; 1921, 258; 1922, 339.

58. The British banned approximately 25 Sikh titles between 1921 and 1924. On repression in Bombay, see *History of the Freedom Movement*, 3 vols. (Bombay: Maharashtra Government, 1965–1971), III, Pt. 1, 490–98.

59. Public despatch, January 12, 1920, GIPOL 1921, 4–I; Montagu to Chelmsford, April 1, 1920, C.C.

fast because Bengalis were allegedly not interested in the issue. If Madras had its way, agitation for similar action might occur in Bengal. The provincial chiefs split on the issue, most of them backing Bengal, and the Indian government concluded the discussion with the threat to block Madras if Willingdon pursued his remission scheme.[60]

Although initially balking at wholesale abandonment of securities, the governments drifted toward a policy of leniency toward the press. Circulars requesting comments on the Montagu proposals evoked a variety of responses, but with two exceptions, administrators felt the time had arrived to reconsider restrictions. The statistics that accompanied the replies also suggested that some administrations were already doing what they could to improve the climate surrounding press–government relations. Madras, Bengal, and the United Provinces had returned most of their securities and were demanding new ones only in very special cases. Delhi and Punjab remained firm in their determination to keep a tight grip on journalists.[61]

Collection of information consumed valuable time, however, and soon Montagu pressed for final action. On November 4, 1920, he warned that unless some action was taken by the first meeting of the Indian Legislative Assembly in January, "we shall have lost the tide." If constructive measures were ready, on the other hand, they would "consolidate Indian opinion which is well worth having on the Government side."[62] The Government of India obviously had to reach a decision soon. As Vincent commented, if Delhi did not modify the Press Act, the Secretary of State and the new legislature would. The central government therefore agreed to appoint a public committee, with an Indian majority, to study the issue. The move would prevent an immediate repeal, and if, as expected, the committee suggested alterations in the law, the new Viceroy (Lord Reading, who assumed office in April 1921) could reap the political benefits.[63]

The decision to form a public press committee came none too soon. One of the initial debates in the Legislative Assembly centered on restrictive legislation. The government blocked the introduction of a bill repealing the 1910 Press Act and then buttressed its position by announcing that a respected member of the Governor General's Council, Tej Bahadur Sapru, would chair a

60. Background on the meeting in GIPOL March 1920, 10D. Willingdon's views on the press and provincial autonomy are surveyed in "Victor Trench," *Lord Willingdon in India*, pp. 42–43, 51–52.
61. Synopses of action in J&P 1919, 4468.
62. Montagu to Chelmsford, November 4, 1920, M.C.
63. Vincent note (December 15, 1920), GIPOL 1921, 4–I.

committee to study press matters and recommend future policy.[64]

The committee began collecting evidence in March and reported in June of 1921. A procession of English and Indian editors testified on all aspects of recent press history. One by one they recounted personal affronts and incidents in which officials had misused discretionary powers. Even pro-British witnesses agreed that restrictive laws undermined the morale of journalists and hampered legitimate criticism of government. Internalized rage against the 1910 Press Act burst forth during almost every testimony.[65] As a result, the committee recommended a radical redrafting of Indian press laws. While denying the effectiveness of controls, it asserted that measures that might have been necessary during emergency were now incompatible with India's new political spirit. The major recommendations consisted of repeal of the 1908 and 1910 acts and the retention of limited aspects of those measures in the penal code. The only major provision continued was the power to seize documents that clearly fell under the sedition clause, 124A: "The confiscation of openly seditious documents in no way, we believe, constitutes an interference with the reasonable liberty of the Press and the openly seditious character of some of the documents which are now circulated in India has convinced us of the necessity of retaining this power as a regular provision of the substantive law."[66] Such confiscations and bans would be contestable in the high courts. A corollary of maintaining the ban on seditious matter was amending the Sea Customs and Postal acts to facilitate the seizures. In addition, the committee suggested retaining a modified version of the 1867 Registration Act. Henceforth, persons registered as printer or publisher were required to be old enough to accept responsibility for publications, and the names of editors were to be printed on the front sheet of newspapers. Finally, fines and terms of imprisonment under the 1867 act were to be reduced sharply.

The committee also considered whether legal protection for Indian princes should be continued. Under the 1910 Press Act, which was slated for repeal, action could be taken against journals or books that "excited disaffection" against princes or brought them into "hatred and contempt." The princes generally refused to give evidence on the matter, but the committee examined documents supplied by the Indian Political Department. On the basis

64. Strategy and proceedings discussed in GIPOL February 1921, 70B.

65. Evidence and report in J&P 1919, 4468. Copy of the report reprinted in G. K. Roy, *Law Relating to Press and Sedition* (1922), pp. 11–23.

66. Roy, *Law* (1922), pp. 19–20.

of that material and testimony from witnesses, it decided that princes did not require special assistance. The report concluded that, since citizens of princely states often had legitimate grievances, any law designed to help princes probably would stifle criticism and change. The only British officer on the committee, Home Member Vincent, agreed with the majority opinion because of insufficient evidence and the Indians' strong feeling on the issue.[67]

The recommendations did not go much further than anticipated. The Indian government was aware of public sentiment and knew that the committee chairman, Sapru, long had been a proponent of the argument that ordinary law, if used effectively, could regulate seditious writings.[68] The Governor General's Council examined the findings and wired Montagu that the report should be accepted. Montagu agreed. Both Lord Reading and Montagu were concerned with one problem, however—protection for princes. Telegrams and letters flashed back and forth, but while gathering more information on the princes' need for protection, the Indian government proceeded with the drafting of a bill.[69]

There then occurred a reversal of policy that foreshadowed a trend at the highest levels of decisionmaking. Montagu had championed press reforms and flexibility toward Indian politicians, but in the summer of 1921 he suddenly changed direction. The reason probably involved the information on Indian unrest that had filtered into the India Office and Parliament. Opposition in the Cabinet and Parliament to the Indian government's strategy of maneuvering and use of minimal force grew steadily in proportion to news of fresh Congress activities. The boycott directed at the visit of the Prince of Wales particularly struck home. Reading seemed to be losing control.[70] Montagu consequently challenged Reading's policies from several directions. For example, he telegraphed disapproval of Delhi's intention to accept most of the recommendations of a committee studying the effect of "repressive laws." Both the Secretary of State and Governor General had agreed to the committee's appointment, but when it called for

67. Vincent note (August 1, 1922), GIPOL 1923, 258. On evaluation within the Punjab, entries in the Thompson diaries (IOL Eur. Mss. F 137), July 1920. I am indebted to Professor Barbara Ramusack for this citation.

68. For example, his notes in GIPOL 1921, 4–I. Low, "Government of India," traces Sapru's role in evolving British strategy.

69. Telegrams of August 4, 28, 1921; Reading to Montagu, July 21, 1921, R.C.

70. Background on pressure from London in the Low article; Waley, *Montagu*, pp. 252–69; Viscount Templewood, *Nine Troubled Years*, pp. 42–48, 80–103. Montagu also was undergoing severe melancholy and illness during this period.

repeal of favored repressive acts, such as the deportation power under Regulation III of 1818, Montagu warned that the substitution of legal process for executive discretion must be undertaken very slowly.[71] Much of Montagu's criticism pertained to the press. According to the India Office, the Government of India was rushing legislation at the risk of alienating traditional allies of the *raj*, the princes. Montagu became insistent that protection be given them, either in the forthcoming bill or in a separate act.[72] He also changed his position on methods to handle the press. Disturbed that Indian authorities seemed lenient on "malignant articles," Montagu demanded accelerated prosecution of offenders.[73]

The pressure from London complicated but basically did not alter the Indian government's political strategy. Reading successfully backed the repressive law committee's report on the grounds that it had been a responsible body and had permitted continuation of measures thought necessary for maintaining order.[74] Reading also circularized Montagu's comments on the press, but in an accompanying minute stated that, given the delicate political situation, care should be taken when applying sanctions. Local governments were confused. Bengal, for example, observed great inconsistencies in messages from London and Delhi. How could officials be lenient and employ vigorous restraints simultaneously? The Punjab replied that, since the gradual relaxing of security demands, it preferred to rely on warning rather than to increase formal press actions.[75]

As to the princes and repeal of the press law, Reading wanted more information on the necessity for their protection before bringing the controversial issue to the new Legislative Assembly. The press bill (introduced on September 15, 1921) accordingly carried no special provisions for the protection of the princes.[76] The measure reproduced the basic suggestions of the study committee. The bill repealed the 1908 and 1910 Press acts and amended Section 99 of the penal code to permit confiscation of printed matter that had been punishable under the 124A sedition clause. It recommended that injured parties could appeal to a

71. Montagu to Reading, November 10, 1921, R.C.

72. Montagu to Reading, November 24, 30, 1921, and noting in J&P 1919, 4468.

73. Expressed in Montagu letters, winter 1921, and documents in GIPOL 1921, 263.

74. Reading to Montagu, October 18, 1921, R.C.

75. Replies in GIPOL 1921, 4–I, 263. In File 263, S. P. O'Donnell noted that if the government prosecuted all those who infringed the letter of the law, the number would be in the hundreds. Minute, October 12, 1921.

76. Background and copy of the bill in J&P 1919, 4468; reproduced in Roy, *Law* (1922), pp. 173–85.

special panel of an appropriate high court. Amendments to existing law also strengthened British options relating to customs and postal seizures and made the suggested changes in the 1867 Registration Act. Accepting the bill as a token of British good will, the legislature passed a slightly modified version in March 1922.

Although the issue of press controls apparently had been resolved, the India Office's obstinacy almost scuttled the reform. While the repeal bill went through a six-month legislative process, resentment at the noninclusion of a princes clause had been mushrooming. A meeting of the Chamber of Princes in November decried the legislation and reminded the British of treaties and earlier pledges. Individual rulers used personal contacts to influence government and parliamentary officials.[77] Montagu warned Reading that such adverse attitudes might force the India Office to insist on a new princely bill, but when the demand came, Montagu was not its author. In March of 1922 he resigned on a non-India issue. His replacement, Lord Peel, adopted a strong stand and told Reading in May that, unless Delhi would guarantee assistance for the princes, he would invoke Section 69 of the Government of India Act and disallow repeal of the press measure.[78]

The question of the princes' protection caught the Indian government in a crossfire. While resenting the threat of disallowal as an infringement on its authority, Reading's main concern was that a veto would constitute "a serious blow to the independence of the Legislature."[79] The alternative was no more appealing. The government knew that, had the repeal measure been tied to support for princes, the Legislative Assembly would have balked. To bring in a special bill now would be more dangerous because of the members' growing independence. During the first sessions of the central legislature, the British and the nonofficial majority that dominated both houses had been in a honeymoon phase. As the legislators gained confidence and voting blocs emerged, however, overt opposition to government came to be articulated freely. Three incidents in England further dissipated the initial spirit of reform and compromise. First, speeches during an attempted censure of the India Office in the House of Commons (February 1922) publicized that many M.P.s and indeed, the Secretary of

77. Proceedings of the Chamber of Princes in J&P 1919, 4468; comments of Reading to Montagu, July 21, 1921, R.C.; noting in GIPOL 1921, 4–I.

78. Despatch 30, May 25, 1922, and minutes, GIPOL 1921, 4–I.

79. July 7, 1922, J&P 1919, 4468. Background on the Indian government's position in GIPOL 1921, 4–I, and 1923, 258.

State, regarded the Indian government as responsible primarily to Parliament. That interpretation conflicted with Indians' view of the 1919 Government of India Act and made them sensitive to their own prerogatives. A month later, Indians lost Montagu, an acclaimed sympathizer, and gained Peel, a House of Lords politician undistinguished in Indian affairs. Shortly thereafter, Prime Minister Lloyd George made a notorious "steel frame" speech on the Indian Civil Service that suggested the British planned to rule the subcontinent indefinitely. Reading attempted to repudiate any shift in policy, but the damage had been done. The Legislative Assembly responded to growing hostility from England with suspicion and great pugnacity.[80]

The Government of India tried to avoid a crisis. In a July dispatch, Reading asked Peel to reconsider the threat of disavowal because of its implications for British–Indian relations. The Secretary of State replied with a lecture on the constitutional authority of the India Office and of Parliament. Although he agreed to let the Press Act stand, he warned that the authorities in Delhi must reexamine new legislation and, if necessary, ram a bill through the Legislative Assembly.[81]

Continuing pressure from London forced a review of the issue, but the Indian government's final decision to prepare a princes' bill actually derived from its study of information that had been accumulating in the Home and Political departments. Numerous political agents pushed for legislation because princely rulers supposedly were facing a massive attack from nationalists based in British India.[82] Statistics reinforced their assessment. Just a handful of documents directed at princely states had come to the notice of the Political Department prior to 1921, but from May 1921 until May 1922, over 150 such articles and books came into circulation.[83] Despite Sapru's bitter dissent, the Council decided that two factors made legislation imperative—prior pledges of support to the princes and the more immediate rationale of preventing the spread of sedition.

The resulting bill basically duplicated sections of the repealed 1910 act. Persons connected with publications that created hatred or disaffection relating to princely states were liable to imprison-

80. Based on study of the Legislative Assembly debates and a survey in *Report of the Administration of Lord Reading, Viceroy and Governor General of India, 1921–6*, pp. 2–14. The informal rules and business of the Assembly are summarized in *Manual of Business and Procedure in the Legislative Assembly*, 2d ed.

81. Despatch, July 7, 1922, and SS telegram, July 31, J&P 1919, 4468.

82. Replies from agents in GIPOL 1923, 258.

83. Note by J. P. Thompson (July 25, 1922), GIPOL 1923, 258.

ment up to five years. To diminish the expected criticism from legislators, the draft carefully stated that legitimate comments on princes would be permitted. Provisions of Section 99 of the penal code and of the Postal Act were to apply to publications that attacked the princes as they had to seditious matter.[84]

Fearing that postponement of the encounter with the Legislative Assembly would accelerate antiprincely writings, Reading immediately presented the Indian States Protection against Disaffection Bill on September 23, 1923. The Assembly reacted sharply against the measure, and on a crucial vote refused, 45 to 41, to permit its introduction. Having foreseen the outcome, for the first time Reading used his reserve power to certify the bill under Section 62B as essential to the defense and interests of India. The legislation then bypassed the Assembly and went to the Council of State. Stunned, but then reassured by Reading that restrictions would be employed only against extremist material, the Council passed the bill.[85]

Although the reaction to the princes' bill died down within six months, other turbulence did not. The Government of India was entering a complex phase of Indian politics armed with traditional punitive weapons under the penal code, but except for the power to ban sedition, without the preventive measures that had been employed for over a decade. Not only had security deposits been repealed, but in an effort to make the reforms survive, the British belatedly had agreed to relinquish the Defence of India and Rowlatt acts. Would the remaining sanctions, plus propaganda and anticipated responsible action by Indian leaders, be sufficient to minimize disorder and permit political progress? The answer to the effect of limited controls depended on a variety of variables, some of which had been important in the press repeal proceedings. The attitudes of the Legislative Assembly certainly would be of vital concern in the future, as would the attention to and participation in political developments by Parliament and the India Office. The House of Commons, for example, had a lengthy debate on the princes' protection act before the Secretary of State gave his assent. Reading could do nothing to speed the acceptance despite his warnings about continued publicity on the matter.[86] There remained the unknown activities of politicians operating outside the normal channels of government. What they

84. Bills contained in GIPOL 1923, 258, and *The Unrepealed Central Acts*, VII, 382–83.

85. Summary drawn from documents in GIPOL 1923, 258, and J&P 1919, 4468. Also, Reading to Peel, December 14, 1922, R.C.

86. Peel to Reading, January 3, February 28, 1923; Reading to Peel, December 12, 1922, and March 1, 22, 1923, R.C.

did would affect decisionmaking and the question as to whether the Indian government could survive without reliance on naked force.

The Lid Comes Off

Three trends between 1922 and 1926 helped focus British strategy toward politics and the press. First, following the end of the non-cooperation campaign in early 1922, the Congress devoted much of its energy to internal affairs and the evolvement of a program acceptable to a range of interests. Whether and how to operate within the legislative process also became a central concern of the Congress. The direction of concern meant that, despite brushfire harassment, the British did not have to contend with the massive agitation of earlier periods.[87]

The government needed such a breathing spell because the decline in fights with the Congress was matched by persistent challenges at the local level of administration. In Punjab, for example, the efforts of the militant Shiromani Gurdwara Parbandak Committee to seize gurdwaras led to numerous conflicts. Since Sikh rajas were immersed in the politics of their community, provincial administrators faced both direct attacks and related moves against Punjab states (especially Patiala).[88] Bengal, Punjab, and United Provinces governments were also forced to deal at different times with a recurrent problem—revolutionary uprisings. All across North India, the bitterness and excitement generated by events associated with non-cooperation became channeled into new organizations such as the Hindustan Republican Association. In the Punjab, the Babbar Akali Dal served as a rallying point for disaffected youth and Sikh extremists. The renewed network of revolutionaries carried out assassinations and raids, the most publicized of which was an attack on a train near Kakori, U.P.[89] The revolutionaries also wrote and secretly distributed works like *The Revolutionary* and a manifesto from the "President in Council, Red Bengal," which called for violence

87. Description in *Report on Reading Administration*, pp. 28–36. For a summary statement on Congress politics, Sitaramayya, *The Indian National Congress*, I, 428–520. Constitutional activities are summarized in *Reports of the Local Governments on the Working of the Reformed Constitution.*

88. Several reports in the Crown Representative Papers (C.R.P., especially 1/29/87, 157) cover the Patiala incidents. General background in Ruchi Ram Sahni, *The Gurdwara Reform Movement*; J&P 1924, 3833; 1926, 3651.

89. Accounts of revolutionary activity include the following: GIPOL 1926, 236–II; J&P 1925, 1869; K. C. Ghosh, *The Roll of Honour*, pp. 376–88; Manmathnath Gupta, *They Lived Dangerously.*

and contained a picture of the goddess Kali killing a European.[90]

In addition to the lull in Congress activity and to the intense but regionalized unrest, a third trend forced itself increasingly on the British—the appearance of two all-India varieties of political activity which threatened the peace of the subcontinent. First, the Comintern set destruction of the British Empire in India as a premier goal. Bolshevik documents began circulating in India around 1919, followed shortly by an influx of Moscow-trained Indians who organized the Communist Party of India and related propaganda agencies. Indian Communists in Berlin also deluged their homeland with journals, posters, and anti-imperialist material. Led by M. N. Roy, they tried to infiltrate the Congress, labor unions, and peasant associations.[91]

The Communist campaign seemed almost negligible, however, compared to another source of disruption, communal violence. Religious controversy had reemerged from a latent stage during the First World War to become a permanent factor in Indian politics. One reason for the renewal of hostilities was the Moplah uprising in 1921, which resulted in the killing and forced conversion to Islam of thousands of Hindus. The Hindu attempt to reconvert through *shuddhi* (purification ceremonies sponsored primarily by the reformist Arya Samaj) had a similar effect. The consequent battles between religious communities took several forms. Hindus and Muslims fought in formal political channels to protect themselves and to undermine religious opponents. Provincial and central legislative debates often became scenes of bitter religious acrimony. Even at the subdistrict level, in elections or municipal proceedings, politicians frequently mobilized along religious lines. "There is nothing of our work," summarized a key British official, "from administration of justice down to digging of drains, in which we do not have to face troubles arising from communal differences."[92] This competition became institutionalized in new or revived organizations. The Hindu Ma-

90. Discussed in J&P 1924, 3021. The 4-page *Revolutionary* viewed "all constitutional agitations with contempt and mockery," and called instead for "organized and armed revolution." A copy is in J&P 1925, 1869.

91. Two C.I.D. confidential studies on the C.P.I., D. Petrie, *Communism in India, 1924–27* (Calcutta: Government of India, 1927), and William Kaye's *Communism in India* (reprint version with notes, Calcutta: Editions Indian, 1972) provide chronological background. Useful from a Communist perspective are Muzaffar Ahmad, *Myself and the Communist Party of India*, and Sukhbir Choudhary, *Peasants' and Workers' Movement in India, 1905–1929* (Delhi: Peoples' Publishing House, 1971). Also, Bose, *Indian Revolutionaries*, pp. 192–220.

92. Hailey note (October 6, 1924) in Hailey Collection, IOL Eur. Mss. E 220. For a survey of the problems, Gene Thursby, "Aspects of Hindu-

hasabha and shuddhi sabhas preached a doctrine of militant self-defense and self-strengthening, *sangathan.* Muslims countered with defense associations, such as the Jam'iat-i-Tabligh-ul-Islam, extensions of the organizational structure and zeal once focused on the *khilafate* issue.

A pronounced increase in communal literature both reflected and contributed to Hindu–Muslim tension. Published attacks among Indian religious groups had been common for at least four decades, but by the 1920s the erratic exchange gave way to persistent warfare by tract and journalistic publications. Produced by dozens of sectarian presses and publishing firms, the controversial material savagely reviewed the history and religious doctrine of opponents. In 1923, for example, Maulvi Abdul Hak commented in a Muslim newspaper, *Paigham-i-Sulah*, that while Hindus often made fun of Muhammad's marriages, they conveniently forgot the sexual practices of Hindu gods.[93] *Vichitra Jivan* exemplified the corresponding viewpoint of the Hindu community. Written by an Arya Samaj preacher and polemicist, Pandit Kalicharan Sharma, *Strange Life* surveyed the formative experiences of Muhammad and the evolution of early Islam. Sharma claimed the book's aim was "not to hurt Muslim feelings," but rather to win adherents away from religious falsehood through reasoning and a "correct" view of history.[94] In addition to emphasizing Muhammad's sexual life and alleged immorality, the book stressed the spread of Islam by the sword. All Muslims, according to the author, were intent on loot, arson, and rape.

Verbal and written conflict eventually became widespread violence. By the mid-1920s, riots occurred on an almost weekly basis. Between 1922 and 1926, over two hundred incidents were reported, the most noteworthy being the Kohat riots of 1924 (leaving 36 dead and driving the Hindu population out of the

---

Muslim Relations in British India" (Ph.D. diss., Duke University, 1972). The annual "moral and material progress reports" capsule yearly events, especially the following: *India in 1924–5* (Calcutta: Government of India, 1925), pp. 300–301; *India in 1923–4* (Calcutta: Government of India, 1924), pp. 258–60. Key files include GIPOL 1924, 243, 249/8; 1925, 140. A contemporary survey is in Hugh McPherson, "Communal Antagonism Between Hindus and Muhammadans," in John Cumming, ed., *Political India, 1832–1932*, pp. 106–23; also *Reports on Working of Constitution*, pp. 190–209, 449–50; Graham, "The Khilafat Movement," pp. 412–505.

93. Quotations and background from Thursby, "Aspects," p. 66. References to sex frequently dealt with *niyoga* (an Arya Samaj marriage arrangement, or to relationships between Brahma and consorts).

94. Background in Thursby, "Aspcts," p. 134. The author received a sentence of two months' rigorous imprisonment and fine.

town) and the 1925 Calcutta riots (140 killed and much arson). Sparked by local issues or concern with symbols (the cow, processional rights, music before religious buildings), the affrays had a devastating cumulative effect on communal relations. To the dismay of officials and nationalists alike, the situation deteriorated with each passing year.[95]

These assorted developments formed the backdrop against which the Government of India attempted a wary transition from colonial bureaucracy to Imperial politician. Direct involvement in legislative maneuvering became a British priority. Within the Indian Legislative Assembly, the government hoped to sustain an atmosphere of constitutional advance combined with careful nurturing of coalitions that were sympathetic to official plans. This effort is nowhere more graphically illustrated than in Reading's 1924 commentary on the Assembly. While facing continuous opposition, he noted, the British had to work as a unit, prepare their homework, and then debate each issue with critics. Care should be taken to supply Indian allies with useful information, with special emphasis on predebate caucusing.[96] At least until early 1926, Reading judged the strategy reasonably successful. Congress—independent groupings formed occasionally, but on the whole, the government had carried many key votes and prevented numerous efforts to undercut its authority.[97] The Indian government pursued this course under frequent pressure from London officials who, not fully appreciating the delicacy of day-to-day negotiations, felt that Delhi's control was inadequate. Central authorities, therefore, faced the ongoing problem of juggling the demands, often conflicting, of Indian and British politicians.[98]

Intensification of propaganda comprised another element of British strategy. The 1919 disturbances, according to a confidential circular, had resulted partially from the infection of popular opinion by rumor and extremist views. Such an interpretation reinforced the growing realization among high officials that the government must clearly place its views and position before the Indian people.[99] Utilizing experience gained in wartime, the

95. Birkenhead, Secretary of State, accurately warned Irwin on his becoming Viceroy in April 1926 that a main anxiety would be "recrudescence of communal strife." Birkenhead to Irwin, May 12, 1926, I.C. Riots discussed in Thursby, "Aspects," pp. 159–243.

96. Reading to Ramsden, June 5, 1924, R.C.

97. Assessment in *Report on Reading Administration*, pp. 1–36.

98. Exemplified by London concern with Indian communism, Birkenhead to Reading, September 2, November 5, 1925, R.C. Also, Templewood, *Troubled Years*, pp. 42–48, 68–103.

99. Note by Rushbrook Williams (December 17, 1920), GIPOL March 1921, 92–93A.

Home Department pressed hard for a centralized publicity/propaganda agency. These urgings bore fruit in the Central Bureau of Information, with Rushbrook Williams as director, and provincial bureaus controlled by local governments. The agencies had three basic functions: supplying official versions of events to journalists, correcting alleged rumor and misrepresentation, and producing and disseminating propaganda. The techniques employed resembled those used earlier (lectures, brochures, film and slide shows), but the content of the propaganda dealt with current problems. In 1921, for example, pamphlets such as *A Straight Talk on the Khilafat Question* were published to counter Pan-Islamic material. Similarly, local bureaus produced propaganda that focused on immediate issues, illustrated by the United Provinces' circulation of two million leaflets, in question and answer form, on non-cooperation and peasant–landlord relations.[100]

The British balanced cultivation of legislative and public support with sporadic resort to coercion. The Government of India attempted to maintain a posture of conciliation, but provincial authorities, who faced more pressing threats and were not burdened with overseeing all aspects of constitutional reforms, showed less restraint. Prosecutions for sedition and for creating disorder occurred in most provinces; approximately thirty journalists were sentenced to jail and/or fined prior to 1926. At least two governments exceeded the normal bounds of punishment. Punjab officers brutalized intransigent Sikhs both in public and in jail, while Bengal asked for and received special powers to conduct summary trials against revolutionaries.[101] The British also seized over 200 pieces of printed matter under Section 99A, primarily on the initiative of local authorities.[102]

The Indian government played a dual role in the application

100. The following GIPOL files contain comments on the system: March 1921, 92–93A; February 1921, 341–354A; July 1921, 241–242A; also, J&P material: 1920, 903; 1919, 2078. The Punjab receives treatment in the July 1920 section of the Thompson Collection (IOL). The British supplemented these tactics with manipulation of placement of official advertising. Discussion in GIPOL February 1921, 40–43B.

101. Descriptions on Punjab in Ruchi Ram Sahni, *Gurdwara*, and Ganda Singh, ed., *Some Confidential Papers of Akali Movement.* Bengal receives treatment in John Broomfield, *Elite Conflict in a Rural Society* (Berkeley: University of California Press, 1968). Both governments also utilized propaganda and "noncoercive tactics"; discussion in GIPOL 1924, 1/11.

102. Two files (GIPOL 1925, 33/25, GIPOL 1933, 25) contain descriptions of many titles; this has been supplemented with statistics from biannual reports on banning. Because the Indian government did not have full information, the estimates probably are very low. GIPOL 1927, 10/98; background in *Freedom Movement in Madhya Pradesh*, pp. 322–28. The banning peaked in 1921 and 1922 (approximately 460 titles) and dropped to 160 in 1923 and 41 in 1924.

of repressive measures. First, it facilitated intelligence, superintended the activities of subordinates, and defended them if necessary against critics in the Legislative Assembly. At the same time, the Governor General and his Council assumed responsibility for preventing disorder that might arise from sources beyond the control of provincial governments. This duty meant paying special attention to all-India or external threats. Adopting a "shielding" policy, the Government of India tried to keep disruptive persons or material from affecting Indian politics.

Communism was a case in point. India supposedly had to be insulated from Bolshevik ideas because they might stimulate "unhealthy" political trends. As one C.I.D. officer commented, a linkage between international activists and Indian patriots had to be prevented at all cost; otherwise, the germ would multiply.[103] The Indian government therefore set up a postal cordon aimed primarily at Communist literature. All Communist or left-leaning publications were banned automatically. When the tactic failed to stop the spread of communism, the British attempted to uproot its leadership through sedition trials—at Cawnpur (1924) and the volatile proceedings at Meerut (1929–1932).[104]

Customs and postal machinery was not directed solely at nationalist or Communist writing, but at almost every outside stimulus that might cause trouble. Agents at the seaports seized books on Ireland, works on Egyptian and Chinese nationalism, a survey of Indian social and religious ideas (R. J. Minney's *Shiva or the Future of India*) and Dan Breen's autobiography.[105] Similar priorities were reflected in official handling of a new medium—movie films—under the 1918 Cinematograph Act. The British banned many American movies because they portrayed the "more seamy" side of Western culture.[106] "The Chinese Bungalow" did not reach the Indian public because it portrayed a Chinese with higher character than a European and introduced "the vexed question of marriages between Western women and

103. Petrie, *Communism*, p. 321. On pre-1921 discussion of Communism and the British Empire, see Frederick Julian Stanwood, "Britain in Central Asia, 1917–1919" (Ph.D. diss., University of California at San Diego, 1971).

104. Trials summarized in Petrie and H. Williamson, *India and Communism* (Calcutta: Government of India, 1933). Two J&P files (1919, 6946; 1925, 572) trace British policy and tactics; also, Choudhary, *Peasants*, pp. 209–64.

105. An incomplete but representative list is in *General Rules and Orders Made Under Enactments in Force in British India*, IV, 103–311.

106. Note by Irwin to Birkenhead, November 3, 1926, I.C. Censorship and its effects evaluated in a massive collection file, J&P 1921, 260. The same power was used to control internally produced but controversial films, such as those on the Sikhs and communalism. J&P 1922, 949. Descriptions taken from File 260.

Orientals." Because racism remained a perennial concern, the mob fight between whites and Indians in "The Man from Brodneys" made its prohibition inevitable. Any description of Asian nationalism or revolution also caused consternation. "The Heir to Genghis Khan" was banned, and the following changes made in "Hutch of U.S.A.": a subtitle, "A revolutionary committee has been formed," was altered to "Our Government is in danger," and "Dreamed of a day when the Government would be a Government of the people by the people" became "Dreamed of a day when peace and contentment would prevail in the land."

Had the quantity and tone of anti-British writings constituted its sole benchmark, by 1926 the Government of India would have been content with the experiment of relaxing restrictions on the Indian press. The cautious screening of external materials, combined with selective prosecution and banning, had from the British point of view minimized seditious activity. Occasionally seizures or arrests fostered controversy in Parliament or in the Indian Legislative Assembly. But the effort to maintain low-keyed control over publications had led to no widespread opposition.[107] When a broader criterion was applied, however, the British painfully realized that relaxation of restraint had been far from successful. Communal violence continued to threaten public order. Only when trying to overwhelm this mushrooming danger did the government regret the lack of the wider powers of the 1910 Press Act.

The Indian government did not know how to ease Hindu-Muslim tension. It brought into play a battery of old techniques for influencing Indians that ranged from private discussions to public warnings, but none seemed to have long-term effect. Renewed efforts focused on conciliation boards and conferences at the provincial level. When coupled with acceleration of prosecutions for breach of the peace and for publishing rumors, the improved communication among religious leaders, it was hoped, would lessen tension. Again a failure.[108]

In desperation, the government decided that the sole alternative open was a vigorous campaign to mute communal writings. If Hindu and Muslim publicists somehow could be prevented from inflaming the population, then perhaps other problems between the communities would be resolved. In the summer of

107. For example, discussion in J&P 1928, 1144. Ironically, the most dramatic confrontation came, not over what the British did, but what they did not do—ban Katherine Mayo's *Mother India*. For background on the incident, see Manoranjan Jha, *Katherine Mayo and India*; also, documents in J&P 1925, 3061.

108. Surveyed in Thursby, "Aspects," pp. 249–78.

1926 the Home Department therefore requested local opinion on a proposal to amend Section 99A of the penal code so that, in the future, material falling under 153A (the class hatred and incitement section) could be seized in addition to sedition.[109] All provincial heads welcomed the proposal, but the Punjab and Bengal urged stronger steps. Noting that newspapers reprinted pamphlets and exaggerated communal issues, the governments warned that proscription would be useless because copies already would have reached the public. The other problem, from their perspective, was that trials on communal issues tended to publicize controversy. The situation could be resolved only by return to expanded executive controls similar to those in the repealed 1910 act.[110]

The central secretariat examined the alternative plans—amendment of 99A or broadening press restrictions—and then opted for the less extreme measure. Arguments against the comprehensive suggestions were an important gauge of how the Indian government viewed the political environment. According to the Home Member, Alexander Muddiman, no type of interference with religious polemics could be guaranteed to improve communal relations. Given this uncertainty, the potential public reaction seemed to override the gamble on thorough controls. A return to the 1910 Press Act was "outside the sphere of practical politics," he concluded, because British opponents might use the issue to rally broad-based popular support. The government feared a confrontation with anti-British forces more strongly than a continuation of Hindu–Muslim violence.[111]

The measure to include action under 153A in 99A—the Code of Criminal Procedure (Third Amendment) Bill—precipitated heated legislative debate in late August 1926. Critics argued that banning would not affect journalists but permitted excessive executive discretion and did not come to terms with the primary causes of communalism.[112] The rapidity with which the speeches deteriorated into accusatory and sectarian diatribes underlined the seriousness of the problem, however, and while all members of the Legislative Assembly (M.L.A.s) did not agree on the bill's wording, they passed it without serious division.

The first adjustment of press laws since 1922 revealed that the Legislative Assembly could evaluate the case for changes in the penal code, and if convinced of a measure's utility, it would

109. Circular 1451/25, June 2, 1926, and background discussion in GIPOL 1926, 236; also, 1927, 77–111.

110. PG and BG replies in GIPOL 1926, 236; 1927, 77–111.

111. Muddiman note (September 11, 1926), GIPOL 1926, 236.

112. For example, arguments on Lajpat Rai. L.A.D., 1926, VIII, 279–309.

enact new restrictions. Discussion leading to the bill's passage also revealed a new development within the bureaucracy. Mounting political pressure was forcing a political reappraisal by at least some local administrators. The Punjab and Bengal governments had balanced the value of reform against the danger of disorder and then called for a return to expanded press controls. They continued to document the need for the move, and as communal relations worsened, their argument received a more sympathetic hearing from the beleaguered Indian government.

The Gathering Storm

Two occurrences intensified Hindu–Muslim conflict after the summer of 1926 and set the stage for renewed debate on limitation of communal literature. First, a Muslim zealot, Rashid, assassinated a leader of the Hindu shuddhi movement, Swami Shraddhanand, on December 23, 1926. The murder triggered a noticeable increase in violence, a condition perpetuated by the appearance of "martyr" writings over the next eighteen months. Prose and poetry eulogized Shraddhanand as a symbol of Hindu self-defense, while gory colored posters depicting his assassination circulated widely through North India.[113] The British employed the newly amended law to ban the most vehement of the martyr productions, but discontent and a new wave of writing built up again during the assassin's trial. Rioting at the time of his execution dramatized the resentment among the Muslim population.[114]

The second occurrence involved an Urdu tract critical of Muhammad, *Rangila Rasul.* The anonymous author of *The Merry Prophet* suggested that the activities of great religious leaders had been associated with a set of ideas and symbols. For example, the founder of the Arya Samaj, Dayanand, had typified celibacy and closely associated himself with the Vedas. Similarly, Muhammad's life and message were tied closely to relationships with women. The remainder of the book explored Muhammad's sexual affairs and poked fun at his view of life.[115] A Lahore bookseller, Rajpal, published the essay in May 1924, and before Muslim objections brought it to official notice, 1,000 copies got

113. For example, *Khun-i-Darvesh* (Lahore: 1927) and *Svami Shraddhanand* (Ajmer: 1927). Background on the murder is in J&P 1924, 3833; 1926, 3651.

114. Discussed in J&P 1926, 3651. Most of the Hailey correspondence during the period pertains to communal problems.

115. Background on the case, and a translation, in J&P 1927, 1513; communal review in *India in 1927–8* (Delhi: Government of India, 1928), pp. 11–26. Rajpal's subsequent murder also led to rioting.

into circulation. Without power to ban the book, the British chose to prosecute Rajpal for inciting religious hatred. His trial dragged on for almost three years because of extensive evidence and appeals. Meanwhile, the case stimulated controversy and a secondary set of "exposés" on Muslim and Hindu saints. A magistrate eventually found Rajpal guilty and sentenced him to 18 months of rigorous imprisonment. The sessions judge also found Rajpal guilty of "raking together" episodes that gave an obnoxious view of Muhammad. On May 4, 1927, however, Justice Dalip Singh of the Lahore High Court ruled that *Rangila Rasul* did not fall under 153A, and he freed the publisher. The surprise verdict left Hindus jeering and Muslims stunned. Ten thousand Muslims attended an open protest meeting in Lahore, and telegrams and petitions poured into the Delhi and Lahore secretariats. The Punjab's governor, William Hailey, prohibited public meetings to prevent further unrest, but when Muslims disobeyed the order, he met with a deputation and tried to calm heightened emotions. If necessary, Hailey promised, the British would amend the law to prevent circulation of material that was blatantly offensive to religious feelings.[116] Shortly afterward, the communal chasm widened when contempt-of-court charges were brought against Muslim papers for their scathing commentary on British justice, in particular, the Christian background of Justice Dalip Singh. To Muslims, his judgment meant that, while their opinions would be punished, Hindu publicists could speak with impunity.[117]

Hailey then decided that only successful prosecution of publications similar to *Rangila Rasul* would calm Muslims and at the same time illuminate the tangled legal issues involved in the earlier verdict. Dalip Singh had argued that, since Section 153A was to prevent attacks on a community "as it exists at the present time" and not to stop "polemics against deceased religious leaders," the Rajpal conviction had been illegal. Hoping to secure an opposite ruling from the High Court, Hailey wired Judge Broadway, then on vacation, to return to Punjab immediately. Broadway and a second English justice, F. W. Skemp, composed a special bench to hear arguments against another hostile essay on Muhammad, an article published in the Hindu *Risala-i-Vartman*.[118] The article, "A Trip to Hell," described the presence of Muhammad in hell and elaborated on his suffering and sins.

116. Secretariat notes, telegrams from PG in GIPOL 1927, 132; 132/II.

117. Hailey to GI, June 23, 1927, in GIPOL 1927, 132.

118. Correspondence in GIPOL 1927, 132–132/II. Also, GIPOL 1928, 7KW.

Much to the relief of government, the judges ruled against the editor and publisher of the journal. The judgment denied the defense, accepted earlier by Justice Dalip Singh, that an attack on a founder of a religion could not be considered a slur on the religion itself. The reversal restored some faith in the British and the court system among Muslims, and when combined with tightening restrictions on public communal utterances, helped prevent reprisals against Hindus in the Lahore vicinity.[119]

Potential loopholes in Section 153A remained, despite the subsidence of the immediate crisis. *Rangila Rasul* was merely one of several cases that related to the use of historical narratives as a means of injuring religious opponents.[120] Shocked by the first judgment, the Punjab and Indian governments laid plans for amendment of the section if the *Vartman* judgments substantiated the *Rangila Rasul* interpretation. The Secretary of State pushed for a revision, whatever the outcome. He argued that publicity over the affair had so confused issues that the law must be clarified. Communiqués from Punjab reinforced his attitude. Punjabis saw the judgment as a sign that, as long as remarks were clothed in historical material, the publishers had nothing to fear from the law.[121] Hailey added that, unless the government faced the problem, the Indians would present their own solutions. Pressure for a new law especially designed to protect Muhammad and other historical figures was mounting, and unless attempts at openly class legislation were sidetracked, a communal explosion could occur.[122]

The Government of India accepted Hailey's arguments and drafted a bill that added a new section to the penal code, 295A, which made it an offense "intentionally to insult or to attempt to insult the religion, or outrage or attempt to outrage the religious feelings of any class."[123] With the concurrence of local governments, the Home Member, James Crerar, introduced the legislation on August 24, 1927. A Select Committee examined all aspects of the measure and suggested modifications both in wording and procedure. The committee preceded *intention* with *deliberate and malicious*, changed *religious feelings* to *religious beliefs*, and limited the offense to verbal and written attacks by

119. Irwin to Birkenhead, August 18, 1927, I.C. The issue did spark further unrest in the N.W.F.P. Discussed in GIPOL 1927, 603.

120. On one such case, *Vichitra Jivan*, see Thursby, "Aspects," pp. 134–46.

121. Hailey to GI, July 25, August 12, 1927, GIPOL 1927, 132. Muslim organizations petitioned for a special law protecting Muhammad.

122. On other historical material, see documents in GIPOL 1929, 27/II.

123. Bill and discussion in GIPOL 1927, 132.

visible representations instead of the earlier vague clause, *by signs*. Further, the Indian government had to sanction prosecutions, and offenses would be tried at the sessions or at the Presidency Magistrates level. Introduction of a case at a relatively high level of the judiciary was considered necessary to prevent prolonged appeals such as had occurred earlier.[124]

Debate on the revised bill assumed a communal character similar to the prior discussion of Section 99A. A few Hindu M.L.A.s labeled the measure a concession to Muslims, while Muslim members took the opportunity to lash out at Hindu revivalist tactics. Few changes were made in the amended version, despite the rhetoric, and the Assembly voted 61 to 26 to pass it. A major reason for the relatively easy passage was that some Hindu stalwarts, most notably Lajpat Rai, supported the bill on the grounds that communal writings had gotten entirely out of hand.[125]

Discussion of religious insults reopened the omnipresent issue of press controls. Although the Punjab government supported the suggested addition to the code, it questioned whether prosecution and slightly amended laws would check communal attacks. Fraud in registration and rapid turnover of editors made close surveillance of the worst offenders difficult. The editorship of the Lahore *Siyasat* had changed ten times, the government observed, and once the *Zamindar* registered a blind, illiterate old man as editor instead of Zafar Ali Khan. Approximately sixty newspapers existed for the primary purpose of attacking religious opponents. Only a tightening of registration procedures and a return to security demands would force the publicists to quit their attacks or to moderate the tone of their journalism.[126] Although Home Department officials shared the Punjabi officials' anxiety about the effectiveness of 295A, they shied from immediately introducing further restrictions. In reviewing the situation in October of 1927, the Home Secretary, Douglas Haig, noted that renewed security arrangements would bring financial pressure to bear on the publishers and perhaps lessen the need to arouse public commotion by prosecutions. Using a massive collection of Punjab material as evidence, he recommended a testing of public opinion through the creation of a legislative committee to study communalism and the law.[127] The secretariat debate

124. GIPOL 1927, 132.

125. Debate reproduced in GIPOL 1927, 132; L.A.D. 1927, IV, 4459–4520, 4575–4612; V, 3924–67.

126. PG to GI, August 6, 1927, GIPOL 1928, 74.

127. Haig notes (October 14, 1927, June 30, 1928), GIPOL 1928, 161.

ended shortly thereafter without action, but not because communal tension had lessened. Rather, the Indian government's focus was diverted from the danger of Hindu–Muslim violence to another cloud that was graying the political skies—a resurgence of challenge by the Congress and revolutionists. The shift of priorities and the reason behind the shift was plain to all. As the 1927–1928 "moral and material progress report" noted, until November 8, 1927, the "main interest of the public and of politicians centered on the Hindu–Muhammadan troubles."[128] On that date, the Viceroy, Lord Irwin, announced the formation and composition of the Indian Statutory Commission.

When enacting the 1919 Government of India Bill, Parliament provided for the calling of a commission within ten years to report on the progress toward representative government. Indian politicians had anticipated the creation of the body since 1924, but the provisions in the final announcement came as a profound shock. Only members from Parliament would sit on a commission whose report would be a guidepost to future constitutional development. The official rationale for limiting to Englishmen membership of the Simon Commission (named for its chairman, John Simon) was that if Indians or bureaucrats became members, they would bring to the evaluation preconceived notions and thereby affect the commission's findings and the readiness with which Parliament would accept its report.[129] In anticipation of an uproar, Irwin met with Indian politicians just prior to the announcement and assured them that their views would be taken seriously. Irwin's plea for understanding and cooperation fell on hostile ears. Indians considered the constitution of the commission a direct insult, an indication of Britain's reluctance to pursue a course of reform.[130]

The Simon Commission disrupted India and caused extensive disorder. Internal differences within the Congress gave way immediately to a united front against the British. The 1927 session of the Congress passed two resolutions which reflected the nationalist mood. The first called for total boycott of the commission. Spurned by government, Indians should not assist what seemed to be a device for perpetuating the *raj*. Specifics included mass demonstrations, propaganda, and attempts to solidify cooperation with other parties so as to make the boycott effective. To clarify any misunderstanding about India's aspirations, the session con-

128. *India in 1927–8*, p. 55.
129. Irwin statement in *India in 1927–8*, pp. 387–92.
130. Indian response summarized in Sitaramayya, *The Indian National Congress*, I, 534–37. Also, *India in 1927–8*, pp. 55–59.

cluded that Indians wanted "complete National Independence."[131]

The Congress boycotted and hampered the commission during 1928, but at a price. Police used force to disperse demonstrations, and arrests mounted. In August, Muslims participated in an All-Parties Conference, which prepared a draft constitution for India premised on independence. The electric political atmosphere spread as the Congress adopted the conference report and stated that if, by December 31, 1929, Parliament had not accepted the constitution, the British would be the target of a new non-cooperation campaign.[132]

While Congress carried out its program, other disillusioned patriots turned to violence as the means for hurrying withdrawal of the British. Explosions and robberies marked the quickening of revolutionary activity. Besides creating turmoil, the organizations prominent in the terrorist wave, such as the Hindustan Socialist Republican Army, launched a substantial drive to distribute extremist literature.[133] Clandestine presses churned out pamphlets, which then were distributed in crowds and local fairs. Frustrated at not reaching a large audience, Punjab revolutionaries headed by Bhagat Singh threw bombs in the Central Legislative Assembly on April 8, 1929, and surrendered without a fight, shouting "Long Live Revolution!" The affair had been carefully staged for publicity purposes. Before entering the Assembly Hall, Bhagat Singh and his colleagues had prepared pictures and propaganda for circulation after the arrest.[134] As anticipated, the bombing and the ensuing conspiracy trial created a furor. Trial antics, including a hunger strike, aroused public interest and contributed to a hardening of sentiment in the press toward the British. Bhagat Singh became a popular hero.[135]

The spirit of disaffection finally influenced the central legisla-

131. Resolutions in Sitaramayya, *The Indian National Congress*, I, 537–41.

132. Sitaramayya, *The Indian National Congress*, I, 558–63.

133. A survey of the activities of the HSRA can be found in the following: J&P 1928, 5164 (judgment and background on the Lahore Conspiracy Case); Gurdev Singh Deol, *Shaheed Bhagat Singh*, pp. 20–25, 41–42; Bipin Chandra, "The Ideological Development of the Revolutionary Terrorists in Northern India in the 1920's," in B.R. Nanda, ed., *Socialism in India*, pp. 163–89. Other organizations and propaganda treated in J&P 1929, 4580.

134. Deol, *Bhagat Singh*, pp. 41–42; Ghosh, *Roll of Honour*, pp. 385–95.

135. Discussed in J&P 1929, 578. Examples of the laudatory literature include V. Nataraja Pillai, *Bhagat Singh Kiranamrutnam*, discussed in GIPOL 1932, 13/IV/A. Typical is this quotation: "Bhagat Singh is the lion that appeared on earth for rendering service to Mother Bharat; the lion that avenged the wrong done to the lion of the Punjab; the lion that disregarded the wicked whites; the lion that said that victory should be achieved by means of war."

ture. Opposition to officialdom grew, and the government suffered setbacks on small and major issues. The Assembly registered disgust with the Simon Commission by refusing to appoint a committee to cooperate in its evaluation of reform. Moreover, legislators rejected a "public safety" bill, which empowered the government to expel non-Indian citizens from the subcontinent without judicial review. The Governor General was finally forced to issue an ordinance rather than continue the attempts to woo Assembly support.[136]

Unable to announce new promises of reform and yet wary of precipitate action that might alienate any remaining Indian support, Governor General Irwin and his colleagues tried to control their tempers and played a waiting game.[137] Despite their alarm at recent developments, they hoped that the political storm would subside without an escalation of British reprisals. This attitude emerged clearly from secretariat debate of renewed press restrictions in June 1928. The government judged that widespread repression was politically unwise and banked instead on fresh reforms as a move against unrest:

> There are really only two ways in which the present very unsatisfactory, and even dangerous, situation can be remedied. One is to attempt to remove the cause, in other words to give a measure of self-government which may be expected to lessen, if it does not remove, this exceedingly bitter spirit and occupy with more useful and practical problems the minds of those who at present devote their whole energies to ceaseless hostility to the British. The other method is to adopt thorough-going measures of control. In popular language, the alternative policies are described as conciliation and repression. I have little belief in attempting at the same time to practice both policies, for the result generally is that the full advance of neither is secured . . . the present time is extremely inopportune for considering a measure of press control, and . . . we must wait and see whether the new measures that are taken as a result of the Statutory Commission's enquiry bring about a natural diminution in this dangerous press propaganda.[138]

Discussion of the press less than a year later evoked the same response. In commenting on a query about the tone of Indian writings, only two governments, the Punjab and Bengal, called for new legislation. Bengal warned of terrorist threats, while the Punjab voiced alarm over deterioration of communal relations.

136. Background in J&P 1928, 3788.

137. An excellent survey of Irwin's orientation is in S. Gopal, *The Viceroyalty of Lord Irwin*, pp. 61–63. Irwin characterized his own goal as being "in India to keep our temper" (quoted in Templewood, *Troubled Years*, p. 44).

138. Haig note (June 20, 1928), GIPOL 1928, 161.

While agreeing to the presence of danger, the Indian government reiterated its opposition to the attractive path of extended controls. Haig argued that the British should keep a low profile until the effect of imminent constitutional decisions became known, and Irwin heartily agreed. Local governments were instructed to increase propaganda and to be judicious in handling political dissent.[139]

As the deadline set by the Congress approached, Irwin attempted to regain initiative with the announcement (October 31, 1929) of a round table conference. The meeting, to be held just after publication of the Simon Commission's findings, would permit full expression of Indian opinion before Parliament decided on India's political future. Coupled with a reaffirmation that the British goal for India was Dominion status, the announcement had the effect of temporarily reviving Indian trust in the government.[140] Several M.P.s became so excited by these events that they proposed a parliamentary resolution to request general amnesty for Indian politicians. The India Office managed to water down the proposal so that Parliament finally thanked Indians for "the evidence [of] cooperation" and asked Irwin's government "to encourage good will by its sympathetic conduct of its administrative and executive functions."[141] The spirit of cooperation, however, proved illusory. When Gandhi met Irwin in December, the Governor General could not commit Parliament to specific measures or a timetable. Gandhi went straight from the conference to the Lahore Congress session, which passed a strong resolution rejecting further negotiations:

> Nothing is to be gained in the existing circumstances by the Congress being represented at the Proposed Round Table Conference. This Congress, therefore, in pursuance of the resolution passed at its session at Calcutta last year, declares that the word "Swaraj" in Article I of the Congress Constitution shall mean Complete Independence, and further declares the entire scheme of the Nehru Committee's Report to have lapsed, and hopes that all Congressmen will henceforth devote their exclusive attention to the attainment of Complete Independence for India. . . . This Congress appeals to the Nation zealously to prosecute the constructive programme of the Congress, and authorises the All-India Congress Committee, whenever it deems fit, to launch upon a programme of Civil Disobedience including non-payment of taxes, whether in selected

139. Notes by Haig (January 28, 1929) and Irwin (January 30, 1929), and local government commentaries, GIPOL 1929, 178.

140. Gopal, *Irwin*, pp. 50–52; Sitaramayya, *The Indian National Congress*, I, 591–600. Irwin had difficulty in developing enough political support in London to be able to make the announcement.

141. Information on debate and background in J&P 1929, 4580.

> areas or otherwise, and under such safeguards as it may consider necessary.[142]

Sympathy and promises had produced nothing tangible, and therefore the Congress resolved to force concessions from the *raj*.

The specter of civil disobedience necessitated a reassessment of British political strategy. Throughout the 1920s, the Indian government had relied on a shifting mix of coercion and conciliation that was calculated to contain disorder but, at the same time, to pave the way for future stability through orderly reform. During the period, bureaucrats had functioned without extensive press restrictions. Coercive powers certainly remained after 1922, but their application depended on British evaluation of political constraints. The government met some challenges such as communism and incitement to violence with banning and prosecution, others, with persuasion and propaganda. Continuous reevaluation of options clearly affected the official response to communal literature. Massive restrictions were not attempted because they might have created more trouble than they solved. The difficulty of ferrying controversial legislation through the obstinate Assembly prevented a return to the 1910 Press Act, a decision reinforced by fear of providing an issue that could be manipulated to mobilize substantial anti-British sentiment. Except for the disturbances over the Simon Commission and the renewed militance of Congress demands, the government might have been able to pursue that course indefinitely. But the realities of Indian politics in 1929 could not be denied. Communalism, terrorist attacks, and the challenges by the Congress seemed to be returning India to the chaos that surrounded the first non-cooperation campaign. In such an emergency, the bureaucracy had no doubts how British authority and public order would be maintained. The question rapidly became, not whether to use force, but where, when, and what kind of repression might be necessary, and for how long.

142. Quoted in Sitaramayya, *The Indian National Congress*, I, 605–6.

Chapter 4

EIGHTEEN YEARS OF CONFRONTATION, 1930–1947

In 1930 the Indian government and the Congress engaged in a struggle that lasted until independence. Although the nationalist challenge fluctuated between militant and dormant phases, the ultimate goal of the Congress remained steadfast. India had to be freed quickly. The British preferred a gradual constitutional transition and, indeed, devoted much attention to making the reforms of 1919 and later those of 1935 viable alternatives to abrupt withdrawal. Because Congress campaigns and other pressures within Indian society threatened public order, however, the bureaucracy developed and used widened powers of repression, most notably in the early 1930s and again in 1942–1944. Coercion and conciliation continued as intertwined elements of British strategy in the subcontinent.

Official handling of the press and Indian publicists varied with the government's fluctuating perception of danger. The 1930–1932 non-cooperation movement evoked controls exceeding any that had been experienced earlier. Congress publications became a prime target for the first time. A crackdown on news about Congress activities, the British reasoned, would disrupt the organization's communication network and isolate nationalist efforts. Although banning, prosecution, and renewed security demands subsided subsequently, the bureaucracy kept and occasionally strengthened the press law. During the 1930s, containment of two persistent threats—religious and Communist literature—received priority, and in 1942, the Quit India struggle brought the Congress back into the British sights.

Except for these periodic outbursts, however, the British moved toward relinquishment of direct controls and relied instead on less formal techniques for affecting the press, such as propaganda and working through Indian news agencies. Forced by circumstances to be increasingly sensitive to political currents, the British had no real choice. Indianization of the political system meant a decrease in bureaucratic prerogatives, particularly in matters relating to the provinces. The lid on Indian publications had come off in 1922, and the British had neither the power nor the will to replace it on a permanent basis.

Tiger by the Tail

Indian politics exploded in early 1930 as the Congress dramatically implemented its Lahore resolve to confront the British. Congressmen throughout the subcontinent celebrated "Total Independence Day" on January 26. The massive demonstrations publicized nationalist goals and attempted to broaden public support. At meetings held in major cities, fiery orators spoke on the evils of foreign domination and then read a declaration of independence. The sole means of removing those who ruined India "economically, politically, culturally, and spiritually," according to the declaration, was withdrawal of "voluntary help" and "non-payment of taxes."[1] Gandhi followed the demonstrations by presenting Governor General Lord Irwin with a list of demands, and when, as expected, Irwin refused to accept them, he launched his program of civil disobedience. As he walked across India with a band of devotees, Gandhi announced plans to break the law that forbade Indians making salt from the sea water. Such action was illegal because the government monopolized the production and taxation of this vital substance. As the "salt march" progressed, local Congressmen organized systematic boycott of English goods and formed action committees to disrupt daily administration.

The experience of the first non-cooperation campaign strongly influenced the British handling of the renewal of challenge by the Congress. The weathering of the previous storm had bolstered British self-confidence and had enhanced the rulers' sense of tactics and timing. Supposedly knowing what to expect and less prone to panic, the British decided from the outset to keep the initiative; they were determined not to be backed into a corner. Each step of the opposition was to be evaluated and then met with calculated response. Premature interference with the Congress might intensify popular sympathy for Gandhi, but hesitancy could permit a snowballing of national sentiment, which would engulf the small foreign bureaucracy.[2]

The Government of India had hammered out a political course

1. Background and the declaration in Pattabhai Sitaramayya, *The History of the Indian National Congress*, I, 614–17. Details on the initial phase of the non-cooperation campaigns in the same volume, 617–61; *India in 1929–30*, pp. 112–13; *India in 1930–31*, pp. 68–77; *The Civil Disobedience Movement, 1930–34* (New Delhi: Government of India, 1934); records in J&P 1929, 2926.

2. An excellent survey of Irwin's strategies is in S. Gopal, *The Viceroyalty of Lord Irwin*. Background documents on policy in J&P 1929, 2926.

well before Gandhi embarked on his salt *satyagraha* (political campaign) in March 1930. The first step was to ensure that the Secretary of State, Wedgewood Benn, gave Delhi full backing. Although wary of acts which might alienate moderate politicians, Benn agreed in advance to support decisions deemed necessary by men in the field.[3] Anticipating such an eventuality, the Home Department began preparing ordinances and legislation that enlarged the government's summary powers.[4] Irwin still clung to the hope that the measures would not be necessary—a grasping at straws that was reflected in his January 30 circular to local governments.

The circular outlined policy toward accelerating Congress agitation. Foremost, public order and bureaucratic authority must be maintained. If the *raj* projected a firm image and successfully countered disorder, the masses would remain loyal. If not, anarchy might develop:

> The Secretary of State has suggested that in dealing with this extremist movement, an endeavor should be made as far as possible to carry moderate opinion with Government in enforcing the law. That is an object the importance of which the Government of India fully realise and commend to the attention of the Local Governments. But they cannot conceal from themselves the fact that it is unlikely that firm action against the extremists will receive open support from the more moderate elements, and while giving due weight to the consideration which the Secretary of State has emphasized, they wish to make it plain that the first duty of Local Governments is to ensure the due maintenance of law and order in the face of this dangerous menace to the foundation of the State.[5]

To achieve this goal, the Indian government emphasized the use of measures already available to subordinates. Banning and selective prosecution should suffice for the moment, especially if local authorities intensified propaganda and worked through loyalist organizations within Indian public life.[6] Irwin gave his men virtually full rein in employing techniques because they alone "could adjust Government action to local conditions." Only prosecutions that affected all of India need be referred to Delhi. In essence, the Government of India advocated localized responses that would hamper the Congress but not escalate conflict. This wait-and-see

3. Telegraphic exchanges between Irwin and Benn, January 1930, I.P. Also, Circular 113, January 30, 1930, J&P 1929, 2926.
4. Background in GIPOL 1929, 240.
5. Circular 113 (January 30, 1930), J&P 1929, 2926.
6. For example, the Indian government suggested use or creation of "counter-Congress organizations," such as Aman Sabhas in the U.P. Earlier reliance on the Sabhas examined in Reeves, "Politics of Order."

attitude already had accounted for one major decision, agreement that the declaration of independence not be banned.[7]

The attempt to avoid mass retaliation against the Congress prevailed for three harrowing months. The British generally ignored breaking of the salt law and arrested few Congressmen. At a point when the strategy seemed to be disorienting the nationalists, however, two events shook British confidence and provoked a more aggressive stance. On the evening of April 8, a gang of well-trained terrorists raided the police armory at Chittagong, killing eight defenders and escaping with numerous weapons. The raid symbolized the dramatic upswing in terrorist activity. Nineteen acts of violence occurred in 1929, rising sharply to seventy-four in 1930.[8] Simultaneously, the North-West Frontier Province burst into flames. On April 23, the arrest of a prominent Pathan political leader, Abdul Gaffar Khan, precipitated violence. An incident of police firing from armored vehicles was followed by a minor mutiny among Indian troops and sporadic uprisings among Pathan tribals.[9]

The mounting violence indicated to the British that watchful moderation had run its course. Support for the Congress had spread further and more quickly than anyone imagined. Boycott and street demonstrations became common, along with a noticeable rise in anti-British sentiment both in cities and in the countryside. Telegrams from the Bombay, Bengal, United Provinces, and Punjab governments warned that their authority was being undermined. To make matters worse, Indian writers seemed determined to further poison the political atmosphere.[10]

Two developments relating to printed matter especially troubled the rulers. First, potentially dangerous writings circulated freely in many parts of India. Dozens of publishing houses specialized in anti-British or pro-Congress literature. In Lucknow, for example, the Hindu Pustak Mandar series included *Mahatma Gandhi's Swadeshi Song*, *The Conditions of Peasants and Workers*, *Poems of Non-Cooperation*, and *British Atrocities*.[11] The

7. Telegrams of January 24–25, 1930, GG to SS, J&P 1929, 2926. On British maneuvers, Gopal, *Irwin*, pp. 54–66. The British also developed fresh propaganda techniques for use during the crisis.

8. Background on terrorist resurgence in GIPOL 1931, 4/36. Also, Gospal, *Irwin*, pp. 66–67; K. C. Ghosh, *The Roll of Honour*, pp. 463–69.

9. Extensive correspondence in GIPOL 1930, 255 I–III. For unofficial interpretations, see Mohammad Yunus, *Frontier Speaks* (banned); Badshah Khan, *My Life and Struggle*; G.L. Zutshi, *Frontier Gandhi.*

10. Secretariat noting and provincial correspondence, GIPOL 1930, 503 I–III.

11. Based on lists of publications appended to tracts banned by the British during 1939. A rapid survey indicates that as many as half came from less than two dozen publishing sources.

Lajpat Rai Martyrdom Series and the Bharat Book Agency at Delhi produced similar material. A more clandestine group of presses printed open appeals for revolution; their tone is well illustrated by this selection from *The War of Freedom of 1857*: "Broad was the fiery red cross with which India started her crusade to Freedom. Hold fast to that red cross, oh ye oppressed peoples, speed on Angel of Revolution, speed on. The country is ready for a holy war to make every child of India free."[12] Caught up in political excitement, publicists who normally would have been cautious now espoused the Congress and sometimes even violence.

The content of writings alarmed the British more than the increased volume of polemics. Authors clothed attacks in historical garb so as to evade existing legal constraints. "Pseudo historians," such as the author of *British Rule in India*, fashioned lengthy tirades into chronological narratives.[13] Other writers were less subtle. Recent events fostered hero cults. Numerous pamphlets eulogized Gandhi and Bhagat Singh, as did colorful posters that were designed to affect the nonliterate population. One such picture showed Bhagat Singh handing his head to "Mother India," and another depicted Gandhi standing at the foot of a "non-cooperation tree" that was adorned with gods and pictorial references to controversial incidents.[14] Political commentators also attributed all communal violence to British divide-and-rule tactics or, as in the following poem by Lal Chand Falak, beat out an inflammatory staccato of indictments against the *raj*:

He who follows religion is a rebel and a mischiefmaker
He who serves the country is a traitor
He who can dare speak the truth
The troubles under sections 124A and 153 are there
He who sympathises with a governed man in his oppressed state is disloyal
He who cuts the throat of his brother receives a title
In British civilization, truths and lies are the same
In British statesmanship, promise and refusal are the same
There is a ban on the body, ban on seeing, ban on the pen and ban on the tongue
Despite these restrictions, they expect cooperation from us.[15]

12. Discussed in GIPOL 1933, 48/4. Much of the literature judged dangerous can be found in a J&P collection file, 1929, 4580.

13. Background in GIPOL 1929, 27/II.

14. *Bhagat's Curious Present* (available in IOL banned Hindi works series, F. 69); *Non-cooperation Tree* (discussed in GIPOL 1930, 28).

15. *Dard-i-Watan* (Lahore: n.d.), pp. 39–40.

Varieties of literature not specifically concerned with the British also posed significant threats to order. Socialist and Communist writings, both from inside and outside India, increased in ferocity. Leftist authors aimed a barrage of tracts at workers and peasants, illustrated by this excerpt:

> The fat bellies which can be seen are swollen with flesh cut from our stomachs
>
> The faces which are red, are red with the blood of the workers which has been shed
>
> Our children cry with hunger, but the capitalist lives in luxury
>
> There is no rag for our loins, but the capitalist wears silk
>
> No one listens to our cry, but the capitalists threaten us
>
> We will cut the nose of capitalism.[16]

Communal literature persisted as a source of disharmony. Alterations of the Press law had temporarily dampened religious attacks, but by 1930, the hostility of the writings had resumed and now probably exceeded the levels in the earlier publications. Tracts and newspapers mirrored growing communal antagonism fed by riots and the inability to make political compromises. One tract, *The Food of the Hindus*, urged boycott of Hindu trade because Muslim patronage would just help the "enemy." To eat from the hands of a Hindu was to risk infection and exposure to filth. In addition, Hindu fairs should be avoided because participants were polytheists and "damned to hell."[17]

In the face of a situation that appeared to be a plunge into anarchy, Irwin quickly consulted with London and provincial chiefs and then activated contingency plans.[18] The British anticipated that mass arrests and a harsh policy toward demonstrations would cripple the Congress. They arrested Gandhi on May 5, then members of the higher echelons of the Congress. On June 30, the government proclaimed the Congress Working Committee an unlawful association. Although Delhi reached the basic decision to rout Congress, as planned, local authorities implemented that policy. In Madras, for example, officers stopped meetings, seized Congress personnel and property, and tried to prevent

16. Selections from *Kirti*, a radical Punjab journal, in GIPOL 1930, 503 I. Also, discussion of extremist writings in J&P 1929, 4580; GIPOL 1931, 4/36.

17. *Ta'am-i-Hunud* (Bareilly: n.d.). Also, see Azhar Usam, *Fughan-i-Muslim* (Delhi: 1933). Discussion in R&R 1930, 720; GIPOL 1931, 4/36.

18. On tightening of controls, documents in the following: J&P 1929, 2926; GIPOL 1930, 503 I–III; *Civil Disobedience*, pp. 1–12; Gopal, *Irwin*, pp. 70–87; *India in 1930–31*, pp. 73–75.

public bodies such as municipal councils from aiding nationalist activities.[19] Over 23,000 Congressmen were in prison by the end of 1930.[20]

Irwin simultaneously promulgated emergency ordinances calculated to strengthen British power drastically. Seven ordinances came into effect between April 19 and July 7. They extended executive prerogative and in effect suspended normal criminal procedure in cases relating to terrorism or disruption of vital services (loosely defined as administration, police, the military, and communications).[21] Two ordinances directly affected the press. Ordinance II (April 27) reestablished a system of security demands and enhanced officials' ability to seize publications. The new restrictions were to cover an assortment of printed matter, not just "blatant sedition." Securities could be seized and books banned if writers incited "hatred," attempted to influence troops, put persons "in fear," caused annoyance, or tampered with the law and payment of revenue. Statements introducing the ordinance claimed that its primary use would be limited to returning India to peace, and called on "sober citizens" to unite with government to achieve that goal.[22] In fact, the Government of India intended to muzzle all segments of the press defying its dictates. Noting that the success of the Congress "depends largely on publicity, and that it is mainly through the Press that publicity is secured," Delhi privately instructed officers to quash any publication that consistently lauded civil disobedience.[23]

A related ordinance—for control of unauthorized news sheets and newspapers—dealt with material that was slipping through loopholes in the law. By halting the output of daily bulletins mimeographed by Congress units, the British hoped to put the nationalist communication network into disarray.[24]

The embattled bureaucracy immediately activated the ordinances. By the end of June, the British had issued formal warnings to 150 publishers and banned approximately 400 books and tracts, 40 posters, and 50 numbers of newspapers.[25] During the

19. M. Venkatarangaiya, ed., *The Freedom Struggle in Andhra Pradesh*, III, 471–81. Summary of British action in *Civil Disobedience*.

20. Documents, GIPOL 1931, 5/45.

21. On ordinances, documents in GIPOL 1930, 503 I–III; J&P 1929, 2926.

22. Copies of ordinance and correspondence on implementation in J&P 1930, 1962; GIPOL 503 I.

23. Telegram to local governments, 1235S (April 25, 1930), GIPOL 1930, 503 I.

24. Documents on the ordinance, GIPOL 1930, 503 III.

25. Based on quarterly reports on proscriptions, 1930, GIPOL. Surveys of banning notifications in provincial gazettes suggest that the official cumulative lists were incomplete. Also, see listing and discussion in GIPOL 1930, 28.

same two-month period, at least 125 newspapers and 153 presses came under security provisions:

Actions under the 1930 Press Ordinances,
April 27th–June 30th, 1930[26]

Newspapers

	Securities	Ceased	Paid	Not started	No information
Madras	18	13	4		1
Bombay	45	13	18	10	4
Bengal	n.a.				
U.P.	13	6			7
Punjab	25	20	5		
Burma	5	5			
Bihar	1	1			
C.P.	2	2			
Assam	4	3		1	
N.W.F.P.	3	3			
Delhi	9	3		2	4
Totals	125	69	27	13	16

Printing Presses

	Securities	Ceased	Paid	Not started	No information
Madras	28	15	5	1	8
Bombay	22	10	6	1	5
Bengal	16	8	7		1
U.P.	19	5	1		13
Punjab	21	16	2		3
Burma	4	4			
C.P.	1	1			
Assam	5		5		
N.W.F.P.	1	1			
Delhi	25	10	5		
Bihar	12	6	1		5
Totals	154	76	32	2	35

The decentralization of supervision over seizures and securities meant that sanctions mirrored the concerns of local administra-

26. Statistics abstracted from notes in GIPOL 1930, 503–I. A similar set of statistics, with modification, is in J&P 1930, 1962.

tions. Although the United Provinces faced sustained attempts to spread Congress messages among the rural population, for example, that government relied on warnings (almost half of the all-India total) and extensive bans (180 items between May and December of 1930) rather than heavy securities.[27] At the other pole, Bombay and Punjab preferred preventive measures such as securities to informal warnings. Criteria for proscription also varied by provinces. Harassed by terrorists (75 attacks in 1930 and 1931), Bengal bans tended to fall heaviest on violent and Congress literature, while Punjab officials most often seized Communist and communal writings. The United Provinces evidently banned all but the most innocuous documents relating to Congress and Gandhi.[28] The central government played a relatively minor role in the decisionmaking behind these press actions. It theoretically superintended the sanctions, but in fact, the Home Department frequently lacked information on the burgeoning restrictions.[29]

The major threat for proscription—nationalist writings—fell into several categories. First, the British usually banned anything by Gandhi or that mentioned him in title or content.[30] Probably overreacting to the threat of danger, the bureaucracy also seized a mass of patriotic poetry associated with the non-cooperation campaign. At least 150 collections of nationalist songs and poems were scooped into the *raj*'s net, especially those with titles referring to independence, freedom, and satyagraha. Approximately half the literature seized in the United Provinces, for instance, bore titles that included one or more of those words.[31] The often vague references to patriotism and sacrifice in the writings did not differ substantially from those which circulated prior to 1930; acting under pressure, however, the bureaucracy judged even apparently innocuous works on politics to be intolerable.

In addition to Gandhiana and patriotic effusions, the government confiscated formal Congress publications like news sheets and handbills. When the organization developed fresh methods of propaganda, such as magic-lantern slides showing contro-

27. Warnings examined in GIPOL 1930, 503 I. Statistics on UP bans drawn from quarterly list in GIPOL 1930, 28 K.W.

28. Reports and tables in GIPOL 1930, 503 I, and sources mentioned in note 25. On terrorist attacks, GIPOL 1931, 4/36.

29. See, for example, the attempts to put together a comprehensive list in response to a legislative question, June 1930 (discussed in GIPOL 1930, 503 I). The India Office staff had even less information.

30. Approximately 75 titles banned in 1930 had Gandhi's name in the title. On material seized earlier, see Bharat Mishra, *Civil Liberty and the Indian National Congress*, pp. 55–58; Dharam Paul Sarin, *Influence of Political Movements on Hindi Literature*.

31. Quarterly lists in GIPOL 1930, 28 K.W.

versial scenes or "Boycott British Goods" labels surreptitiously affixed to mail articles, they too were banned.[32] Finally, the rulers attempted to prevent the circulation of the reports on the Congress inquiry into riots in Cawnpur and Peshawar. In both instances, the Indian committees that studied the disturbances sharply criticized the British.[33]

New administrative difficulties accompanied the wholesale interference with Indian political writings. The perennial problem of coordinating local actions emerged again, sometimes, as in the case of the Peshawar disturbances inquiry, with devastating results. The central government had monitored the activities of the Congress Peshawar committee (headed by Bhai Jhaverbhai Patel) for months, but at the last moment arrangements with Punjab and United Provinces officials for confiscation of their report collapsed. Copies reached the press, and a boxload circulated in England.[34] Although efforts to seize the findings on the Cawnpur inquiry were successful, coordination and strategy in preparation for the ban forced the undertaking of voluminous correspondence with the United Provinces government.[35]

Communication with agents and Indian princes also became more troublesome. Mounting criticism of the princes' support for the British and conditions within the states had developed alongside the surge of Congress activism. Rulers wielded dictatorial power to crush dissent in their domains, but they depended on British help to stem external challenges.[36] Occasionally the Imperial Political Department did intervene to prevent circulation of journals, such as Gandhi's *Young India*, within the states, but generally the government preferred to avoid bans and court cases if possible. The Delhi *Riyasta*'s attack on the Nawab of Bhopal, for example, brought a warning instead of prosecution.[37] Likewise, Punjab and Delhi authorities declined to ban a controversial study by the Indian States People's Conference, *Indictment of Patiala*, despite claims of political agents that if such attacks

32. On the magic lanterns, GIPOL 1932, 117. One slogan read, "Ruling and sucking blood are the functions of the same government." Another showed a child being flogged by an East India Company employee. On the labels, J&P 1931, 3433.

33. Cawnpur riot report discussed in J&P 1931, 1522; GIPOL 1933, 43; Peshawar, J&P 1930, 2464.

34. GI telegram, May 26, 1930, and notes in J&P 1930, 2464. Similar incidents reviewed in GIPOL 1930, 168.

35. Notes by H. Williamson (April 21, 1933) and H. G. Haigh (April 22, 1933), GIPOL 1933, 54.

36. See, for example, the account of Mulk Raj Saraf, *Fifty Years as a Journalist*, p. 59. Background on controls in the states and British–prince relations in Barbara Neil Ramusack, "Indian Princes as Imperial Politicians, 1914–1939," PhD. diss., University of Michigan, 1969.

37. Discussed in CRP, R/1/29/601.

undermined the princes, their territories would become centers of sedition. Prosecution supposedly would publicize Patiala's conduct, according to the Home Department, and for the time being, it was hoped that warnings and informal pressure could contain the most virulent of the antiprince material.[38]

The situation in London brought other complications. The expectations and policies of the India Office constantly had to be taken into account. Conflicting pressures made Secretary of State Benn ambivalent toward press measures. A majority of M.P.s feared that the Indian government might be too lax toward the Congress and terrorism, but a small, vocal group kept raising the issue of repression in the Commons question period. On May 19, 1930, for example, one member pointedly asked Benn "if he remembers some of the very eloquent speeches which we have heard from him with regard to freedom of the press?"[39] The Secretary's inclination to defend men on the firing line, frequently without possessing full information, was balanced in turn by his determination to make the Round Table Conference a success. If coercion became prevalent, chances for negotiations and orderly constitutional advance might be lost.[40]

Benn therefore remained in public a defender of Indian policy but in private he urged caution. Moreover, the India Office used its very limited powers to assist in preventing "dangerous" books from reaching India, illustrated by its handling of A.C. Osborn's *Must Britain Lose India*? A retired army surgeon who once served in India, Osborn joined the English Socialist party and became extremely critical of imperialist attitudes. His study high-lighted the errors of British rule and also gave a sympathetic picture of India that was meant to counter that of *Mother India*. Upon reviewing an advance copy of the volume, the Under Secretary of State, Arthur Hirtzel, labeled Osborn as "one of those disgusting birds who like to foul their own nests" and urged steps to keep copies from India.[41] The India Council considered revoking Osborn's pension but finally avoided that step because of possible reaction from the army and the English public. The success of informal pressure on the publisher, Alfred Knopf of New York, or of a protest to the United States through the Foreign Office, seemed equally remote. The only course open, therefore, was a

38. Documents in CRP, R/1/29/545.
39. Debate summary and related documents, J&P 1930, 1962.
40. Earl of Birkenhead, *Halifax*, pp. 268–312; Viscount Templewood, *Nine Troubled Years*, pp. 79–80.
41. Hirtzel note (April 10, 1930), J&P 1930, 1602. The following description based on documents in the file. Also, comments in GIPOL 1930, 29/II.

warning to Delhi, accompanied by a strong suggestion of interception under Sea Customs provisions. Another example of constraints on help from London occurred in August 1930, when the report on the Peshawar inquiry reached England. The Secretary of State rejected a request from India that its circulation be stopped. Such a seizure would draw too much criticism. All the India Office could do was prepare a contradicting note for circulation as propaganda to leading newspapers and U.S. press correspondents.[42]

Such episodes were minor compared with an issue that threatened to cause a public break between London and Delhi—censorship of Indian news reports. The second non-cooperation campaign drew much international attention. To the discomfort of Indian authorities, the Congress acquired the knack of influencing foreign correspondents (especially Americans), to the extent that their telegraphed stories tended to be pronationalist. The Indian government attempted to stem the unfavorable reports in late April of 1930 by stopping telegrams and censoring dispatches. These actions boomeranged within a month. The United Press and *The Herald Tribune* roared at the unaccustomed suppression of news, and the latter published a mutilated story as evidence of tampering. Parliament also debated the censorship. As often happened, the India Office lacked background on what Indian officials were doing, and after telegraphic exchanges, insisted that surveillance be abandoned. Although Irwin agreed hesitantly, local governments apparently continued the practice through the rest of 1930.[43]

Indian politics had reached a sensitive juncture in the winter of 1930. Agitation by the Congress, while still active, had lost its initial momentum, and press restrictions seemed to have moderated the most virulent of anti-British writings.[44] Local governments nevertheless argued that continuation of the trend required renewal of the soon-to-expire emergency ordinances or their replacement by permanent legislation. The center agreed that the possibility of fresh unrest did seem to warrant firm action. After promulgating another round of ordinances in October, Irwin

42. Telegram, SS to GI (August 29, 1930), and background notes, J&P 1930, 2464. The India Office also questioned bans on some items. See discussion of F. D. Walker, *India and Her People* (W. Johnston note, April 30, 1931), R&R 1938, 2129.

43. Telegram, SS to GI, May 31, 1930, and reply, June 8, 1930. Also, subsequent minutes. J&P 1930, 2088.

44. For example, comments in *United Provinces Administration Report, 1931–2*, p. 82; PG letter 2922 (April 27, 1931), GIPOL 1931, 13/XI. Surveys on politics are in the following: *India in 1931–2*; Sitaramayya, *The Indian National Congress*, I, 671–720; John Cumming, ed., *Political India, 1832–1932*, pp. 301–18.

presented the Legislative Assembly with an expanded version of the notorious 1910 Press Act.[45]

At the same time, Irwin appreciated that only a political settlement, not force, would foster long-term peace. The awaited report of the Simon Commission afforded little hope of reconciliation with educated Indians. A compromise document, the report recommended virtually full autonomy for the provinces but unassailable British control at the center. The commission did not mention Dominion status, thus affirming suspicions that England was backing away from the announced goal of self-government.[46] Resolved to keep open the remaining avenue to a constitutional settlement, the Indian government declared that the report would not constrict discussions at the Round Table Conference.

Irwin went a step further. Non-cooperation had demonstrated the appeal of the Congress and legitimized the party's claim to represent a substantial spectrum of Indian political interests. Conducting meaningful high-level talks on India's future without Congress participation would be an exercise in futility. The Governor General therefore renewed efforts to negotiate with Gandhi. The Congress leader agreed to private talks. Months of intricate maneuvering between the two men culminated in the Delhi settlement of March 5, 1931.[47] Civil disobedience was suspended. Other Congress activities, most notably picketing and the boycott of British goods, would continue under the terms of the pact, but with the stated goal of developing Indian industry rather than as a political weapon. In return, Irwin promised to withdraw all ordinances except those on terrorism and to free civilians whose offenses had not included violence. Although the symbol of satyagraha, the Salt Act, was not altered, Irwin agreed to permit villagers near natural salt deposits to collect salt for domestic consumption. Besides a few tangible concessions, the Congress won recognition as an integral participant in any future negotiations. The British secured a temporary halt to disobedience and Gandhi's willingness, under the right circumstances, to attend the Second Round Table Conference.[48]

Although the uneasy truce persisted through 1931, fundamental problems plagued British–Congress cooperation. Gandhi and Irwin could not control their far-flung troops. Many Con-

45. Correspondence in J&P 1930, 1962; GIPOL 1931, 13/6, K.W.

46. Maurice Gwyer, ed., *Speeches and Documents on the Indian Constitution, 1921–47*, I, 211–19; Gopal, *Irwin*, pp. 90–91.

47. Excellent survey in Gopal, *Irwin*, pp. 91–107; also, documents in GIPOL 1931, 4/41.

48. Analysis and a copy of the pact in Gopal, *Irwin*, pp. 107–13, 140–44.

gressmen lacked Gandhi's trust in Irwin and sporadically pursued their own programs. Terrorists continued to attack. During 1931, for example, over a hundred incidents occurred in Bengal and Rajputana.[49] The Government of India also would not or—more accurately—could not guarantee the commitment of subordinates both to the spirit and the letter of the pact. The decentralized bureaucracy dealt with crises as in the past, with the result that reports of real or imagined oppression flowed into Congress headquarters.[50] Perhaps subsequent Gandhi–Irwin talks might have smoothed relations, but in mid-April the sympathetic Viceroy retired. His successor, the former Governor of Bombay and Madras, Lord Willingdon, tended toward a law-and-order approach in negotiations with the Congress. That Willingdon viewed Gandhi as "a little *bania* who is the most astute and opportunist politician I have ever met" certainly did little to facilitate the open communication that had characterized the Gandhi–Irwin exchanges.[51]

Neither Irwin nor Willingdon could have removed a primary block to continued Congress quiescence, however—the refusal of home authorities to take another stride toward Indian self-government. The August elections had brought to the House of Commons a conservative majority that was interested in stamping out terrorism and other overt challenges to the *raj*.[52] Given their attitude, reforms beyond the suggestions of the Simon Commission appeared most unlikely. The Government of India thus was trapped in the now familiar cycle of being unable to meet rising Indian aspirations with more than empty promises. Gandhi sensed the drift of affairs and almost absented himself from the September Round Table session. Willingdon convinced Gandhi to go to London, but the possibility of resolving differences there remained slim.[53]

Amidst breaches in the Delhi Pact and frustrating relations with Gandhi, Willingdon reassessed the strategy of his predecessor. Although propaganda had been disseminated widely, pro-

49. Discussion in GIPOL 1931, 4/36, 5/41.

50. For two interpretations of the problems, see Sitaramayya, *The Indian National Congress*, I, 786–851; *India in 1931–2*, pp. 3–25. Several local governments bitterly opposed negotiations and moderation in applying sanctions. See, for example, PG to GI, January 31, 1931, GIPOL 1931, 5/41.

51. Birkenhead, *Halifax*, p. 318. For Willingdon's political stance, see his correspondence with Samuel Hoare, October 1931–July 1932, H.C. Also, Templewood, *Troubled Years*, pp. 79–80; comments on order in *India in 1931–2*, pp. 32–35, 46–47.

52. Hoare's analysis in Hoare to Willingdon, December 17, 1931, H.C. Also, Templewood, *Troubled Years*, p. 79.

53. Sitaramayya, *The Indian National Congress*, I, 819–28.

British slide shows, posters, and pamphlets reportedly had little effect on the popular appeal of the Congress. Terrorism and communal tension had not abated, and in most instances, messages from local governments attributed the unrest to the press. Evidence suggested that emergency ordinances tended only to bottle up the hostility of nationalist and religious writers. Once controls lapsed after the Delhi settlement, pent-up feelings burst forth again.[54]

The resulting discussions between Willingdon and the new Secretary of State, Samuel Hoare, high-lighted the political considerations that affected Delhi and London. The India Council placed priority on ending communal unrest and creating a climate of opinion favorable to negotiations in the Round Table forum. The Government of India's main concerns included the control of terrorism and avoidance of an irreparable rupture with the Congress. Both governments appreciated that the attitude of the House of Commons might be decisive. Appeasement in India could alienate vital support for reforms, but conversely, continued unrest might reinforce the conservatives' claim that India was ill-prepared for constitutional change.[55]

Willingdon reached a major decision on strategy by September 1931. Preparing for the worst, he instructed the Home Department to draft fresh emergency ordinances, which would empower the I.C.S. to "knock out" any opponent.[56] The department also drew up a press bill that had more limited scope than the one before the Legislative Assembly. The Indian Emergency Powers Bill, XXIII of 1931, had three main provisions. First, it reestablished security demands for publications inciting violence. The Secretary of State had urged that the securities also be applied to class hatred and communal literature, but the Indian government felt that a measure which was clearly aimed at terrorism stood the best chance of enactment.[57] The provisions would lapse in three years—a point that emphasized the measure's special, crisis-related function. Finally, the bill authorized imprisonment for distributors of terrorist literature and unauthorized news sheets.

The Government of India moved cautiously to ensure the bill's passage. Prior to its introduction, Home Department officials pre-

54. Emerson note (August 30, 1931) and reports from local governments, GIPOL 1931, 4/36. For one discussion of propaganda, see documents in GIPOL 1932, 35/31.

55. Background in GIPOL 1931, 4/36; J&P 1930, 4977.

56. Note by R. Peel (August 28, 1931), GI telegram (September 5, 1931), J&P 1930, 4977.

57. Telegram, GG to SS (September 1, 1931), and copies of the bill, J&P 1930, 4977.

pared a list of terrorist writings and discussed them and the need for controls with Gandhi. If Gandhi publicly denounced the legislation, the Delhi settlement might crumble overnight. Gandhi proved receptive, however, and agreed that the worst varieties of radical material must be taken out of circulation.[58] Willingdon similarly developed support among other leaders, including prominent M.L.A.s. Legislative allies had examples of terrorist material in their hands before the introduction of the bill on September 7. The preparations paid off. Although it protested, the Congress did not denounce the restrictions as a serious breach of the Delhi Pact. The legislature, in general, agreed to the bill, probably influenced by official willingness to debate issues at length and to compromise.[59] During five days of discussion, the government bench successfully defended the bill as an emergency measure with a narrow scope. Speaker after speaker quoted from the writings in question and drowned out the cries of opponents, who argued that the restrictions were unnecessary. The vote in favor of the legislation, 55 to 24, surprised Willingdon and pleased him immensely.[60]

The Governor General soon found that he needed more than special legislation in order to survive politically. As feared, the Round Table Conference achieved little. Gandhi returned home disillusioned but apparently still committed to working out a solution with Willingdon.[61] The deterioration of the agreement in his absence, however, permitted no room for negotiation. Militants in the Congress had intensified their disruptive efforts in the United Provinces and Peshawar, and the British had responded with force. According to the Home Member, Crerar, "the whole of the Working Committee were unanimous in clamouring for war," and after futile telegraph exchanges with Willingdon, Gandhi succumbed to the radicalism ascendant in the Congress. The Congress resumed its program of civil disobedience on January 3, 1932.[62]

The British gave Gandhi no time to move. On January 4, Willingdon promulgated four ordinances—the Emergency Pow-

58. Emerson notes (August 30, September 4, 1931), GIPOL 1931, 4/36.

59. For example, the government accepted the Select Committee recommendation that the bill be limited to one year. L.A.D., 1931, V, 65–66, 300–340, 347–82; VI, 1176–84, 1273–1326, 1927–75, 1416–64, 1469–92.

60. Willingdon to Hoare, October 6, 1931, H.C. The government had planned to certify the bill if necessary.

61. Birkenhead, *Halifax*, p. 317.

62. Crerar to Irwin, January 5, 1932; I.P. Background on incidents in *India in 1931–2*, pp. 24–32; Sitaramayya, *The Indian National Congress*, I, 842–75; Cumming, *Political India*, pp. 301–18.

ers Ordinance that expanded the 1931 Press Act to deal with material on civil disobedience, the Unlawful Instigation Ordinance aimed primarily at no-tax efforts, the Unlawful Association Ordinance used to seize Congress funds and buildings, and the Prevention of Molestation and Boycotting Ordinance. The British threw Gandhi and thousands of his followers in jail, and in isolated cases, nationalist processions were dispersed by police gunfire.[63]

Willingdon did not stop with this summary blow to the Congress. Using the crisis as justification, he made extended executive powers part of the criminal code. On November 15, 1932, the Government of India introduced the Criminal Law Amendment Bill, which encompassed most of the special provisions of existing ordinances. The bill gave local governments almost total control over the press, the power to establish summary tribunals, and over-all authority to outlaw associations. The speech to introduce the measure broadcast the government's intent. If the legislature chose to enact a "pale shadow" of the restrictions, Willingdon would find another means of securing powers to deal with unrest. The Assembly debated the issue but, mindful of the warning, finally gave the government what it wanted.[64]

From 1932 to 1934, the British openly pursued a dual policy that consisted of "vigorous maintenance of law and order" coupled with "active progress towards the introduction of constitutional reforms."[65] In the eyes of government, both goals were achieved. The civil disobedience movement weakened until, by 1934, Gandhi suspended the campaign in favor of "individual satyagraha." Simultaneously, a compromise Government of India bill made its way through parliamentary debate and culminated in the passage of new constitutional guidelines in 1935.[66]

The application of press laws reflected both aspects of British policy. As the table on the following page indicates, the cumulative application of security demands was heavy. The British banned approximately 1,000 pieces of printed matter during the same period.[67]

It would be misleading, however, to assume that most of the

63. *India in 1931–2*, pp. 41–66.

64. Haig comment, L.A.D. 1932, VII, 2091. Documents and discussion relating to the Act in J&P 1932, 3094. Willingdon also anticipated having to certify the bill. W. to Hoare, June 30, 1932, H.C.

65. "Dual policy" quotation and summation from *India in 1932–33*, p. 1. Also, see "Victor Trench," *Lord Willingdon in India*, pp. 152–68.

66. An accessible survey of events is in Sitaramayya, *The Indian National Congress*, I, 856–1021. On the problems underlying passage of the Government of India Bill, Templewood, *Troubled Years*, pp. 68–103.

67. Based on data in J&P 1932, 616, with additional material taken from L.A.D. and quarterly reports in GIPOL, 1932–4.

Security Demands on Presses and Newspapers, October 1931–February 1935.[68]

	Securities	Deposited	Forfeited	Ceased	Securities Waived, n.i.
Madras	28	12	1	12	3
Bombay	140	48	4	67	21
Bengal	55	13	6	12	24
U.P.	43	5	1	25	12
Punjab	198	28	3	112	55
Burma	7	5		2	
Bihar-O	5	2		3	
C.P.	3	1			2
Assam	2			2	
N.W.F.P.	11	1		8	2
Coorg	1	1			
Delhi	20	8	2	11	
Ajmer	3			2	1
Merwara	11				11
Totals	527	124	17	256	131

press actions involved the Congress. Because the government believed that maintenance of order in January 1932 demanded the destruction of the nationalist infrastructure, the bulk of material seized or placed under security then related to Congress activities.[69] Not so in 1933 and 1934. British perception of danger altered with time. As the Congress agitation subsided, the bureaucracy turned its widened authority toward other sources of trouble.

Communal literature received high priority. The Congress militancy unexpectedly placed new strains on already shaky Hindu–Muslim relations. In several instances, demand for boycott sparked rioting reminiscent of that which accompanied the partition of Bengal in 1903–1905.[70] The communal press played up sectional tensions and helped spread antagonism throughout North India. The British reacted with traditional weapons. Brute force put down disturbances, and proscription became more prevalent. Approximately half the printed matter banned between

68. Ibid.

69. Based on lists in J&P 1932, 616, and collection files GIPOL. The Government of India did not have complete records on all banned material.

70. Background on the 1930–1931 riots in *India in 1930–31*, pp. 119–20. Also, survey of communal situation in *A History of the Hindu-Muslim Problem in India* (Allahabad: Cawnpore Riots Enquiry Committee, 1933; banned by the British).

1933 and 1935 dealt with religious controversy.[71] Preventive measures also intensified. For at least a decade, officials had urged resumption of security demands as a means of controlling the tone of communal writings. Although detailed background on securities is not available, scattered records in Home Political proceedings suggest that, once the bureaucracy regained preventive sanctions, they were used widely. In Punjab, for example, 98 of the 135 newspapers under security had been involved in religious issues.[72]

Non-cooperation also provided the opportunity to neutralize the threat of a source of ferment both inside and outside India—communism. The Government of India attacked on two fronts. First, it tried to break the Communist grip on labor unions and peasant associations through prosecutions and aid from Indian opponents of the C.P.I.[73] More relevant for this study, the British moved toward a blanket ban on leftist and Communist-related literature. Many such publications had been banned since 1927, but in 1932 fresh notifications under the Sea Customs and Emergency Powers acts extended confiscation to any work containing documents from the Comintern or an "affiliate." The latter category was aimed at the assortment of clubs and societies in England that sporadically issued propaganda on Indian economic and political affairs.[74] Customs officials paid new attention to suspected Socialist publications. Of the 175 items seized while entering India between 1932 and 1934, for example, at least 150 titles were Communist or by "known sympathizers."[75] The temporary lapse of sanctity of the mails during the non-cooperation fight aided the British in their anti-Communist drive. Inspection of first-class mail from Europe occurred regularly, a move the government justified by the argument that India

71. Based on lists of titles in GIPOL, 1931–1935.

72. *Report on the Punjab Press, 1933* (Lahore: Punjab Government, 1935); *Report on the Punjab Press, 1934* (Lahore: Punjab Government, 1935). Other provincial actions discussed in *History of the Freedom Movement in Madhya Pradesh* (Nagpur: Madhya Pradesh Government, 1950), pp. 388–407; Mrinal Kanti Bose, *The Press and Its Problems*, pp. 57–63. Bengal particularly curtailed publications, censoring reports on legislative debates and trial proceedings.

73. Policy exemplified in GI circular (April 29, 1935), J&P Collection file 117–B–1. Background in H. Williamson, *Communism in India* (Calcutta: Government of India, c. 1935).

74. File on banning of the CPI and CPI publications, GIPOL 1932, 29/6.

75. Based on statistics from scattered GIPOL files, and 1937, 41/10. CPI publications also were prominent among titles banned within India. In January–March 1934, for example, a list of proscribed works included 8 titles on communism, a life of Lenin, studies relating to peasant and workers movements, and copies of three leftist newspapers. GIPOL 1934, 37/6.

had enough domestic problems without the added danger of outside agitation.[76]

There has been a tendency among participants and historians to emphasize the dimensions of coercion and control in the British response to events after the end of the Delhi Pact. Often forgotten is that preparations for constitutional change played a role equal to that of the law-and-order imperative in deciding the range and phases of restrictions. Indianization of the bureaucracy and the legislatures made justification of suppressing nationalist sentiment increasingly difficult, no matter how repulsive those ideas might be to a veteran I.C.S. officer. If the British intended to hold India at any cost, broad reliance on force made sense; if Indians were to become partners in government, those same controls were outdated and illogical. Accordingly, the long-term trend from 1922 had been growing toleration of Indian dissent. The heightening of political activism in 1930 and 1932–1933 tended to cloud the trend, but even then, the nature of permitted writings suggested a mellowing of British attitudes. At the height of the 1932 crackdown, political literature circulated, which probably would have been seized previously. Only a small percentage of tracts in the Hindi Sahitya Mandir and Political Series published by Prabhu Narayan Misra, Gaya, for example, came under ban. Untouched were controversial works on Shivaji, the Congress, Tilak, Indian national spirit, a history of Indian-made cloth and boycott, and a children's reader designed to disseminate Gandhian ideals among the young.[77] The groundswell of nationalist writings would not be countered effectively either by propaganda or any measure short of total repression. The British had reached the limits of their power, and they knew it.[78]

This knowledge did not cause the Government of India to shy away from preserving order. When the British nervously approached the hurdles of reform in 1910 and 1919, their position had been buttressed by new reserve powers. A similar situation pertained in 1934. Impressed by the experience in 1922–1929 of having to meet unforeseen challenges without such weapons, the bureaucracy did not intend to surrender the extraordinary

76. Evaluation of anti-Communist tactics in Williamson, *Communism in India.*

77. Based on lists of publications abstracted from covers of publications and checked against lists of proscriptions; also, a cross-check between quarterly lists of publications from Punjab, Bengal and UP, 1932–1934, and proscription lists.

78. For example, the discussion of repression and debates over a stronger press law in Bengal, J&P 1930, 4977; Circular 13/4/3 (December 20, 1932), J&P 1932, 3094. A survey of press controls is found in GIPOL 1931, 4/36; on propaganda, see GIPOL 1932, 123.

sanctions acquired in the recent struggle with the Congress. Survival in an uncharted phase of constitutional transition seemed to dictate that executive prerogatives be kept, strengthened, and used if necessary.

Between Storms

Political developments in India from 1934 to 1939 resembled those of the 1920s in that, for a brief time, no single danger threatened disruption of conditions in the subcontinent. Riots and anti-British agitation occurred, but the *raj*'s primary foe, the Congress, avoided systematic civil disobedience. As earlier, the Indian government divided its attention between cultivating Indian supporters and jockeying back and forth with challengers. Both methods were frequently applied within legislative arenas.

The essential difference between conditions in the two decades arose from the changed constitution and the attitudes of political actors toward those changes. The principles underlying the 1935 Government of India Act had been evident before its signing by the King on August 2, 1935. While publicized as a "great stride" in transferring power to Indians, the act made clear that the foreign rulers anticipated controlling the subcontinent for an undetermined period.[79] The "stride" consisted of an end to dyarchy at the provincial level and the initiation of a new federal structure at the center. In the future, an electorate enlarged by four fold would choose representatives to local assemblies, who then would form governments responsible primarily to the legislatures. No subject was to be reserved solely for British discretion. Arrangements for a federation, to be inaugurated after a designated number of princely rulers executed instruments of accession, provided for a dyarchic executive branch similar to that which operated in the provinces under the 1919 Act. Aided by "counsellors," the Governor General would retain charge of defense, eccelesiastical affairs, external matters, and tribal problems. A Council of Ministers responsible to the Federal Legislature would assist him in the remaining areas. The new legislature was to be bicameral, with Indian states allotted 40 per cent of the seats in the upper house (Council of State) and 33⅓ per cent of the seats in the lower house (Federal Assembly). The remainder would be filled either through direct elections within territorial constituencies (Council) or by indirect elections in

79. Summary of Hoare speech on the Act, quoted in Maurice Gwyer and A. Appardori, eds., *Speeches and Documents*, I, 323. Additional information on the bill is in Gwyer, I, xxxix–xlv, 270–382; Bijoy Prasad Singh Roy, *Parliamentary Government in India*, pp. 186–281.

provincial legislatures (Assembly). Other provisions included the establishment of a Federal Court, abolition of the Secretary of State's Council in London (to be replaced by a group of "advisers"), and a time schedule, the main thrust of which was that while provincial autonomy came into force as soon as elections could be held, the provisions of the 1919 Act pertaining to the center would continue until formation of the federation.

Despite the new structures, safeguards permeated the revised constitution. The British-appointed governors of the provinces had special responsibilities (and reserve powers) in critical areas such as protection of minorities. The Indian Civil Service (by 1937, composed of 1,893 British and 1,319 Indian officers) became known as the "Secretary of State's Services," distinctly indicating to whom they owed final responsibility. The Governor General maintained substantial supervision over central operations and, in an emergency, over provincial subjects. His "master," Parliament, would continue to exert ultimate control over what happened in India.

How the new constitution functioned would rest on the attitudes and actions of Indian politicians, the princes, and the bureaucracy. Before the act came into operation, the Government of India tried to anticipate problems and to create an atmosphere conducive to integrating those three elements within the system.

To increase the possibility that the Congress would cooperate in elections, the Indian government deliberately avoided precipitating conflicts with Gandhi or the All-India Working Committee. The British removed the ban on most Congress organizations in June of 1934 and followed this action by the release of noncooperation prisoners and the return of seized Congress assets. Surveillance and harassment of Congress workers persisted in Bengal, but overt hostility to the organization tended to be muted. Badly needing to restore its scattered forces, the Congress kept clear of civil disturbance. During the 1935 Independence Day celebrations, for example, the Working Committee issued these instructions: "As Civil Disobedience has been suspended by the Congress, the proceedings of the day should not be in breach of the Ordinances, or other laws or orders promulgated by local authority."[80] The Congress focused rather on thorough reorganization of its structure in preparation for elections. In the 1935 contest—the last supposedly to be conducted under the 1919 Act—the Congress won handily in the central

80. Quoted in Pattabhai Sitaramayya, *The Indian National Congress*, I, 1005. He also discusses the relaxation of controls and the Bengal exception (pp. 958–1013). On the general issue of Independence Day celebrations, GIPOL 1937, 4/1.

and many provincial elections. Temporarily "marking time," Congress bitterly criticized the provisions of the new constitution but indicated that under the appropriate conditions, its members would contest future elections.[81]

The role of the princes in the new scheme was more problematic. The Chamber of Princes and their representatives at the Round Table conferences tentatively agreed that the federation plans might be workable. The Government of India realized, however, that efforts of organizations in British India to undercut the princes' power made them wary of permanent participation in a legislative arrangement that might work to their disadvantage. Established in 1927, the All-India States People's Conference had in particular attacked princely administration. The conference, along with the Congress, circulated propaganda about the states and defended the position that the non-British areas must be fully a part of any union:

> The Congress stands for the same political and economic freedom in the States as the rest of India, and considers the States as an integral part of India, which cannot be separated. "Purna Swaraj" or Complete Independence, which is the objective of the Congress, is for the whole of India inclusive of the States, for the integrity and unity of India must be maintained in subjection. The only kind of federation that can be acceptable to the Congress, is one in which the States participate as free units enjoying the measure of democratic freedom as the rest of India.[82]

The communal spiral also affected order within the states. In Kashmir, for example, militant Punjabi Muslims continued agitating against the Hindu administration, while in Hyderabad, the Arya Samaj fought heated battles with Muslims.[83] Except for several actions under the 1922 Indian States Protection Against Disaffection measure and banning of antiprince literature, the British had been able to give the states little assistance in preserving order.[84]

81. "Marking Time" is the appropriate Sitaramayya chapter heading for this period. On Congress politics between 1935 and 1937, Sitaramayya, *The Indian National Congress*, II, 1–50.

82. Quoted in Rajendra Lal Handa, *History of Freedom Struggle in Princely States*, p. 192. On the conference, also see Ramusack's unpublished study of the princely states, cited in note 36.

83. Background on the Ahrar agitation, Kashmir, in J&P 1934, 3998; Prem Nath Bazaz, *The History of Struggle for Freedom in Kashmir*, pp. 151–67; Barbara Ramusack, "Exotic Imports or Homegrown Riots: The Kashmir Disturbances of the Early 1930's" (unpub. study presented at the Punjab Conference, Philadelphia, 1971). On Hyderabad, Handa, *Freedom Struggle*, pp. 239–48; Swami Ramanath Tirtha, *Memoirs of Hyderabad Freedom Struggle* (Bombay: Popular Prakashan, 1967).

84. Note on press actions, 1923–1932, in CRP R/1/29/914. The

The situation in Kashmir and several smaller states had deteriorated to the point in 1933 that the government decided new legislation was necessary. The discussions of forthcoming reforms colored consideration of such a move. According to the secretaries of the Home and Political departments, the value of the princes as British allies and, indeed, their willingness to join a federation, hinged on whether the government would effectively support their regimes. A comprehensive bill defending the princes would bolster their political image and help reduce anxiety over closer association with British India. The bill had to be passed quickly, the secretariat noted because, although its enactment might be difficult due to the mood of the present legislature, the anticipated federal legislature undoubtedly would be a more stubborn roadblock.[85]

After intense consultation with princes and local governments, the Government of India presented the Indian States (Protection) Bill to the Legislative Assembly on September 6, 1933. The first two sections, to become effective immediately, dealt with conspiracy and the press. Anyone who conspired to "overawe, by means of criminal force or the show of criminal force, the Administration of any State in India" could be punished with imprisonment up to seven years and a fine. Further, the bill added the bringing of "hatred or contempt or . . . disaffection" toward any state to the list of offenses under the Press Emergency Powers Act, thus making publications on the states liable to security demands and seizures.[86] The remaining sections, to be triggered by appropriate notifications and ordinances, empowered magistrates to prevent assemblies for the purpose of proceeding into non-British areas and prohibited acts that potentially could create administrative problems for the princes. Hoping to get the bill through the Assembly without certification, the British accepted compromise amendments, such as an explanatory note that "statements of fact made without malicious intention and without attempting to excite hatred, contempt or disaffection" should be permitted.[87] This tactic softened some criticism from M.L.A.s. Although opposition continued on the grounds that the bill curtailed legitimate criticism, the measure passed by a comfortable margin, 75 to 28.

Despite official efforts to facilitate the princes' embracing the

---

Princes Protection Act was judged a virtually "dead letter." Bose, *Press*, p. 57.

85. Discussion in CRP R/1/29/914. Of particular importance are notes by C. M. Trivedi (July 29, 1932) and M. G. Hallett (July 12, 1932).

86. L.A.D., 1934, IV, 320–62. Bill in *Unrepealed Acts*, IX, 201–3.

87. Haig comment, L.A.D., IV, 320, 362. The British also agreed to have security and forfeiture procedures reviewed by the center.

federal scheme, their distrust kept postponing a final decision. The former issue of British paramountcy revived and became subsumed in the question as to whether princes would permit federal authorities to intervene in their affairs. Occasional interference ultimately might lead to a decline of suzerainty.[88] Hardening Congress attitudes toward the princes reinforced those fears. Before and just after the passage of the 1935 Act, the Congress had identified with reforms and political movements in the states but had not intruded directly. It changed course in 1937 and made militant gestures toward several states. As a result, the princes did not join the Federation, and except for the Court and ancillary services, the Federation never actually functioned.[89]

How would the British and Indian politicians interact in the new reform era? Continuation of law and order remained a key question for the Indian government. Provincial autonomy transferred control of the police, intelligence, and punitive actions to Indians. The Government of India resolved the problem of securing intelligence by strengthening the central C.I.D. and meticulously working with governors to forestall conflict with Indian-dominated ministries. Application of criminal law was more ticklish. The government eventually decided to keep reserve power to handle affairs in central territories (primarily Delhi) and in the provinces if local administration collapsed.[90]

The center had considerable opportunity to evolve new patterns and relationships with the provinces because the initial elections under the 1935 Act were not conducted until 1937. However, one matter had to be dealt with immediately. The three-year limit on the 1932 Emergency Powers Act meant that it would expire on December 19, 1935. Although reliance on emergency provisions had diminished, the thought of giving up executive power greatly disturbed the bureaucracy. India in 1935 might be somewhat tranquil, but what of tomorrow?[91] Responding to governors' calls for extension of security demands and penalties for illegal publication, Willingdon telegraphed London for permission to proceed with a bill that would make permanent all sections of the expiring law. Current threats to

88. On the changed Congress posture, general background in Barbara Ramusack, "Indian Princes." Also, Sitaramayya, *The Indian National Congress*, II, 97, 107–8; Handa, *Freedom Struggle*, pp. 110–18, 239–48.

89. Summary in Reginald Coupland, *The Constitutional Problem in India*, Pt. II, 1–60, 80.

90. On intelligence and other problems caused by the act, documents in J&P 1936, 2124.

91. Correspondence from local governments, responding to GI circular (April 29, 1935), J&P Collection 117–B–1.

security, such as communism, would be used to justify the legislation, but the Government of India frankly wanted the powers to meet any future disturbance, including a revival of Congress militancy.[92] The Secretary of State felt the issue was so important that he referred the telegram to a special India Council committee. The India Council agreed on the need for a bill but added that any measure should close the loopholes that were evident in other press regulations. This approach was seconded by the Cabinet, but Willingdon's argument that amendments would only hamper passage won out.[93]

Opting for extension of the Emergency Powers Act rather than bogging down in tedious debate over amendments, the Delhi authorities turned to ferrying the bill through the central legislature. The Council of State tended to support official measures, but the Legislative Assembly was another matter. There the government seats (50) and Congress members (55) offset each other. Independents (22) might join the British in extreme emergency, but that condition did not exist in 1935.[94] Willingdon planned his strategy accordingly. "Inciteful" material would be circulated to friends in the Assembly, and then the Home Member, Craik, would call for the bill's immediate consideration, on the grounds that an extension of current law did not justify study by a Select Committee. If the Assembly insisted on such a committee, the government would permit the delaying tactic and also minor amendment. Compromise might change enough votes to ensure passage. On the other hand, if the Assembly remained adamant, the Governor General would "recommend" the bill and thereby force a vote without delay. The Assembly would, it was hoped, appreciate the gravity of the situation and support the bill, but if not, Willingdon was ready to certify the legislation as vital "for the safety, tranquility or interest of British India."[95]

The hostile attitude of M.L.A.s confirmed the government's premonitions. The introduction of the Criminal Law Amendment Bill on September 2 precipitated extensive debate between officials and a Congress–Independent coalition. The majority of the Assembly rejected the argument that terrorism and alleged Communist plots justified special provisions. When the Assembly refused either to enact the bill or send it to committee, the Governor General "recommended" the measure. On the 12th and

92. Telegram to SS, June 14, 1935, J&P 117–B–1.
93. Telegrams between SS and GG, August 1935, J&P 117–B–1. Also, report of the Committee on the Press Act, same file.
94. Coupland, *Constitutional Problem*, II, 8. Jinnah and Muslims tended to align with Congress on all but the most basic communal issues.
95. Telegram to SS, August 26, 1935, J&P 117–B–1.

16th, both groups debating the issue took off their gloves. When Congressmen claimed that a "yellow leaflet of 25 pages" (a reference to the collection of excerpts circulating among M.L.A.s) did not warrant controls, Craik exploded. Clutching a dossier of 429 pages of material, which he said would "turn [the] stomach" of any "reasonable" person, the Home Member asked rhetorically whether the Assembly was ready to loosen "those forces of chaos and anarchy which produced such misery and such economic loss in 1931 and 1932?"[96] "Yes," the majority replied. Suspecting the government's motives and unimpressed with appeals to order, on September 16 the Assembly rejected the bill, 69 to 57. Everyone knew what would follow. Willingdon certified the measure, and on September 26, it passed the Council of State.

The drama did not cease with enactment. Under the 1919 Government of India Act, certified legislation had to be printed as a command paper and lie eight sitting days before houses of Parliament. While the remaining days of the former act ticked away, the India Office realized in horror that Parliament might not be able to meet this legal obligation. If that happened, and the act were not signed before December 18, many press controls would lapse. After repeatedly calculating Parliament's schedule, the London staff decided that, since the House of Lords met only three days a week, another method of ensuring controls had to be found. Fortunately, the Government of India had at hand an escape clause hitherto unused—a clause that permitted the Secretary of State to declare a state of emergency in India and thus negate the requirement of parliamentary discussion. He now declared a state of emergency, and the new bill became law hours prior to the expiration of press provisions.[97]

The Government of India did not employ the controls widely between 1935 and 1939 despite the determined struggle to keep them. Two political factors helped account for its restraint. First, the mounting sensitivity of Indians to bans and press security embarrassed the British and publicized issues. Editorials censured press actions, while the Indian Civil Liberties Union made bans a matter of primary concern.[98] Legislators proved especially troublesome over the principle of press freedom. Although they could not rescind bans, their questioning tended to reinforce British awareness of the new constitutional setting in which the *raj* had to function. A general disdain for interference was spread-

96. L.A.D., 1935, V, 944. Debates in V, 883–950, 1059–62. Also, background in J&P 117–B–1.

97. Background in J&P 117–B–1.

98. Correspondence with I.C.L.U., GIPOL 1938, 41/56.

ing rapidly, as illustrated by a private discussion between an M.L.A., S. Satyamurti, and the Home Department. In August of 1938, Satyamurti sent the department documents on banning along with a moderate statement that, while admitting the need for occasional controls, stated that most banned works were innocuous and should be deproscribed: "India has now reached a stage politically that she can be allowed to read most of the books which are now proscribed without any harm to anybody."[99] The official reply was polite but vague. Confidentially, however, the secretariat noted that Satyamurti had made several good points. Some officers went so far as to urge systematic deproscribing, even though, were local governments contacted, the result probably would be "a collection of eleven conflicting opinions about each book."[100]

Legislators supplemented personal inquiry by high-lighting the issue of press controls during question hour. M.L.A.s kept asking to see copies of banned works, with the promise, of course, that they would not divulge the content. The government refused, but clothed many of its refusals with attempts at levity. For example, Home Member Craik commented that he wished to avoid exposing "the morals of Honourable Members to such temptations."[101] Other harassment ranged from questioning the nature and results of British policy (for example, did not bans perpetuate smuggling?) to blow-by-blow encounters on the propriety of specific cases.[102] The seizure of Communist and Socialist writings from abroad sparked the fiercest fights. Legislators pricked the government with questions like, Had *The Brothers Karamazov* been confiscated, and if so, why?[103] At other times, as for example in 1938, the challenges became very bitter. Socialist sympathizers dug in on the banning of books (*Fascism and Social Revolution* and *World Politics, 1918–1936*), which they stated were recommended reading in English schools. The Home Member made no reply except to note weakly that circumstances in England and India differed. N. M. Joshi then sarcastically inquired whether "The Government of India also ban books that

99. Satyamurti letter to J. A. Thorne, Home Dept. Secretary (August 27, 1938), GIPOL 1938, 41/56.

100. Note by Thorne (October 11, 1938), GIPOL 1938, 41/56.

101. L.A.D., 1936, VII, 1775. As a rule, the Indian government refused to supply the material or lists, which in fact often were faulty, in any event.

102. In reply to the smuggling comment, the government commented that the same argument would "apply to the removal of restriction on the importation of opium." L.A.D., 1938, IV, 539.

103. L.A.D., 1936, VIII, 2309–10.

propagate Fascist ideas, or has Fascism become the creed of the Government of India?", which drew the answer, "We have not reached that stage."[104]

Such questioning kept the British aware that repression would be scrutinized and probably contributed to hesitancy at moving in that direction. The effect of a second factor, the fragility of relations with the Congress, is easier to demonstrate. Local instances of struggle between bureaucrats and nationalists continued, but, on the whole, the Government of India urged caution in handling Congress. In September 1936, for example, the Governor of the United Provinces ordered a raid on Congress headquarters in Allahabad but then, under pressure from the Home Department, he did an about-face and declined to prosecute Congressmen for publishing an illegal newsletter. In fact, the case resulted in Jawaharlal Nehru's receiving permission to print the propaganda newsletter on a regular basis.[105]

Another illustration of British caution concerned the notorious Congress declaration of independence. The Bombay government wanted to outlaw the declaration and prosecute local Congressmen during the 1935 Jubilee celebration of the Congress. Delhi replied that the declaration probably would not be read aloud, and anyway, it was five years old. Seizure would only intensify sympathy for Congress programs. Bombay had permission to seize seditious books but not those which expressed "mere advocacy of independence."[106] The issue took another turn in January of 1937 when Nehru issued instructions for Congressmen to celebrate Independence Day by reading a slightly altered pledge in open meetings. Interpreting the move as a kite to test British authority, the Indian government refused to ignore the challenge and ordered arrests and banning of the pledge. Although local governments agreed, several (most notably, Madras and the United Provinces) warned that the action would merely increase Congress popularity. A Congress backdown at the last moment prevented the clash, and during 1937, all governments happily canceled proscription of the declaration. When the annual Independence Day celebrations occurred again in 1938, the Government of India counseled the authorities to maintain a low profile and issued no general instructions on official reaction to local ceremonies.[107]

104. L.A.D., 1938, IV, 536–38.

105. Correspondence in J&P 1936, 3903.

106. GI to Bombay, November 13, 1935, J&P Collection 117–C–41. IO staff agreed that Bombay unnecessarily had been "worked up." Peel note (December 5, 1935).

107. Documents and background in GIPOL 1937, 4/1.

While central authorities occasionally initiated actions against the Congress, their main concern was with other publications that presented an external threat to India. Between 1935 and 1938, Customs seized approximately 450 titles, most of which tended to be Communist or contained Socialist themes. The works of John Strachey, Mulk Raj Anand, Agnes Smedley, and R. P. Dutt, for example, fell snare either to Customs or postal inspection centers dotting India.[108] One exception, *The Face of Mother India* by Katherine Mayo, was especially controversial. Mayo's anti-Hindu bias surfaced repeatedly in the volume. She poked fun at the notion of a Hindu golden past and denounced Bengali politicians as effete intellectuals. Muslims were portrayed as masculine but relegated to a low state by Hindu oppressors. The book placed the Indian government in a quandary. Much of Mayo's text could be propaganda against the Congress, Home Secretary Hallett noted, and on the whole, the narrative had "a substratum of truth."[109] Mayo's handling of controversial topics such as the Cawnpur riots (complete with pictures) and the resulting persistent clamor in the Legislative Assembly nevertheless made the book too inflammatory to remain in circulation. On January 17, 1936, the government banned the volume, on the grounds that it contributed to religious tension. Other noteworthy materials seized by the central government included scattered writings critical of the princes and a report on Hindu–Muslim relations in Bahawalpur.[110]

As in the past, the decisions of local officials accounted for most restrictions on Indian publications. Each governor and his secretariat evolved strategies to meet immediate political problems. This decentralization in decisionmaking accounted for varying degrees of repression and interference with Congress operations.[111] Securities and banning followed the same pattern. All governments were committed to put down communism, while those of Bihar, Punjab, and the United Provinces used warnings and selective press actions to control peasant agitations. Terrorism remained a burning issue for Bengal. Of the approximately 175 Indian titles confiscated between 1935 and mid-1937, about half dealt with religion.[112]

108. Drawn from scattered GIPOL files; also, 1937, 41/10.

109. Note by Hallett (January 4, 1936), GIPOL 1936, 36/41.

110. Banning of the communal report surveyed in GIPOL 1937, 37/1. Attitudes toward the states exemplified in CRP 1/29/1083, 1795.

111. Background on provincial policies in Sitaramayya, *The Indian National Congress*, II, 19–20; K. K. Datta, *History of the Freedom Movement in Bihar*, II, 235–78; discussion in L.A.D.: 1936, I, 471–512; VII, 1494; 1937, V, 1615, VI, 2054–55.

112. Based on documents relating to bans and security, included in the

A review of banned material in Punjab illustrates the variety of topics judged dangerous by a provincial government. First, at least ten banned items (primarily posters and handbills) and four newspapers under security related to communism. The provincial party rebounded from each wave of repression with new journals and illicit publications, the tone of which is typified by the lengthy title of a 1935 flyer: "Labourers of the World Unite, May the Communist Party Live, May the British Government's Ship Sink."[113] Some pamphleteers tried to reach the workers; other publicists explored economic problems and the difficulties of reconciling nationalist fervor with international Communist doctrine. Religious conflict in Punjab stimulated a Communist drive to replace religion with other issues, a theme in this poster:

> Labourers and peasants of the world, unite yourselves and overthrow Imperialism. Government which plays holi with the blood of the masses and its henchmen—Hindu, Sikh and Muslim capitalists—seeing the peace of India being burned with fire set by them, feel pleased just as Nero felt happy on seeing Rome destroyed. These capitalists have looted Hindu, Muslim and Sikh masses, and have created trouble in the whole country. Having misled the people in the name of religion, they have made them enemies of each other. Their object is that the masses will continue to cut each other's throat while the capitalists continue to suck their blood, and the Government, which continues to riddle their chests with bullets, rules on. In short, the people never have the opportunity to study the struggle for their rights. O starving labourers and peasants. Rise up and understand the motives of the capitalists, understand the policy of a government thirsting for your blood, and move toward class struggle in order to dash to the ground the hopes of the government and its henchmen. Long live Hindu, Muslim and Sikh alliance. Down with Hindu–Muslim boycott. Down with the capitalists. Down with the government which thirsts for Indian blood.[114]

Religious controversy also affected publications not directed specifically at other communities. Banned nationalist literature in Punjab, for example, had a peculiar mixture of anti-British and communal sentiment. One set of tracts narrated the exploits of an imaginary hero, Harphul Singh Jat. The many tales of his

---

following GIPOL files: 1935, 37/1–2; 1936, 37/1–2; 1937, 37/1. In 1935, 23 titles were seized under 99–A, 62, under the Emergency Powers Act; in 1936, 15 and 61; in 1937 (until July), a total of 29 proscriptions.

113. A translation and discussion in GIPOL 1935, 37/2.

114. *Inkilabi Nara* (n.p.: n.d.), included in GIPOL 1935, 37/2. Also *Vartman Rajat Halat Te Mazdur Kisanon Da Farz* (Amritsar: 1935), same file.

bloody encounters with police officers and Muslim butchers usually were presented in melodramatic, spicy dialogue, such as this conversation between him and an old woman:

> *Lady:* O Darling, bloodthirsty butchers live here, O Darling we are so weak and helpless. O Butchers, they daily slaughter the poor cows.
>
> *Harphul:* I will become a Kshyatria (warrior). I will remove forever the sufferings of cows and cause mourning among butchers. With Durga's help I will crush our oppressors just as I have crushed the British officials.[115]

Publications on the princely states were a similar blend of communal and secular politics.[116]

Finally, the Punjab government prohibited a range of literature produced by the various factional struggles in the region. Polemics often were aimed at other religions, but a surprising number of the banned titles dealt with controversies within a community. The Arya Samaj, for example, reserved its most virulent language for Hindu opponents. The Samaj–Sanatan Dharm conflict fostered exchanges of pamphlets, which sometimes culminated in violence. A favorite Arya Samaj tactic was "exposure" of conservative Hindus' defense of the Puranas as sacred literature (complete with copious translations of passages relating to sex).[117] Sanatan writings tended to be equally intense and derogatory. One proscribed tract, *A Shoe on the Head of the Arya Samaj*, included a section entitled "Dayanand was an Abuser of Saints," a second questioning the character of the Samaj's founder, and a third surveying his views on sex.[118]

Two bitter controversies among Muslims also led to banning. The obscenity and personal attacks in Sunni–Shia exchanges easily matched the tone of the Arya–Sanatan contests. A proscribed Sunni work in the form of a dialogue, for example, quoted the *Encyclopedia Britannica* and missionary studies as "unbiased authorities" in labeling Shias "butchers" and "innovators in religion."[119] The most heated discussions among Punjabi Muslims centered on the Ahmadiya sect, whose founder claimed special

115. Selections from *Ath Nawan Kissa Surma Harphul Singh Daku* (Lahore: c. 1936), GIPOL 1936, 37/2. Other examples of this trend and other material discussed in Part Two of this volume.

116. For example, *Hyderabad Neb Arya Samaj Andolan* (Delhi: n.d.); *Kashmir De Zulum* (Multan: n.d.); *Husain-i-Mazlum* (Lahore: 1936), GIPOL 1936, 37/2.

117. For example, Mansa Ram, *Puranik Pol Prakash* (Lahore: 1936).

118. *Arya Samaj Ke Shir Par Sansar Ka Juta* (Delhi: 1938); *Surapnakha Ke Himayati Ki Nak Kat Gai* (Bhivani: 1936); *Shiv Puja Aur Dayanand Ki Talim* (Amritsar: 1937).

119. *Kahar-i-Khudai Bar Sare Ibne Sabia* (Ferozepur: c. 1938).

knowledge of Islamic truth and even messianic authority. One representative Ahmadiya tract, *The Cutter of the Nose of the Vile Shias*, tried to show that the Shias were heretical and indulged in unnatural sexual acts.[120] Ahrars, a militant group operating from central Punjab, spearheaded the Muslim counterattack. Banned tracts claimed that Ahmadiyas drank wine, ate pork, fornicated, and in general, sold the Muslim community into British slavery.[121]

Local administrations such as the Punjab therefore used the press laws to deal with a diversity of threats to order. Although the introduction of provincial autonomy in mid-1937 led to a reduction in instances of security demands and banning, the pattern persisted.

The Congress emerged from the first general elections under the 1935 Government of India Act dominant in all legislatures except Punjab, Bengal, Assam, and Sind. The nationalist victory transformed center–province relations and created new problems for the British. Until 1937, men-on-the-spot and Delhi shared a common viewpoint and usually acted in concert, but now as a Home Department official noted, "We thus have the political party forming the Government in the majority of the Provinces pledging itself to continuance of the struggle to sever the British connection."[122] The transition threatened to disrupt the flow of intelligence reports and information vital to central operations. Imperial C.I.D. officers had to withdraw from postal inspection posts, and security arrangements had to be slowly and, at times painfully, renegotiated with local governments. The Government of India maintained authority to ban material from outside sources and publications from centrally administered areas or affecting princely states, but suppression of all other printed matter rested essentially with Indian-dominated administrations.[123]

The Congress also had to adjust and deal with issues implicit in its transition from political party to responsible governor. The initial nationalist action after gaining control of the assemblies and police functions was to overturn former British decisions.

120. *Kati-ul-Anaf-ul-Shia-ul-Shaniah* (Lahore: 1935), GIPOL.

121. For example, *Hazliat-i-Mirza* (Sialkot: 1936), GIPOL 1936, 37/2. Background on Ahrar–Ahmadiya controversies in J&P 1934, 3998; also, Spencer Lavan, "The Ahmadiya Movement" (Ph.D. diss., McGill University, 1970), pp. 278–317. The latter contains an excellent description of the tract warfare prominent in the period.

122. Undated note by John Ewart, GIPOL 1937, 4/1.

123. On the technical and philosophical problems inherent in a new phase of power transfer, see documents in the following GIPOL files: 1937, 51/8; 1938, 32/6, 53/1. Published background in Coupland, *Constitutional Problem*, II,193–94; Sitaramayya, *The Indian National Congress*, II, 91–93.

Having stated the intention to remove vestiges of repression upon accepting office, in most areas the Congress ministries lifted bans on associations and returned securities. Deproscription also became common. Non-Congress ministries followed approximately the same course.[124] The provincial governments nevertheless soon found that they confronted the same problems of order that had long plagued the British, and like the colonial power, they began to utilize available machinery to combat lawlessness. Occasionally, labour, *kisan* (peasant), and terrorist literature fell victim to the inherited press regulations. More frequently, however, the governments aimed at communal literature. Hindu–Muslim riots continued to occur regularly in 1938 and 1939. A few Congress governments such as Bombay and the United Provinces attempted to stem the tide by prohibiting especially virulent writings, but others, unsure about how to handle the religious warfare, turned to the All-India Working Committee for guidance.[125] The Indian ministries therefore tolerated more criticism and propaganda than their predecessors, but when necessary, political pressure and inherited British assumptions on maintaining peace and order overrode theoretical commitment to freedom of the press.

Coercion ultimately sparked a debate within the highest echelon of the Congress. The left wing, headed by Nehru, urged that the All-India Working Committee denounce ministers who employed repressive techniques, but Gandhi defended the imperative to put down sedition and disorder. The matter was settled in the fall of 1938 when the Committee sent Congress governments this resolution:

> Inasmuch as people, including a few Congressmen, have been found in the name of civil liberty to advocate murder, arson, looting and class war by violent means, and several newspapers are carrying on a campaign of falsehood and violence calculated to incite the readers to violence and to lead to communal conflicts, the Congress warns the public that civil liberty does not cover acts of, or incitements to, violence or promulgation of palpable falsehoods. In spite, therefore, of the Congress policy of civil liberty remaining unchanged, the Congress will, consistently with its tradition, support measures that may be undertaken by the Congress Governments for the defense of life and property.[126]

124. For example, deproscription in Bihar discussed in GIPOL 1938, 37/2.

125. Some of the problems of the first year of Congress ministries surveyed in Sitaramayya, *The Indian National Congress*, II, 59–71; Coupland, *Constitutional Problem*, Pt. II, 126–33.

126. Sitaramayya, *The Indian National Congress*, II, 91–93; Coupland, *Constitutional Problem*, Pt. II, 134.

The ministers put the policy into effect immediately. With regard to communal disturbance, little distinguished the repression in Congress provinces from that in other provinces or indeed in earlier administrations.[127] Because communal problems crossed provincial boundaries, local governments also attempted to coordinate their action. In May of 1939, Home Ministers from all states except Madras, the Central Provinces, and Assam met at Simla and agreed "to undertake a concerted campaign against propaganda of a communal nature and against incitement to violence of any kind whatever."[128]

Although the original Congress plan in accepting office had been to fight the new constitution, it is evident that by 1939 cooperation between elected representatives and the British had expanded and was moving toward a working relationship. Satisfied that provincial authorities reasonably maintained order, the central government tended to avoid meddling in local matters. In fact, the British were prepared to go far in preventing a schism with Congress ministries. During the Congress agitation in 1938 over conditions in Hyderabad, for example, the Governor General agreed to Bombay's contention that the Indian States Protection Act should not be used so long as the nationalists used only nonviolent techniques.[129]

Experiments in self-government might have proceeded further except for events in Europe. The prospect of another World War polarized Indian politics. The attitudes of educated Indians had changed since they rallied to the British side in 1914. Frustrated by Britain's apparent reluctance to transfer power, the Congress had taken the stand since 1935 that it would oppose India's participation in "an imperialist war."[130] This position was unacceptable to the Indian government, and fearing what might happen if war broke out, Viceroy Lord Linlithgow began to prepare for any eventuality. First, a new section (126) was inserted in the 1935 Act authorizing the center, in case of war, to direct provincial ministers on key issues and enabling the central legislature to make laws in the provincial field. The amendment abruptly reversed the trend toward decentralization. The Secre-

127. Summarized in Coupland, *Constitutional Problem*, Pt. II, 134, but documented more fully in the discussion of individual regimes later in the volume. Background on particular decisions found in the following: Gopinath Srivastava, *When Congress Ruled* (Lucknow: Upper India Publishing House, n.d.); *Five Years of Provincial Autonomy in the Punjab* (Lahore: Punjab Government, 1944).

128. Coupland, *Constitutional Problem*, Pt. II, 136.

129. Correspondence in CRP 1/29/1803.

130. Congress policy reviewed in Sitaramayya, *The Indian National Congress*, II, 124–25; Coupland, *Constitutional Problem*, Pt. II, 208–9.

tary of State's promise that the British did not intend to undermine the authority of local governments fell on deaf ears. The Congress passed a resolution warning of its determination to resist by every possible means a return to unitary, British-dominated administration.[131] When the situation in Europe worsened in the summer of 1939, the Government of India sent Indian troops to Egypt and Singapore. Disturbed by this military deployment, the Congress called on M.L.A.s to boycott the next session of the central assembly and notified provincial committees to prepare for resistance to the war effort.[132]

On September 3, Linlithgow announced that India was at war with Germany and proclaimed a state of emergency. Days later, the government introduced the Defence of India Bill, which legitimized a wide range of wartime powers. The Assembly debated the bill for four days, but because Congress had withdrawn from the legislature, the measure passed on September 19 without serious opposition. The Congress ministries in nine provinces then denounced the declaration of war and resigned.[133] Within a short span of time, therefore, any hope of continued entente with Indian nationalists disappeared. The British were on yet another collision course with the Congress and Mahatma Gandhi.

A Turbulent Path to Independence

The means of political control available to the British in 1940 resembled those which had operated during the earlier war. The Defence of India Act bolstered central authority and gave reserve powers for use when existing regulations on matters such as banning seemed ineffective. Internment, special tribunals, and apparatus for supervising almost every aspect of Indian economic and public life reappeared. Censorship again became prominent, probably more elaborate than in 1915 because of the immediate Japanese threat. The structure for censorship consisted of a small coordinating group at the top (the Chief Censor, the Director of Public Information, and an additional secretary of the Home Department) and censors and advisory committees in each province. The committees had the task of cultivating press co-operation and furnishing recommendations on specific articles or sanctions. They received administrative support from special press officers and their staffs, who had the primary responsibility

131. Gwyer, *Speeches and Documents*, I, lii; Coupland, *Constitutional Problem*, Pt. II, 209–10.
132. Coupland, *Constitutional Problem*, Pt. II, 210.
133. Early stages of Congress policy and the last months of 1939 summarized in Coupland, *Constitutional Problems*, Pt. II, 211–36; Sitaramayya, *The Indian National Congress*, II, 125–44.

for surveying printed matter. The Government of India theoretically issued guidelines on censorship and coordinated all censoring activities; in practice, however, the decisionmaking devolved to men caught up in daily problems.[134]

The system of controls and censoring looked adequate on paper, but making the mechanisms work proved nightmarish. Integration of wartime measures into ongoing administration raised innumerable problems and tensions, many of which required months to untangle.[135] During this initial phase of testing and adjustment, censors and customs officers tended to be concerned primarily with material on military operations or affecting public morale (specifically, pacifist writings).[136] The Government of India avoided comprehensive suppression of news or writings on domestic politics. That policy derived from British ambivalence toward applying the Defence of India Act. When enacting the bill, the government had insisted that widened executive privilege would not be used in wholesale fashion to deal with local crises. Despite occasional censoring of stories on or by the Congress, therefore, the Imperial Home Department abstained from acts that might belie a public commitment. In January of 1941, for example, press advisers permitted publication of the notorious Congress independence pledge, and local governments were requested not to outlaw independence celebrations.[137] The incident also reflected a related rationale for minimizing conflict with political opponents. The Government of India kept trying to develop support for the war effort from many segments of Indian society, including potentially the Congress. A major breach was to be avoided if at all possible.[138]

Interaction between the *raj* and the Congress took several forms between 1940 and 1942. Both developed extensive propaganda. While the Congress attempted to win support from sympathetic foreign newsmen, its main thrust was toward the Indian masses. Preaching teams visited rural areas, and Congress presses emitted innumerable tracts denouncing the war.[139] British propaganda had two goals. A newly created agency, the Central Board

134. Key files on the censorship system include the following: GIPOL 18/14/41; 14/20/41; 3/5A/41; 3/27/41.

135. Note by B. J. Kirchener (September 19, 1941), GIPOL 18/14, 1941. Also, documents in 1942, 47/2; 1943, 33/33.

136. Circulars and other documents in GIPOL 1941, 3/7; 1941, 41/20.

137. Circular 3/7 (January 17, 1941) and telegram, Viceroy to Home Department (January 2, 1941), GIPOL 1941, 3/7.

138. Ibid.

139. Congress propaganda discussed in Sitaramayya, *The Indian National Congress*, II, 166–309; P. N. Chopra, *Rafi Ahmad Kidwa*, p. 73; K. K. Datta, *Bihar*, III, 342–85.

of Information, distributed material among the Allies and especially in the United States. The British anticipated that such propaganda would neutralize the often pro-Indian news in Western papers.[140] To reach the Indian public, the government could rely on tract literature and hourly broadcasts from the officially controlled radio stations.[141]

The two rivals also negotiated long and hard to bridge the political impasse. The most dramatic discussions occurred in March of 1942, when Sir Stafford Cripps visited India and tried to work out a constitutional compromise. As a result of his mission, the government became committed to the principle of India becoming a Dominion immediately after the war and to an interim arrangement whereby Indians' role in administration would be expanded. Moreover, the British conceded that Indians would play the dominant role in framing a new constitution. As often happened, however, the nationalists' expectations far exceeded what the government could deliver. Involvement in the war was irreversible, and the rulers had no intention of immediate constitutional shifts. When the Congress reiterated the demand for substantial transfer of power in the midst of the war, the talks broke down.[142]

Increasingly the government and the Congress clashed in the streets. Gandhi cooly escalated a campaign against the bureaucracy. The first phase consisted of individual acts of law-breaking, generally connected with freedom of speech, followed in 1941 by group civil disobedience. Each step evoked an equally calculated application of repression by the British. In its refusal to permit open breaches of the peace, the government imprisoned over 20,000 Congressmen. The central secretariat, however, still hoped "to keep the temperature as low as possible" despite these arrests.[143] A full-scale attack on opponents would be postponed until activities by the Congress seemed about to unleash anarchy.

The British had been formulating plans to meet such a crisis since 1940. In August of that year, Linlithgow sent London a draft of a "revolutionary movement" (later, "emergency powers")

140. Discussed in Chaman Lal, *British Propaganda in America* (Allahabad: Kitab Mahal, 1945); also documents in GIPOL 1940, 3/16, and Sitaramayya, *The Indian National Congress*, II, 736–56.

141. J&P Collection file 104/B; background in GIPOL 1940, 3/16.

142. Sitaramayya, *The Indian National Congress*, II, 310–31; Coupland, *Constitutional Problem*, Pt. II, 263–86.

143. Note summarizing tactics, undated, in GIPOL 1940, 3/25. Also see discussion in Datta, *Bihar*, Vols. II–III. Documents and specific rules are in P. Ramanath Ayyar, ed., *The Indian Ordinances, 1939–1944, With Notes* (Mylapor: Madras Law Journal Office, 1944); *The Defence of India Act, 1939, and The Rules Made Thereunder* (Delhi: Government of India, 1944).

ordinance, which provided for mass arrests and total control of mass communications. The ordinance had a dual purpose. First, it would obviate using the Defence of India Act against antigovernment forces as well as opponents of the war effort.[144] A second motive was to immobilize Congress or, as Home Member Maxwell noted, "to crush the Congress finally as a political organization."[145] A decisive blow would eliminate Congress influence and at the same time graphically underline British determination to remain master of Indian politics.

The secret proposal triggered heated debate among top British officers. Some, such as the Governor of the United Provinces, felt the ordinance unwieldy and politically dangerous:

> If we are out to smash the Congress as a political party in this country, we alienate all the support we might get from its half-hearted supporters. I do not question the desirability of smashing the Congress but I submit that this is not the way to do it. . . . Having said that the future constitution of India will, subject to certain safeguards, be decided by Indians themselves, it seems anomalous for us to go out and smash the Congress on any other ground but that they are interfering in the war.[146]

The Home government also had reservations. The War Cabinet feared the result of a total break with the Congress and insisted that any reserve powers be applied only to maintain public order and the war campaign. Linlithgow eventually received permission to promulgate the ordinance in a crisis, but the months of discussion clearly showed that it must be used with tact and an eye to postwar conditions.[147]

British strategy involved elements besides maneuvering with Congress. Sustaining support from important blocs of Indians remained a concern. Political mobilization had produced many divergent groupings and parties, including the Muslim League, the Sikh League, the untouchables headed by Dr. Ambedkar (a Mahar with a doctorate from Columbia University and wide political experience), and the Hindu Mahasabha. Winning their cooperation required delicate handling. To help achieve this goal, representatives of these groups were included on both the Imperial Defence Council and the expanded Viceroy's Executive Council.

144. Major files on preparations include J&P 117/B/13; GIPOL 1940, 3/16, 3/31. A description is in Francis G. Hutchins, *Spontaneous Revolution* (Delhi: Manohar, 1971), pp. 188–96.

145. Maxwell letter, April 25, 1940, GIPOL 1940, 3/13.

146. Maurice Hallett to Maxwell, October 10, 1940, GIPOL 1940, 3/18.

147. Documents in J&P 117/B/13.

The Legislative Assembly also influenced the government's political game plan. The frequent resignations by Congress M.L.A.s smoothed passage of necessary legislation, but the central authorities continued to face stubborn resistance in the Assembly to its policies. The most repeated charge was that Defence of India sanctions had been employed against the Congress for activities unrelated to the war. The Home Member usually replied either that he could not question the decisions of local governments in that regard, or that under certain circumstances, Congressmen had attempted to undermine the war effort.[148]

The British appreciated that the outcome of their attempt to contain the Congress and build support for the government rested largely on the attitude of the press. If newspapers sided with Gandhi, they could spread his message and help precipitate a confrontation; on the other hand, a cooperative press would aid wartime appeals, communication, and publicity. Unable to predict in which direction journalists might move, the bureaucracy instinctively censured reference to inflammatory Congress announcements or to unpleasant events such as a hunger strike in Calcutta.[149] That approach soon changed, however, because of public outcry. Newspapermen had become accustomed to widened freedom of expression since 1934, and they were not willing to acquiesce quietly. Following negotiations with a young but active press organization, the Indian Newspaper Editors' Conference, in later 1940, the government developed oblique means of directing press opinion. Editors agreed to regulate the industry from within through provincial press committees in return for relaxed controls. The committees would try to minimize emphasis on controversial subjects and to serve as a go-between if conflict arose between the British and a particular newspaper. From the beginning, the makeshift arrangements threatened to break down because local governments pursued their usual policies, often banning or censoring with little regard for the "gentleman's agreement." The Editors' Conference repeatedly remonstrated over such cases. Sometimes the Governor General declined to intervene; on other occasions, he counseled moderation toward the press. Neither side was happy with the results of the experiment, but banning and censorship remained at a low level until the political explosions of 1942.[150]

148. For example, discussion in L.A.D., 1940, I, 463–65; 1941, I, 534–35.

149. Documents in J&P 127/2; GIPOL 1941, 41/20.

150. Survey on the system and its problems in GIPOL 1941, 3/27; 1942, 3/13, Pts. 1–2. Indian evaluations in Sitaramayya, *The Indian National Congress*, II; K. Rama Rao, *The Pen As My Sword*, pp. 146–66;

The emergence of a Japanese threat to India set the stage for a final showdown between the government and the Congress. Rangoon fell in the spring of 1942, and bombs began exploding along India's eastern borders. Gandhi decided that the safety of the country and her freedom depended on a rapid evacuation by the British, and therefore he and the Congress resolved to force that move. On August 8, 1942, the All-India Congress Committee authorized Gandhi to take whatever steps he deemed necessary to make the British "Quit India." That the rulers were by no stretch of the imagination prepared to do. Menaced by the rapid Japanese advance and on the verge of losing political control, the Government of India struck before Gandhi could launch his campaign. Most Congress leaders had been imprisoned by August 10, and a tight news cordon was imposed throughout India.[151]

The action precipitated a wave of violence such as no one had anticipated. Without the stabilizing influence of Gandhi, local Congressmen initiated their own programs of confrontation and sabotage. Some planning underlay the attacks, but the records suggest that the anarchy prevalent throughout the remainder of 1942 tended to be a spontaneous reaction to wartime conditions and British oppression. Official control over large areas of Bihar and the United Provinces wholly disappeared for several weeks. Numerous atrocities occurred as police and the army battled nationalist rebels. The Indian government pulled no punches in crushing the insurgency, and in the end, the lingering might of the *raj* won out. Over 100,000 political prisoners sat in jail, countless offices and private residences had been destroyed, and the death toll exceeded a thousand.[152]

In addition to death and destruction, the Quit India movement also unleashed a barrage of emergency press measures. Detailed instructions on handling of news and comments on domestic pol-

---

Bose, *Press*, pp. 107–20; *Report of the First U.P. Press Conference Held at Lucknow on July 31 and August 1, 1942* (Lucknow: Chalapathi Rau, 1942).

151. Final negotiations and the British response summarized in Hutchins, *Revolution*, pp. 207–12. The revolutionary movement ordinance did not come into effect because most provincial governments preferred to use Defence of India regulations to meet the uprisings.

152. The attacks and incidents discussed in the following: Francis G. Hutchins, *Spontaneous Revolution: The Quit India Movement*, pp. 212–17, 267–311; R. H. Niblett, *The Congress Rebellion at Azamgarh; Congress Responsibility for the Disturbances, 1942–3* (Delhi: Government of India, 1943); *India Ravaged* (Madras: Indian Express, 1943, banned); Datta, *Bihar*, Vol. III. On the suffering of individuals, Niranjan Sen, *Bengal's Forgotten Warriors* (Bombay: Peoples' Publishing House, 1942).

itics already had been circulated prior to August. Censors and district officers were warned to cooperate in eliminating any printed matter that favored opponents of the British, referred to setbacks of the government, or reported trials and arrests in such a fashion as to create an atmosphere of "martyrdom."[153] Attempts to disrupt Congress contact with a mass audience had had a trial run from April 1942 onward in the form of systematic bans on Working Committee resolutions, but these were nothing compared to the massive censorship that surrounded Quit India incidents. The British blacked out all news on demonstrations and Congress activities.[154]

Expanded censorship brought the *raj* to the threshold of renewed conflict with Indian journalists. Eighty-four periodicals suspended publication to protest the stringency of censorial demands.[155] Within two weeks, the Standing Committee of the All-India Newspaper Editors' Conference met and presented an ultimatum. Either the policy of permitting journalists to police themselves be resumed, or the committee would call a general newspaper strike. The government responded by attempting to apply financial pressure on individual papers, but clearly the editors held political leverage. Threatened with a potentially united front that would paralyze communications, the Governor General and his Council opted for compromise; over-all prohibition of news on the disturbances had been removed by early September, and local governments were requested to use restraint and conciliation in press matters. The editors in turn agreed to ask provincial advisory groups to work more closely with censors in preventing inflammatory reports. Local arrangements and difficulties varied with each province, but the agreement apparently worked to the satisfaction of both parties. As the Governor General noted in a telegram to London on December 15, 1942, "the press throughout India is now working under restrictions voluntarily imposed and is at least as 'free' as the press in any country at war."[156]

Indirect controls through the advisory system persisted as a core element in government policy during the remainder of the war. Cooperation by newspaper committees minimized circulation of "dangerous" material and at the same time freed bureaucrats

153. Memoranda in GIPOL 1942, 3/16 K.W.

154. Documents on GI response in GIPOL 1942, 3/16.

155. Lists and notes in GIPOL 1942, 3/105.

156. Governor General to Secretary of State, telegram (December 15, 1942), GIPOL 1942, 3/13, Pt. II. The file contains much of the correspondence relevant to this summary.

to focus much of the censorship apparatus on commentary sent to or from India. Occasionally, militant papers or snap judgments by the British jeopardized relations with news organizations, but a spirit of give and take tended to steer the arrangements past major shoals.[157] The Imperial Home Department religiously read proceedings of the various advisory groups and the Editors' Conference, and when disagreement arose, attempted to suggest workable solutions. The informal controls became regularized to the point that, by 1944, the Home Secretary, Richard Tottenham, regularly met with editors and shared in their deliberations. Tottenham often went into such sessions with a prepared strategy and "bargaining counters."[158]

The British buttressed the advisory scheme with other strategies and sanctions. Censorship continued until 1945, but generally the bureaucracy preferred a less visible means of control such as warnings and the withholding of a commodity that was scarce in wartime, newsprint. In December of 1942, for example, a Home Department official, S. L. Oliver, had several private talks with P. C. Joshi, editor of the Communist *Peoples War* and, from at least the British viewpoint, moderated the paper's stance.[159] In addition, the government's publicity program intensified after the first shock of the August uprising. The Government of India sent out elaborate memoranda on neutralizing the psychological effect of the Quit India movement. Propaganda should high-light four themes: 1. the promise of independence, to be given after the war; 2. the presence of the threat of Japan to the Indian people; 3. the discrediting of the Congress; 4. the cultivation of loyalty and support from specific groups (for example, Sikhs and untouchables).[160] The circulars also included draft documents and pictures, such as a cartoon showing a British soldier leaving a house, a Congressman waving goodbye, and a Japanese coming in the back door (the caption read, "Babuji, look who is coming"). Another "model" pictured Hitler, Tito, Mussolini, and Tojo at microphones, in unison chanting "I vote for the Congress resolutions." Both the central and provincial governments prepared

157. Quote from Sitaramayya, *The Indian National Congress*, II, 735. Background on the conference and press problems in GIPOL 1943, 33/4; L.A.D. 1942, III, 163–64; Sitaramayya, II, 721–35. Resolutions of the Conference on journalist–British relations can be found in *Resolutions of the All-India Newspapers Editor's Conference from 1940–1967* (Delhi: A.N.E.C., 1967).

158. Tottenham note (March 16, 1943), GIPOL 1944, 33/8; also, documents in GIPOL 1943, 33/42.

159. Minute by S. J. L. Oliver (December 16, 1942), in GIPOL 1942, 7/17.

160. Circular 28/5/42 (July17, 1942), GIPOL 1942, 3/11.

numerous official and clandestine political commentaries for distribution to the public.[161]

The brutality and repression in 1942 has clouded another more peaceable dimension of Indian politics during the war years. The sporadic but persistent transfer of power continued to be matched by a diminishing of British controls over the press and public movements. Propaganda, indirect supervision, and influence received preference over reliance on open force. Substantial gaps in records and faulty communication among administrative units after 1940 make a thorough assessment of British restrictions virtually impossible, but at least banning of Indian publications slowed. Less than three dozen items were proscribed between 1943 and 1945.[162] With the exception of a comprehensive ban on official Congress publications, major instances of British restrictions related primarily to writings from outside India and not to the domestic. Censors and customs officials seized approximately seven hundred works at Indian ports of entry.[163] The anti-imperialist productions of Reginald Reynolds (for example, *The New Indian Rope Trick* and *White Sahibs in India*) fell prey to customs, as did Nazi and Communist literature and material from the Watchtower Bible and Tract Society. The latter organization had been outlawed also in Canada, Australia, and New Zealand because of its pacifist orientation and work with troops.[164] The Government of India did ban the Congress and in general kept militant nationalists away from public activities until 1944, but once the Quit India movement had been broken, on the whole other political parties operated as normally as might be expected in a wartime colonial setting.[165]

By early 1945, British reevaluation of Indian political trends led to a further relaxation of bans on political protest and printed opinion.[166] On the one hand, mounting opposition to actions under emergency powers came from the courts and the central legis-

161. Examples taken from propaganda memoranda in GIPOL 1942, 3/11. Other efforts surveyed in GIPOL 1943, 48/6.

162. Based on handlists prepared from GIPOL indexes, 1942–1945, and research in specific files. For important discussion of principles operating, see GIPOL 1943, 37/1–37/10. Banning of particular Congress titles evaluated in GIPOL 1942, 3/49; 1943, 37/2, 3/7.

163. Statistics based on collection files on application of censorship and seizure by customs, GIPOL. The system receives treatment in the following: 1944, 41/2, 41/7; 1945, 41/1. The government almost banned Pendrel Moon's *Strangers in India* (background, GIPOL 1944, 20/15).

164. Reynolds's books evaluated in GIPOL 1944, 41/1; Watchtower series in 1944, 56/44.

165. See, for example, discussion of politics and raids on Congress headquarters, GIPOL 1943, 3/7; 1944, 24/3, 33/19.

166. Exemplified by permitting papers "blowing off steam" when

lature. The High and Federal courts criticized the executive branch's overbearing methods in specific cases. The judiciary declared some laws illegal and set limits on the application of others, a development aptly described in an Assembly debate by Pandit L. K. Maitra: "At present there is a sort of race going on between the judiciary and the executive in this country. The executive makes rules. The judiciary says that the rules are *ultra vires*. Then immediately the executive brings in another rule."[167] To the government's dismay, the Federal Court also began to bring Indian sedition law into line with that pertaining to Britain. Its liberal constructions and tendency to champion freedom of the press placed restraints on handling of newspapers or books.[168]

The Legislative Assembly seconded efforts to limit executive authority. Wartime controls had directly affected many M.L.A.s, and they were angry. The British unconsciously had contributed to the emergence of an unlikely coalition on the subject by applying the Defence of India Act to prevent communal disturbances. Thus, radicals from each religious sect joined with nationalists in denouncing the government.[169] The Viceroy was well aware of legislative sentiment and took it into consideration. In particular, the government hesitated to approach the Assembly with fresh restrictions. By late 1943, for example, loopholes and problems in existing press laws had become so general that the Home Department confidentially considered a revised press act. The Governor General stopped the discussion by noting that the Assembly would reject the measure. The resulting confrontation would only be "troublesome" and cause "a stink."[170] The anti-British spirit eventually took definite form during the 1944 budget debate when, for the first time in war, the legislature passed a censure motion. Speaker after speaker rose to recount examples of British *zulum* (oppressive action) toward the press, and more than one harkened back to the debate over the Defence of India

---

Gandhi was released in May, 1944, GIPOL 1944, 33/19. Also, shifting priorities for banning discussed in GIPOL 1943, 7/16; 1944, 37/3.

167. L.A.D., 1944, II, 1117. Summary statement in Sitaramayya, *The Indian National Congress*, II, vi–cxxxvi.

168. The following GIPOL files document the frustrations and altered handling of cases because of various judicial decisions: 1943, 91/43; 1944, 49/5 (especially Legal Advisor opinion, April 10, 1944).

169. For example, debates in 1941, II, 1345; 1942, I, 168–70; 1944, II, 1115–38. One case that caused particular consternation involved the banning of *Satyarth Prakash* in Sind by a Muslim-dominated legislature. GIPOL 1943, 37/9; S. Chandra, *The Case of Satyarth Prakash in Sind* (Delhi: Arya Pratinidhi Sabha, 1947). From 1943 onward, press files often concluded with the statement that intervention would create too much commotion or "bad publicity."

170. Notes by Home Department Officials and the Governor General in GIPOL 1943, 33/33.

Act when the government vowed that the legislation would be applied cautiously. In his last public debate before retirement, Home Member Maxwell pleaded that the bureaucracy be given the benefit of the doubt, but he was shouted down.[171]

Exposés of British missteps coincided with diminishing danger of a Japanese invasion and the gradual return of Congressmen to the legislative arena. Invasion and the crisis of 1942 no longer threatened, and now Indians impatiently expected the British to fulfill their promises. The Congress had not been destroyed, as evidenced by its resurgence upon release of prominent leaders in late 1944. That organization, and the Muslim League, which had flourished in the war period, clearly would be critical determinants of India's political future. After the winter elections of 1945, the Congress resumed control of all but three provincial legislatures, and shortly thereafter, the "fomentors of sedition," Jawaharlal Nehru, Rajendra Prasad, and Sardar Patel, accepted portfolios in the central government. Nehru symbolized the transfer of power on that occasion by conducting a press conference in Hindi.[172]

Continued censorship and repression of political commentary became meaningless under such circumstances. Press advisers interfered infrequently with news reports, and most controls ended with the cessation of the war. Less than thirty books and individual numbers of papers were seized subsequently, and those generally with the acquiescence or active assent of Indian leaders. For example, the editor of the *Daily Herald*, K. Rama Rao, has recounted that while the British wanted to curtail his aggressive editorials, they demanded security only after intercepting a note from Nehru that criticized the newspaper's biting tone.[173] Congress continually made freedom of expression a cardinal point in election manifestoes, and upon taking office in 1946, the new ministries returned securities such as that of the *Herald*. The Congress victory also led to deproscribing books, most notably in Bombay where approximately 70 titles returned to circulation.[174]

Although the British remained central in politics until August of 1947, they accepted the fact that the tide against controls was irreversible. Perhaps the best illustration of the official stance toward political rhetoric is the manner in which the bureaucracy

171. L.A.D., 1944, II, 1115–38.

172. On changing circumstances and shifts in government policy, Hutchins, *Revolution*, pp. 311–33; Rama Rao, *Pen*, pp. 194–209; Rajendralal Handa, *Leaves From a Diary*, Pt. 1, 65–67.

173. Rao, *Pen*, pp. 208–9.

174. Alterations in controls and banning discussed in GIPOL 1945, 33/19, 33/29. A detailed treatment of deproscription is not possible because GIPOL files for 1946–1947 are closed to foreign scholars.

approached the annual question of the Congress pledge. The pledge of independence had been legal before the second non-cooperation campaign, then banned for two years, and later permitted again because "academic advocacy" of freedom did not constitute a major threat. In 1943, the Home Department felt that, since the Congress had been outlawed, the pledge too should be forbidden. The manner of prohibition, however, signaled a shift of priorities. Local governments were ordered to take action against presses that printed the pledge but not to ban it formally because of "bad publicity."[175] This order lapsed in 1944, and although quiet efforts were made to prevent wide circulation and demonstrations arising from the pledge, the Government of India henceforth adopted a hands-off policy.[176]

The initiative and power that remained in British hands was directed, not toward the press, but toward the communal rioting, which spread like brushfire. The suspicions and tension between adherents to the various religions were at least partially suppressed by wartime restrictions; they now resurfaced and took their toll. In the year before independence, central and provincial authorities desperately tried to contain communalism through stringent public order ordinances, but to no avail. Pressure from Indian nationalists had brought the subcontinent to the eve of freedom, but ironically, a variety of religious warfare that denied many of the Congress's political assumptions furnished the final impetus for an accelerated British withdrawal. The foreign bureaucracy resolved the problems and contradictions inherent in its rule by quitting India. The task of maintaining order and the difficult choice between dismantling or using the accumulated apparatus for controlling controversial writings, now passed to the British government's successors in India and Pakistan.

175. Tottenham notes (January 1, 1943) and Circular 3/3 (January 16, 1943), GIPOL 1943, 3/3.

176. R. F. Mudie minute (January 11, 1945), and Circular X/153 (January 18, 1945), GIPOL 1945, 3/1.

Chapter 5

THE LEGACY

The British orientation toward Indian publications must be viewed in terms of changing political circumstances and the government's over-all response to those changes. The gradual transition toward independence during the twentieth century placed new restraints on the bureaucracy. The most obvious effects involved formal structures. Indians became prominent in decision-making and in legislative arenas. By 1937, the Government of India had lost much immediate authority over provincial administration. The shifts meant that the rulers had to be concerned increasingly with elections, political parties, and legislative tactics. At the same time, the ideological underpinning of the *raj* was being transformed. The movement from autocracy to democracy necessitated the British replacing their self-image as authority figures with that of knowledgeable political leaders. Similarly, the concepts of "power" and "orders to be obeyed" shifted toward "influence" and "winning cooperation."

The new sense of accountability and political participation in turn created conflict within the inner circles of government. Although imperial bureaucrats devised an assortment of experiments designed to slow or at least to influence the direction of political change, they remained ambivalent toward their own role and the notion of Indian partnership. Developing a crisis psychology in response to terrorism, assaults by the Congress, and tension between Hindus and Muslims, the British fastened upon the maintenance of law and order as the ultimate rationale for their continuing presence in the subcontinent. This decision led to marked discrepancies between announced goals and practice, most notably the repression occasioned by the non-cooperation and the Quit India campaigns.

From the viewpoint of the Government of India, anti-British and communal literature contributed to disorder in two ways. First, political writings created an atmosphere conducive to the spread of ill feelings and violence. The bureaucracy assumed that espousal of revolution or attacks on the administration demoralized those who came in contact with such printed material. Although the assumptions were not tested thoroughly, enough evidence accumulated to spport the link between publications and deed. Revolutionary tracts did indeed affect young men, and certainly religious polemics intensified communal hostility.[1] The government also judged bulletins, posters, and newspapers as vital to the flow of information among Indian groups, and for that reason, seizure of Congress material in 1932 and 1942 was partially intended to disrupt the nationalists' communication network.

Officialdom had several options in handling Indian books and newspapers. Authors could have been permitted to write whatever they chose, bound only by fear of prosecution and a sense of responsibility. If freedom of expression was misused, propaganda and related efforts like subsidizing progovernment publications might counterbalance the bad effects. Finally, the bureaucracy could employ a combination of preventive and punitive measures to contain controversial writings. The Government of India attempted all these approaches, but while propaganda and a hands-off policy seemed ineffective, controls remained a vital part of British strategy.

Four decades of experimentation with press restrictions produced a set of interconnected laws and bureaucratic apparatus. The procedure for maintaining surveillance over Indian publications had been routinized by 1914, as had standardization of reports and other intelligence documents connected with the press. Although the system underwent great stress after 1937 because of expanded provincial autonomy, the rudiments continued until independence.[2] The two basic provisions of the 1910 Press Act—banning and securities—became the models for subsequent legislation. The power to declare writings illegal remained constant despite fluctuations in specific laws that related to changing political conditions. The 1922 reforms narrowed the grounds for banning, but soon religious tracts and then other types of controversial material once again fell within the scope of the banning provisions. The temporary lapse of security demands upset the bureaucracy. Once they regained that method of repression in 1930, the British never yielded it. Provincial autonomy led to repeal of local press laws, but within three years, the Defence of India Act reinstated the authority of the center if local min-

1. The effects of such writings in one province are examined by N. G. Barrier in a forthcoming volume edited by Kenneth W. Jones and Eric Gustafson, *Sources for Punjab History: An Exploratory Bibliography* (Delhi: Manohar, 1974). Also, see discussion of related matters in *Report of the Press Laws Enquiry Committee* (Delhi: Government of India, 1948).

2. For example, the confidential press reports from each province supposedly lapsed after 1935. Discussion in GIPOL 1934, 53/3; also, GIPOL 1937, 36/1; 1938, 53/1. The weekly sets of translations from vernacular papers ended at approximately the same time.

istries did not deal satisfactorily with problems of law and order. With the exception of brief relaxation of legal restraints during the 1920s, therefore, the bureaucracy kept the legal power to demand securities, to ban works, and to seize printed matter at customs and in the mails.

If the legal basis for press controls was fairly consistent after 1910, implementation of the laws varied widely in time and locale. Technical problems persisted as a source of tension and misunderstanding within administrative circles. Government units (police, customs, postal inspectors, and censors) had difficulty coordinating decisions and presenting a united front. Squabbles over jurisdiction and responsibility were commonplace. Many difficulties arose from the alternative sanctions that could be employed in specific cases. Authors and publishers might be prosecuted and/or their writings confiscated under a variety of provisions of the penal code or press law. Which lever to pull, if any, required time-consuming evaluation and planning.[3] Moreover, definitions often created problems. Debate over what constituted a "closed cover" in the mails, or if a politically inscribed *dhoti* (loincloth) could be dealt with under the Press Act were not isolated incidents. New situations or propaganda techniques forced continued discussion on the meaning of legal terms. Whether or not gramophone records of Congress speeches constituted a document as defined in the Emergency Powers Act, for example, led to tedious correspondence within the bureaucracy. Similarly, as late as 1940, the government was still trying to resolve the question of whether items banned in one province automatically could be considered illegal throughout India.[4]

This study suggests that at least five elements accounted for how and when the British relied on repression of publications as a political tactic. The first lay outside the subcontinent. Parliament and a parade of Secretaries of State exhibited no consistent attitude toward freedom of the Indian press. Rather, home concerns depended on the party in power, the personalities of India Office officials, and the situation both in Europe and in India. Alternate cries for repression or conciliation came from London, sometimes from the same individual such as Morley or Montagu.

3. When discussing Fisher's *That Strange Little Brown Man Gandhi*, for instance, the Home Department decided to ban the work but not notify it under Sea Customs provisions because the latter might generate too much publicity. Documents in GIPOL 1932, 29/8. A reversal of sanctions in another case, *India Marches Past*, discussed in GIPOL 1933, 35/13.

4. Correspondence and circular 126/34 (November 5, 1934), GIPOL 1934, 126. The government finally decided that the records were documents and should be banned because they potentially reached large audiences with the "spoken word."

The India Office forced no major alteration of press policy, with the possible exception of pressure for protecting princes and repeal of the 1910 Act; however, the Indian government always appreciated that decisions would receive careful review and occasional public debate in England. The potential responses of home politicians and public opinion narrowed the options open to administrators in India. The press could not be totally subdued nor wholly freed of restraint.

Had Parliament given the Governor General free rein, he and his associates would have been forced to come to terms with the differing approaches of local officials. From the outset, the provinces contributed heavily to formulation of press laws. More importantly, they implemented those regulations in response to regional conditions. A few concerns tended to be constant, such as communal conflict in Punjab and U.P., revolutionary activity in Bengal, or the Kisan problems in U.P. and Bihar, but more often than not, local officials devised their own political strategies and were given latitude in putting them into effect. Publications thought dangerous in Punjab or Bengal could be and occasionally were permitted to circulate in Bombay or Madras. The central government held ultimate authority over its subordinates, but only rarely did the Governor General intervene, despite signs of miscalculation. The localized nature of decisions on special bans and securities meant that there was not one but many press policies.

A third element in the political system, the judiciary, played a growing role in decisionmaking. Although the British-dominated courts occasionally disrupted government tactics prior to 1937 (most notably with regard to the *Zamindar/Comrade* prosecutions c. 1912–1914 and communal writings in the 1920s), common assumptions about law and order permeated the executive and judicial branches of Indian administration. This helped account for the infrequency with which Indian publicists turned to the courts for redress.[5] Behind the scenes, however, the government worked hard to minimize such appeals by carefully avoiding prosecutions or bans if the courts seemed likely to interfere. This dimension of British rule becomes more prominent in the 1930s and 1940s when, as a result of Indianization of the judiciary and the changing constitution, the courts began liberalizing their interpretation of press freedoms. Judicial constraints increasingly appeared in discussion on the secretariat level of particular cases.

5. *The Press Laws Enquiry Committee Report* (pp. 31–36), for example, indicated that in most provinces, appeals to courts were rare.

Indian politicians also vitally influenced British–press relations. Beginning with Minto, each viceroy included the anticipated response of Indian legislators in calculations concerning press laws. The Government of India never relinquished ultimate authority to promulgate emergency measures, but the soul-searching that preceded any act that might antagonize the legislature or the issuance of an ordinance underlined how seriously the government viewed legislative politics. The steady independence of the Central Legislative Assembly after 1921 reinforced official hesitancy to widen reliance on coercion. Interference with books and newspapers would be reviewed at every turn.

Politicians in the streets caused far more anxiety within the I.C.S. than those debating in the legislature. The Government of India spent much time responding to the initiatives of revolutionaries, communal leaders, and Congressmen. The British never fully controlled Indian political developments. Some threats could be dissipated with negotiation, others had to be met with force. The rhythm of press securities and bans reflected the constant interaction between government and antigovernment forces. Such exchanges help to explain the bursts of restrictions and the type of printed matter banned; Congress publications circulated freely one year, and the next, became illegal. An especially lively essay on Hinduism by a Muslim theologian might be available for seventy years, only to be banned because of a sudden heightening of Hindu–Muslim tension.[6]

Final determination of what constituted a threat to order and how that threat should be countered depended on the British themselves. At any given point in time, the bureaucracy had a sense of whether or not an item was dangerous, an evaluation based on reviews of pressures and variables affecting events. The Government of India was an important factor in the evaluation because only the center had the information and ultimately the authority to make all-India decisions. Until 1937, circulars and other instructions from the Governor General and Council fixed the guidelines and boundaries influencing action by provincial governments. After 1937, the ministries still operated in tandem with the center. The study of political developments changed with time. The Government of India tended to curtail freedom of expression during the two wars and in the periods of confrontation with the Congress. The dominant trend from 1921 onward, however, lay in the direction of relaxed controls. The transfer of power increased the government's toleration of public

6. For example, Shaikh Salim, *Katha Salwi*, a Muslim satire on Hinduism first published in 1852 and banned in reprint version, 1911.

criticism. Only violent writings and direct challenges to order were consistently subject to control. A demand for home rule, thought to be seditious in 1916, might be viewed as innocuous in 1945, for example, but a call for nonpayment of taxes or for political assassination could never be permitted to circulate.[7] All participants in Indian politics appreciated the drift of events by the 1940s. The militancy of the press, the restlessness of legislatures, and the growing legal resistance to executive action—these pointed to the futility of maintaining the repressive measures that had been resorted to one last time during the Second World War.

In retrospect, the British attempts to control Indian publicists had few long-term consequences. The bureaucracy did manage to exert legal restraint on approximately 2,000 newspapers between 1907 and 1947 and seized 8,000 to 10,000 individual titles. This action had immediate, tactical value. The government met challenges at key junctures by striking at the most visible features involved in unrest—organizations and printed matter. The Congress communication network was damaged in 1932, and in 1942 censorship resulted in an almost total news blackout on Quit India activities. Moreover, repression or the threat of repression had a psychological effect. Numerous journalists and politicians have noted the sudden—albeit short-lived—acquiescence of Indian publicists in the face of possible reprisals.[8] Controls temporarily tended to moderate the tone of the press and set limits on what was acceptable. They also gave the British a breathing spell and provided a sense of security in stormy conditions.

The colonial rulers nevertheless had neither the will nor the power necessary to maintain extensive controls when emergencies subsided. Once the lid came off, the groundswell of inciting publications, whether communal or anti-British, soon confronted the *raj* with a fresh crisis. Controls could not stem the tide of nationalism, nor did they appreciably affect Indian politicians. Polemical literature grew out of feelings over which the British had little influence. Banning and security demands dealt with symptoms, but the permanent solution to India's complex social, religious, and political problems awaited an end to foreign domination.

When the British withdrew, they transferred to India and Pakistan the legal and administrative apparatus accumulated in

7. Illustrated by the discussions of B. D. Basu's *India Under the British Crown*, GIPOL 1933, 48/6.

8. Illustrated by discussion in K. Rama Rao, *The Pen As My Sword*; J. Natarajan, *History of Indian Journalism*; Pattabhai Sitaramayya, *The History of the Indian National Congress*, II.

a forty-year struggle with the press. Indians already had experience working that machinery. Indian members of the I.C.S. aided the British in 1932 and 1942 and in those critical years helped to crush elements of disorder.[9] While in office, the Congress ministries championed a more lenient policy toward dissent, but when threatened by unrest, they too fell back on initiatives made possible by local press ordinances and the Defence of India Act. The same pattern persisted after independence. The chaos created by partition and the problems inherent in a rapid transfer of power led the Indian and Pakistan governments to rely heavily on force as a means of ensuring political stability. Police firings and security demands were common.[10] Once public life settled down, however, politicians had to decide if safeguards initiated by the British should remain permanently in South Asian politics.

The two countries pursued different courses. Pakistan kept most of the inherited regulations and added substantially to official power through enactment of the Public Safety (1949) and Security of Pakistan (1952) bills. In a continuing atmosphere of political turmoil, newspapers were censored, forced out of business, or brought under stringent security provisions. Freedom of the Pakistan press improved somewhat after 1956, but each subsequent crisis has been accompanied by a reversion to the type of controls under British rule.[11]

India also maintained significant press laws in the form of an amended penal code and special legislation such as the Press (Objectional Matters) Act, but restrictions have been exercised infrequently. Three factors have reinforced the trend toward relaxation of controls. First, the Indian judiciary interpreted the new constitution so as to limit official controls of printed opinion. The courts struck down precensorship and attempts to establish permanent security arrangements.[12] In addition, the emergence

9. An excellent description of the ambiguities and rationale involved in such action is found in N. B. Bonarjee, *Under Two Masters*, pp. 186–222.

10. K. L. Gauba, *Inside Pakistan*, pp. 109–10, 178–93; S. M. A. Feroze, *Press in Pakistan*, pp. 145–48; Majid Nizami, *The Press in Pakistan*, pp. 55–58; Rajendralal Handa, *Leaves From a Diary*, Pt. IV, 37. Local activities survey in *Chief Ministers Speak* (New Delhi: All India Congress Committee, c. 1950).

11. No solid research on press controls in Pakistan is available. Interpretation based on comments in Feroze and Nizami. Also valuable is *The Report of the Pakistan Press Committee* (Lahore: Pakistan Government, 1959).

12. Described in A. G. Noorani, "Freedom of the Press and the Constitution," in Noorani, ed., *Freedom of the Press in India*, pp. 24–35; Bharat Mishra, *Civil Liberty and the Indian National Congress*, pp. 83–120; *Report of the Press Commission* (Delhi: Government of India, 1954), I, 350–407.

of strong press associations has helped check bureaucratic interference. The All-India Newspaper Editors' Conference and the All-India Federation of Working Journalists, for example, have lobbied extensively on matters relating to freedom of expression. The A.N.E.C. played an especially significant role in the deliberations of the 1948 Press Law Enquiry Committee and its successor, the 1953 Press Commission.[13] Finally, India's relative stability has permitted the Congress government to proceed in a fashion consistent with the liberal policies championed during the British period. Communal incidents and labor disputes continue to generate sporadic bans and prosecution, and in emergencies such as the wars with Pakistan and China, the Indian and state governments have curtailed some press and civil liberties.[14] On the whole, however, India has been moving from the shadow of control of information toward an open society in which expression of a variety of views is permissible and even encouraged.

The British actions against Indian publications produced two final legacies. First, the formerly banned literature remains a source of bureaucratic controversy. According to the Indian Home Department's interpretation, the responsibility for deproscription resides with the provincial (now state) government that initially banned the work. The local administrations have not pursued that course, largely because of complicated procedure and lack of information on what actually has been banned and why. The works outlawed for colonial reasons therefore are technically proscribed even today.[15] In addition to inadvertently creating a lingering legal problem, British controls had one beneficial result. Although proscription removed a substantial amount of Indian literature from circulation, the process also led to the preservation of many works that probably would have been scattered and lost. Attempts to meet political challenge thus have produced a cultural heritage that should make possible a reevaluation of many yet uncharted facets of nation building in modern South Asia.

13. For example, *Press Law Committee*, p. 32. Also, background in Natarajan, *Indian Journalism*, pp. 174–75; Mishra, *Civil Liberty*, pp. 118–19. Branches of various civil liberty groups and unions played a similar role.

14. Noorani, *Freedom of the Press*, pp. 25–33, 126–36.

15. Based on interviews with officials at the National Archives of India, November 1968.

Part Two

A GUIDE TO BANNED LITERATURE

Section 1

COLLECTIONS OF BANNED LITERATURE IN INDIA AND ENGLAND

The British preserved four major collections of proscribed material, two each in India and England. A brief survey of how and why the sets came into existence is relevant because idiosyncrasies have developed in the depositories containing somewhat different types of publications.

The bureaucratic need to refer to previous legal action accounted largely for the attempts to collect copies of proscribed works. Secretariats often had to provide information on bans in response to questions from other bureaucrats, legislative assemblies, and persons in London. The central and provincial governments considered the controversial printed matter as much a part of their record system as departmental files and correspondence. It is unclear as to whether state officials maintained their references sets after 1947, but the Government of India did.[1] The copies in the Imperial Home–Political proceedings are now housed in the National Archives of India, New Delhi. The archives also hold a smaller set, the remnants of the Home Department's confidential library, which was transferred after 1947.

The Delhi collections currently are being deproscribed, a lengthy process because individual states must be consulted on release of titles. Although the material has as yet received little attention, the Home–Political annual index serves as a guide to the copies in the records, and a detailed handlist of the library holdings can be seen on request.

The conviction among British librarians that banned publications constituted a vital element of Indian literary output led to

1. The Punjab Records remained with the West Pakistan government; supposedly the C.I.D. records were destroyed after 1947. Some of the state governments probably maintain confidential libraries, and those may include proscribed works. I am indebted to the Director of the National Archives and especially Miss Dhan Keswani, R. C. Gupta, J. C. Srivastava, and Sourin Roy for assistance in working with the NAI collection.

the preservation of two additional sets in London. Proscribed material initially was not included in shipment of Indian books to the copyright depositories, the India Office Library, and the British Museum. In April of 1914, however, the Bombay government raised the issue of whether they should receive copies. The Government of India replied negatively, but the British Museum insisted on its legal right to possess all titles, not just those judged "safe" by the bureaucracy. At the same time, the museum's trustees offered to lock up controversial items until their integration into the public library might be unobjectionable. The India Office agreed, and the Secretary of State called for a reconsideration of the question because of the literary and "perhaps pathological" interest of banned writings. The Government of India reversed its decision and instructed local authorities to send proscribed items to London.[2] Most secretariats shipped two copies directly to the India Office, which kept one and sent the other to the British Museum. The Punjab apparently dispatched copies straight to the museum.[3] These arrangements were constantly disrupted; nevertheless, correspondence suggests that a stream of banned literature reached both depositories between 1914 and 1947.

The India Office Library opened its proscribed material in the summer of 1968. Although originally mailed in packets, the material had been thrown loose into trunks with little regard for organization or preservation of identifying documents. The staff of the India Office now have divided the tracts by language and have prepared rough handlists. The lists and specific items can be seen either in the general or special reading rooms. Further information on the literature is available in the Records section, particularly in the files of the Judicial and Public Committee and the Register and Records Committee.[4]

The British Museum also has made public its banned material. Museum officials kept the items in their original packets and placed them in cabinets. There the packets remained until the staff sorted them out and prepared handlists in 1968. Because the lists include a reference to every item, scholars easily can request material for use in the Student's Room of the Department of Oriental Printed Books and Manuscripts. As with the India Office Records, the museum's archives contain correspon-

2. Note by M. Seton, November 13, 1914, and correspondence in Register and Records, 3336 of 1914. Also discussions in Minutes of the Trustees of the British Museum, 1914–1926 (BM Archives).

3. Discussion in R&R 1930, 1382. Also background in 1932, 1955; 1930, 720.

4. Further information may be obtained from Miss J. R. Watson and Mrs. Usha Tripathi, India Office Library, Blackfriars Road, London.

dence, with descriptions of pamphlets, background of authors, and translations of controversial passages.[5]

Inadequate bibliographic control over the total range of banned publications makes impossible a final evaluation of what has and has not been preserved. The collections are nevertheless substantial, as indicated by this table on the holdings of the three libraries:

Banned Works in the National Archives of India, the British Museum, and the India Office Library[6]

Bengali	99	95	32
Gujarati	40	49	69
Hindi	581	216	594
Hindi-Hindustani		320	
Marathi	65	65	55
English		152	121
Panjabi	60	51	24
Urdu	190	168	110
Dravidian	110	53	61
Mis.	109	400	29
Total	1244	1569	1095

Each of the collections has a distinct character despite similarities and duplication. Provincial authorities apparently sent items to the Home Department until the 1920s, at which time the Keeper of Records became responsible for their maintenance.[7] The bulk of the material in the National Archives in India is in the Home–Political Keep-with (depository) section. The library set, basically second copies or titles saved for a special purpose, tends to cluster around the two non-cooperation campaigns. Books and longer works are heavily represented, with a small proportion of tracts and poetry. In addition, several bundles of periodicals (chiefly Socialist and Communist journals) have been preserved.[8]

5. Further information on banned material (15010.f.8) may be obtained from Dr. G. E. Marrison, Assistant Keeper of the Department.

6. Based on handlists of the various depositories. The "Hindi-Hindustani" reference in the BM lists is to Hindi materials written either in the nastaliq or devanagri script.

7. Correspondence in R&R 1930, 1382, especially Education circular March 18, 1931, and Bombay to GOI, May 12, 1931.

8. For example, the IOL has an almost complete set of *Kirti*, a Communist publication in Punjab, c. 1929–1930.

The librarians in England could preserve only the materials each provincial government chose to send. The initial shipments in 1914 contained both current and earlier banned titles. Both institutions received approximately the same material, probably a truly representative sampling of the printed matter proscribed between 1910 and 1914.[9] Dislocations caused by the First World War resulted in gaps in the collections. Shipments resumed after 1920, with the result that the India Office and British Museum held an abundance of tracts relating to Gandhi's first non-cooperation effort. The system lapsed again after 1922. Only the United Provinces consistently sent material to London.[10] Other governments had little interest in preserving the banned titles, a sentiment that was agreeable to the overworked India Office staff. In 1930, the India Office Library even suggested that shipments be totally abandoned.[11] The British Museum repeated its demand for copies, however, and eventually the libraries, together, demanded a more efficient dispatch of materials. After 1931, the British Museum became the primary depository for banned works. If only one copy arrived in London, the India Office was content to let it go to the museum.[12] The correspondence of the libraries indicates that, until 1947, the material collected came essentially through direct communication between personnel and provincial governments. The Second World War interfered again, and thus neither the India Office nor the British Museum has more than a handful of publications from the post-1940 period.

The London collections also have other characteristics. First, both contain large assortments of tracts—polemic titles 4 to 16 pages in length. The low price of the tracts (generally under 4 annas) reflected their purpose, the broadcasting of opinion among the widest possible audience. Second, neither library has many copies of newspapers. Apparently, individual numbers were not sent home regularly. Both have posters, although the British Museum seems to have the wider range. The museum is definitely stronger in holdings from particular provinces, such as the Pun-

9. Correspondence in R&R 1930, 1382. Approximately 75% of the first 300 items banned can be found in the two collections.

10. Notes in R&R 1930, 1382, especially IOL to BM, August 22, 1930.

11. The India Office preferred to keep only works in English. In fact, it had a difficult time trying to deal with the flood of vernacular materials in 1931–1932. For example, no library staff member could read Hindi well enough to catalogue the Hindi tracts in 1932. Discussion in R&R 1932, 1392.

12. For example, Circular 30–9, October 28, 1940, in R&R 1930, 1382, and also, discussion in R&R 1931, 2143.

jab, and in English-language publications.[13] The most obvious gap in the collections and in the following guide is the wide range of publications produced by Socialist and Communist organizations after approximately 1930. The British automatically banned any item associated with Socialist thought. This in essence meant that hundreds of books and tracts published in the West tended to be banned through appropriate Sea Customs Act clauses. While maintaining a checklist of such material, however, the Government of India made no attempt to preserve copies because of its ready availability in the British Museum or other depositories.

The Scope and Arrangement of the Guide

Several criteria determined the material to be discussed in the following sections. First, emphasis has been placed on the holdings of the official depositories plus items collected by the author and available on film with the South Asia Microfilm Project.[14] Second, only nonserial publications that could be examined at first hand have been included. The Bibliography does not treat two varieties of printed matter, the smattering of newspapers and the Keep-with materials of the National Archives, which were unavailable while the study was in preparation. There is one exception, however, to this limitation on the materials that are covered. If a work could not be traced, but was treated or translated in British proceedings, that information seemed to justify a citation. Finally, the author's language skills and the pressures of the time and space have narrowed coverage to English and North Indian vernaculars (Hindi, Urdu, Panjabi). The list thus comprises a comprehensive guide to the nonserial publications in specific languages and available either in the original form or described in official records. I hope to examine the remaining vernacular material and that in the Keep-with section of the National Archives at a future date.

Transliteration of Indian languages has posed a number of difficult problems. The various libraries have their own systems of romanization, while the Government of India apparently

13. There seems to be no explanation as to why the IOL does not have an extensive English-language section of proscribed works. Either the set was misplaced, perhaps during the war, or individual items were dispersed in the regular collection.

14. I was able to purchase several sets of the material from bookdealers in Lahore and Delhi during a visit in 1965, and over the last eight years stray titles have fallen into my hands. The 450 items in my collection and filmed by SAMP primarily reproduce the material available in Delhi and London. A positive film shortly will be placed with the Nehru Memorial Museum and Library, New Delhi.

changed its usage frequently. In this study, I have tried to romanize simply and along lines easily recognizable by scholars who are familiar with the languages. Diacritical marks have been omitted for two reasons: First, the British references left them out, and unless every title could be checked, adding marks would perpetuate inaccuracies because the originals may have been spelled in unorthodox fashion; second, conversations with Indian and Western scholars suggested that incorrect diacritical marks create unnecessary difficulties for those who know the vernaculars. These arguments also weighed against the temptation to standardize or to attempt to put British citations back into the vernacular character. If Western words, such as *Congress* and *English*, are used in titles, they have been reproduced as they would appear in English rather than in the varied forms caused by transliteration into Hindi or Urdu. Otherwise, the transliteration of names of printing presses, publishers, and authors has been based primarily on information from the title pages. I apologize in advance to relatives or associates of authors whose titles or names may appear in strange spellings. Although I have tried to eliminate inconsistencies, they still may remain in cases in which works were published in more than one language or in which references have been based solely on background in the records.

The banned works have been arranged in three sections (Religion; Anti-British and Secular Politics/Biography and Collected Works; and Patriotic Poetry), further subdivided by subject or issue. Many titles do not fit neatly into one category, but cross-listing and subject/author indexes should facilitate use of the guide.

Bibliographic information is arranged according to the following format:

a. *Title and Language*. G, Panjabi in Gurmukhi script; H, Hindi; P, Panjabi in Arabic script; U, Urdu. Works are listed alphabetically by title within each subsection because many are anonymous. This approach also precludes the need for a separate title index.

b. *Author*. The spelling of the names of authors as printed in the records or on title pages has been accepted. No attempt is made to sort out individuals on the basis of external evidence. Many items are anonymous, and in these instances, title information will be followed immediately by place of publication and publisher.

c. *Place of Publication, Publisher, Press, Date, and Pagination*. If the author or editor is also publisher, that will be indicated by a notation (pub.) after his name, and the information will not be repeated later. District or princely states, in parentheses, follow the place of publication when the information is available or appropriate.

d. *Location.* The following symbols are used:

BM—British Museum

CRL—Center for Research Libraries, Chicago, the depository for the South Asia Microform Project

GIPOL—Government of India Home Political file

IOL—India Office Library Collection

IOR—India Office Records Collection

J&P—Judicial and Public Committee file, IOR

NAI—National Archives of India Library Collection

PIB—Proscribed Indian Books, British Museum Collection

R.A.—Readily available in many libraries

R&L—Records and Library Committee file, IOR

R&R—Registry and Records Committee file, IOR

Exact references will be provided if a title has been catalogued (for example, PIB 41 indicates that the item can be found in British Museum, File 41; similarly, IOL F 1 is an appropriate India Office citation). Translations or abstracts will be indicated by "trans."

e. *Annotation and Cross References.* The degree of comment varies with the material and source of information. When background is not available, or if the title is self-explanatory, only approximate translations of the title will be given. Since most patriotic poems and songs are repetitive, no elaborate annotation is necessary except for occasional translation of titles. Cross references follow the commentary, or if there is no annotation, the location. Readers also should refer to the indexes for related works.

Section 2

RELIGIOUS CONTROVERSY

This section contains references to titles that deal primarily with religion and communal issues. Other materials related to similar topics (anti-British and revolutionary works) are in the third section. For example, literature on the princely state of Hyderabad sometimes dealt with Hindu–Muslim problems and is therefore included here as religious writings, or at other times with nationalist programs, which are discussed in Section 3. Cross-references are frequent because the subject categories are not always exclusive. Publications written by or against a particular sect have been placed together (for example, the Arya Samaj subsection contains both the organization's publications as well as anti-Samaj polemics by the Sanatan Dharm and the Dev Samaj). The material has been arranged by title. Posters and handbills (one- or two-page sheets) are grouped at the end of each subsection. Detailed discussion of format and abbreviations are in Section 1 of this Part.

Ahmadiya[1]

Balaghat-i-Hak (U). Sheikh Ahmad Husain. Lahore: Haji Badar-ul-Din Attar, Himayati Islam Press, 1936. 8pp. IOL 113; PIB 85; GIPOL 1936, 37/2.

Interpretation of Truth. Anti-Ahmadiya tract accusing its founder of being "a leading member of the Satanic Society."

Bayat-i-Razvan Ki Hakikat (U). Ghulam Muhammad, pub. Lahore: 1939. 36pp. IOL 51; CRL.

Ahmadiya tract, critical of other Muslim sects.

Gur Bachan (P). Manzur Ahmad Manzur. Qadian: Muhammad Inayatullah, Cooperative Steam Press, 1935. 8pp. PIB 101; CRL.

1. A Muslim reform and revivalist sect, founded by Mirza Ghulam Ahmad (1839–1908) and known for its attacks on other Muslims, Hindus, Sikhs, and Christians. The standard work on the sect is H. A. Walter, *The Ahmadiya Movement.* A new study, soon to be published, treats the Ahmadiyas in a more detailed and scholarly fashion: Spencer Lavan, "The Ahmadiya Movement" (Ph.D. diss., McGill University, 1970).

Ahmadiya tract, calling Muslims back to the sect's version of Islam, and claiming Guru Nanak was a Muslim.

Hansi Ka Gol Gappa Urf Qadianvala (U). Ahmad Yar Khan, pub. Lahore: Nami Press, 1935. App. 30pp. NAI; GIPOL 1935, 37/2.

Anti-Ahmadiya tract by the Secretary of the Majlis-i-Ahrar-i-Islam, Lahore.[2] In addition to charging the Ahmadiyas with helping send fellow Muslims to jail, the author defends a revolutionary, Bhagat Singh.

Hazliat-i-Mirza (U). Muhammad Shafi Sialkoti. Sialkot: Javid Book Depot, 1936. Trans. in GIPOL 1936, 37/2.

Absurdities of Mirza. Ahrar attack on Ahmadiyas. Focuses on how the sect allegedly undercut Islam: "Look at the hair-splitting and faith-consuming activities of the muddle-headed Swadeshi prophet of Qadian, who is a lover of tonic water, electuary and pearls, who sits on sofas and carpets, rides in motor cars, sows seeds of mischief, and teaches the lessons of slavery." The author says that the British created communal tension and use Ahmadiyas as a means of dividing Muslims.

Judgement of the Lahore High Court in the Case of the Murder of M. Fakhar-ud-Din of Qadian. Qadian: Bait-ul-Qadian, n.d. 10pp. PIB 114.

Judgment and commentary on a trial concerning the murder of a former Ahmadiya who left the sect because of factional strife and formed his own. The murderer, Aziz Ahmad, was convicted and hanged. Court record, pictures.

Kati-ul-Anaf-ul-Shia-ul-Shaniah (U). Lahore: Mohammad Yamin. Cooperative Steam Press, 1935. 32pp. PIB 107; CRL; GIPOL 1935, 37/2.

The Cutter of the Nose of the Vile Shias. Two-part Ahmadiya work. The first quotes from Shia writings in an effort to prove the sect heretical; the second hits at the alleged sexual and "unnatural" acts of Shias.

Khatam-i-Nabuvat (P). Abdul Vahid Haji, pub. Sialkot: Kaumi Press, c. 1935. 68pp. PIB 141; GIPOL 1935, 37/2.

Anti-Ahmadiya, anti-Christian. Claims that Ghulam Ahmad, founder of the sect, lived in filth and died "fittingly" in a latrine.

Khenchvan Ilham (P). Abdul Latif ("Afzal"). Gujrat: Iqbal

2. The Ahrars, a militant Muslim movement centered in Punjab, reputed for their attacks on Ahmadiyas and also on Hindu administrators of Kashmir.

Steam Press, c. 1936. 8pp. IOL 114; PIB 173; GIPOL 1936, 37/2.

Stretched Revelations. Ahrar attack on Ahmadiyas. Suggests that Ghulam Ahmad drank wine, ate pork, was a son of Satan, and a fool. Concludes with the note that the Ahrars will not be subjugated by the British–Ahmadiya coalition: "If the government proscribes this pamphlet, we have more ammunition."

Khenchvan Nabi (P). Abdul Karim ("Rahi"). Lahore: Alamgir Electric Press, 1934. 8pp. PIB 173; CRL; GIPOL 1935, 37/2.

Ahrar denunciation of Ahmadiyas. Labels Ghulam Ahmad and the sect traitors to Islam, questions their sex life.

Kukrun Ghun (P). Khadim Abdul Amin Muhammad Ibrahim. Lahore: Abdul Hamid, Feroz Printing Works, c. 1936. 8pp. PIB 157; GIPOL 1937, 37/1.

Anti-Ahmadiya, on sex life and ideas of founder.

Kya Mirza-i-Qadiani Aurat Thi Ya Mard? (U). Lahore: Hafiz Abdul Rahim, Gilani Electric Press, 1935. GIPOL 1935, 37/2.

A very controversial and strong attack on Ghulam Ahmad.

Mazhabi Daku (U). Amritsar: Mabahala Book Depot, Sanai Press, n.d. 136+18pp. IOL 87; PIB 95.

Novel on the Ahmadiya movement, with Ghulam Ahmad and his followers portrayed as lecherous men.

Mubahash-i-Tarak Mavalat (U). Delhi: Akhbari Itfak Hakai Press, n.d. 34pp. CRL.

Anti-Ahmadiya discussion between Syed Khafair Ullah (Ahmadiya) and Syed Abdul-ul-Barkat.

Muhammadi Gola (P). Ghulam Mohammad Khan ("Shok"), pub. Amritsar: Aftab Barki Press, 1930. 4 parts, 8pp. each. Pt. 1, PIB 29; Pts. 2–3, PIB 70; CRL; Pt. 4, PIB 70. Full treatment in GIPOL 1932, 114, 116.

Virulent Anti-Ahmadiya propaganda.

Navan Kisa Mirzaiyan (P). Muhammad Ramzan Caragh Din. Lahore: Inkilab Steam Press, 1933. 8pp. PIB 19.

Anti-Ahmadiya poetry. Examines nature of Muslim orthodoxy against backdrop of the sect's conduct, theology.

Nikamma Nabi Bam Tirtali Dave (U). Khadim Abdul Amin Muhammad Ibrahim, pub. Lyallpur: George Electric Press, n.d. Another ed., Lyallpur: Anjuman Ahl Hadith, 1937. 8pp. PIB 160; CRL; GIPOL 1937, 37/1.

Attack on the allegedly pro-British policies of the Ahmadiyas. According to the author, when Sikhs fought Muslims in Lahore, the Qadian newspaper supported official efforts to maintain peace. Calls Ghulam Ahmad a coward, badmash (very bad person), and a "foolish prophet with 43 claims." Apparently a regular commentator on the sect: "I have printed three books in his repudiation. In one I have made him crow like a cock; in one I have composed a poem in rhymes. I have become an enemy of the Prophet's enemy."

Panjabi Nabi (U). Pastor Peter Ditta Zahir, pub. Amritsar: Sanai Barki Press, 1936. 12pp. GIPOL 1936, 37/2.
The Panjabi Prophet. M.E. Mission criticism of the sect. Tries to show that Ghulam Ahmad was a megalomaniac, then describes his activities.

Qadian Ke Sar Yashrabi Gola (U). Ahmad Yar Khan. Lahore: Punjab National Steam Press, n.d., 2d printing. 8pp. PIB 101.
Attack on the Ahmadiyas and the sect's founder.

Rahmat Ullah Mahajit Batala-i-Yad-i-Raftgan (U). Muhammad Ibrahim Bhata. Gurdaspur: Majilis Ahrar Islam, 1938. 25 pp. CRL.
Anti-Ahmadiya.

Savalat-i-Muhammadiya (U). Maulvi Hafiz Muhammad Abdul Salam. Lucknow: Umdat-ul-Mutaba Press, c. 1934. 68pp. CRL; GIPOL 1935, 37/1.
Details on a Muslim-Ahmadiya controversy and background on a resulting court case.

Svadeshi Nabi Ki Lash (P). Karim Bakhsh. Lyallpur: Partap Electric Press, c. 1936. GIPOL 1936, 37/2.
Corpse of the Indigenous Prophet. Anti-Ahmadiya preface by a former member of the sect, followed by patriotic poems.

Qadian Main Panjtan Pak (U). Sayed Amdad Ullah, n.d. 1p. IOL 31, PIB 102.
Anti-Ahmadiya poster.

Arya Samaj[3]

Adarsh-i-Dayanand (U). Munishvar Dev. Rawalpindi: Arya Publicity Bureau, Lakshmi Art Steam Press, 1937. GIPOL 1937, 37/1.

3. A revivalist Hindu organization, founded by Dayanand Saraswati

Arya rejoinder to *Asli Sangit Dayanand*. Strongly anti-Sanatan Dharm,[4] critical of Puranic literature.

Aina-i-Islam (U). Hari Singh Khalifa. Delhi: Hamdard Electric Press, c. 1935. 136pp. IOL 170; NAI; PIB 105; CRL.
Mirror of Islam. Anti-Muslim work by an Arya propagandist just recently recovered from an assassination attempt.

Arya Samaj Aur Mussalman (U). Mahmud Qureshi. Madras: Shahi Electric Press, 1939. 32pp. CRL.
Criticism of Arya Samaj communal policies.

Arya Samaj Aur Uski Islah (U). Swami Raj Narayan. Lahore: Alamkir Press, 1937. 16pp. IOL 119; PIB 121; NAI.
Sanatanist abuse of the Arya Samaj.

Arya Samaj Ke Sir Par Sansar Ka Juta (H). Atma Ram Sharma ("Shok"). Delhi: Atma Ram Sharma, National Printing and Publishing House, 1938. 16pp. IOL B 281; CRL.
The People's Shoe on the Head of the Arya Samaj. A Sanatanist tract with sections entitled "Dayanand Was an Abuser of Saints," and "A Shoe on the Head of the Arya Samaj's Domestic Policy" (references to drinking and marriage).

Arya Samaj Ki Nak Men Nakel (H). Badri Singh ("Tanvar"). Bhivani (Hissar): Jai Narayan Sharma, Sri Ambika Printing Works, 1937. 52pp. NAI 65; PIB 25; CRL; GIPOL 1937, 27/1.
A Nail in the Nose of the Arya Samaj. Primarily Sanatanist poems already banned.

Aryon Ka Danka (H). Mahadev Sharma, ed. Calcutta: Ram Narayan Trivedi, 1937. 39pp. NAI 94; PIB 134; CRL.
Drums of the Aryas. Praise of the sect's tenets and attacks on other religions, particularly Islam.

Ashuddhi Tor Ved Ki Hakikat (U). Lucknow: Gentlemen Book Depot, c. 1928. 16pp. CRL.
Attack on Arya Samaj and Dayanand.

(1824–1883), which became a driving force behind militant Hindu activities such as shuddhi (reclamation and reconversion) and sangathan (self-strengthening). Background in Lala Lajpat Rai, *A History of the Arya Samaj*; Kenneth W. Jones, "Communalism in the Punjab," *The Journal of Asian Studies*, 28 (1968–1969), 39–54.

4. Sanatan Dharm Sabhas were conservative Hindu organizations created in part to contest the changes of Hinduism advocated by reform sects such as the Arya Samaj. The sabhas tended to accept the Puranas as a vital element of Hinduism's sacred writings (a point denounced by the

Astak Va Nastik Ki Partal Bajavab Kaljug Insan Ke Libas Men (H, U). Pandit Munishvar Dev Sidhant. Rawalpindi: Arya Publicity Bureau, Lakshmi Art Steam Press, c. 1937. 8pp. PIB 152 (H); CRL (U); GIPOL 1937, 37/1.

Justification of Samaj doctrines in reply to Gopal Misra's *Kaljug Insan Ke Libas Men.* Attack on Sanatanists, with denunciations of Puranic practices relating to adultery, meat-eating, and relations with prostitutes. Judged obscene and inflammatory by the British.

Dev Sabha Men Vedon Ki Appeal (H). Akhiland Sharma. Cawnpur: Kamta Prasad Dikshit, Fine Art Printing Press (Etawah), 1930, 2d ed. 70pp. NAI 7; CRL; R&R 1930, 720.

Reprint of articles in the *Hindu*, 1928. Arya attack on the Dev Samaj, in the form of a court case.[5]

Dev Samaj Ke Mutalik Inkshafa (U). Rai Sahib Jhangi Ram. Lahore: Azad Hind Press, c. 1923. 255pp. CRL.

Some Revealing Facts about the Dev Samaj. Arya Samaj attack.

Deva Dutt Darpan (H). Agra: D. D. Varma, Prem Pustakalya, 1927. 358pp. NAI 160; PIB 22; R&R 1930, 720.

Criticism of Islam and Christianity by an Arya Samaj preacher.

Din-i-Islam Aur Uski Ishait (U). Lahore: 1927. 32pp. PIB 54; CRL.

The Muslim Religion and Its Spread. Arya Samaj opinion on Islam.

Dhol Ke Pol (U). Pandit Munishvar Dev. Rawalpindi: Arya Publicity Bureau, 1937. GIPOL 1937, 37/1.

Criticism of the Dev Samaj, Puranas, in reply to *Kaljug Insan Ke Libas Men.*

Islam-i-Bahshat Ki Hakikat (U). Lakshman, Arya Updeshak. Delhi: Arya Sahitya Patshala, n.d. 404pp. NAI; PIB 79; CRL.

The Truth about the Islamic Concept of Paradise.

Arya Samaj, which itself stressed the Vedas as the bedrock of Hindu theology).

5. Another Hindu sect, founded in the 19th century, with strong claims about divine truth and inspiration usually repugnant both to the Sanatan Dharm and the Arya Samaj. Background on this and other Punjab sects in J. N. Farquhar, *Modern Religious Movements in India.*

Jebi Pistol (U). Prem Candra, Lahore pub. Lahore: Guru Datt Bhavan, 1937. 352pp. NAI; GIPOL 1937, 37/1.

Collection of Anti-Sanatanist commentaries, many already banned, and judged by the government to be a "foul link in a chain of Arya Samaj publications."

Khun-i-Darvesh (U). Kishan Cand Ziba. Lahore: Lajpat Rai and Sons, Mercantile Press, 1927. 114pp. PIB 62.

Drama on the life of Swami Shraddhanand, an assassinated Arya leader.

Main Ne Islam Kyo Chora (U). Mahasha Gyan Indar. Delhi: Omkar Press, 1925. 75pp. IOL 137.

Controversial Arya attack on Islam and the Koran by a Muslim convert.

Mere Pachis Minute (H). Pandit Mansa Ram. Bhivani (Hissar): Arya Samaj, Ambika Printing Works, c. 1937. 27pp. NAI, CRL.

Statement by an Arya speaker who claimed that he was beaten while participating in a religious debate.

Misraji Insan Ka Libas Men (U). Prem Candra. Lahore: Arya Pratinidhi Sabha, Hindu Art Press, 1937. 48pp. PIB 25; CRL; GIPOL 1937, 37/1.

Reply to Gopal Misra's *Kaljug Insan Ke Libas Men*, attempts to expose Puranic literature and sexual orientation of the Sanatan Dharm.

Pandit Buddh Dev Ka Juta Rishi Dayanand Ke Sir Par (H). Pandit Madhavacarya. Meerut: Atma Ram Sharma, Dharm Press, 1936. 80pp. IOL B 334; NAI 95; PIB 46; CRL.

On a Hyderabad debate between an Arya Samaj preacher, Buddh Dev, and the author (a Sanatanist). Buddh Dev hit a representation of Dayanand to prove that the Samaj's founder was not sacred (the debate centered on idol worship). Madhavacarya attacked Samajists for always going around beating people with shoes (figurative expression referring to insults) and being repulsive to other religions.

Puranik Dharm Ka Janza Urf Puranic Phakkar Ka Munh Kala (U). Vishva Mittar, pub. Amritsar: Aftab Electric Press, c. 1936. 113pp. NAI 190; PIB 152; CRL; GIPOL 1937, 37/1.

Attack on Sanatanists and especially Hindu publicists such as Gopal Misra: "It has become common with our Puranic brethren to reply to objections raised by the learned Arya Samajists against the absurd, stupid and immoral writings of the Puranas, by levelling absurd and baseless charges at the great personality of Rishi Dayanand." Pointing out Sanatan "absurdities," the author claimed "Sanatan Dharm" actually was a term with sexual connotations.

Puranik Pol Prakash (H). Pandit Mansa Ram, Arya Updeshak. Lahore: Bhim Sen Varma, Arya Sahitya Mandir, Jagjit Electric Press, 1936. 1307+4pp. NAI 140; PIB 46+215.

An Exposé of Puranic Hollowness, a reply to Kalu Ram Shastri's *Death of the Arya Samaj*. The tone of the tract is indicated by Mansa Ram's claim that "the Sanatanist religion is a mixture of several things; all rotten and defiling matter finds a place in it." Urdu version, *Puranik Pop Par Vedic Top* (Delhi: Candra Gupta Press, 1224pp.) in IOL 67, PIB 19.

Rampuja Urf Shaitan Ki Talim (U). Peshawar: c. 1937. GIPOL 1937, 37/1.

Sanatan tract, attacked Dayanand "in hell" and questioned the character of the Samaj's founder.

Sanatan Dharm Vijai (U). Khunja Lal, Lal Bhardvaj. Amritsar: Sahnai Electric Press, 1932. 248pp. PIB 19; CRL.

Victory of the Sanatan Dharm. Strongly anti-Arya Samaj.

Shashtrath, Arya Samaj Ka Khul Mandi (U). Pandit Mansa Ram. Lahore: Updeshak Svantranand, Aftab Electric Press, 1931. 127pp. CRL.

Religious Debate, The Arya Samaj's Open Shops. Samaj views of orthodox Hindus and particularly the Sanatan Dharm. Contains caustic comments on Sanatan approaches to women, literature, and magic.

Shivpuja Aur Dayanand Ki Ta'lim (U). Gopal Misra. Amritsar: Nazir Printing Press, 1937. GIPOL 1937, 37/1.

Sanatanist tract on the theme that Dayanand worshipped Shiva. The following quote reflects the tone: "It is my firm belief that a Hindu can never produce such an unworthy son as Swami Dayanand who employs filthy language in respect to his parents. I call him a Rishi in the sense that he was a master of sexual science. He was not a seer, but a butcher of hymns." Misra concluded with a letter to Pandit Mehr Chand Sharma, editor of the *Arya Vir*, criticizing *niyog* (special form of Arya marriage) and a poem: "The Arya Samajists call brave a coward who became upset on seeing a mouse."

Stri Shiksha (H). Shiv Sharma. Bareilly: Vidyabhushan Sharma, Arya Young Men's Association, King Press, 1927. 15pp. PIB 22; CRL.

Commentary on female education by an Arya preacher, who claimed that the British tried to prevent girls from attending school.

Surapnakha Ka Bara Bhai Arthat Pakhandi Pop Ki Behayai (H). Pandit Mansa Ram. Bhivani (Hissar): Pol Parkash Mandal, Sarvanand Press, 1936. 16pp. PIB 158; CRL.

Anti-Sanatanist, with particular reference to the writings of Badri Singh.

Surapnakha Ke Himayati Ki Nak Kat Gai (H). Thakur Badri Singh. Bhivani (Hissar): Lakshmi Narayan, Ambika Printing Press, 1936. 6pp. NAI 47; PIB 158; CRL.

Sanatanist tract, with controversial comments such as "The celibates of the Gurukula (Arya Samaj School) enjoy sex with she-asses. Is this the Vedic school? Dayanand has written that in order to become rich, one must practice intercourse with bulls.

Svami Dayanand Krit Granth Ved Anukul Hain (U). Swami Svatranand. Amritsar: Mahasha Ram Das, Arya Pustakalya, Aftab Electric Press, 1932. 1+279pp. PIB 19.

Exposition of Arya principles coupled with a strong diatribe on the Sanatan Dharm.

Svami Shraddhanand (H). Ram Singhasan Tivari. Ajmer: Diamond Jubilee Press, 1927. 20pp. IOL B 107; NAI 46; PIB 112; CRL.

Poetry on the life and murder of Shraddhanand, an Arya leader.

Vartman Bharat (H). Somdatt Sharma, pub. Lahore: Vidya Prakash Press, 1930. 224pp. NAI 161; PIB 67; CRL; GIPOL 1932, 114.

Arya Samaj production, by a former principal of a Sanatan College who converted to the Samaj. Poems on the Arya school system, Kashmir, education. Apparently banned because of criticism of Muslims and the Sanatan Dharm.

Sacrificial Scene of Swami Shraddhanand (H, U, English). Amritsar: Master Brothers, n.d. Poster. CRL.

Gory picture of Shraddhanand's murder on December 23, 1926, multicolored. In addition to the major scene in which the Arya Samajist lies bleeding while associates grapple with his

Muslim assassin, the poster has three other scenes: Shraddhanand leading a group of Sikhs and Hindus, an angel killing a Muslim, and Dayanand standing with Krishna.

Christianity

Bhonchal Bir Lashkar (U). Rawalpindi: Muhammad Abdul Razak Hashani, Lakshmi Art Steam Press, 1934. 16pp. PIB 158; CRL.
Anti-Christian tract by a Muslim publicist.

End of Axis Powers: Comfort All That Mourn. J. F. Rutherford. Bombay: Watchtower, Uniform Printing Press, 1941. 19pp. IOL; NAI 15; PIB 5.
Jehovah's Witnesses tract urging trust in God and suggesting that all men steer clear of politics because of the imminent end of world governments. Links Christianity and England.

The Finished Mystery. Pastor Russell. Brooklyn: International Bible Students Association, 1917. 592pp. NAI; GIPOL 1919, 370–89A.
Jehovah's Witnesses interpretation of parts of the Bible dealing with last events of the world, supposedly to occur in 1917.

Injil Se Baithaka Bazi Yani Kutiniti Ka Kam (H). Surya Narayan Singh, pub. Mirzapur: Visvi Sadi Printing Press, 1944. 10pp. NAI 51; PIB 210; CRL.
Attack on Christianity and the Bible. Claims that the Bible had been altered through the centuries to support various political ideas and regimes.

Padri Sahab Se Bacho (H, U). Ganga Prasad Upadhyaya, ed. Allahabad: Arya Samaj, Sarju Press, 1941. 8pp. H: PIB 132, 215; IOL B 161. U: IOL 174; PIB 215.
Avoid the Missionaries. Anti-Christian tract.

Pagans and Christians. W. W. Strickland. London: George Sandring, 1908. GIPOL Feb. 1911, 36–40A; R.A.
Criticism of Christian missionary activity, banned in 1911.

Shuddhi Se Nak Men Dam (H). Dayal Jhalu. Lucknow: Talukdar Press, 1920. R&R 1930, 720.
Primarily an Arya Samaj reply to Kutub-ud-Din's *Shuddhi Ka Kunch* (Christian tract attacking Hindu reconversion efforts). Also contains anti-Muslim material.

Hindu-Muslim[6]

Bahadur Rajput (U). Shanti Narayan Puri ("Shad"), trans., ed. Amritsar: Bharat Pustak Bhandar, Vazir-i-Hind Press, 1940. 192pp. IOL 178; PIB 215; CRL.

Exploits of Mahrattas and Shivaji, translated from Bengali. Fictitious account that stressed Hindu confrontation with Muslims, atrocities of Aurangzeb.

Bahadurane Hind (H). Ganesh Prasad Varma, ed., pub. Benares: Ramesh Press, 1939. 182pp. IOL B 26; NAI 88; PIB 3.

Historical sketches compiled from numerous books. Covers India, A.D. 570–1786, with attention to Muslim rule. Hindu nationalist viewpoint, highly critical of Muslim policies.

Balidan Citravali (H). Ram Gopal Vidyalankar, ed. 2 eds. Lahore: Govind Ram Hasand Varma, c. 1927. Calcutta: Vedic Press, c. 1927. 30pp. CRL.

On Hindu heroes, with pictures such as that of Guru Govind Singh's sons being walled up alive by Muslims. Colored illustrations.

Bharat Ki Dasha Ka Bhavishya Sudhar (H). Gorishankar ("Brahmacarya"). Bombay: Shiv Lakshman Range, c. 1941. 48pp. IOL B 166; PIB 134; CRL.

The Future Reformation of India's Condition. Partially autobiographical. Deals with communal relations, sharply anti-Muslim.

Calcutta Men Mussalmanon Par Aryon Ka Zulam (U). Motiullah, pub. Cawnpur: Razzaki Press, 1926. 2pp. R&R 1930, 720.

Two poems on Hindu–Muslim riots. Calls for Muslim unity.

Caman Islam Ki Sair (H). Shiva Sharma, Mahaopdeshak. Lucknow: Shyama Lala Satyadev Varma, Shukla Printing Press, 1930. 80pp. NAI 8; PIB 14; CRL.

A Visit to the Garden of Islam. A Hindu document written because Muslim preachers maintained in debates that this or that was not in their traditions. Severe indictment of Muslim history, theology.

6. For background on the communal situation after 1900, see the following: W. C. Smith, *Modern Islam in India*; Gene Thursby, "Aspects of Hindu–Muslim Relations in British India" (Ph.D. diss., Duke University, 1972); Hugh McPherson, "Communal Antagonism Between Hindus and Muhammadans," in John Cumming, ed., *Political India, 1832–1932*, pp. 106–23.

Can the Hindus Rule India? James Johnston. London: P. S. King and Son, 1935. xv+144pp. IOL T 16167; R.A.

A pro-Muslim discussion which argues that India is multinational, and consequently, Hindus should not be permitted to dominate the political system. The author, a retired I.C.S. officer, discusses Hindus' alleged treatment of Muslims and untouchables.

Cand Mussalmanon Ki Harkatain (H). Raghubar Dayal ("Arya"). Cawnpur: Narayan Press, 1928. 12pp. IOL B 327; NAI 122; PIB 22; CRL.

Bad Actions of a Few Muslims. Charges that Muslims oppressed Hindus and ridiculed the Hindu religion.

Chatpati Bhajan (H). Calcutta: Baidik Press, 1933. GIPOL 1933, 48/4.

Controversial poetry on Hindu–Muslim relations. Pro-Hindu; eulogizes Swami Shraddhanand.

Din Nagar (Zila Gurdaspur) Ke Pakistan Virodhi Sammelan (H). Candra Gupta Vedalankar, ed. Delhi: Prakash Candra Arya, 1941. 21pp. NAI 145.

Speech at an anti-Pakistan conference, Punjab.

The Face of Mother India. Katherine Mayo. London: Hamish Hamilton, 1935. App. 250pp. (primarily pictures). R.A.

Pro-Muslim review of Indian history, contemporary problems. Mayo spent much time on Mughal rulers, and then labeled Bengali Hindus as cowards. She also noted that Hindus sponsor child marriage, a theme in her earlier studies, and therefore were physically inferior to Muslims. Several paragraphs and pictures on Hindu–Muslim problems, riots (Moplah). Also, pictures, commentary on Kali worship, sacrifice of goats, assassinations, and terrorism. All in all, a very controversial book written from a naive viewpoint.[7]

Fughan-i-Muslim (U). Azhar Usmani ("Panapati"). Delhi: Anjuman-i-Islamiya tract 14, Bombay Electric Job Press, Delhi, 1933. 15pp. NAI; PIB 88; CRL.

Wail of the Muslims. Criticism of Hindu administration in Karnal, Punjab. Mentions alleged injustices and appeals to the British for redress, although noting that "just as it is silly to play a flute before a buffalo, so it is equally useless to call on Hindus for justice."

Government Bahavalpur Ki Ghair Manulishat: Javab (U). Multan City: Nau Bahar Press, 1936. GIPOL 1936, 37/2.

7. Background on Mayo in Manoranjan Jha, *Katherine Mayo and India.*

Defends Hindu Sabha activity in the princely state after a Muslim ruler arrested Hindu leaders.

Hamare Kaumi Hero (U). Bhai Parmanand. Lahore: Hindu Book Shop, n.d. 124pp. CRL.

Pro-Hindu study of national heroes (focus on Krishna, Kabir, Guru Nanak and Shivaji). Passages provocative both to Sikhs and Muslims.

Hinduism vs. Islam, or Islamic Teachings Scrutinized Through Hindu Eyes. Pandit Jnani. Madras: Arya Samaj, 1936. 16pp. NAI; CRL.

Criticizes Muslim theology, ethics, social values.

A History of the Hindu-Muslim Problem in India. Bhagvan Das, ed. Allahabad: Sundar Lal (Secretary, Cawnpur Riots Enquiry Committee), 1933. v+536pp. NAI 24; PIB 39; CRL. Urdu, Hindi versions, PIB 28.

Report of the Congress inquiry into the 1931 communal riots at Cawnpur. Presents the nationalist interpretation of the growth of communalism as well as detailed information on the riots. Charges the government with using divide-and-rule policy and suggests remedies to improve Hindu–Muslim relations.

Imam Hasan Aur Husain Ki Tarikh Yani Tazia Ka Itihas (U). Agra: Kashi Ram Jeval, Fah-i-Am Press, 1937. 8pp. IOL 94; PIB 77.

Attack on Islam in the form of a dialogue between Maulana Abdul Misri and Swami Parmanand. Particularly critical of Muslim historiography and customs, such as pilgrimages to Mecca.

Kalam al-Rahman Veda Hai Ya Quran (U). Pandit Dharm Bhikshu. Lucknow: Vishnu Svarup Vidyarthi, Dayanand Press, 1930. 392pp. PIB 45.

Questions the validity of the Koran as received knowledge and claims only the Vedas are true. Also, critical of contemporary Muslim leaders.

Katha Salvi (U). Shaikh Salim. Delhi: reprint, c. 1912. 8pp. IOL Urdu 1060 (earlier edition).

Muslim satire on Hinduism, first published in 1852 and banned when reprinted six decades later.

Khuni Cawnpur (U). Muhammad Ibrahim, pub. Bombay: Rahim Press, n.d. 8pp. IOL 126; PIB 183.

Story of communal conflict; pro-Muslim.

Khuni Coffin (H). Muhammad Matin Shamshi Naziri. Allahabad: Bhavisya Press, n.d. 11pp. PIB 154; CRL.

Poetry on Hindu–Muslim relations; call for unity against the British.

Khutba-i-Sadarat (U). Lala Kidar Nath. Ambala: Mujba Model Printing Press, 1928. 8pp. CRL.

Speech at Punjab Hindu conference, 1926. Anti-Muslim; goes into socioeconomic condition of Punjab Hindu minority.

Mister Jinnah Aur Inkishaf-i-Hakikat (U). Lahore: Giani Lal Singh Samundri, Propaganda Secretary, Sat Sangh Sabha, c. 1936. GIPOL 1936, 37/2.

Emphasis on Sikh and Hindu martyrdom; background on the agitation over the Sikh gurdwara at Shahidganj, Lahore.[8]

Muslim Faryad (U). Ahmad Husain. Meerut: Afak Press, n.d. 8pp. CRL.

Cry of the Muslims. Discussion of Muslim conditions in Hindu-majority regions.

Muslim-i-Khabeda Uth (U). Abdul Rahman. Cawnpur: Muhammad Abdul Karim, Intazami Press, c. 1930. 4pp. PIB 45.

Prose urging "lethargic" Muslims "to awake," lead a simple and pure life, and avoid contacts with Hindus.

Phajite Ka Gol Gappa (H). Master Gupta Jhalu, pub. Lucknow: Shukla Printing Press, 1924. 30pp. CRL; R&R 1930, 720.

Strongly anti-Muslim, a reply to *Gola Bel.* According to the author, Muslims always loot, burn and rape. After warning Hindus, the work makes fun of Muslims in the areas of sex and cleanliness. Muslims are challenged "to drink a cup of wine of Shuddi (convert), only then will you become a man from a brute."

The Real Sevaji. Saiyid Taffazzul Daud Sayeed Khan. Allahabad: Popular Printing Works, 1935. iv+224pp. NAI; PIB 35; CRL.

Muslim viewpoint of Shivaji, Mughal–Maratha relations. Also, comments on contemporary communal problems. Copies confiscated prior to binding.

Report of the Enquiry Committee Appointed by the Provincial Hindu Sabha, Lahore, To Enquire in the Bahawalpur Affairs.

8. The incident surveyed in Ganda Singh, *History of the Gurdwara Shahidganj, Lahore, From Its Origins to November 1935.*

Lahore: Punjab Hindu Sabha, c. 1937. 24+66+11pp. NAI; PIB 82; CRL.

Describes harassment of Hindus following a hartal in the princely state. Charts, evidence, lists of punishment meted out by the Muslim ruler.

Report of the Kudchi Inquiry Committee, Bombay, 1930. Bombay: 1930. 32pp. NAI; PIB 72; CRL.

Background on communal rioting in an incident in which Muslims in a South Bombay village were charged with exploiting the minority Jain community.

Report on Manzilar and Sukkur (Sind) Riots. Lal Cand Tirthdas, ed., pub. New Delhi: Hindu Mission Press, c. 1940. 16pp. NAI; PIB 3; CRL.

Details of alleged Muslim attacks on Hindus, February 1940. The author, a Sind Hindu Sabha leader, served as director of the Arya Samaj activities in Hyderabad. On the last page, a picture of a Mahasabha leader, V. D. Savarkar, calling for a day of mourning.

Risala Nau Muslim Da (P, U). Ghazi Muhammad Jamal. Sargodha: Akhtar Press, 1934. GIPOL 1934, 37/5.

Muslim attacks on Hindu views concerning cattle and other matters. Hindus supposedly made children drink unclean matter, visited the dirty Ganges for purification (at Hardwar "filled with prostitutes"), and practiced polytheism.

Sacitra Hasan Bin Sabbah (H). Prem Cand (formerly Shaikh Anamul-Hak); Devendranath Shastri, trans. Delhi: Murari Tract Society, Devidyal Printing Works, 1927. 62+2pp. IOL B 145.

Biography of a Muslim general and background on atrocities he allegedly committed on Hindus. Contemporary material on Hindu–Muslim relations.

Savan Ka Sahar (H). Sankhta Prasad, Govind Prasad, Kanhaiya Lal. Benares: Pandit Prabhu Narayan Misra, Sri Press, 1931. 16pp. IOL B 178, 407; PIB 6, 63.

On the 1930 Benares riots and communal tension. The concluding poems praise nationalism and the wearing of homespun cloth.

Ta'am-i-Hunud (U). Muhammad Basit Yarkhan. Bareilly: Mahmud-ul-Matabi Press, c. 1929. R&R 1930, 720.

Muslim tract on the theme of pollution from Hindus because

of their unclean practices. Also attacks shuddhi (conversion) and calls for a boycott of Islam's enemies.

Tarana-i-Shahidi Talif Kardat (P, U). Imam Din, pub. Gujrat (Punjab): Ikbal Electric Press, n.d. 8pp. IOL 50; PIB 51.
Survey of Muslim conditions, anti-Hindu.

Tuphat al-Hind (U). Nazir Husain. Delhi: Rahmani Press, c. 1925. 116pp. PIB 71.
Muslim interpretation of recent Indian history.

Vijai Pataka (H). Ramcandra Sharma ("Vir"). Sagar (M.P.): Akhil Bharatiya Ardash Hindu Sangh, Shanti Press (Agra), 1943. 264pp. IOL B 22; NAI 67; PIB 215; CRL.
Review of Indian history, plays up Muslim atrocities and Hindu heroes. Particularly critical of Muslim cooperation with the British.

Why Bloodshed in Sind? Sayyad Ali Muhammad Rashdi, Secretary Sind Muslim League. Lahore: Sind Provincial Muslim League, Calcutta Art Printing Press, c. 1941. 18pp. NAI; PIB 139; CRL.
History of agitation by Hindus and Muslims, 1937, at Sukkur (Sind) over control and use of a mosque.

Yadgar-i-Karbala Urf Bombay Ka Khuni Moharram (U). Muhammad Hafiz-ul-Din. Bombay: c. 1932. 8pp. IOL 129; PIB 183.
Poetry on Bombay communal riots.

Gomata Ka Sandesh (H). Ayodha Das. n.i. 1p. PIB 120.
Yellow poster urging Hindus to boycott Muslims. References to cow protection.

Masleh Shahidganj (U). Lahore: Gianai Lal Singh, n.d. GIPOL 1937, 37/1.
Poster on communal tension in Lahore revolving around control of holy places.

Sri Avodhyaji Ki Sacci Yatra (H). Gopal Das. Benares: Ramesvar Press, n.d. 1p. IOL B 436; PIB 126.
Handbill supporting cow protection; anti-Muslim.

Virbhogya Vasundhara (H). Rashtra Sevak. Bareilly: Bansal Press, 1946. 1p. IOL F 8; PIB 35.
Large handbill with quotations from Vedic texts. Appeals for Hindus to protect the cow and return India to past glories.

Hyderabad[9]

Arya Satyagraha (H). Satyadev Vidyalankar, pub. Delhi: Arjun Press, 1942. t.c., 290pp. PIB 207; CRL.

Detailed account of Arya Samaj and Congress activities in the princely state.

Hyderabad Bhajnavali (H). Tulsi Ram. Ferozepur: Madan Jit Arya, Goldsberry Electric Press, 1939. 4pp. IOL F 108; NAI 28; PIB 167; CRL.

Songs on the Arya Samaj and Hyderabad.

Hyderabad Neb Arya Samaj Andolan (H). Delhi: Hamdard Electric Press, n.d. 72pp. CRL.

On origin and activities of Arya Samaj agitation in Hyderabad. Speeches, songs, narrative.

Nazi Rule of the Nizam of Hyderabad. Hyderabad Civil Liberties Committee, London. London: Hyderabad Civil Liberties Committee, Wheatley-Farringdon, c. 1939. 12pp. CRL.

A propaganda pamphlet attempting to demonstrate that the Nizam "is deliberately attempting to stifle the rights and liberties of his 12,000,000 Hindu subjects." Narrative plus documents from newspapers and speeches.

Nizam Defence Examined and Exposed. International Aryan League. Delhi: Imperial Fine Art Press, c. 1939. t.c., 104pp. CRL.

A rejoinder to *The Arya Samaj in Hyderabad*, an official document which in turn was a response to the Samaj's *The Case of Arya Samaj in Hyderabad State.* The detailed case studies suggest that the Nizam, not the Arya Samaj, precipitated communal conflict.

Nizam Hyderabad Ke Dharm Yudh Ka Itihas (H). Govind Ram, ed. Delhi: Arya Sahitya Bhavan, Oriental Arts Press, c. 1939. 212pp. PIB 132; CRL.

History of Arya activities in Hyderabad, pictures.

Nizam Hyderabad Ke Satyagraha Ka Itihas (H). Tej Singh Varma. Mathur: Hindi Pustakalaya, c. 1942. 31pp. NAI 1.

Epic poem on Arya Samaj campaign.

Siasat-i-Momin (U). Abdul Samad Siraj-ul-Din, ed., pub. Hyderabad: Ibrahim Marke Press, c. 1930. 48pp. IOL 215;

9. Events in Hyderabad, a Muslim princely state, surveyed in N. Ramesan, ed., *The Freedom Struggle in Hyderabad.* Also useful is *Arya Satyagraha and Arya Requirements.*

NAI; PIB 64A; CRL.

Discussion of Islamic states, Indian politics, and the nature of the Hyderabad government. Anti-Christian, anti-Hindu.

Islam

Balae Huma (U). Asar Zuberi. Aminabad: Umdal al-Mutalabae, 1940. 31pp. PIB 200; CRL.

On Muslim history, deals with famous battles and compares them with contemporary struggles.

Dard-i-Vatan (U). Usmani Hamid, pub. Karachi: Abbasi Electric Litho Press, 1930, also a Delhi ed. 32pp. IOL 130; NAI 171; PIB 183; CRL.

Muslim grievances against the British, call for Hindu–Muslim unity.

Ilam-i-Masharki Ki Kahaniya (U). Munshi Zahur al-Hasan. Delhi: Lala Girdhari Lal, n.d. 24pp. CRL.

History of political leaders, particularly Khaksar and other Muslim politicians.

Islam Ke Gale Par Churi Ya Vafadari Ka Sila (U). Peshawar: Muhammad Azad Ghulami, c. 1931. App. 15pp., pictures. PIB 9; NAI; CRL.

The Reward for Loyalty is a Sword at the Throat of Islam. On the Khidmatgar, Redshirt movement in Peshawar.[10] Notes that while Sikhs were giving up their lives for religious causes, "how disgraceful it is for the Muslims to live."

Jamait-i-Ulama-i-Hind Ki Cand Aham Khidmat Ka Mukhtasar Razkara (U). Abdul Halim Sadik. Delhi: Mahbub Ulmatabae Electric Press, 1940. 42pp. IOL 132; PIB 132.

Short review of the activities of the Jamait-i-Ulama-i-Hind; critique of British policy toward Muslims.

Kanpur Ki Khuni Dastan (U). Khvaja Hasan Nazami. Meerut: Tauhid Press, 1913. 31pp. IOL 41.

The Bloody Massacre of Cawnpur. A description of protests over demolition of the Cawnpur mosque.[11]

10. Led by Abdul Ghafar Khan, the Pathan-based political party known as the "Redshirts" attempted to control the North-West Frontier Province. Generally adopting nonviolent techniques, the Redshirts nevertheless became involved in several bloody clashes with the British, 1929–1935. Background in Badshah Khan, *My Life and Struggle*, and G. L. Zutshi, *Frontier Gandhi.*

11. Partial destruction of a mosque in Cawnpur, U.P., sparked the cry, "Islam in Danger!" and became a major component of *khilafate* propaganda prior to 1914. Background on the incident and the Pan-Islam movement

Khan Abdul Kyum Khan (U). Mirza Sardar Beg. Lahore: Alamgir Electric Press, c. 1934. 8pp. IOL 112; PIB 150; CRL; GIPOL 1934, 36/6.

Poetry on conflict among Muslims over the nature of orthodoxy.

Khun-i-Harmin (U). Sayyad Ghafur Shah. Meerut: Hashami Press, 1921, 4th ed. 64pp. IOL 90; PIB 37.

On problems faced by orthodox Muslims when traveling on the *haj*. Critical of British, foreign treatment.

Kissa Ashik-i-Rasul (U). Ghulam Muhammad, pub. Lahore: Cooperative Steam Press, 1934. 8pp. CRL; GIPOL 1934, 37/6.

Background on Ghazi Muhammad Siddiq who killed an anti-Muslim speaker. Turns him into a martyr, asks all true Muslims to emulate his fervor.

Mohammed: A Biography. R. F. Dibble. London: Hutchinson and Co., n.d. 254pp. R.A.

Critical of Islam and its founder; banned when negotiations to prevent its circulation in India broke down.

Mutihida Kaumiat Aur Islam (U). Maulana Sayed Husain Ahmad. Delhi: Sultan-ul-Hak, Khoja Electric Press, 3d printing, n.d. 80pp. IOL 176; NAI; PIB 215; CRL.

A tract calling for Muslim unity and attacking virtually every kind of political activity not directed toward helping the community. Denounces the British, Hindus, Jains, and the Congress.

Paigham-i-Zindagi (U). Abdul Rahim Aziz, pub. Amritsar: Sanai Electric Press, c. 1939. 8pp. IOL 110; PIB 181.

Muslim attack on Hinduism, Sikhism, and British administration.

Rangila Rasul (H, U). Baldev Prasad Sharma. Benares: Hari Press, n.d. 47pp. PIB 22; J&P 1927, 1513.

Notorious attack on Islam and the Prophet.[12]

Sada-i-Bazgasht (U). Mirza Fahim Beg Cughtai. Agra: Notice Press, c. 1922. 8pp. IOL 115.

Criticism of British attitude toward Muslims.

Side-Lights on Muslim Politics. Zia-ul-Islam. Karachi: Pakistan Publishers, 1946. t.c., 7+104pp. CRL.

---

in Gail Minault Graham, "The Khilafat Movement" (Ph.D. diss., University of Pennsylvania, 1972).

12. Incident examined fully in Gene Thursby, "Aspects of Hindu–Muslim Relations in British India," Ph.D. diss., Duke University, 1972.

Pro-Muslim League series of articles. Strong denunciation of opponents, both Muslim and Hindu.

Twelve Against the Gods. William Bolitho. London: Penguin Books, 1939. 278pp. R.A.

Biographical sketches of historical figures, including a controversial commentary on Muhammad.

Vajh Zahur-i-Koran Majid (U). Hari Singh Khalifa. Delhi: Asmi Press, 1936. 32pp. IOL 171; NAI; PIB 83.

Criticism of the Koran and Islamic practice.

Vicitra Jivan (H). Kali Caran Sharma, Arya Updeshak. Moradabad: Vedic Pustakalya, 1925. 260pp. NAI 167; CRL; R&R 1930, 720.

Full-scale attack on Islam and especially Muhammad. Allegedly a response to similar criticism of Hindu deities. Plays up religious wars, sex life of Muhammad.[13]

Zarurati Hadish (U). Sialkot: Jamait-ul-Muslimin, Ikbal Electric Press, 1934. 8pp. PIB 86; CRL; GIPOL 1934, 37/5.

The Necessity for Tradition. A request for Muslims to unite against enemies (Hindus). Also argues for a re-evaluation of tradition and an expurgation of sexual references from sacred literature. Copious quotations from Puranas, trying to prove that Hindus, not Muslims, linked sex closely with religion.

Kaho Takabar (U). Khvaja Hasan Nazami. Meerut: Tauhid Press, 1913. 1p. IOL 6.

Poster protesting demolition of the Cawnpur mosque.

Mussalmanon Ko Jang-i-Azadi Men Hissa Lene Ki Davat (U). Maulana Husain Ahmad. Saharanpur: Congress Committee, Faruki Press, 1930. 1p. IOL 183; PIB 74.

Handbill calling for Muslims to join in the "war of freedom."

Paigham Janab Maulana Kadri Mohammad Ishak Saheb (U). Mohammad Ishak Ahmad. Allahabad: Government Press, c. 1932. 1p. IOL 29; PIB 47.

By the dictator, Jamait-ul-Ulama, Saharanpur, the handbill calls on Muslims to distrust the British and to join the Congress.

Kashmir[14]

Halat-i-Kashmir (P). Maulvi Muhammad Mahtab Ali. Lahore: Karimi Press, 1931. 9pp. PIB 6; CRL.

13. Thursby, "Aspects."

14. Background on Kashmir, ruled by a Hindu family, can be found in Barbara Neil Ramusack, "Exotic Imports or Homegrown Riots: The

Poetry on the "bloody lives of the oppressed peoples of Kashmir." Attacks allegedly pro-Hindu policies of the Kashmir prince.

Inside Kashmir. Prem Nath Bazaz, pub. Srinigar: Kashmir Publishing Co., Lion Press (Lahore), 1941. t.c., 412pp. NAI 33; PIB 215.

Historical study of economic and political conditions, with attention to agitation and the communal situation.

Kashmir De Zulm (P). Hafiz Amir Bakhsh Soz, Multani, pub. Multan: 1931. 8pp. IOL; CRL; GIPOL 1932, 149.

Poetry on Kashmir. One poem consists of a dialogue between husband and wife, with the husband finally leaving home to go to Kashmir and become a martyr for Islam. A second deals with alleged atrocities against Muslims.

Mussalman Voh Hai Je Na Dogra Se Dara Na Gore Se (U). Maulana Habib-ul-Rahman, president, Majlis Ahrar-i-Islam, Punjab. n.i. c. 1931. GIPOL 1932, 117.

The Muslim is He Who Neither Fears the Dogra Nor the Whites. Series of Ahrar statements on Kashmir; calls for united action against the British and the Hindu-controlled Kashmir government.

Safina-i-Nuh (U). Babu Faqir Ullah Khan, ed. Srinigar: Muhammad Nazir, 1932. GIPOL 1932, 150.

Lengthy treatise on Muslims in Kashmir, both prose and poetry.

Tere Kurban Mani Kashmir Ko Jane Vale (U). Attaullah Khan Ghaznavi. Lahore: Punjab Press, 1932. GIPOL 1932, 117.

On plight of Kashmir Muslims; hostile to the Raja of Kashmir and British support of his regime.

Zulum Utte Zulam Urf Kashmir Da Hal (P). "Feroze." Amritsar: Sanai Press, 1931. 8pp. IOL; PIB 6.

Muslim condemnation of Kashmir administration.

Khilafate[15]

Al-Balagh (U). Suleman Ashraf ("Bihari"). Aligarh: Muhammad Faruki, Ahmadi Press, n.d. 47pp. IOL 133; PIB 54.

Kashmir Disturbances of the Early 1930's" (paper presented at the Punjab Conference, 1971). Also, Prem Nath Bazaz, *The History of Struggle for Freedom in Kashmir.*

15. Discussion in Graham, "The Khilafat Movement."

Account of the khilafate movement in Turkey and its contribution to Islamic unity.

Ah-i-Mazluman (U). Saharanpur: Sheikh Anvar Ahmad, Faruki Press, n.d. 16pp. IOL 148; PIB 37.
Sigh of the Oppressed. Khilafate poetry.

Angrezon Da Tattu Almaruf Phauj Police Ki Naukari Haram (U). Hafiz Abdul Haq. Sialkot: Musaffar Al-Din, n.d. 8pp. CRL.
The Touts (Spies) of the British. A call for Muslims to withdraw from the army and police. The author claims that Islamic principles forbid work for the British.

Boycott (U). Maulana Abul Kalam Azad. Meerut: Mushtak Ahmad Nizami, Hashami Press, c. 1921 (4th printing). 12pp. IOL 106; PIB 37.
Statement urging Muslim boycott of foreign goods.

Come Over into Macedonia and Help Us. Constantinople: Le Comité de Publication, D.A.C.B., 1913. Reproduced as a supplement to the *Comrade*, May–June 1913. Trans., discussion in J&P 1915, 935.
Controversial khilafate tract.

Dard-i-Khilafat Yani Kalam-i-Ahmad (U). Natya Fikar Haji Ahmad, pub. Aligarh: Herat Press, c. 1920. 16pp. IOL 44; PIB 153.
Pro-khilafate poetry.

Gariyan-i-Hind (U). Muhammad Jamil-ul-Din, ed., pub. Bijnour: Nijat Machine Press, n.d. 16pp. IOL 153; PIB 56.
Khilafate poetry.

Gulshan-i-Khilafat (U). Master Abdul Sattar. Dharmpur: Sheikh Allahi Bakhsh, Kaumi Press, 1922. 16pp. IOL 152; PIB 56.
Khilafate poetry.

Islam-i-Jhanda (U). Riaz-ul-Din. Amora: Lakshmi Narayan, 1921. 8pp. IOL 190; PIB 37.
Khilafate poetry.

Islam Ki Faryad (U). Wali Muhammad. Delhi: Miverya Press, 1921. 8pp. IOL 142; R&R 1922, 1110.
Khilafate poetry.

Jahan-i-Islam (U). Usaf Manvah, ed. Lucknow: Amadi Press, 1939. 4pp. IOL 14.

Anti-British, khilafate poetry. Apparently reprints of material circulating two decades earlier.

Kaum-i-Taran: Azadi Ka Nuskha (U). Muhammad Haidar. Pilibhit: Bashir-ul-Avam Press, 1921. 8pp. IOL 108; PIB 52.
Khilafate poetry.

Khutba-i-Sadarat (U). Mahmud al-Hashan. Deoband: Kasmi Press, 1920. 12pp. IOL 54; PIB 52; R&R 1922, 1110.
Presidential address by Maulana Mahmud al-Hashan Deobandi on the occasion of the opening of Jamia Millia Islamia, October 29, 1920. The speech is an important appeal for Muslims to non-cooperate peacefully. Hindu–Muslim unity and protection for Muslim holy places receives attention.

Nazam-i-Vajahat (U). Vajahat Hasain. Lahore: Rafa-i-Am Press, 1914. 168pp. IOL 131; PIB 305.
Collection of Pan-Islamic poems, relating chiefly to the Balkan wars, by a former assistant editor of the *Zamindar*. Also attacks Italy and, according to the British, tended to inflame old hatreds.

Nirah-i-Jang (P). Syed Ali Husain, ed., pub. Lyallpur: Narindar Electric Press, c. 1931. 8pp. PIB 162; GIPOL 1932, 117.
The War Cry, Pan-Islamic and khilafate poems.

Phida-i-Kaum (U). Ahmad Husain. Moradabad: Matbua Printing House, c. 1921. 8pp. IOL 145; PIB 37.
Patriotic poetry, addressed principally to Muslims.

Shahan Shah-i-Kabul, pt. 1–2 (U). Hafiz Zahir Ahmad, Shahranpur, ed. Saharanpur: Faruki Press, c. 1920. R&R 1930, 720.
Five poems on Turkey, Pan-Islam. Message supposedly from the Amir of Afghanistan to the Emperor of India, another, the Ali brothers addressing the inhabitants of Karachi.

Tarana-i-Khilafat (U). Maulvi Misbah-ul-Islam Siddiki Aziz. Deoband: Kasimi Press, c. 1920. 16pp. IOL 43.
On Rowlatt Act, Punjab atrocities, khilafate movement. Calls on Muslims to join with Hindus and participate in a freedom struggle.

Tark-i-Muvalat Par Mofassal Tavsera (U). Maulvi Shabbir Ahmad Usmani. Deoband: Habibur Rahman, Kasimi Press, 1921. 24pp. IOL 53; PIB 52.
Detailed treatment of the non-cooperation and khilafate movements. Calls for ulemas to lead Muslims against the British,

supports communal unity. Appended is a speech by Maulana Mahmud al-Hashan.

Tark Muvalat Par Takrir Zabardast (U). Muhammad Mubarak Husain Mahdudi, pub. Meerut: Shams-ul-Mutaba Press, c. 1921. R&R 1922, 1110.

Pro-Muslim statement, *A Powerful Speech on the Non-Cooperation Movement.*

Angrezon Ka Zulam Aur Iraki Mukatal (U). Muhammad Jamal, n.i. 2pp. IOL 10.

The Tyranny of the English and the Iraqi Massacre. Probably an appeal to Shias to join non-cooperation efforts.

Bulbulan-i-Haryat Ke Tarane (U). Jaunpur: Jaunpur Khilafate Committee, Jadu Press, c. 1921. 1p. IOL 47; PIB 153.

Hazrat Sheikh-ul-Hind Maula Mahmud-ul-Husain Sahib Rahmut Ullah Ka Ek Zaruri Khat (U). Masud Ali Nadvi, Khilafate Committee, Aligarh, pub. Aligarh: Maraf Press, c. 1921. 1p. IOL 5; PIB 56.

Hindi Bhaion Ko Ek Mushfahana Nasihat (U). Muhammad Jamal. n.i. 2pp. IOL 7

Muhban-i-Vatan Se Iltaja (U). Muhammad Jamal. n.i. 2pp. IOL 9.

Rasul Allah Ke Roz-i-Mubarak Par Bolabari (U). n.i. 2pp. IOL 8.

This and the above five posters, handbills, contain poetry, anti-British themes.

Ulama Hind Ka Mutafika Fatva (U). Muhammad Mohsin. Shaharanpur: Dehra Dun Khilafat Committee, Bharatiya Press (Dehra Dun), 1921. 2pp. IOL 25; PIB 52; CRL; R&R 1922, 1110.

The United Fatwa of Indian Ulema. Fatwa signed by some 500 ulemas in 1921, endorsing non-cooperation and even civil disobedience.

Sikhism, Sikh Politics

Akali Bhabak (G). Patiala: Bhai Nihal Singh, Khalsa Agency, n.d. 80pp. IOL; NAI; CRL.

Poetry, prose on Gurdwara reforms and incidents at Nabha.[16]

16. Survey of Sikh reform efforts and the Nabha incident involving Sikh martyrdom in Ruchi Ram Sahni, *The Gurdwara Reform Movement and the Sikh Awakening.*

Akali Darshan (H). Cawnpur: Shiv Narayan Misra ("Pratap"), n.d. 100pp. CRL.
Lives of Akali leaders and Sikh martyrs; history of campaigns.

Akaliyon Ka Adarsh Satyagraha (H). Babu Sampuranand. Benares: Hindi Sahitya Mandir, Sri Lakshmi Narayan Press, 1932. 84pp. CRL.
Survey of Akali and Sikh movements, picture of Akali with his head split open.

All for Law and Order. Amritsar: Shromani Gurdwara Parbandak Committee, Onkar Press, 1922. 16pp. CRL.
Criticism of British treatment of Akalis.

Angrezon Ne Nabha Kikun Lita Arthat Tarikh Nabha (G). Harnam Singh ("Mast Panchi"). Amritsar: Punjab Khalsa Press, n.d. 210pp. PIB 61; CRL.
Why the British Took Over Nabha. Study of Sikh affairs and nationalism in Punjab.

Azad Di Garj (G). Rattan Singh. Patiala: Sajan Singh, Punjab Khalsa Press (Amritsar), 1924. 41pp. PIB 80; CRL.
The Roar of Freedom. Review of recent Sikh history and British policy toward Sikhism. Focus on the case of Ratan Singh, who was sentenced to five years for writing *Baghi Sikh Ki Sarkar.*

Azadi Di Khic (G). Bhagi Bhag Singh ("Nidharak"), pub. Amritsar: Coronation Press, c. 1924. 8pp. IOL; PIB 64A; CRL.
Poetry on gurdwara reforms by a member of a *jatha* (confrontation group).

Baghi Ki Ki Sarkar? (G). Bhai Rattan Singh ("Azad"), pub. Amritsar: Punjab Khalsa Press, n.d. 64pp. PIB 64A; CRL.
What is the Government of the Revolutionary Sikh? On Sikh politics and the princely states.

Bal Updesh (G). Lyallpur: Masat Ram, Om Prakash, 1938. 65pp. PIB 118; CRL.
Picture of gurus' torture, then primer with political themes.

Bhram Nivaran Arthat Kya Sikh Hinduon Ke Rakshak Hain? (H). Narayan Lal Gupta, pub. Delhi: Candra Printing Press, c. 1942. 26pp. PIB 134.
Rejects claim that Sikhs were the traditional protectors of Hindus, trying to show that Sikhs always sided with Muslims.

Bijli Di Karak (G). Darshan Singh ("Daljit"). Amritsar: Khalsa Azad Agency, Onkar Press, c. 1922. 64pp. CRL.
Sound of Thunder. On Akali politics and gurdwara reform.

A Brief Account of Military Sikh's Struggle for Religious Freedom. Gurmukh Singh, ed. Hyderabad (Sind): Sind Sikh Publicity Committee, Bharatvasi Press, 1921. 4pp. J&P 1920, 122.

On Sikhs imprisoned for wearing kirpans (short ceremonial swords).

Dukhan De Kirne (G). Feroz Din ("Sharif"), pub. Amritsar: Punjab Khalsa Press, n.d. 80pp. PIB 64A, CRL.

On massacres of Sikhs at Guru Ka Bagh, other encounters with officials.

Dukhi Parja Patiala Utte Navin Sahar Sati (G). Ujager Singh ("Bhaura"). Amritsar: Akash Bani Press, 1936. GIPOL 1936, 37/2.

On the princely state of Patiala and Akali Dal politics. Claims that the Raja paid Akalis Rs. 15,000 to support him, and that he secured the money through pressure on peasants.

Government Allegations Against the Sikhs Refuted. Hyderabad (Sind): Sind Sikh Publicity Committee, Bharatvasi Press, c. 1922. 80 pp. NAI; CRL; J&P 1920, 122.

Sikh version of their political activities, the incidents at Nankana.

Gupat Hukamnama Pathsahi, Kalghidhar Da Avtar (G). Bela Singh Akali. Amritsar: Sricandar Press, n.d. 34pp. PIB 88; CRL.

Poetry against orthodox Sikhs by leaders of the Udasis sect.[17] Contends that Sri Chand was a guru after Guru Govind; very controversial.

Guru Ghar Ki Durga Bhagti (U). Lal Cand Dhunna. Amritsar: Jagan Nath Handa, Sanai Electric Press, 1934. Muphat Dharm Prachar series 63 (Sanatan Dharm). 18pp. PIB 86; CRL.

Allegedly a Sanatanist call for Sikh–Hindu unity but, in fact, a charge that Guru Govind Singh worshipped the goddess Durga.

Guru Ka Bagh. Sikh Tract Society, no. 43. Amritsar: Sikh Tract Society, 1922. vii, 48+iiipp. CRL. Univ. of Calif., Berkeley.

Criticism of British handling of Sikh politicians.

Hirde Vedhak Bad Nasib Bharat De Bacchian Te Hoe: Zulman Da Asli Photo Asli Arthat Sarhe Itihas Shahide Da Khuni Coffin

17. A Sikh sect, supposedly founded by a relative of Guru Nanak, and highly controversial.

(G). Ranjit Singh ("Talvar"). Amritsar: Gurdwara Press, c. 1922. 128pp. IOL; NAI 25; CRL.

A Real Picture of Oppression, Or a Full History of the Martyrs' Bloody Coffin. Fictitious travel journal in which nationalism and religious sacrifice are discussed (attention to Sikh reformers and Akali activities).

The Jaito Affair. Amritsar: Shromani Gurdwara Parbandak Committee, 1924. 24pp. NAI; CRL.

Affair has been pasted over *Killing* on the title page, an apparent effort to minimize the chance of banning. Recounts the tribulations of Sikh groups trying to "capture" a shrine in the princely state Nabha.[18]

Jaito De Atyacar (G). Amritsar: Punjab Khalsa Press, c. 1922. 24pp. PIB 163.

Vivid description of the Jaito morchas (marches), poetry.

Jaito Vic Khun De Parnale Arthat Sakhti Da Har (G). Bhag Singh ("Nidharak"), pub. Amritsar: Coronation Printing Works, n.d. 111pp. IOL; CRL.

Poetry on Jaito.

Jivan Birtant Master Mota Singhji (G). Gyani Gurmukh Singh. Jullundur City: Desh Sevak Book Agency, Khalsa National Press, 1923. 144pp. PIB 163; CRL.

Life of Mota Singh, an educator and politician, leader of the Shromani Gurdwara Parbandak Committee and the Central Sikh League. Also contains his articles.

Kaidi Bir Bhag, Pt. 1 (G). Avatar Singh ("Azad"). Amritsar: Punjab Khalsa Press, c. 1924. 128pp. IOL; PIB 64A.

Poetry on Nabha, Sikh patriotism, Gurdwara reform.

Kala Te Gore De Saval Javab, Arthat Gora Shahi De Dhol Da Pol (G). Ranjit Singh ("Tajvar"). Amritsar: Akali Press, n.d. 16pp. NAI 191; PIB 64A; CRL.

An Answer to Black and White, or the Hollowness of Drums. A dialogue on British rule. Also references to Sikh problems, Nabha incident.

Kalgidhar Da Zahur (G). Ram Ganga Singh, Akali. Amritsar: Simla Printing Press, 1933. 36pp. CRL.

Interpretation of Guru Govind's teachings, stress on Sikh militarism.

18. Jaito discussed in Sahni, *Gurdwara*; Ganda Singh, *Some Confidential Papers of the Akali Movement.*

Kaumi Kahanian Arthat Dardan De Hanju, Pt. 1 (G). Pritam Singh, ed., pub. Amritsar: Khalsa Sevak Agency, Nirank Press, n.d. 88pp. NAI 154; PIB 64A, 163; CRL.

Collection of stories and accounts relating to Gurdwara reform and Sikh–British confrontation.

Khun Karhan (G). Ranjit Singh ("Tajvar"), pub. Amritsar: Gurdvara Press, n.d. 128pp. PIB 163A.

Anti-British, anti-Muslim novel.

Naukar Shahi Di Chati Vich Shantmai Gola (G). Bhai Bhag Singh ("Azad"), pub. Amritsar: Gurcaran Agency, Coronation Printing Works, c. 1924. 24pp. CRL.

Poetry, prose on Sikh politics and Gurdwara reforms.

Pardhangi Address (G). Rulia Singh, Lal Singh. Amritsar: Akash Bani Press, c. 1937. 26+16pp. PIB 180; CRL.

Speeches at Shahidi (martyrs) conference, on March 25, 1937. Focuses on Patiala, Akali politics, and the martyrdom of a leader in Patiala, Seva Singh. Attacks Tara Singh and the Akalis.

Patiale Di Sikhi Da Namuna (G). Patiala: Secretary of the Akali Jatha, Bharat Printing Press (Moga), 1936. GIPOL 1936, 37/1.

Attacks Patiala and charges Akali Dal and Tara Singh with compromise and use of foul propaganda. Claims Tara Singh should be ashamed proclaiming "the Patiala cigarette smoker to be the contractor of Sikhism."

Report of the Guru-Ka-Bagh Congress Enquiry Committee. Ruchi Ram Sahni, ed., pub. Lahore: Hindi Press, 1924. 68+xxi+352pp. 44 photographs. CRL.

Report on a massacre of Sikh reformers. Includes documents, evidence.[19]

Sakhti Da Har (G). Bhag Singh ("Nidharak"), pub. Amritsar: Coronation Press, 1924. 110 pp. PIB 64A.

The Flood of Oppression. Poetry on Sikh politics, Jaito.

Sant Khalsa Arthat Tavarikh Namdhari (G). Harnam Singh Svaich, Ludhiana, pub. Ludhiana: Satguru Ram Hari Press, 1936 (2d ed.). 36+34pp. PIB 174; CRL; GIPOL 1936, 37/1.

History in verse of Kukas and the life of Ram Singh, founder

19. Singh, *Some Confidential Papers.* The incident involved a massacre of Sikh reformers by the Hindu manager of the sacred Sikh shrine at Guru-Ka-Bagh.

of the Sikh sect.[20] The work apparently has two purposes. First, it tries to inflame Sikh militancy by referring to past bravery: "The British and Muslims mercilessly kill cows in your presence, O Sikhs, why are you alive in this world." Also, attempts to ingratiate the Kuka group with the rest of the Sikh community by underlining their alleged role as "freedom fighters."

Sardar Rattan Singh Azad Di Garj (G). Amritsar: Sardar Sajan Singh, Khalsa Press, c. 1924. 41pp. IOL; CRL; GIPOL 1924, 33/11.

Written statement in a sedition case over Rattan Singh's *Baghi Sikh Ki Sarkar?* The following indicates the tone of the tract: "If we had not sacrificed our bodies, minds and wealth and had not gone abroad and made other countries slaves of the English, we would never have suffered the hardships which are entailed on us these days while we are engaged in religious work [Nankana *Morcha*]. If the Sikhs had not obliterated all trace of the 1857 mutiny insurgents, not even a spot of the English would now be left. But such was our fate. We were misled into loving snakes."

Shahadat Namah; Khalsa Manzum (U). Naubat Rai Bali. New Delhi: Gurumat Vidayala, 1935. 32pp. PIB 99; CRL.

Controversial study on Sikhism; plays up militancy and spirit of martyrdom.

Shahid Sardar Seva Singhji Ashram: Adarsh Unnati No. 1 (G). Hari Singh ("Gardi"), pub. Patiala: Praja Mandal Riayasat, Punjab Literary Press, c. 1936. 20pp. IOL; PIB 120; CRL.

Eulogic study of the life of Seva Singh Thikrivala, who died in a Patiala jail. Critical of Patiala state administration.

Shahidi Di Khic. Gurbaksh Singh, pub. Amritsar: Punjab Khalsa Press, n.d. 8pp. IOL; NAI 193; CRL.

The Appeal of Martyrs, on reforms and Sikh politics.

Shahidi Parvane (G). Autar Singh ("Azad"). Amritsar: Khalsa Dramatic Agency, Punjab Khalsa Press, 1924. 32pp. PIB 64A; CRL.

On Sikh reforms, with attention to Nankana campaign. Ends with a call to fight the government and bureaucratic rule: "We shall never obey laws that interfere with our freedom and shall know no peace until we have attained religious and political independence."

20. One of the earliest Sikh reforming groups, the Kukas claimed their own guru and frequently were involved in struggles with other Sikhs. Background on the Kukas and the milieu of reform within the community in N. G. Barrier, *The Sikhs and Their Literature*.

Shahidi Sakka Jaito (G). Bhag Singh ("Akali"), pub. Amritsar: Sud Printing Press, n.d. 8pp. IOL; NAI 194; PIB 64A; CRL.

Poetry on the Jaito campaign.

Shahidi Yatra (G). Rattan Singh ("Azad"). Amritsar: Khalsa Dramatic Agency, Punjab Khalsa Press, 1924. 24pp. NAI 73; PIB 64A; CRL.

Drama on Sikh martyrdom because of Gurdwara reforms, review of four hundred years of Sikh history.

Shantmai Gola (G). Bhag Singh ("Azad"), pub. Amritsar: Gurcaran Agency, Coronation Printing Works (also Punjab Khalsa Press), n.d. 24pp. IOL; NAI; PIB 64A; CRL.

The Peaceful Bomb. Poetry on Sikh and Akali Dal activities.

Sikh Mazhab Aur Kesh (U). Gyani Vahid Husain. Qadian: Steam Press, 1936. 54pp. PIB 91; CRL.

The Sikh Religion and Hair. Criticism of Sikh practices and Akali, Sikh patriotic songs.

Udasin Panth Samiksha Aur Srautmuni Caritamrit-Dhvantadivakar, Pt. 1 (H). Maharaj Ava Dutt, ed. Jullundur: Svami Narayan Giri, Standard Press, c. 1939. 75pp. IOL B 83; NAI 185; PIB 92.

Tract on Sikh and Hindu religious practices, critical of the Arya Samaj and supporting the Udasis sect.

Zulam De Ban (G). Harnam Singh ("Mast Panchi"), pub. Amritsar: Sud Printing Press, c. 1924. 32pp. IOL; PIB 163; CRL.

Poetry on Sikh politics and non-cooperation, 1913–1923. Reviews incidents such as Rakabganj, Jallianwala Bagh, Nankana, and Budge Budge.[21]

Khalsaji Pind Jathe Banae Ate Bakaida Shastar Abhias Sikhe (G). Amritsar: Shromani Akali Dal, Guru Ram Das Printing Press, 1935. GIPOL 1935, 37/2.

Akali poster criticizing Muslim–British connections. Beginning with a call for Sikhs "to organize jathas in every village and learn the art of weapons," the author says that Muslims have been preparing to oppress Sikhs as in the past.

Patiala Di Sikhi Da Namunda Parje Ghatak Master Patiala Samjhote Di Mitti Palit (G). Patiala: Secretary of Akali Jatha, Bharat Printing Press (Moag), c. 1922. GIPOL 1936, 37/2.

21. The origins and major events involved in Sikh resurgence discussed in Barrier, *Sikhs*; Sahni, *Gurdwara.*

Poster on Patiala and Akali Dal. Compares the Raja with Aurangzeb in terms of practicing oppression on his subjects.

Sri Guru Nanak Devji in Mecca (H, G). Lahore: Arorbans Press, n.d. 1p. PIB 166.
Colored picture of Guru Nanak moving a mosque, an incident the British judged "inciting."

Zulam Di Had Hogai Nankan Shahivallan Sikhan Nun Khula Challenge (G). Amritsar: Shromani Akali Dal, Onkar Press, 1930. 1p. GIPOL 1930, 171.
Poster on police firing at Sisganj Gurdwara, Delhi. Call for prayers and non-violent meetings to oppose the British and Muslims.

Sunni-Shia

Asli Zalil-i-Nur (U). Kazi Fazal Ahmad. Ludhiana: Islah Electric Press, c. 1938 (2d printing). 28pp. IOL 93; PIB 169.
Anti-Shia tract, with extensive Koranic quotations.

Chappan Churi Ulmaruph Durra-i-Hazrat Umar (U). Muhammad Ata Khan. Saharanpur: Akhtar Hind Press, c. 1934. 242+8pp. IOL 42; PIB 69; GIPOL 1934, 37/5.
Sunni theological tract, anti-Shia.

Dur-i-Muhammadi (U). Maulana Maulvi Muhammad. Delhi: Azadi Electric Press, n.d. (5th printing). 8pp. IOL 95; PIB 70.
Sunni criticism of parts of the Koran and Shias.

Durzad Hazar (P). Ciragh-ul-Din Lahori. Lahore: Koh-i-Nur Press, n.d. 24pp. IOL 181.
Sunni tract, anti-Hindu and anti-Shia.

Husain-i-Mazlum (U). Shaukat, Lahori. Lahore: Kazi Habib Ullah, Sabir Electric Press, 1936. 48pp. CRL; GIPOL 1936, 37/2.
Sunni tract attacking Shias, in the form of a dialogue. Uses the *Encyclopedia Britannica* as an "unbiased," Christian authority in charging Shias with butchery and being "innovators of religion." Ends with a demand for a Shia boycott.

Indiva Vishiya Bagaval Aimmatul Mirza (U). Ghulam Haidar. Multan: c. 1939. 32pp. CRL.
Anti-Shia work, on Muharram and other Shia practices.

Intabah Shia Bakval Ulama Almarzia (U). Maulvi Ghulam Haidar. Multan: Nav Bahar Electric Press, c. 1938. 32pp. IOL 139; PIB 155.
Anti-Shia tract.

Kahar-i-Khudai Bar Sare Ibne Sabai (U). Alam Syed Husain Shah. Ferozepur: Steam Press, c. 1938. 52pp. CRL.
Fury of the Gods. Sunni attack on the Shias.

Kehr-i-Khudai (U). Syed Husain Shah. Ferozepur: Ferozepur Steam Press, 1937. 52pp. PIB 143; CRL.
Divine Vengeance. On Sunni–Shia quarrels.

Mahashar-i-Lucknow (U). Akhtar Mirza, Gen. Secretary, Jamait-i-Ahrar-i-Islam. Barelli: Ibrahim Husain, Alaram Press, n.d. 8pp. IOL 52; PIB 32.
Ahrar attack on Shias.

Mo'aviya Par Javaz Lanet Ke Sharan Dalael (U). Khalil Ahmad Chisti. Benares: Electric Machine Press, n.d. 92pp. CRL.
Defense of Shia festivals and ideology against Sunni propaganda.

Nur-i-Hidayat (U). Zahur Shah. Lahore: Sabar Electric Press, c. 1939 (6th printing). 64pp. IOL 134; NAI.
Theological treatise aimed at Shias.

Shahidon Ki Shan Ke Mutalik Sunnion Ka Iman Mutabik Talim-i-Kuran (U). Maulana Maulvi Abulnani. Lahore: Muslim Printing Press, c. 1937. 8pp. IOL 92; PIB 155.
Anti-Shia tract.

Tarikh-i-Shia (U). Mohammad Anvar Ali Khan. Mirzapur: Majak Jadid Press, 1940. 8pp. PIB 3; CRL.
Anti-Shia tract.

Zulfikar-i-Safdari (P). Inayat Ali Shah, Sialkoti. Lahore: Rajput Printing Press, c. 1913. 508pp. PIB 66.
Voluminous book on the first three Caliphs of Islam. Shia treatise, with obscene references offensive to Sunnis.

Miscellaneous

Akida-i-Islam (U). Abdul Wahi Haji. Lahore: Sevak Steam Press, n.d. 2 pts. 204+93pp. IOL 70; PIB 192.
Criticism of non-Muslim Indian religions, plus Christianity, Judaism.

Anukampa Vicar (H). Javahar Acharya. Bvyavart (Rajputana): Manmal Surana, Sasta Sahitya Press (Ajmer), 1930. 352pp. PIB 70.
Strong criticism of Jainism.

Dipmalika Ki Prasidi (H). Ajmer: Sri Ratna Prabhakar, Adarsh Press, n.d. 63pp. PIB 215.
Reply to K. L. Bafna's *Paryushanon Ki Bhent.* Attacks Jain opponents.

Exclusion of Hindus from America Due to British Influence. San Francisco: Ghadar, 1916. 23pp. IOL.
Charges the British with pressing U.S. officials to limit immigration of Hindus and to expel especially noisy opponents of colonial policy.

Morcha (U). Abdul Vahid. Sialkot: Matluba-i-Kaumi Press, n.d. 16 pts. app. 400pp. IOL 68–86; PIB 16.
Collection of essays on Christianity, Islam. Also anti-Ahmadiya.

Mulk Aur Kaum Ki Halat (U). Babu Jhuman Lal Jaini. Saharanpur: Faruki Press, c. 1921. 42pp. IOL 88; PIB 37.
Appeal to Jains to join in anti-British activities.

Social Conquest of the Hindu Race. Lala Har Dayal. Calcutta: 1910. Also, San Francisco, 1910. 22pp. IOL.[22]
Reprint from an article in *Modern Review*, 6:3 (September 1909), 239–48. Shrewd analysis of the relationship between Hindu religious thought and Indian political awareness. Argues that the British assumed the role of Brahman and continued domination of the Hindu masses. Focuses on why Hinduism supposedly went into decay and suggests how to reclaim past glory. Apparently banned only when reprinted as a tract.

Sri Sabda Bodha Prakash (U). Svami Hans Das. Ajmer: Pittha Ram, Rajputana Press, 1925. 315pp. PIB 70.
Metaphysics and study of Hinduism; not clear why banned.

Why Should the Devadasi Institution in the Hindu Temples Be Abolished? S. Muthvlakshmi Reddi. Chintadripet (Madras): Central Co-operative Printing Works, c. 1923. 14pp. IOL.
Speech on temple girls and their evolution into prostitutes.

22. I am indebted to Professor Emily Brown, University of Northern Iowa, for background on this title. Her study of Har Dayal, to be published shortly by the University of Arizona Press, will be the standard biography of an important Indian politician and philosopher.

Yad-i-Raftagan (U). Rahmat Ullah Mahajir. Gurdaspur: Muhammad Ibrahim, President, Majlis-i-Ahrar-i-Islam. Yogi Raj Press, 1938. 24pp. NAI; PIB 155; CRL.

Ahrar work attacking Shias and Ahmadiyas. Apparently sparked by the murder of an Ahrar leader, Haji Abdul Ghani.

Section 3

NATIONALIST, SECULAR POLITICS

This section on nationalist and secular printed matter is the largest and has been the most difficult to organize. Many works contain material that overlaps logical subject-headings, and therefore the reader is urged to examine the entire section or to use the various indexes. Related publications have been placed under one heading in an effort to minimize categories. Labor and Kisan (peasant) titles have been lumped together, for example, as have studies on British administration and recent Indian history. There is a separate heading for nationalist biography, but the substantial number of items on certain individuals (Gandhi, Bhagat Singh) or a group of revolutionaries (those involved in highly publicized conspiracy cases) warranted additional categories. As in Section 2, cross-references are frequent, items are arranged by title, and posters and handbills are grouped at the end of each subsection. Discussion of format and abbreviations can be found in the introduction to Part Two.

Bhagat Singh[1]

Amar Shahid Bhagat Singh (H). Calcutta: Sarasvati Pustak Agency, n.d. 16pp. IOL B 192; PIB 1.

Amar Shahid Deshbhakt Sardar Bhagat Singh (H). Badri Prasad Sharma ("Prem"). Mathur: Hindi Sahitya Mandir, Prabhakar Press, 1939. 64pp. IOL B 58.

Azadi Ka Ciragh (H). Benares: Babu Ram Candra Dev, Satyanam Press, c. 1931. 16pp. IOL B 112; GIPOL 1932, 208.
Collection of poems on Bhagat Singh, many banned previously.

Bali Vedi Par (H). "Yuvak Hraday," pub. n.i., c. 1931. 32pp. IOL B 351; PIB 8; GIPOL 1932, 116.

1. Bhagat Singh (1909–1931), a revolutionary who helped found the Hindustan Socialist Republican Army. On April 8, 1929, he was arrested for throwing a bomb in the Central Legislative Assembly. He and two associates, Sukhdev and Rajguru, were hanged for murder on March 23, 1931. Bhagat Singh quickly became a folk hero among Indian nationalists.

On the Sacrificial Stake by "Young Heart." Poetry on Bhagat Singh and other revolutionaries.

Bhagat Singh (H). Harash Datt Pandey ("'Shyam"). Cawnpur: Rameshvar Prasad Pandey, Sursari Press, 1938 (2d ed.). 32pp. IOL B 325; PIB 31.
Poetic biography of Bhagat Singh.

Bhagat Singh Ki Birta (H). Calcutta: Radhe Sham Pustakalya, c. 1931. 16pp. PIB 1; CRL.

Camakte Sitare (H). Raja Ram Nagar, ed., pub. Allahabad: Allahabad Union Steam Press, 1931. 8pp. IOL B 390; PIB 27; CRL.
Twinkling Stars. Patriotic poems on martyrs, especially Bhagat Singh.

Kajali Bombcase Urf Bhagat Singh Ki Phansi (H). Prabhu Narayan Misra, ed., pub. Benares: Sri Press, 1931. 16pp. IOL B 106; PIB 27.
Contains several poems on the life of Bhagat Singh.

Lahore Shadyantra Arthat Sardar Bhagat Singh (H). Benares: Kuber Singh, 1930. 208pp. IOL B 27; PIB 1.
Life of Bhagat Singh, generally excerpts from newspapers.

Mardana Bhagat Singh (H). Aligarh: Prabhu Dyal Dandevala, Rajendra Printing Press (Delhi), c. 1931. 16pp. PIB 8.
Poetry on Bhagat Singh.

Pyara Bhagat Singh (U). Mehar Ilam al-Din, pub. Lahore: Sanatan Dharm Press, c. 1931. 8pp. PIB 8; GIPOL 1932, 4.
Collection of poems on Bhagat Singh's personality, exploits.

Rashtriya Alha, Bhagat Singh Ki Larai (H). Comrade Surya Prasad. Cawnpur: Brahmin Press, 1940. 24pp. CRL.
Survey of Bhagat Singh's activities, also comments on agrarian conditions.

Sardar Bhagat Singh (H). Agra: K. L. Gupta, Adarsh Press, c. 1931. 40pp. IOL B 376; NAI 4; PIB 8; CRL.
Short biography, with poems praising Bhagat Singh's bravery.

Sardar Bhagat Singh. Jitendra Nath Sanyal, pub. Agra: Fine Art Printing Cottage, 1931. 129pp. English. PIB 8; NAI.
Detailed biography, eulogic in tone.

Savan Bam Case (H). Markande Mahadrij. Benares: Gauri Shankar Prasad, Arjun Press, n.d. 16pp. IOL B 386; PIB 27.
Poems on Bhagat Singh, revolutionaries.

Shahid Bhagat Singh (H). Calcutta: Shamhhu Prasad Misra, 1931. 16pp. IOL B 338; PIB 1.
Poems, prose on Bhagat Singh.

Shahid Sardar Bhagat Singh (H). Jaycandra Vidyalankar. Lahore: c. 1931. 16pp. IOL B 352; PIB 8; J&P 1931, 4245.
Poetry, prose on Bhagat Singh's life.

Shahid Sardar Bhagat Singh (H). Candravati Devi. Lahore: 1931. GIPOL 1931, 4/36.
Life of Bhagat Singh based on letters, conversations, manuscripts. Apparently detailed, filled with anecdotes.

Shahide Vatan (H). Calcutta: Bhartiya Pustakalya, n.d. 16pp. IOL B 235; PIB 1.
Poetry, primarily on Bhagat Singh.

Sirdar Bhagat Singh. C. S. Venu, pub. Madras: Kesari Printing Works, 1931. 80pp. English. PIB 38, CRL.
Eulogic biography.

Virlap (P). Amar Nath Ahluvalia. Lahore: Sanatan Dharm Steam Press, Lahore: c. 1931. 8pp. PIB 8; CRL; GIPOL 1932, 116.
Poetry, prose on Bhagat Singh.

Bhagat Singh, Rajguru, Sukhdev Memorial Fund Men Arthak Sahaita Dijive (H). Sushila Ghose. Cawnpur: Narayan Press, 1931. 1p. IOL F 100; PIB 27.
Poster appealing for contributions, primarily to honor Bhagat Singh.

Bhagat's Curious Present (H, E). Cawnpur: Ganga Narayan Beharilal, 1931. 1p. PIB 27; CRL.
Poster, Bhagat Singh giving his head to Mother India, who has a spear by her side. Caption: "Mother, For Thy Freedom's Sake, I Offer My Life."

The End: Bhagat Singh on a Cross. Ferozepur: Ram Saran. 1p. CRL.
Green and black poster. In addition to Bhagat Singh, pictures of other nationalists such as Tilak are scattered throughout the poster.

Inkilab Zindabad. Lahore: c. 1930. 1p. English. PIB 9. Similar poster, IOL F 55; PIB 37.
Poster in red ink on Bhagat Singh and revolution. Denounces nonviolence as ineffective and demands "blood for blood."

Sardar Bhagat Singh on the Scaffold. Lahore: Rattan Printing Press, n.d. 1p. IOL; PIB 42.

Poster of Bhagat Singh preparing to hang, as usual portrayed with a smile on his face.

Sardar Bhagat Singh's Wonderful Presentation (H, English). Cawnpur: Shyam Sundar Lal, 1931. 1p. IOL F 66; PIB 27; CRL.

Picture of Bhagat Singh giving his head to Mother India, with blood spurting from his trunk. Surrealistic, in black and white.

Boycott, Swadeshi[2]

A Brave Warning. n.i. GIPOL 1909, March 148–150A.

Circular on British finances and promissory notes. The anonymous author claims that foreign currency is unstable and calls on Indians both to rid themselves of the notes and to eliminate the British. Financial supporters of the *raj* are judged traitors.

Jang-i-Garha Malmal (U). Tohpha Ram Vaish. Khoria: Sudarshan Printing Works, n.d. 16pp. IOL 120; PIB 47.

Poetry on boycott and the necessity of using Indian-made products.

The Light of Swadeshism. Devi Prasad Mookerji. Bombay: Crown Electric Printing Works, 1908. 40pp. NAI.

On use of Indian products and the necessity for Hindu–Muslim national unity. Ends with a fiery religious appeal for a fight to rid India of "hideous poverty and degeneracy" and the cause of the condition, "blood-sucking countries."

Svadeshi Andolan Aur Boycott (H). Madhavrav Sapre. Nagpur: Vasudev Rao Limaye, Desh Sevak Press, 1906. 68pp. IOL F 103; PIB 140.

Essays on swadeshi and boycott, primarily reprinted from Tilak's *Kesari*.

British Adalat Bahishkar Divas (H). Benares: Satyagraha Sangram, 1932. 1p. IOL B 179; PIB 65.

Poster calling for revolt, militant boycott.

2. The swadeshi (buy only Indian goods) movement and boycott became prominent first in 1903–1906 over the issue of the partition of Bengal. Gandhi and the Congress made boycott a favorite political weapon.

Videshi Kapron Ko Chordo (U). Lakshmi Narayan Sharma. Aligarh: Aligarh Congress Committee, Riaz Press, n.d. 1p. PIB 52; R&R 1922, 1110. *Videshi Kapade Chordo* (H). Lakshmi Narayan Sharma. Aligarh: Sreni Press, n.d. 1p. IOL F 41.

Give Up Foreign Clothes, posters calling for boycott.

British Administration, India's Problems

Ag Ka Gola (H). Sevak Kundan Lal, ed. Lucknow: Ramesh Fine Arts Press, c. 1940. 9pp. PIB 138; CRL.

Poetry on India's rural conditions under the British, associates the freedom struggle with the Mahabharata wars.

Agle Sat Sal (H). Satya Bhakta. Cawnpur: Socialist Books Shop, c. 1922. 2 pts. 208pp. NAI 176; PIB 22; R&R 1930, 720.

Deals with the condition of India and makes predictions on its future, including independence in seven years, Hindu–Muslim unity, and Bolsheviks leading the country.

Angan Di Gavahi (H, G, U). San Francisco: Hindustan Ghadar, Yugantar Ashram, 1915. 48pp. H: IOL F 42; CRL; G: IOL; CRL. U: IOL 63; CRL.

Evidence of Statistics, #3 in the Ghadar series. Detailed study of alleged British exploitation of India.

Angare (U). Syed Sajjad Zahir, Ahmad Ali, pub. Lucknow: Nizami Press, c. 1933. 134pp. PIB 47; CRL; GIPOL 1933, 48/4.

Red Hot Coals. Short stories on the negative aspects of British rule.

Angrezi Raj Vic Praja De Dukh Di Kahani (G). San Francisco: Hindustan Ghadar, 1915. 32pp. IOL; CRL.

An account of the people's suffering under British rule.

Angrezi Siksha Se Bharatiya Sabhyata Ka Nas (H). Govind Ram Hasanand, ed. Calcutta: Vedic Press, c. 1934. 16pp. GIPOL 1934, 37/6.

The Ruin of Indian Civilization through English Education. Primarily, passages from letters of Sir Charles Trevelyan which pertain to the British goal of cultural conquest.

Angrezon Ki Bolati Band (H, U). Babu Ram Dunerya, pub. Agra: J&S Press, n.d. 16pp. H: IOL B 394; NAI 57; PIB 21; CRL. U: IOL 118.

An End to British Speeches. Poetry denouncing British rule and claims about Indian prosperity.

Angrezon Ki Daimphul (H). Lucknow: Gokarram Prasad Gupta, Nishad Printing Press, c. 1923. 8pp. IOL B 355, PIB 56.

British Damfoolery. Poems on British rule and alleged atrocities.

The Appeal of India to the President of the United States. Ram Chandra. San Francisco: 1917. 6+1pp. R. A. Stanford, New York Public.

Denunciation of British administration and a call for U.S. aid to Indian nationalists.

Arz (H). Shiva Lal Varyu. Jhansi: Anand Press, 1930. 24pp. PIB 21.

Request to the King of England on "misunderstandings" of I.C.S. officers in India. Some correspondence with bureaucrats appended, including documents in English.

Aupniveshik Prashna (H). S. P. Tripathi. Allahabad: Bhishma Arya, Madho Printing Works, c. 1937. 28pp. IOL B 307; NAI 27; PIB 100; CRL.

Short essays on the "colonial problem" and effects of imperialism.

Barbad-i-Hind (U). Govind Ram Sethi ("Shad"). Lahore: Narayan Datt Saighal, Washington Press, c. 1928. 64pp. PIB 26; CRL.

Barbadi Hind (H). Govind Ram Sethi ("Shad"). Lahore: Narayan Datt Saighal, Virjanand Press, c. 1926. 64pp. NAI; PIB 26; CRL.

India's Destruction. Historical drama illustrating how British merchants and bureaucrats caused India's fall from greatness. The final section focuses on the 1857 Mutiny.

Bharat Men Angrezi Rajya (H). Catur Sen Shastri. Delhi: Devi Dayal Printing Press, 1932. 323pp. PIB 42; CRL.

Nationalist commentary on British rule, with attention to the importance and effect of the nonviolence campaign for Indian independence.

Bharat Men Angrezi Rajya (H). Allahabad: R. Saighal, Fine Art Printing Press, c. 1929. 2 pts. 1+696pp. NAI 72; CRL; J&P 1929, 4580.

Nationalist interpretation of British rule, emphasizing Indian unity, imperialist oppression. The first part covers pre-1800 events, the second, 1800–1857. The Mutiny is portrayed as the first united effort to free India. Possibly by Pandit Sundar Lal.

Bharatvarsh Ka Itihas (H). "Ek Itihas Premi" (Lover of History). Benares: Gyan Mandal, 1925. 332pp. NAI 150.

Indian history from a nationalist viewpoint. Possibly an edited version of Bhai Parmanand's *History of India.*

British Government Aur Azadi Ki Lahar (U). Lahore: Caranjilal, Bande Mataram Press, c. 1930. 16pp. CRL.

One section (in English) involves British policies and the need to unify and throw out imperialists: "Every Indian wants the downfall of the English Empire; Between an Indian and an Englishman, a difference which we know; the Indians will be pleased to their entire; when they see themselves that out of India the English go." Another refers to British divide-and-rule policy and communal unity: "To you Hindus and Mohamedans, there is a request of mine, which when acted upon will prove most useful. That is, you should live like brothers, you both are the real sons of God."

British Justice and Honesty: Addressed to the People of England and India. Walter William Strickland. Milano: Walter William Strickland, 1913. 12pp. R.A.

British Rule in India Condemned by the British Themselves. London, Geneva: Indian National Party, 1915. 68pp. English, other European languages. CRL.

Excerpts from English commentaries on British rule. Filled with misquoted and, according to the British, nonexistent material.

The Case for India. Will Durant. Mysore: Mysore Congress Committee, 1939. 219pp. NAI.

Appraisal of India's economic and political condition. Condemns "bleeding" of the country and challenges the usual arguments favoring British rule. Reprinted to commemorate the 52d Congress session, Tripuri.

Condition of India. Indian League. London: 1934. GIPOL 1934, 35/3.

On politics and civil rights, with an introduction by Bertrand Russell.

Delhi Ka Rajnaitak Itihas (H). Rajendra Prasad. Delhi: Delhi District Congress Committee, Arjun Electric Printing Press, 1935. 217+223pp. PIB 215.

Political history of events in Delhi, with synopsis of earlier decisions by British administrators.

Desh Ki Bat (H). Dev Narayan Divedi. Calcutta: Adarsh Hindu Pustakalaya, 1932. 360pp. NAI; PIB 1; CRL.

Account of India's past, present condition. Emphasis on Western exploitation.

Desh Ki Bat (H). Mahadev Prasad Misra. Trans. from Bengali, Rav Vishnu Paradhkar. Calcutta: Metcalf Press, 1910. 452pp. IOL B 7; PIB 198.

Account of India's condition, similar to the Divedi study.

Devastated Bihar Through Jawaharlal's Lenses. Lucknow: Mohanlal Saksena, 1934. 75pp. CRL.

On the 1934 Bihar earthquake, suggests British mishandling of the disaster.

District Political Conference Banda Zila Jullundur, Presidential Speech (U). Sardar Naranjan Singh. Jullundur: Popular Press, 1936. GIPOL 1936, 37/2.

Address at a Jullundur political conference, July 1936. On rural conditions and British exploitation. Quotes Digby and other critics of foreign rule; pro-Congress.

Dum Kati Sarkar (H). Cawnpur: Ram Govind Misra, Narayan Press, 1922. 7pp. IOL B 209; PIB 56.

Government with a Cut-Tail, anti-British poetry.

The Emancipation of India. H. M. Hyndman. London: Twentieth Century Press, 1911. 16pp. IOL.

A reply to an article by John Morley in *The Nineteenth Century*. A Socialist leader, Hyndman had attacked Morley's ideas on the condition of India and its political progress. When the editor rejected the rejoinder, Hyndman published his essay independently.

A Few Facts About British Rule in India. San Francisco: Hindustan Ghadar, 1915. 12pp. CRL.

Focus on economic policies. Begins with "Why does India hate the British? The answer follows." Addressed to a Western audience.

Ghulam Za Zaher, Ghulam Ki Atma (U). Har Dayal. San Francisco: Hindustan Ghadar Press, n.d. 16pp. IOL 64.

Two essays on the enslavement of India by the British.

India. Richard Congreve, ed., with introduction by Shyamji Krishnavarma. London: A. Bonner, 1907. 40pp.

Commentary on the problems of confrontation between Western civilization and Indian administration. Highly critical of British rule, with a subtitle "Denying England's Right to Retain Her Indian Possessions." Originally published in 1857.

India in Bondage: Her Right to Freedom. Jabez Thomas Sunderland. Calcutta: R. Chatterjee, Prabasi Press, 1928 (2d ed.). New York edition, Lewis Copeland, 1932. xxii+589pp. J&P 1929, 2422, 4580. R.A.

Pro-Indian survey of politics and civilization. Points out harmful effects of British rule. The author, a British Unitarian, spent time in the subcontinent.

India: Her Position Today. G. S. Dara, pub. London: c. 1926. 32pp. BM 08023.dd.30.

The author (editor of *Hind*, a London newspaper), publishes extracts, speeches, quotations relating to Akali activities, the Congress, Gandhi, and British rule. The front page of the work has a photograph of Indians caught in famine, down to skin and bone, with this caption: "The Rightful Owners of Kohinur and the Peacock Throne" (artifacts alegedly taken from India by Englishmen).

India under British Rule. Sati Sadan Gyan, ed. Benares: Deshbandhu Palli Sanskar Samiti, Arjun Press, n.d. 40pp. NAI; PIB 71; CRL.

Part of the "National Propaganda Series." Statistics and narrative on the decline of indigenous industry during British occupation and its revival under Gandhi's programs.

Insaf Ka Khun (U). Pandit Shiv Lal Vismil, Lyallpuri. Lyallpur: Narendar Electric Press, 1931. 32pp. PIB 8; CRL.

The Blood of Justice. Alleged samples of British misrule. Presents the case of Bal Devi Singh, who reported an officer who killed a worker while driving. Singh was immediately jailed. Also, examines the case of a European dog biting an Indian (who was then jailed for three years on accusations by the hysterical owner). Charges use of bayonets, calls for revolution.

Jab Angrez Ave (H). Akshay Kumar Maitrey. Ajmer: Sasta Sahitya Mandal, Sasta Sahitya Press, 1930. 272pp. IOL B 41.

When the British Came. History of India from nationalist viewpoint.

Jansamudai Ki Ram Kahani (H). Radhakrishna Toshnival. Ajmer: Rajasthan Hindi Upasna Mandir, Adarsh Press, 1937. 60pp. IOL B 299; PIB 119.

Indian history, with critique of the British and Muslim rulers.

Jvala Mukhi Arthat Dabi Hui Ag (H). Gopinath Vaid. Bijnour: Congress Committee, Caitanya Printing Press, 1930. 12pp. IOL B 202; PIB 72; CRL.

Volcano or the Flames of Suppressed Fire. Political tract written in simple Hindi for distribution to villagers. Offered as a model for contacting the masses; focuses on how a "swarm of locusts," the British, ravaged India.

Khuni Ghadar (P). Thakur Singh, pub. Amritsar: Sud Printing Press, c. 1924. 320pp. GIPOL 1925, 33/11.
Reinterpretation of recent Indian history. Attention paid to the actions of Warren Hastings, exploitation of indigo, British atrocities during the 1857 Mutiny, and treatment of Dhuleep Singh (deposed son of Ranjit Singh, ruler of Punjab).

Khuni Raj (H). Ashpha Kulla Khan. Delhi: Pathak and Co., c. 1930. 130pp. IOL B 133.
Criticism of British rule; short biographies of national heroes.

Koza Men Darya (U). Babu Ram Garg. Muzaffanagar: Svarajya Press, also, Hamdard Press, c. 1920 (2d printing). 24pp. IOL 157; PIB 56.
Anti-British prose on economic conditions of working class and British exploitation.

Mamla Na Den Da Morcha (P). Lahore: c. 1931. GIPOL 1932, 149.
Charges British with being parasites who eat eggs, drink, run cars, are racist, and earn money in India and then send it to England. Some attention to land revenue and conditions among peasants. Ends with a call for total revolt.

The Methods of the Indian Police in the 20th Century. San Francisco: Hindustan Ghadar, 1915. 30pp. CRL; J&P 1910, 1714.
Originally published in *Nation*, 1910. Series of case studies designed to highlight British savagery.

Must England Lose India? Arthur Carre Osburn. New York: Alfred Knopf, 1930. 280pp. J&P 1930, 1602. R.A.
Critique of British administration by a former military officer stationed in India.

The New Indian Rope Trick. Reginald Reynolds. London: Indian Freedom Campaign Committee, 1944. 16pp. GIPOL 1944, 41/1.
Focuses on Indian national debt, indicts British rule.

An Open Letter to Count Leo Tolstoy in Reply to his "Letter to a Hindoo." Tarak Nath Das. New York: Free Hindustan, 1909. 47pp. IOL.

On Indian conditions, filled with quotations from British documents and other Western sources.

Opinions of English Socialist Leaders on British Rule in India. Indian National Party. Stockholm: c. 1916. 24 pp. NY.P.
A collection of anti-British commentaries.

Proclamation of Liberty. n.p. n.d. c. 1913. 9pp. IOL.
On British domination; plays up famine and economic exploitation and ends with the claim that India has been turned into the land of the white man.

Pyam-i-Ali (P). Syed Ali Husain Ali. Lyallpur: Narendar Electric Press, c. 1931. GIPOL 1932, 13–14A.
Fiery poetry on British rule. Hits imperialism, tyranny. Ends with a challenge to kill all Englishmen, who are enemies of the Muslim faith and the Indian nation.

The Ruin of India By British Rule. Henry Max Hyndman. London: 20th Century Press, 1907. 16pp. IOL; BM 8023.cc.35; J&P 1907, 2198.
Report of the Socialist Democratic Federation to the International Socialist Congress, Stuttgart. Focus on economic exploitation.

Self-Government for India, Demanded by the Indian National Congress and the All-India Moslem League, Lucknow, December 1916. Stockholm: Indian Nationalist Committee, c. 1917. 76pp. IOL.
Introduction and documents from the 1916 Unity meeting of the Congress and League. Strong indictment of British rule and especially economic and cultural repression.

Shahid-i-Azadi (U). Ram Manohar Lohia. Delhi: Muktba Jamial, Mahbub-ul-Mataba Electric Press, 1938 (2d printing). 83pp. IOL 177; NAI; CRL.
Essays on the nature of freedom and India's position under the British.

Sidelights on India. John D. Barry. San Francisco: 1912. 15pp. IOL; University of California; CRL (Xerox).
Articles, reprinted from the *San Francisco Bulletin*, based on an interchange between Barry and Har Dayal.[3] Discusses darbars (extravagant public audiences), conditions in India.

3. Background on Har Dayal, a leading publicist in the U.S., can be found in Dharmavira, *Har Dayal*, and Emily Brown's forthcoming biography, to be published by the University of Arizona Press.

Some American Opinion on British Rule in India. Stockholm: Indian Nationalist Committee, 1917. 68pp. IOL.

Short introduction on the evils of British rule, then quotes from William Bryan, Hearst, and La Follette.

Tarikh-i-Hind (U). Bhai Parmanand. San Francisco: Hindustan Ghadar, c. 1918. 384pp. IOL 66; PIB 206; CRL. Also, reprinted on numerous occasions.

History of India, interspersed with criticism of the British and "vilification" (according to the I.C.S. reviewer). The chapter on the 1857 Mutiny was judged especially dangerous, as was the account of Sikh revivalism and the 1871 outbreak of a Sikh sect, the Kukas, in the Punjab.

The White Terror in India, Being the Second Appeal of the Savarkar Release Committee. Guy Alfred, ed. London: Savarkar Release Committee, 1910. 4pp. IOL.

On British policies toward politics and press controls in India. Concludes with a call for working-class unity and rebellion.

Why India is in Revolt against British Rule. London: Indian National Party, 1916 (8th ed.). 32pp. IOL; CRL; Berkeley.

Lengthy indictment of British rule, with details and comments by Englishmen.

William Jennings Bryan on British Rule in India. n.i. 14pp. CRL; GIPOL 1910, 127–130A. Also, Urdu version, IOL 60.

Excerpts from articles by the Secretary of State, U.S.A., highly critical of British rule. Charges Indian government with worse repression than Russia.

Zabt Shudah Kitab Bharat Men Angrez Raj (U). n.i., c. 1930. 8 pp. PIB 29.

Survey of British rule, emphasis on alleged atrocities.

Abru Sarkar Ki (H). Gorakhpur: Madhav Tripathi, Seva Press, n.d. 1p. IOL F 113; PIB 56; R&R 1930, 720.

Dignity of Government. Handbill on British oppression.

Atyacari Naukarshahi Se Kuch Mahatvapuran Prashna (H). "Ek Rashtriya Premi" (A Lover of the Nation). Calcutta: c. 1931. IOL F 21; PIB 9.

Mimeographed condemnation of British rule, *Some Important Questions to the Oppressive Bureaucracy.*

The Balance Sheet of British Rule in India. San Francisco: Hindustan Ghadar, n.d. 1p. CRL.

Extract from the revolutionary Ghadar journal, on the "drain theory" of British economic policy and alleged exploitation.

Bandar Bant (G). n.i., c. 1932. 2pp. PIB 9; CRL.
Broadsheet charging the British with divide and rule.

Bharat Ki Loot (H). Deva Narayan Varma. n.i. 1p. IOL F 56; PIB 63.
Pictures of Europeans taking food from starving Indians. Quotes from Englishmen such as Charles Elliott, James Mill, Digby.

Dhysan Se Parhiye (H). Kanhaiya Lal Gautam. n.i. 1p. PIB 67.
Poster with anti-British commentary.

Ghadar (H). Delhi: Sarasvati Pustak Bhandar, Congress Press, n.d. 1p. IOL F 81.
Large poster, app. 2′×3′. In the form of questions and answers on British rule.

Svarajya Kaise Milega (H). Radha Mohan Gokulji. Cawnpur: Brahman Press, 1931. 1p. IOL F 89; PIB 74.
Observations on India's poverty and the necessity of freedom.

Communism, Socialism[4]

Atyacari Shasan Ka Ant (H). "Suresh," ed. Delhi: Lakshman Pathik, Rajendra Printing Press, c. 1931. 92pp. IOL B 65; PIB 42; CRL.
The End of the Rule of Tyranny. A Communist tract with extracts from books on the Russian revolution, and a discussion of the Indian situation. Focus on revolutionary movements in India and the potential for mass uprising.

Bharatiya Samyavadi Dal (H). Satya Bhakta, ed. Cawnpur: Indian Communist Party, Shakti Press, c. 1924. 2pp. CRL.
The Indian Communist Party. Similar to an English-language information sheet providing background on the party, rules.

Bihar Communist Party Ka Elan (H). Calcutta: Bihar Communist Party, n.d. 4pp. PIB.
Anti-British appeal, call for revolution.

4. Two official overviews of the Communist and Socialist efforts in India are D. Petrie, *Communism in India, 1924–27* and H. Williamson, *India and Communism*. Both C.I.D. handbooks are being reprinted with critical notes. Other items relating to the Socialist activities can be found under the appropriate subjects in the Index to this volume. Many tracts in the "British Administration" subsection, for example, contain a leftist viewpoint.

The Black Prince of Wardha. Pulakesh De. Calcutta: Premendra Biswas, Patheya Printing Works, 1939. GIPOL 1939, 37/28.

Attack on Gandhi as "satanic" and the "Black Rasputin of India," an imperialist tool. Supports communism and a "red revolution."

Bolshevik Communist (H). United Provinces Communist Party, c. 1937. 8pp. IOL F 60.

On the Spanish civil war and its implication for India.

Bolshevism Kya Hai? (H). "Vyakhit Hradaya" (Pinched Heart). Allahabad: Ram Mohan Lal, Diamond Printing Works, 1931. 40pp. IOL B 385; NAI 80; PIB 8; CRL.

Communist tract on Lenin. Communist theory, and the nature of revolution.

Communist International De Hisse Hindustan Communist Party De Arzi Niyaman Da Kharara (G). n.i. 11pp. GIPOL 1936, 37/2.

Provisional draft rules and regulations of the C.P.I. Emphasis on militancy, careful organization, and discipline. A call for union support and avoidance of Gandhi, M. N. Roy, and other political organizations.

Communist Manifesto Arthat Samishtvad Ki Asli Sidhant (H). Karl Marx, Frederick Engels, trans., Ayodhya Prasad. Jhansi: Shram Jivi Sahitya Prakashak Mandal, Matra Bhunsi Printing House, 1934. 56pp. IOL B 326; PIB 104. Urdu version, IOL 175.

Translation of the Communist Manifesto.

Communist Party Ke Sangathan Ke Sidhant (H). Bombay: Communist Party of India, People's Publishing House, c. 1931. 47pp. NAI 114; CRL.

On the principles of the party, resolutions and proceedings of the Third Congress of the Comintern.

The Communist Reply. Bombay: Workers' Literature Publishing Company, c. 1933. 60pp. PIB 10; CRL; GIPOL 1933, 48/3.

Abridged edition of the joint statement of eighteen Communists accused in the Meerut Conspiracy case. General defense of the defendants, based on a Communist view of society, capitalism, and revolution.

Comrade M. N. Roy: A Few Words About His Life and Work. n.i. 8pp. photocopy, NAI 12.

Brief biography of Roy up to his 1931 imprisonment.[5]

Comrade Muzaffar Ahmad. Saumyendra Nath Tagore. Calcutta: Rabi Press, c. 1935. 8pp. PIB 109.

Background on Ahmad and Indian communism, c. 1921–1935.[6]

Duniya De Mazduro Ek Ho Jao (H, G). Amritsar: Punjab Communist Party, 1935. 8pp. PIB 159; GIPOL 1935, 37/2.

Communist bulletin addressed to "labourers of the world." Calls for the establishment of a Soviet Republic in India, confiscation of land, eight-hour day. Workers are asked to "read, paste and pass on" the cyclostyled message. Subtitle: "May the Congress Party live, May the British Ship Sink."

Essay on Religion. Lenin, ed. by Gopal Panjabi. Agra: Socialist Literature Publishing Company, n.d. 19pp. NAI.

Marxist view that organized religion supports tyranny over workers and peasants. The editor suggests that religious problems are crucial in India and urges that nationalists meditate on the essay.

Ham Bhukhe Nange Kyon Hain? (H). Cawnpur: Mazdur Kisan Pustakmala Karyalaya, 1935. 32pp. IOL B 197; NAI 178; PIB 98; CRL.

Why are We Hungry and Naked? Communist tract on the effects of British imperialism.

I Accuse. Manabendra Nath Roy. New York: Roy Defence Committee, 1932. 30pp. Hoover Library.

Statements during Cawnpur conspiracy trial, with introduction by Aswani Kumar Sharma.

India in Transition. Manabendra Nath Roy, with Abani Mukherji, collaborator. Geneva: J. B. Target, 1922. 241pp. NAI.[7]

English version of a Russian work first published in 1921. Examines material forces contributing to class struggle in India, and evaluates nationalist movements and the possibility of cooperation with the masses.

5. Manabendra Nath Roy (1887–1954) was a leading Communist in both national and international circles before breaking with the party. Background in his autobiographical account, *M. N. Roy's Memoirs.*

6. Muzaffar Ahmad helped form the Communist Party of India. His account of the early stages of the C.P.I., *Myself and the Communist Party of India, 1920–1929*, and John Patrick Haithcox, *Communism and Nationalism in India*, constitute two of the most important sources on the period.

7. Reprinted, along with *What Do We Want?*, in *India in Transition* (Delhi: Nachiketa, 1971).

The Indian Communist Party. Satya Bhakta, ed. Cawnpur: Indian Communist Party, Brahman Press, c. 1924. 3pp. PIB 71; CRL.

Manifesto, objects, with membership blank appended.

The International Socialist Congresses, Speeches and Resolutions on India (private circulation only). Indian Nationalist Committee, c. 1911. 13pp. IOL; CRL.

Jute-Mill Workers' Strike: Manifesto. Barrackpore: District Committee of the Bolshevik Party, 1940. 3pp. GIPOL 1940, 37/91.

Background on the strike and a call for a united front against British rule. Also circulated in Hindi.

Karl Marx Aur Frederick Engels Ka Mushtarika Ishtimali Manshur (U). Lahore: Ripon Press, c. 1941. 64pp. PIB 186.

Translation of the Communist Manifesto, with notes.

Krantikari Andolan Aur Rashtriya Vikas (H). Manmath Gupta. Lucknow: Left Wing Publishing House, n.d. 28pp. NAI 157; PIB 3; CRL.

"Red Tract One." On the Communist contribution to nationalism and world revolution. Also indictment of the Congress.

Lal Jhanda Aur Inkilab Hindustan (U). Ram Singh Chavla. Sialkot: Naujavan Bharat Sabha, Mukbul-i-Am Press (Lahore), 1930. 8pp. PIB 62; CRL.

Communist commentary on British rule; call for worker–peasant cooperation.

Manifesto of the Labour Party on War and Federation. Calcutta: Labour Party, Sri Sarasvati Press, 1939. 5pp. GIPOL 1940, 37/3.

Attacks British and Indian participation in the war, opposes federation with princes. Ends with a call for "mass struggle."

M. N. Roy. Poona: Young Socialist League, c. 1935. 25pp. PIB 11.

Sketches on Roy by Nehru, other nationalists. Includes an article by Roy on the Comintern.

Mustakbil Siasiat-i-Hind (U). Ferozuddin Mansur. Lahore: Tandon and Company, 1932. 96pp. PIB 6; CRL; GIPOL 1932, 207.

The Future of Indian Politics from Communist perspective. Discusses British rule, critical of "limited independence" ideas of Congress.

National War Committee's Manifesto to the Workers and Peasants of Bengal. Calcutta: B. G. Press, 1940. 4pp. GIPOL 1940, 37/28.

Anti-Congress, socialist statement which calls for an end to landlordism and British rule and a resurgence of worker–peasant cooperation.

On the Eve of October Revolution, With a Note by Krishnaswami. V. Lenin. Agra: Socialist Literature Publishing Company, 1938. 220pp. IOL.

Survey of Russian politics, followed by Krishnaswami's Socialist analysis of India's conditions and requirements.

Sada-i-Dard (U). Ali Husain Shah, pub. Sialkot: Ranjit Electric Press, n.d. 15pp. IOL 173; PIB 81; CRL.

Voice of Pain. Communist tract on economic conditions.

Samyavad Ki Or (H). Bhupendra Sanyal, pub. Allahabad: Sri Neva Press, 1936. 114pp. NAI 127; PIB 83.

Communist study on world revolution, Russian experience, and its application to India. Sections on India include land programs, Hindu–Muslim relations.

The Second Imperialist War. G. Adhikari. Madras: B. Srinivas Rao, Jesu Press, c. 1939. 10pp. GIPOL 1939, 37/43.

Comparison of the first and second world wars. Pro-Soviet Union; attacks capitalism and demands a "real" anti-Fascist government.

Students' Role in the Anti-Imperialist Struggle. Calcutta: Hindustan Political Syndicate, 1939. 8pp. GIPOL 1940, 37/8.

Communist statement, both anti-imperialist and anti-Fascist.

To All Anti-Imperialist Fighters Gathering Storm. Communist Party of India, 1936. 16pp. NAI.

Discusses the 1935 Indian reforms as an "imperialist trick." Also calls for class struggle and renewed support for communism.

What Do We Want? Manabendra Nath Roy. Geneva: J. B. Target, 1922. 43pp. NAI.[8]

Sections on political independence, economic and social emancipation. Very critical of the role of religion in the Congress.

Chatkal Railway Loha Karkhane Vagairah Ke Majahuri Ke Pas Communist Party Ka Ishtahar (H). Calcutta: Bengal Communist Committee, n.d. 1p. PIB 132.

Handbill on railway conditions; opposes payment of taxes.

8. Reprinted in *India in Transition.*

Lal Dhandora (G). Lahore: Punjab Communist Party, c. 1935. 1p. GIPOL 1936, 37/2.

Poster addressed to "Labourers of the World," opposes anti-labour laws and attacks on the Communist Party.

Sarkar Ki Larai Men Canda Mat Do Rupaye Men Char Anna Marghi Mata Liye Hartala Karo (H). n.i. 1p. PIB 135.

Communist exposé on British rule and conditions in factories. Calls for hartals, open revolt.

Vartman Rajat Halat Te Mazdur Kisanon Da Farz, Hindustan Communist Party De Panjab Committee Da Am Janta Nun Sandes (G). Amritsar: Punjab Communist Party, 1935. GIPOL 1935, 37/1.

The Present Political Situation and the Duty of Workers and Farmers. A Communist appeal for unity of the masses against British "police rule."

What and Whom Do We Stand For? Benares: Jai Prakash Narayan, Gayanmandal Press, c. 1935. 2pp. IOL; PIB 84.

Poster containing a policy statement of the All India Congress Socialist party.

Workers, Students and Citizens of Calcutta. Calcutta: 1930. 1p. J&P 1929, 4580; GIPOL 1930, 171.

Communist charge, in poster form, that the Congress and satyagraha actually support imperialism. "Instead of a revolution of tens of millions, the Congress leaders stage a slavish submissive campaign of a few thousands in places far away from the working class centers and agrarian provinces." Gandhi supposedly asked for "bourgeois" support to "prevent the revolution of the toiling masses." Ends with a call for a mass strike.

Conspiracy Cases[9]

Chittagong.

Album: Dead and Alleged Accused of the Chittagong Armoury Raid Case. n.i. 10pp. PIB 7; CRL.

Pictures of men involved in the April 18, 1930, raid. Comments on revolutionaries.

Kakori.

Inkilab Ke Parvane Phansi Ki Pujari (U). Lahore: Sant Ram, Inkilab Steam Press, c. 1930. 71pp. NAI; CRL.

9. Major conspiracy cases are discussed in the following: James Campbell Ker, *Political Troubles in India, 1907–1917*; Jogesh Chandra Chatterji, *In Search of Freedom*; Manmathnath Gupta, *They Lived Danger-*

Lives of members of the Kakori gang, including Ram Prasad Bismil, Rajendra Nath Lahiri, Roshan Singh, Ashfaq Ullah Khan, Satendra Kumar Bose, Kanhai Lal Datt, Madan Lal.

Jazbaye Shahid Yani Kakori Shahidon Da Paigam (H). Jubbulpur: Ram Kumar Sharma, 1930. 8pp. IOL B 363.
Poems on Kakori raids, martyrs.

Jazbae Vatan (H). Panna Lal Gujarati, ed. Calcutta: Krishnarjun Press, 1931. 10pp. IOL B 82; PIB 1; GIPOL 1932, 117.
Seventeen poems on Kakori incidents.

Kakori Ke Shahid (H). Cawnpur: Partap Karyalaya, Partap Press, 1929. GIPOL 1929, 27/1.
Tenth in a series, on the Kakori gang. Charges police brutality; gives lives of conspirators. Fifteen pictures, trial excerpts.

Kakori Ki Bhent (H). Delhi: Lakshman Pathik, c. 1937. 272pp. NAI 149.
Pictures and narrative on the Kakori conspiracy, background on revolutionaries.

Mata Ki Car Ansu (U). Multan: Naujavan Bharat Society, Iqbal Karki Press, 1929. 32pp. PIB 26; CRL.
Biographical sketches of revolutionaries involved in the Kakori raids.

Lahore (1929–1930).
Anmola Lal (U). M. S. Kavi Panchi. Lahore: Ram Ditta Mal and Sons, 1931. 8pp. CRL; GIPOL 1932, 12/IVA.
Anti-British poems on Hari Kishan, Bhagat Singh, Raj Guru, *Priceless Gems.*

Lahore Ke Shahid (H). Jubbulpur: Azad Granthmala, Raja Gokuldas Printing Works, n.d. 38pp. IOL B 335; PIB 50.
Life of the Lahore conspirators. Prose and pictures.

Lahore Ki Phansi (H). Bamlat, ed., pub. Benares: Sri Yantralaya, 1931. 15pp. IOL B 400; NAI 98; PIB 27.

Lahore Ki Suli (H). Prabhu Narayan Misra, ed., pub. Benares: Shri Press, 1931. 15pp. IOL B 383; NAI 104; PIB 8.

Shahidon Ki Ahen (H). Vishambhar Nath, ed., pub. Mirzapur: Vishvanath Press, 1931. 16pp. IOL B 193; PIB 1.
Three collections of poetry on the lives and actions of the Lahore conspirators.

---

ously; K. C. Ghosh, *The Roll of Honour*; Jagdish Sharma, *Encyclopaedia of India's Struggle for Freedom.*

Shama Azadi Ke Tin Parvane (U). Lahore: Narain Dutt Saighal, 1936 (2d ed.). 32pp. PIB 110; CRL.
Lives, utterances, eulogic poetry on Lahore Bomb Case participants.

Sukh Dev, Bhagat Singh Aur Raj Guru Ke Phansi (H). Calcutta: Shambu Prasad Misra, n.d. 16pp. PIB 1; CRL.
Poetry on the lives, death of the three leaders in the conspiracy.

Azadi Ke Divane (H). n.i. PIB 9.
Picture of the three conspirators hearing the death sentence and laughing.

Bhagat Singh and His Companions Being Carried to Paradise (H, English). Lahore: Punjab Dramatic Pictures, Arorbans Press, n.d. 1p. IOL F 84; PIB 8.
Conspirators moving toward heaven and being greeted by Lajpat Rai and other nationalists.

Founders of Liberty (H, English). Lahore: Punjab Dramatic Pictures, n.d. PIB 27.
Picture of hanging conspirators, view of Mother India in background.

Heroes Sacrifice (H). Lahore: Krishna Picture House, n.d. 1p. IOL F 72; PIB 8.
Picture of Sikhs transporting three hanged men to Mother India, who sits in the middle of a lake. The Congress flag flies in the sky.

Mister Bhagat Singh, Raj Guru and Sukhdeva Hearing the Sentence of Hanging with Pleasure (H, English). Lahore: Arorbans Press, n.d. 1p. IOL F 63; PIB 27; CRL.

Mister Raj Guru, Sardar Bhagat Singh and Mister Sukh Dev (H, English). Lahore, n.i. 1p. IOL F 62; PIB 27.
Smiling conspirators, obviously unafraid of death.

Sardar Bhagat Singh's Wonderful Presentation (H, English). Cawnpur: Shyam Sundar Lal, n.d. 1p. PIB 27.
Bhagat Singh handing his head to Mother India. Similar representation in *Bhagat's Curious Gift* (H). Cawnpur: Ganga Narain Behari Lal, n.d. 1p. PIB 27.

Three Indian Heroes in Prison (H, English). Cawnpur: Shyam Sundar Lal, 1931. 1p. IOL F 65; PIB 27; CRL.
Bhagat Singh, Sukh Dev, Raj Guru behind bars, looking very brave.

Mainpuri.

Kranti Ke Mandir Men (H). Brahmacari Indra, Indradev Singh. Mainpuri: Desh Bandhu Pustak Bhandar, 1929. 176pp. IOL B 37; NAI 141; PIB 22; CRL.

Short biographies of revolutionaries, reproducing material generally banned in earlier works.

Foreign Affairs, International Politics

America Ko Svadhinta Kaise Mili (H). Svami Atmanand. Lucknow: Somdeo Sharma: Phoenix Printing Press, 1917. 201pp. IOL B 5; PIB 57; CRL.

How America Got Independence. Suggests similar patterns for India.

Asia Ki Kranti (H). Satya Narain Shastri. Ajmer: Sasta Sahitya Mandal, Sasta Sahitya Press, c. 1932. 444pp. IOL B 34; PIB 33; NAI 130.

Discussion of nationalism and revolution in Asia, emphasis on applying lessons to India.

An Attack on the Indian Rupee; Portuguese Fascism Exposed. Bombay: Goa Congress Committee, 1944. 14pp. NAI.

Sharp criticism of customs policy and currency manipulation by the Salazar regime. Claims British complicity.

Bhawani Dayal Sanyasi: A Public Worker of South Africa. Prem Narayan Agarwal. Etawah: Indian Colonial Association, Fine Art Printing Press, 1939. vi+180+xlii. NAI; PIB 30; CRL.

Biography of an Arya Samajist and Congress (born in Johannesburg in 1892) who helped lead Indians in South Africa. On Hindu reform efforts, racism, atrocities in South Africa. Appendix includes a report on a Hindu conference.

Bolshevik Rus (H). Shiv Narain Tandoh. Cawnpur: Pratap Karyalaya, Pratap Press, 1932. 401pp. IOL B 39; NAI 15; PIB 23.

History of Bolshevik revolution in Russia.

China in Revolt. S. K. Vidyarthi (alias, M. N. Roy). Bombay: Vanguard Publishing Co., n.d. 80pp. NAI; PIB 72.

Marxist view of China, 1923–1927.

Comrade Dimitroff (H). Benares: Jangju Press, n.d. 16pp. IOL B 195.

Life of a Russian revolutionary.

Comrade Lenin (H). Bombay: Kamgar Vardamaya Pracarak Mandal, n.d. 16pp. CRL.

Life of Lenin and discussion of his ideology.

De Valera (H). Uma Datt Sharma. Calcutta: Hari Har Pustak Bhandar, Sarasvati Press (Benares), 1932. 206pp. IOL B 6; NAI 129; PIB 65.

Biography of an Irish nationalist; emphasis on agitational techniques.

Denationalisation of Goans. Bombay: Goa Congress Committee, Padma Publications, 1944. 62pp. NAI 14.

Charges Portugal with oppression. Attempt to rewrite Goan history.

An Egyptian Opinion: Egypt and the Right of Nations. Shamsy Ali. Geneva: 1918. 30pp. BM 08026.bb.23; CRL.

Condemnation of British policies toward Turkey, Egypt.

Ek Khuli Cithi Benam Asquith Sahib (U). M. Fahami. Geneva: Sadar Anjuman-i-Committee Berar Misaryan Dar Europe, 1915. 4pp. IOL 58.

Open letter to Asquith on British rule in Egypt.

Hamare Zamane Ki Gulami (H). Tolstoi. Vaijnath Mahdaya, trans. Ajmer: Sasta Sahitya Mandal, c. 1932. 92pp. IOL B 18; NAI 179; PIB 58; CRL.

Translation of Tolstoi's *The Slavery of Our Time*, with commentary.

India and China. "An Internationalist" (Philip Spratt). Bombay: Shantaram S. Mirajker, 1927. 38pp. NAI 24; PIB 72; CRL.

Based on articles from the *National Herald*, Marxian viewpoint. Written shortly after the Gauhati Congress, at a time when Chinese nationalists were successful, the essay explores similarities between Indian and Chinese nationalist tactics.[10]

Ireland Da Svatantra Yudh; Darbar Lari 4 (H, G). Amritsar: Darbar and Company, Onkar Press, 1929. 120pp. PIB 178; CRL.

Ireland's War of Independence. Notes on revolution and tactics.

Krantikari Hitler (H). Aditya Kumar Vajpei. Etawah: Hindu Press, 1940. 140pp. NAI 60; PIB 200; CRL.

10. Also, see Spratt's autobiographical version, *Blowing Up India*.

Supports *Hitler the Revolutionary* and criticizes the "weak" policies of the Congress. The author traces Hitler's rise to power and the Nazi role in nation-building.

Lenin Samrajyavad (H). Pandit Jivan Ram Sharma, trans. Benares: Narendra Deo, Lakshmi Narayan Press, c. 1934. 179 pp. IOL B 17; NAI 142; PIB 69.
Life of Lenin, background on international communism.

Meri Kahani (*Atmakatha*) (H). Dan Breen, ed. by Bhagat Singh. Lahore: 1931. 89pp. IOL B 28; PIB 27, 42; CRL.
Edited autobiography of Dan Breen, stress on Irish politics.

Nazi Germany and Soviet Russia. Freda Utley. Bombay: S. B. Chawan, n.d. 45pp. NAI.
Reprint from Utley's autobiography, noting parallels between the political system under Stalin and Hitler.

On the People's Front. G. Dimitroff. Agra: Socialist Literature Publishing Company, c. 1940. 20pp. IOL; NAI; PIB 3.
Communist tract on international communism, with note by B. Srinivas Rao on application to local situations. Anti-Trotsky.

Palestine Ki Azadi (U). Delhi: L. C. Bandi, Secretary, Youth Study Circle. n.d. 8pp. IOL 125; NAI; CRL.
Marxist tract on Arab unity.

Pardhinon Ki Vijaya Yatra (H). Munshi Navajadik Lal Srivastava. Chunar: Narendra Publishing House, Hindi Sahitya Press (Allahabad), 1937. 488pp. IOL B 11; NAI 14; PIB 32.
Stories of revolutionary, nationalist efforts in 36 countries.

Roger Casement and India. Stockholm: Indian Nationalist Committee, 1917. 24pp. CRL; IOL.
On Irish nationalism and the relationship between Irish and Indian politics.

Rusi Baghion Ki Dastanen (P). San Francisco: Hindustan Ghadar, Yugantar Ashram, 1915. 63pp. IOL 62; CRL.
Stories of Russian Rebels, presented as inspiration to Indian nationalists. Also published as *Rus Ghadarian De Samachar* (1917, 64pp.).

Rus Ki 5 Varshiya Ayojana (H). Thakur Rajbahadur Sinha, trans., ed. 2 editions, both Sahitya Mandal, Delhi: c. 1932. Abridged, 20pp. IOL B 4; NAI 153; PIB 18. Full version, 640pp. PIB 18.
Russia's Five Year Plan, with commentary. The editor pro-

vides a pro-Russian view so as to counter the anti-Russian propaganda allegedly circulated by the British.

Rus Ki Hutatmayen (H). Rajeshvar Prasad, Narayan Singh. Patna: Bharti Publishing House, c. 1932. 188pp. IOL B 31; PIB 24; CRL.

Great Personalities of Russia. Reflections on Indian and Russian history. The authors urge that Russian tactics be tried in Indian politics.

Samajik Kuritiyan (H). Madhav Prasad Misra, trans., ed. Ajmer: Sasta Sahitya Mandal, 1932. 278pp. IOL B 19; PIB 58; NAI 168; CRL.

South African Horrors: A Drama in Five Scenes. n.i. 2pp. J&P 1914, 1302; CRL.

A melodrama, similar to the "Simon Legree" dramas in the U.S. Reprinted from *Kistna Patrika* (Telegu), Mausilapatam. Emphasis on exploitation, racism.

Soviet Rus Ke Musalmanon Par Ahsanat-i-Bagayat (U). Khushidil Khan Hevat. Karachi: Valou Litho Press, c. 1941. 4pp. IOL 32; PIB 139.

Pro-Russian tract, claims that Russia has contributed to world-wide Muslim unity while other European powers have manipulated religious diversity for imperialistic reasons.

Teachings of Karl Marx. V. Lenin. Allahabad: Socialist Book Club, 1939. 72pp. IOL; NAI.

Exposition of Marxist views on class struggle.

Wage, Labour and Capital. Karl Marx. Agra: Socialist Literature Publishing House, c. 1939. 60pp. PIB 3.

Gandhi

Angrezon Se Meri Appeal (H). M. K. Gandhi. New Delhi: Sasta Sahitya Mandir, Hindustan Times Press, 1942. 88pp. PIB 204.

Appeal for the British to leave India in the interest of the world. Gandhi judges such a move necessary to check fascism.

Drama Mahatma Gandhi (U). Mauzari Barelavi. Bareilly: Rohilkand Electric Press, n.d. 86pp. IOL 136; NAI; PIB 6; CRL.

Play on Gandhi's life, political campaigns. Tries to show how religious prejudice injures Indian unity.

Gandhi (U). Hansraj Safari. Amritsar: Arjan Press, n.d. 8pp. CRL.

Poetry on Gandhi, eulogic.

Gandhi Gayan (P). Pandit Dev Raj Dev, ed., pub. Lahore: Bharat Newspaper Press, 1930. 24pp. PIB 29; CRL; GIPOL 1932, 114.

Poems on Gandhi and nationalism; claims that Bhagat Singh should be an inspiration to his "timid Panjabi brothers."

Gandhi in South Africa. Saumyendra Tagore. Calcutta: Calcutta Printing Works, n.d. GIPOL 1934, 37/6.

Attempts to show that Gandhi supported British imperialism and was a friend of capitalism. Attacks him for helping the British and being afraid to denounce the caste system. The author also labels the Hindu–Muslim controversies as religious differences that could be overcome by emphasis on class struggle. In a final essay, he says that Gandhi is not modern and lacks the knowledge to shake India from her sleep.

Gandhi Gospel. M. K. Gandhi. Basanta Kumar Chatterjee, ed. Calcutta: Jawaharlal Bakshi, Rati Press, c. 1932. 32pp. PIB 7; CRL.

Selections from Gandhi's publications.

Gandhi Ki Jai. V. A. Sundaram. Madras: Hindi Pracar Press, 1931. 4pp. English. CRL; GIPOL 1930, 171.

Tract on Gandhi. Compares him with Jesus and says that God sent Gandhi to India. Typical of the eulogic material: "England is pig-headed. She is mad with wounded vanity. Her politicians are bullies. She is showing her mailed fist and talks again of steel frames. But Gandhi knows his mind and his art. He has put his head into the lion's mouth."

Indian Home Rule (also, *Hind Swaraj*). M. K. Gandhi, pub. Phoenix (Natal): International Printing Press, 1910. 128pp. GIPOL August 1910, 96–103A. Many editions, R.A.

English version of a Gujarati book published prior to 1910 and promptly banned by the government. Examines Indian problems and the nature of administration in India.

Kali Kartuten (H). M. K. Gandhi. Calcutta: Sita Ram Seksaria, Pravasi Press, c. 1930. 56pp. IOL B 450; NAI 120; PIB 70; CRL.

Gandhi essays reprinted from various sources.

Lenin Aur Gandhi (H). Thakur Rajbahadur Sinha, trans. Delhi: Sahitya Mandal, 1932. 472pp. IOL B 2; PIB 18.

Biographies, with comparisons.

Man Moh Lia Langotivale Has Has Ke (P). Gojra Mandi. n.i. GIPOL 1932, 13/4.

The Man Clad in a Loincloth Has Won Our Heart with a Smiling Face. On Gandhi's life. Also, surveys recent Punjab political history.

Quit India. M. K. Gandhi. Bombay: Padma Publications, 1943 (2d ed). 78pp. PIB 204; various editions, R.A.

Gandhi's famous challenge to the British. Outlines the rationale for the Quit India movement.

Mahatma Gandhi Ka Astar (H). Sidh Gopal Shukla, pub. Cawnpur: Bharatiya Press, n.d. 1p. IOL F 78; PIB 51; R&R 1922, 1110.

Broadside on Gandhi and his program.

That Strange Little Man Gandhi. Frederick B. Fisher. New York: R. Long, 1932. viii+239. Various reprints. RA.

Balanced assessment of Gandhi and the development of Indian nationalism, probably banned because of its favorable comments and the book's appearance in the midst of a non-cooperation campaign.

German Propaganda[11]

Behind the Veil in Persia: British Documents. Amsterdam: C. L. Van Langen Huysen, 1917. 164pp. CRL.

Alleged exposé of British imperialism (with Russian collaboration) in the Persian Gulf.

Duniya Ki Jang Ka Pahla Sal (U). n.i., c. 1915. 4pp. IOL 56; PIB 215.

Pro-German material circulated during the first year of the First World War. Addressed primarily to Muslims.

German Camp Men Hindustani Sipahi (H). n.i. 8pp. IOL F 29.

Anti-British, with pictures and prose on condition of prisoners in German camps.

German Ke Tamadan Aur Jang (U). Berlin: Masharki Akhbari Daftar, 1914. 44pp. IOL 57.

Plays up in favorable light German policy toward Asians, Muslims.

11. Chapter 3, in this volume, describes some aspects of German and Indian propaganda. Additional background is in Arun Coomer Bose, *Indian Revolutionaries Abroad, 1905–1922*; discussion of German propaganda in Eur. Mss. E. 288 (IOL).

British Atrocities in Persia. n.i. CRL.

Pictures of the British hanging Persian nationalists. One photo shows a nationalist cut to pieces and skewered, with his chest carved out.

Hindustani Sipahiyo (U). n.i. 1p. IOL 59.

Poster calling on Indian soldiers to revolt. Copies were dropped by German planes among Indian troops in France.

Nrasanta Jo Rusi Sipahiyon Ne German Nivsiyon Aur Yuddha (H). Berlin: 1915. 4pp. IOL F 104.

Handwritten, lithographed material for distribution among Indian troops.

Harphul Singh Daku

Asli Sangit Julanivale Ki Virta Urf Jat Harphul Singh Ka Dusra Hissa (H, U). Lakhmi Cand. Delhi: Shambhu Dayal, Dina Nath Press, c. 1934. 24pp. H: PIB 146; GIPOL 1935, 27/2. U: IOL 138; PIB 147.

Fictitious account of a Sikh robber–patriot, Harphul Singh, who saves cows and redresses the wrongs perpetrated by butchers and government officials.

Ath Ati Rasila Upnias Parupkari Harphul Singh, Hissa Paihla (G). Pandit Jaggat Ram, Ferozepur, ed. Moga: Mangal Singh, Bharat Printing Press, c. 1936. 56pp. PIB 160; CRL; GIPOL 1937, 37/1.

Ath Navan Kissa Surma Harphul Singh Daku (G). Shambhu Datta, ed., pub. Shahdara (Hissar, Punjab): Panjabi Printing Press (Lahore), c. 1936. 24pp. PIB 164; GIPOL 1936, 37/2.

New Episodes of Harphul Singh. Stress on cow protection and killing bureaucrats.

Harphul Jat Julani Ka Tisra Bhag (H). Man Singh Jogi. Delhi: Shambu Dayal, Dina Nath Press, n.d. 24pp. CRL.

Surman Harphul Singh Daku (G). Shambhu Datta, ed. Lahore: Ram Das Bhatia, c. 1936. 39pp. PIB 164pp.; CRL.

More Harphul Singh tales. In one episode, the Mother Goddess Durga protects the dacoit from the police.

Mutiny of 1857

Baghi Ki Beti (H). Munishvar Datt Avasthi. Benares: Chaudhri and Sons, Mathura Printing Press, 1932. 190pp. IOL B 21; PIB 65; CRL; GIPOL 1932, 208.

Fiction on events during 1857 in the Benares region.

Hindustan Socialist Republican Association, Fourth Manifesto: War of Freedom of 1857. n.i. GIPOL 1933, 48/4.

A comparison of the 1857 Mutiny with the 1921 non-cooperation campaign. Both supposedly were brave attempts, and both failed because Indians lacked unity, due to caste, religion, traditions, and personal resolve. The solution? "We have to annihilate the sins of ages from our organization." The conclusion indicates the tone of the tract: "Broad was the fiery red cross with which India started on her crusade to Freedom. Hold fast to that Red cross, oh ye oppressed people of India, speed on, Angel of revolution, speed on."[12]

Indian War of Independence. V. D. Savarkar. London: 1909. 451pp. Various editions. R.A.

Reinterpretation of the mutiny, one of the first examples of the "national revolt" thesis. Paints mutineers as heroes and ends with an exhortation to take up the cause of freedom and submerge differences. Some day "the sword of Hindustan . . . shall flash even at the gates of London." Originally written in Marathi but translated and printed in English (London and Holland). Background in GIPOL May 1910, 1A; July 1915, 56–72A; banned 1909, again in Lahore when reprinted in 1930.

Itihasik Ghatna (H). Prof. Manoranjan. Aligarh: Prabhu Dayal Dandevale, Svadhin Press (Delhi), c. 1930. 8pp. IOL B 418; NAI 19; PIB 70.

Poems on the 1857 Mutiny and Kumar Singh, a famous rebel.

Jhansi Ki Rani (H). Sudar Ram Misra ("Cakra"). 2 eds.; Cawnpur: Jai Press, c. 1938 (3d ed.). 8pp. IOL B 61; PIB 31. Agra: Kesari Press, c. 1930. 16pp. IOL B 229; NAI 113; CRL.

Poetry on the Mutiny, the Rani of Jhansi.

Nagon Ki Rani (H). Nathu Ram Dvivedi. Cawnpur: Bhagvan Pustakalya, 1939. 16pp. NAI 31; PIB 3; CRL.

Odes on the 1857 events, attempts to show how freedom can be won.

The Revolt of 1857. Baroda: Jyoti Publishing House, c. 1942. 52pp. NAI; CRL.

Nationalist account of the mutiny, written during the Quit India movement. Based on the Gujarati edition of *Bharat Men Angrezi Raj* by Sundar Lal.

12. The Hindustan Socialist Republican Association was a loosely constructed organization of revolutionaries operating in North India. Background in Gurdev Singh Deol, *Shaheed Bhagat Singh: A Biography*; essays in B. R. Nanda, ed., *Socialism in India.*

Rise, Awake, Be Ready. Hindustan Socialist Republican Association, c. 1933. app. 4pp. GIPOL 1933, 48/3.

Review of the 1857 Mutiny. Appeal to youth. Attention to divisive factors undercutting Indian national unity.

Lakshmi Bai. n.d. n.p. 1pp. IOL.

Postcard on the Rani of Jhansi and the Mutiny. A revolutionary challenge is on the back, a portrait of the Rani on the front.

Nationalism, Congress

Azadi Ki Larai (H). Lakshmi Cand Gupta. Saharanpur: Sital Prasad Vidyarthi, Shanti Press, 1939. 380pp. NAI 132; PIB 3; CRL.

Two parts bound together, a history of Indian nationalism with focus on revolution and Gandhi.

Balidan (H). Rameshvar Pandey Prasad. Ajmer: Onkar Press, n.d. 16pp. IOL B 206; PIB 149.

Call for Indians to sacrifice for freedom.

Chathi Pothi (H). Ram Das Gour, ed. Calcutta: Hindi Pustak Agency, c. 1923. 271pp. NAI 180.

Collection of essays on India, nationalism, current politics.

Cingariyan (H). Becan Sharma Pandey ("Ugra"). Calcutta: Mahadeo Prasad Seth, Balkrishan Press, c. 1928. 241pp. IOL B 138; NAI 138; PIB 63.

Short stories, anecdotes on patriotism.

Congress Ke Prastava, 1884–1932 (H). Kanhaiya Lal, ed. Benares: Navyug Prakashan Mandir, 1931. 645pp. IOL B 35; NAI 147; PIB 6.

Background on Congress sessions, detailed index.

Demand of India for Self Government. Stockholm: Indian Muslim Patriots League, 1917. 24pp. New York Public Library.

Emphasis on communal harmony and resistance to the British. On the title page, "No world peace without peoples' freedom."

Gulam Santanon Ke Nam Svarg Se Purkon Se Chitthi (H). Ram Narayan Garval ("Mastana"). Cawnpur: Pitambar Lal Singhal, National Press, n.d. 8pp. IOL B 416; NAI 124; PIB 70; CRL.

A letter supposedly from "relatives in heaven" about nationalism and the need for sacrifice.

Hartal (H). Rasabhacaran Jain. Delhi: Indra Prastha Pustak Bhandar, Bharat Printing Works, 1931. 176pp. IOL B 24; NAI 134; PIB 42; CRL.

Nationalist novel on the theme of opposition to British rule.

India in World Politics. Tarak Nath Das. Calcutta: S. N. Shaw, Sarasvaty Press, 1931 (2d ed.). 298pp. PIB 7; CRL.

On a variety of subjects including Indian history, religion, administration, Pan-Islam and Pan-Asianism. Appeals to the world for India's freedom.

India's Problem and Its Solution. Manabendra Nath Roy. Geneva: 1922. 55pp. NAI (photocopy); R.A.

Claims that India's freedom struggle is a social upheaval directed not only at the British but also at a heritage of religious superstition and social bondage. Criticizes the Congress and argues that nationalism needs fresh leadership and mass appeal.

Khaddar Posh Athva Kranti Ki Jaya (H). "Pran." n.i., 1930. 48pp. IOL B 396; NAI 21; PIB 21; CRL.

The Wearer of Khadi (homespun). A drama on nationalism.

Kranti Ka Bugle (H). Asha Ram. Allahabad: J. R. Tripathi, Madho Printing Works, n.d. 8pp. IOL B 119; PIB 31.

Prose on the struggle against British rule.

Krantikari Kahaniyan (H). Pandeya Becan Sharma ("Ugra"). Benares: Sahitya Sevak Karalaya, Shri Sita Ram Press, 1939. 202pp. PIB 208.

Revolutionary Tales. Plays up atrocities and Indian patriotism.

Mahatma Gandhi Gita (H). Kanhaiya Lal Thakur, pub. Benares: Shambu Printing Works, 1920. 32pp. IOL B 261; PIB 51.

Lengthy poem on nationalism and Gandhi. The couplet on the title page is representative of the spirit of this and similar tracts: "We used to get ministerships in past days by studying up to the sixth standard, but now we fail even to secure an ordinary job under the *raj*, no matter whether we are B.A. or M.A."

Mahila Rashtriya Bugle (H). Cawnpur: Ram Lal Pandey, Director, Cawnpur Satyagraha Committee, Agraval Press, c. 1930. 16pp. IOL B 76; PIB 29.

Nationalist poetry addressed to women.

An Open Letter to the Right Honorable David Lloyd George. Lala Lajpat Rai. New York: B. W. Huebsch, 1917. 62pp. CRL; J&P 1917, 1522.

Primarily a discussion of India's economics, politics.

An Open Letter to the Right Honorable Edwin Samuel Montagu. Lala Lajpat Rai. New York: B. W. Huebsch, 1917. 33pp. CRL; J&P 1917, 5122.

On reforms and conditions in India.

Parole Par (H). Vrajendranath Gaur. Lucknow: Sevak Ram Nagar, Shivaji Book Depot, 1943. 160pp. IOL B 362; NAI 133; PIB 215.

Anti-British novel, emphasis on nationalist values.

Piyam-i-Bedari (U). Nau Bahar Singh, Hissari. Delhi: Candar Gupta Press, c. 1932. 20+4pp. IOL 166; PIB 9.

Poetry on the gallows and martyrdom: "O executioner. Serve us with the cup of martyrdom, we covet it."

The Political Future of India. Lala Lajpat Rai. New York: B. W. Huebsch, 1919. xxviii+237pp. CRL; R.A.

Significant statement on revolutionaries, politics, repression in Punjab.

Prem Pathik (H). Babu Kedar Nath Singh, ed., pub. Benares: Hitcintak Press, 1921. 16pp. IOL B 189; PIB 51; R&R 1922, 1110.

Primarily songs reproduced from *Pratap* and *Prem.* Ends with "Learn the tales of dogs and rats from school readers and abusive language from Police Sub-Inspectors."

Pushpanjali (H). Benares: Lakshman Pathak, n.d. 267pp. PIB 42.

Nationalist, religious, and historical poems.

Rajyakranti Aur Bharatiya (H). Vitthal Caturvedi. Kankhal: Gurukul Press, n.d. 23pp. IOL B 253; NAI 115; PIB 27; CRL.

Discussion of politics and religious conditions in India.

Rasa Aur Alankara (H). Kishori Vajpey Das. Bombay: Hindi Granth Karalaya, New Bharat Printing Press, 1931. 87pp. NAI 78; PIB 125.

Discussion of words, metaphors, with nationalist examples.

Rashtriya Git Sangrah (H). Sukhlal Singh ("Vaid"), President, Congress Committee, Hazaribagh, U.P., pub. Hazaribagh: Samacar Press, 1930. 13pp. IOL B 204; PIB 70.

Three pages of prose on books published and activities of the Congress, followed by patriotic poems.

Reflections on the Political Situation in India. Lala Lajpat Rai. New York: c. 1915. 75pp. CRL.

Views on politics, suggestions for reform. The first section, personal reflections, was republished by the Indian Nationalist Committee, Leipzig (44pp.).

Samar Yatra Aur Anya Kahaniyan (H). Prem Cand. Benares: Sarasvati Press, 1932. 189pp. IOL B 3; PIB 65.

Short stories, primarily on reform except with several references to nationalist themes and incidents.

Shahid Prabhat (H). Brahm Dev Narayan Singh. Monghyr: Bharti Sahitya Bhandar, Tara Printing Works, c. 1931. 86pp. IOL B 36; PIB 6.

Four short sketches on patriotism and nationalism.

Sharat Sahitya: Path Ke Davedar (H). Sarat Cand Chattopadhyaya. Bombay: 1939. 343pp. NAI 136; CRL.

Novel with a nationalist setting.

Struggling India. N. Ramamurti. Berhampur (Ganjam), Vegu Jukka Printing Works, 1929. v+343pp. NAI; PIB 9; CRL.

History of Congress leadership and programs, critical of moderates and the government. The author was editor of a paper, *Andhravani*, Vizagapatam.

Svaraj Gitanjali (H). Caturvedi Shailendra. Benares: Som Datt Sharma, Lahri Press, 1923. 3 pts. 58+6; 48+6; 54+6pp. Pt. 1: IOL B 165; PIB 42, 177. Pt. 2: IOL B 180, 443; PIB 42, 177. Pt. 3: IOL B 443; PIB 42, 177.

Extensive collection of poems on nationalism and patriotic movements.

Takarir-i-Ajit (U). Ajit Singh. Lal Cand Falak, ed. Lahore: Bande Mataram Book Agency, Sevak Machine Press, 1909. 28pp. CRL.

Speeches of Ajit Singh, five lectures on radical politics.

Taklivala Gandhi Arthat Azadi De Git (U). Dev Raj Dev. Lahore: Ram Ditta Mal, Girdhar Steam Press, c. 1931. 16pp. PIB 29; GIPOL 1932, 114.

Background on Gandhi, nationalist campaigns.

Young India. Lala Lajpat Rai. Many editions; originally published in New York, 1915. 263pp. R.A.; reprinted 1966.

Classic nationalist review of modern Indian history. Upon learning of the book, the British banned it because of its glorification of "the martyrdom of those who used the bomb and revolver and vilified the British, whose object in India was represented to be plunder, and who after the Mutiny tortured men, women and children."

Yug Dharma (H). Haribhav Upadhyaya. Ajmer: Sasta Sahitya Mandir, Sahitya Press, 1931. 266pp. IOL B 16; PIB 27.
Essays on Indian problems from a nationalist viewpoint. Supports non-cooperation.

Congress Ko Samrajvavad Virodhi Sanstha Banao Congress Memberon Se Appeal (H). Sajjad Zahir, et al. Allahabad: Sri Seqa Press, 1937. 2pp. IOL F 95; PIB 148.
An Appeal To Make the Congress an "Anti-Imperialist" Organization. A handbill stressing militancy and united action.

Hindustan Azad Jama'at (U). Deo Narain Pande. Calcutta: Indian Freedom Party, Siraji Press, 1928. 1p. PIB 71; R&R 1930, 720.
A poster on the Indian freedom movement.

Non-Cooperation Tree and Mahatma Gandhi (H, English). Lahore: Saghal and Sons, n.d. 1p. PIB 170.
A picture filled with symbols including figures of nationalists, goddesses, council chambers, Krishna, and jail.

The Right Path to Liberty (H, U, English). Lahore: Saghal and Sons, 1931. 1p. PIB 27; CRL.
Black-and-white poster, with pictures of jail, Krishna, and the march to the sea. Also this poem: "Doth Ye Remember, O Krishna, Thy promises made in Gita?" "Yes, Mother (India), I remember. The gulf is being paved. A little more sacrifice and the road will be completed." Gandhi, Nehru, Sikhs also prominent.

Struggle for Freedom (H, G, U). Cawnpur: Shyam Sundar Lal, n.d. 1p. Similar version, Lahore: Saghal and Sons, n.d. IOL F 64; PIB 170.
Poster with many pictures and images. Includes a "Goddess of Freedom," a "Jail Ditch," Gandhi, and British atrocities (including use of planes, guns, bombs).

Nationalist Biography[13]

Bandi Jivan (H). Sacindra Nath Sanyal, pub. 2 eds. Lahore: Vidhya Prakash Press, c. 1922. Allahabad: Standard Press, c.

13. Reference works relating to revolutionaries include the following: Sharma, *Encyclopaedia*; Ghosh, *Roll of Honour*; S. P. Sen, *Dictionary of National Biography*.

1922. 2 pts. 120+157pp. IOL B 32 (Pt. 1); NAI 18+162; PIB 21; CRL.

Autobiographical account of a revolutionary, originally published in Bengali journals and translated by Lalli Prasad Pandey. The first volume discusses revolutionary activities during the First World War; the second, changes among revolutionaries after the war. Sanyal (1893–1943) was transported to the Andamans for involvement in North India conspiracies, later was re-arrested for cooperation with Japan.

Candra Shekhar Azad (H). Harsha Datt Pandey ("Shyam"). Cawnpur: Bombay Pustakalya, Prabhat Press, c. 1938. 32pp. IOL B 270; PIB 31.

Poetry on the life of Azad (1906–1931), a revolutionary leader of the Hindustan Socialist Republican army who participated in various raids, including the ambush of the Kakori Mail, and died in a shoot-out with political officers.

Deshpriya Jatindra Mohan Sen Gupta. Calcutta: Modern Book Agency, Sri Gauranga Press, 1933. vi+158pp. PIB 28; CRL.

An English-language biography of a Bengal politician who worked with labor, coolie agitation. Writings appended.

The Eight Days Interlude. Pandit Jawaharlal Nehru. Delhi: Javahar Press, 1930. 22pp. PIB 64; CRL. Also, Hindi version, *Jail Ke Bahar Ke Ath Din.* Delhi: 1930. IOL F 37; PIB 64. Urdu version, *Mohlat Ki Ath Din.* Delhi: 1930. PIB 64; CRL.

Statements on Indian politics issued by Nehru when released from jail after serving eight days in 1930.

Hindustan Socialist Republican Association, In Memory of Pandit Chandra Shekhar Azad, 2nd Manifesto of 1933. n.i. GIPOL 1933, 48/4.

Short life of Azad, who died in a gun battle on February 27, 1931. Calls on Indians to make the soil fertile with English blood and reproduce the "Cawnpur wheel" (where Indians were massacred during the Mutiny) in every village "where John Bull breathes."

Janbaz Savarkar Ya Maratha Inkilab Pasant (H, U). Lahore: Pandit Satya Dev Sidhant, Mercantile Press, 1931. 120pp. PIB 8.

Biography (1883–1966), with background on revolutionaries transported to the Andamans and those operating outside India.

Jatin Das—The Martyr. G. S. Venu. Madras: C. S. Cunniah, Sundaram Press, 1931. Martyrs of Liberty Series, #4. 55pp. PIB 38; CRL.

Life of a nationalist (1904–1929) who died in a hunger strike.

Mera Uddeshya (H). Kumari Vina Das. n.i. 6pp. IOL F 126; PIB 9.

Patriotic justification of the author's effort to kill the Governor of Bengal.

Mister Hari Kishanji Ki Phansi (H, G, U). Indra Singh, ed., pub. Amritsar: Moti Printing Press, 1932. 8pp. H: PIB 8; CRL. U: PIB 8; CRL. G: CRL.

Eulogic life of a revolutionary, Hari Kishan.

Ram Prasad Bismil (H). Nathu Ram Dvivedi ("Shankh"). Cawnpur: Bombay Pustakalya, Prabhat Press, c. 1941. 16pp. PIB 134; CRL.

Eulogic poetry, background on Bismil (?–1927), a terrorist and member of the Hindustan Socialist Republican Association who after participating in several raids was executed.

Shahid Azad (H). Allahabad: Union Job Press, n.d. 16pp. IOL B 378; NAI; PIB 8; CRL.

Poetry on the life, death of Chandar Shekhar Azad.

Shahid Azam Jatindra Nath Das (U). Atma Ram Sharma ("Shok"). Delhi: Satya Sangh Ashram, Tej Press, n.d. 128pp. IOL 162; PIB 64; CRL.

Biographical sketch of a nationalist (1904–1929) who died fasting in jail, followed by a drama on his life.

Sri Candra Shekhar Azad Ki Jivani (H). Baldev Prasad Sharma, ed. Benares: Adarsh Pustak Bhandar, Sri Yantrakalya, 1931. 56pp. IOL B 345; NAI 181.

Poetry, prose on Azad's life.

Sri Jatindra Nath Das Ki Sankhipt Jivani (H). Shivcaran Lal, ed., pub. Gorakhpur: Gorakhpur Printing Press, 1930. 14pp. IOL B 241; NAI 97; PIB 64; CRL.

Background on the life and ideology of Jatindra Nath Das, a prominent nationalist.

Vilayat Men Phansi (H). Narayan Garg, ed. Delhi: Naujavan Granthmala, J. B. Press, 1929. 16pp. IOL B 183.

Life of Madan Lal Dhingra, a revolutionary who killed a high-ranking British official in London and died on the gallows, 1909.

Bharat Ka Singh Pinjre Men (H, English). Cawnpur: Shyam Sundar Lal, Lakshmi Bilas Press, n.d. 1p. PIB 27, 67; CRL.

Picture of Batukeswar Datta, a revolutionary transported for life because of involvement in Punjab bombings. He is portrayed standing in prison wearing chains.

Candra Shekhar Azad Ki Yad Men (H). Allahabad: Allahabad District Committee, Communist Party, n.d. 2pp. IOL F 52; PIB 159.

Poster on Chandra Shekhar Azad, appeal for funds.

Do Bhai Kela Pinjre Men (H). Cawnpur: Babu Lal Bhargava: Coronation Press, n.d. 1p. IOL F 79.

Picture of Bhagat Singh and Batukeswar Datta.

The Good Fight He Fought for India's Independence. Calcutta: 1931. 1p. IOL.

Picture, eulogy of Benoy Bose (a revolutionary who killed several Englishmen and then killed himself at capture in December 1930).

In the Heart of Mr. B. K. Dutt (H, English). Lahore: Arorbans Press, n.d. 1p. IOL F 61; PIB 27; CRL.

Prisoners opening their chests to reveal other prisoners inside.

Kranti Saphal Ho (H). Cawnpur: Rashtriya Sahitya Pracarak Mandal, 1930. 1p. PIB 70.

Pictures of Batukeswar Datta, Bhagat Singh. Quotations from their speeches, poetry.

Sachitra (H). n.i. PIB 42.

Picture of Ram Prasad Bismil hanging, while British officers stand, smoke, and laugh.

Vir Shivram Raj Guru (H). Lahore: Hindi Brothers, n.d. IOL F 71; PIB 64.

Picture of Rajguru, with patriotic poetry.

Nationalist Biography: Anthologies

Asiran-i-Watan (U). Ram Narayan Mushtak. Lucknow: Vidya Bhandar Press, 1931. 380pp. NAI; PIB 6.

Biographical sketches on approximately 350 nationalists.

Azadi Ke Divane (H). Vidhyabhaskar Shukla. Allahabad: Pandit Surya Sahai Dikshit (prop., Yugantar Pustak Mandir), Allahabad Printing Works, 1930. 227pp. IOL B 14; PIB 22; CRL.

The Devotees of Freedom, first in a series of "mutiny" books. Includes lives of the following: Maharaj Nand Kumar, Bahadur Shah, Khudi Ram Bose, Kanhai Lal Datt, Madan Lal Dhingra, Master Amir Chand, Sufi Amba Prasad, Kartar Singh, Satyendra Kumar Basu, Yatindranath Mukherji, Sohan Lal Pathak, Bhai Bhag Singh, Harnam Singh, Balwant Singh.

Azadi Ke Shahid (H). Sachindranath Sanyal. Cawnpur: P. N. Sushil Sanchalak, Hindi Sahitya Press, 1939. 121pp. IOL B 30; NAI 91; PIB 31; CRL.

Biographies of these revolutionaries: Chapekar Bandhu, Khudi Ram Bose, Satyendra Kumar Bose, Kanhai Lal Datt, Ganda Lal Dikshit, Madan Lal Dhingra, Amir Chand, Bhai Balmokand, Bhai Bhag Singh, Kartar Singh, Sufi Amba Prasad, Yatendranath Mukherji, Shyamji Krishnavarma, Banta Singh, Ram Raju.

Jail Ke Yatri (H). Calcutta: Vishva Mitra Karalaya, Visva Mitra Press, 1922. 304pp. NAI 55; PIB 55; CRL.

A Jail Trip, background on the imprisonment of numerous Indian leaders. Sketches include Tilak, Aurobindo, Lajpat Rai, Gandhi, the Ali brothers, Kitchelew, Bhai Parmanand, Abul Kalam Azad. Urges patriots to sacrifice, even welcoming prison or death.

Katal Begana Urf Shahidan-i-Vatan (U). Lahore: Ram Prasad, n.d. 174pp. NAI; PIB 8; CRL.

Slaughter of the Innocents or Martyrs of the Nation. Sections on Lajpat Rai, Bhagat Singh, other patriots.

Lahore Ke Shahid (H). Brij Lal Jain, ed. Delhi: Balidan Book Depot, 1931. 165pp. PIB 42; CRL.

Lives and political survey of Bhagat Singh, Sukh Dev, Raj Guru, Jatindra Nath Das. Exhortations to revolution interspersed.

Shahidi Jivan, 1st pt. (G). Kirpal Singh ("Panchi"). Amritsar: Azad Khalsa Pardeshi Press, 1930. 216pp. PIB 26; CRL.

Background on the Kuka sect, various revolutionaries (with pictures); Rash Behari Bose, Balmokand, Khudi Ram Bose, Satyendra Kumar Bose, Pandit Mohanlal, Bhai Jagat Singh, Kartar Singh. Primarily focused on participants in the 1914–1915 Ghadar-related outbreak.

Shahidon Ki Toli (H). Benares: Harsha Vardon Shukla, Mata Bhasha Mandir, Pramod Press, 1931. 288pp. PIB 200; CRL.

Lives of nationalists, beginning with Mutiny figures (Bahadur Shah, Nand Kumar, Tantia Topi) and ending with members of the Kakori conspiracy. Background on Khudi Ram Bose, Kanhai Lal Dutt, Madan Lal Dhingra, Master Amir Nand, Sufi

Amba Prasad, Bhai Balmokand, Satyendra Kumar Basu, Kartar Singh, Yatendra Nath Mukherji, Vishnu Ganesh Pingle, Sohan Lal Pathak, Kunvar Pratap Singh, Bhai Bhag Singh, Bhai Vatan Singh, Balvant Singh, Harnam Singh, Banta Singh, Mathur Singh, Baryam Singh, Gopi Mohan Saha, Ganda Lal Dikshit, Ram Prasad Bismil.

Zinda Shahid Babe (G, U). Amritsar: Varma Electric Press, Sudharak Press, n.d. 16pp. G: NAI; PIB 182; CRL. U: NAI; CRL.
Sketches of leaders involved in the 1914–1915 outbreak of revolution in the Punjab. Attention paid to jail conditions.

Arbind Mandir (H). Cawnpur: Lala Sundar Lal Jain, n.d. 1p. IOL F 83.
Pictures of revolutionaries, with Aurobindo Ghose standing in the middle. Patriotic poetry included.

Azad Mandir (H, English). Cawnpur: Shyam Sundar Lal, n.d. 1p. IOL F 68; PIB 27; CRL.
Black-and-white poster with pictures of Bhagat Singh, B. K. Dutt, Roshan Lal, Ram Prasad Bismil, Sukh Dev.

Pathans, Redshirts[14]

Frontier Gandhi. C. S. Venu. Madras: Kesari Printing Works, n.d. 24pp. CRL.
Short biography of Abdul Ghaffar Khan; background on politics along the North-West frontier.

Frontier Speaks. Mohammad Yunus. Lahore: Minerva Book Shop, c. 1941. 248pp. NAI, reprinted frequently. R.A.
History of Pathan activism, with attention to the role of Abdul Ghaffar Khan.

The Frontier Tragedy. Peshawar: Khilifat Committee, 1932. iii+55pp. CRL.
"An account of the inhuman acts of repression and terrorism, blockades, loot, incendiarism and massacres." On Congress activities on the frontier and alleged British repression. Pictures, narrative.

Kaumi Chigha (U). Peshawar: Ahmad Khan, 1931. GIPOL 1932, 121/VA.

14. The "Redshirts," or followers of Abdul Ghaffar Khan in the North-West Frontier Province, mixed regional loyalties with a militant brand of Indian nationalism. Except for scattered biographical treatments of its leader, the movement has received little scholarly attention.

Discussion of Pathan–British relations. Appeals to the tribal sense of identity and religion. Strongly anticapitalist; also contains comments such as, "Oh Pathans, you have kicked your kingdom, now go begging."

Peshavar Ka Hatyakand (H). Cawnpur: Ram Gopal Shukla, Rashtriya Pracarak Mandal, V. P. Press, 1930. 7pp. IOL B 171; NAI; PIB 64, 70; CRL.
Prose and poetry on the British firing at crowds, April 1930.

Report of the Peshawar Enquiry Committee Appointed by the Working Committee of the Indian National Congress. Allahabad: Allahabad Law Journal Press, 1930. 306pp. NAI; CRL; J&P 1930, 2464. Also, Hindi version, 64pp. IOL F 46; PIB 64; CRL.
Report of events following firing by armored cars, April 1930. Background on Redshirt and Congress politics. A strong indictment of the British. Discussion of the incidents and reports in GIPOL 1930, 255 I–III.

Sarhadi Sher (G). M. S. Panchi. Lahore: Lala Ram Ditt Mal and Sons, Virjanand Press, c. 1930. 8pp. PIB 8.
Poetry on the Redshirts, North-West Frontier Province events.

Police, Military, Indian Officials

Bihar Ke Police Hartaliyon Ki Fariyad (H). Sri Ramvriksha Benipuri. Patna: Ajit Kumar Mitra, 1947. 16pp. CRL.
On work stoppage by Bihar Indian policemen. An appeal for soldiers to support their countrymen.

Coloured Victims of the Great War: Their Groanings and Grievances At the Feet of the Crown and the Country. L. R. Sharma, ed. Delhi: Invalid Soldiers' Association, J. B. Press, n.d. 54pp. NAI; PIB 59; CRL.
Charges against British military administration, especially attacks on discharge procedure. Claims that foreigners used Indians and then kicked them out of service without compensation.

Gram Panchayat Pradipika (H). Pandit Durga Shankar Mehta. Seoni: Sahitya Bhushan, Manoranjan Press, 1929. 73pp. IOL B 264.
On village panchayats and the lives of Indians. Attacks honorary magistrates, calls on patriots to free their local government from indirect British control.

The Methods of the Indian Police in the 20th Century. Frederic Mackarness. San Francisco: Hindustan Ghadar Office, c. 1915. 30pp. CRL; Berkeley.

Severe indictment of British police activities, including accounts of alleged atrocities and brutality. Directed toward a Western audience.

Phauji Elan (H). Mohar Candra ("Masta"), ed., pub. Delhi: Sreni Press, n.d. 16pp. IOL B 225.
Patriotic poetry aimed at soldiers.

Police Ka Atyacar (H). Thakar Sabhun. Delhi: Ciranji Lal Vidyarthi, c. 1930. 16pp. IOL B 111; NAI 45; PIB 29; CRL.
Poetry on "tyranny of the police."

Police Ke Bhaiyon (H). Allahabad: United Provinces Congress Committee, c. 1932. 4pp. IOL F 7.
Appeal to Indian policemen to quit and aid the Congress.

Vidhar Ke Police Hartaliyon Ki Phariyad (H). Patna: c. 1947. 16pp. CRL.
Background on the 1947 police hartal (work stoppage) in Bihar.

Bashindgan-i-Delhi Ka Paigham, Police Ke Sipahiyon Ke Nam (U). n.i. 1p. IOL 30.
Message to policemen, calling for non-cooperation and resignation from British service.

He Hindustan Sipayo (H). n.i. 1p. IOL F 105.
Call for Indian troops to revolt.

Long Live Revolution. Kartar Singh. Erahvan: Republic Press, c. 1929. 2pp. IOL B 203.
Handbill containing resolutions of the Congress; high-lights the call for military and police to resign.

Police Karamcariyon Se Appeal (H). Indumati Goyanka. Calcutta: Rashtriya Mahila Samiti, 1931. 1p. IOL F 90; J&P 1929, 4580.
Poster on boycott and military revolt.

Police Ki Kartut (H). Benares: Pancayan Press, c. 1930. 1p. IOL F 54; PIB 67.
Poster, with poetry on misdeeds of the police.

Police Phauj Aur C.I.D. Ke Hindustani Karamcariyon Se Appeal (H). Kanhaiya Lal Gautam. n.i. 1p. IOL F 3.
Call for Indians to withdraw from the police, army.

Polisva (H). Ram Dvivedi. Baliya: c. 1920. 1p. IOL F 12.
Poster attacking the police.

Princely States[15]

Choose, Oh Indian Princes. London: c. 1909. 13pp. NAI; CRL; GIPOL January 1910, 165–166A; July 1915, 56–72A.

Tract aiming at cultivating support among princes for revolution. Threatens a strict accounting on the basis of princely responses.

Civic Suppression in Hyderabad. "A Hyderabadi Citizen." Hyderabad Peoples' Condition Series, #4. Poona: Raghavendra Rao Sharma, 1938. 15pp. CRL.

On internal politics, one of an eight-item series. Others include *Under the Rule of His Exalted Highness*, *Publicity Campaign Against the People*, *Moslem Attitudes in Hyderabad*, *Problem of Political Prisoners.*

Kashmir. Bombay, All India States Peoples' Conference, 1939. 54pp. NAI; CRL.

Sympathetic treatment of Kashmir nationalist movement, pointing out its relation to the wider struggle in British India and urging public support.

Main Ne Ek Crore Rupiya Kaise (U). Delhi: Shaikh Zia-ul-Haq, Khvaja Electric Press, 1936. GIPOL 1936, 37/1.

On scandals within Kashmir, attacks the private life of the Maharaja, Hari Singh, and his British supporters.

Riyasat Malerkotla Aur Uska Hukamran (U). Lahore: Rifah-i-Am Steam Press, 1931. GIPOL 1932, 117.

Collection of articles from *Riyasta Duniya* (a journal, *World of the Princes*), which attacks zamindars, princes. Primarily on Punjab states.

An Alarm Signal to Indian Princes. Princes Welfare League. Amritsar: M. S. Madan, Secretary of the League. Siala Printing Press, 1931. GIPOL 1932, 117.

Attacks on the Maharaja of Patiala, a poster claiming that the ruler, "the greatest intriguer on earth—has come out with his torpedo scheme to wreck the Federation of India ship." Calls for vengeance because Patiala allegedly hurt the Chamber of Princes by attacking Bikaner, causing communal trouble in Bhopal.

Revolution, Violence

Ah-i-Farang Ki Karistanina (U). Ram Nath. Rawalpindi:

15. The most analytic treatment of politics in the states is in Barbara Neil Ramusack, "Indian Princes as Imperial Politicians." Also, see Rajendra Lal Handa, *History of Freedom Struggle in Princely States.*

Chanan Lal Anand, Aman Sarhad Electric Press, c. 1931. GIPOL 1932, 117.

Call for revolution, bitter criticism of British rule.

Azad (H). Baldev Prasad Sharma. Benares: Adarsh Pustak Mandir, c. 1932. 56pp. NAI 181.

Background, prose and poetry, on conspiracy cases and incidents such as bombing of trains.

Azadi Ki Nazmen (U). Sabat Hussan, ed. Lucknow: Umda-ul-Mataba Press, 1940. 192pp. IOL 172; PIB 200.

Revolutionary poems, with a preface by Rafi Ahmad Kidvai.

Bande Mataram (H). Benares: Yuvak Hriday, Sarasvati Press, c. 1929. 16pp. R&R 1930, 720.

Series of revolutionary poems, such as the following: "Bharat will no more be an asylum of slaves, it would be free, free. The time is coming nigh. Now blood of Indians is at the boiling point, we would stop the tyrant from causing more repression. We are ready to sacrifice our lives at the altar of the tri-colour flag."

Bharat Men Sashatra Kranti Ceshta Ka Romancarkari Itihas (H). Manmath Nath Gupta. Allahabad: Samyavadi Pustak Mandir, Nagri Press, 1939. 376pp. NAI 144; PIB 14; CRL.

History of revolution in India, with attention to major court cases. Chapters on Punjab, Muslim activities, Kakori, Mainpur, the 1929 Lahore conspiracy (Bhagat Singh and company). Pictures. Translated and reprinted as *History of the Indian Revolutionary Movement* (Bombay: Somaiya, 1972).

Bharat San 57 Ke Bad (H). Shankar Lal Tivari. Benares: 1939. 283pp. NAI 68; PIB 31; CRL.

History of revolution in India, detailed index. Contains brief biographical sketches.

Bharatiya Atankavad Ka Itihas (H). Acarya Candra Shekhar Shastri. Cawnpur: Sahitya Mandir, 1939. 704pp. IOL B 8; NAI 139; PIB 15.

History of revolutionary activities, index.

Bhukhi Duniyan (H). Benares: Satya Narayan Singh, n.d. 20pp. NAI 106; CRL.

The Hungry World, background on revolutionary activities.

The Constitution of the Federated Republics of India. n.p.: Kabul Congress Committee, 1926. vi+56pp. CRL.

Pro-Russian, Pan-Asian document, first published in Urdu

and banned, then altered slightly in English form and banned again. Call for world revolution, critical of Gandhi.

The Cult of Violence. n.i.c. 1931. 13pp. IOL; NAI 9; PIB 13.
Attack on nonviolence, with comments such as "Let every drop of Indian blood be paid with streams of English blood." Ends with "Long Live the Revolution!"

Dard-i-Vatan (U). Om Prakash Sahni, ed. Lahore: Om Prakash Sahni, Panjabi Press, 1930. 55pp. GIPOL 1930, 28.
Poems by revolutionaries written for young people "whose hearts are not yet inclined toward national work." On martial law, British oppression. Uses a theme involving a flower garden to discuss martyrdom, heroics.

Desh Bhakti Ke Git (H). Ram Candra. San Francisco: Hindustan Ghadar, 1916. 32pp. IOL F 43; CRL.
Revolutionary poems, stress on religious unity, economic problems.

Ghadar (H). Rashbacaran Jain. Delhi: Hindi Pustak Karyalaya, 1930. 184pp. IOL B 25; NAI 117; PIB 55; CRL.
Revolutionary novel on Marathi–British relations.

Ghadar Ki Gunj (U, G). San Francisco: Hindustan Ghadar, Yugantar Press, 1914, 1916. 3 pts. 32pp. G: IOL (1–3); PIB 215 (1, 2); CRL (1, 2). U: IOL 65–66 (1, 2).
The title page of *Echo of Mutiny* is decorated with a woman (probably a representative of Kali) standing over India with a half-drawn sword: "The Sword of Mutiny is in the Hand of India." Patriotic poetry on Sikhs, British misdeeds, Indian heroes. Ends with the challenge to "Be a Martyr."

Ghadar Party Da Janam Din (U, G). San Francisco: Hindustan Ghadar, 1922, 1923. 32pp. G:NAI 132; CRL. U: CRL.
The Ghadar Birthday. Reprints from articles in the first issues, 1913. Poems, articles on British policy in Egypt and India.

Hindustan Socialist Republication Association, Manifesto One: The Philosophy of the Bomb. n.i. 4pp. PIB 71; CRL.
Allegedly issued by a leader of the Association, Kartar Singh, the tract denounces Gandhi and says that violent revolution alone will achieve independence.

Hindustanion Ki Nam Khuli Chitthi (U). San Francisco: Hindustan Ghadar, 1923. 16pp. PIB 168; CRL.
Open Letter in the Name of Indians. Accusations against alleged British atrocities and a call for revolt.

India Against Britain. Ram Chandra. San Francisco: Hindustan Ghadar, 1916. 62pp. CRL; Berkeley.

Excerpts and pictures on Ghadar activities, primarily extracts from American newspapers.

India and World-Peace: A Protest against the Dutch–Scandinavian Socialist Committee's Peace Programme. Stockholm: Indian Nationalist Committee, 1918. 15pp. IOL.

On Indian revolutionaries, and a strong defense of using every measure to attain independence.

India Arise. n.i., c. 1912. 4pp. IOL.

Call for revolt, a very bitter statement probably issued by the Hindustan Ghadar party (San Francisco).

Mangu Di Maut: Sadhu Singh Te Mangal Singh (G). Natha Singh. Ludhiana: Sant Sardar Das, 1936. 8pp. IOL; PIB 111; CRL.

Poetry on an imaginary fight between Sadhu Singh (pro-British) and Mangal Singh (a nationalist). Mangal Singh eventually dies.

Navan Zamane Ke Naven Adarshya (G, U). Har Dayal, pub. San Francisco: 1914. 47pp. G: IOL; CRL. U: IOL 61.

Two essays on politics and Indian economic conditions, *A Little Knowledge is a Dangerous Thing* and *New Times Demand New Remedies*. Representative of Ghadar literature.

Panjab Ki Maharani (H). Becan Sharma Pandey ("Ugra"). Lucknow: Ganga Granthmala, Fine Art Press, 1939. 78pp. NAI; PIB 215; CRL.

Stories about revolutionaries who opposed tyranny in India. Primarily historical, based in the Punjab region.

Parsang Rattan Singh Rakranvala: First Part (G). Amritsar: Bhai Dalip Singh, Punjab Printing Press, 1933. GIPOL 1933, 48/3.

Dialogue between Rattan Singh, a Babbar Akali leader in Punjab, and his sister, on an episode with police. Ends with a shoot-out.

Parvana (U). Gorakhpur: Muhammad Kulban Varis Khan, Masik Press, 1929. 50pp. IOL 159; NAI; PIB 45; J&P 1929, 4858.

Articles reprinted from a revolutionary paper, *Masik*. Attacks moderates, contains letters from "martyrs," members of the Indian Republican Army. Call to destroy the British, "to hell with the Nehru Report and the Nair Committee report (on nationalism, internal problems within Congress, and British rule). . . . We will kill others and die ourselves."

Rakta Dhavarj Natak (H). n.i. 55pp. PIB 125; CRL.
Revolutionary drama, *The Bloody Flag.*

Rakta Kund Athva Krantikariyon Ka Shadyantra (H). Aligarh: Ganga Lahiri Sharma, Sudharak Pustakalya, c. 1932. 184pp. IOL B 1; PIB 1; CRL.
Pool of Blood or Revolutionary Conspiracies, a novel on the Russian revolution. Presented as a model for Indian youth.

The Revolutionary. Kartar Singh, Vijay Kumar, ed. n.i. 4pp. NAI; PIB 162; CRL.
Supposedly the first number of a revolutionary newspaper, January 1, 1925, but in fact, a manifesto. Calls for a Federal Republic of India. Because the British used the sword to conquer India, Indians should rely on force to attain freedom: "This party views all constitutional agitations in the country with contempt and ridicule. It is a mockery to say that India's salvation can be achieved through constitutional means. . . . [It can come] only by organised and armed revolution."

Sansar Ki Vhisana Rajya Krantiyan (H). Shankar Lal Tivari. Benares: Chaudhuri and Sons, Arjun Press, 1939. 241pp. IOL B 15; NAI 145; PIB 3.
History of world revolution, with notes on relevance for India.

Shabash (U). Har Dayal. San Francisco: Hindustan Ghadar, 1913. 4pp. IOL; NAI (Shyamaji Krishnavarma collection); background in GIPOL June 1914, 75–77A.
Also referred to frequently as the "Yugantar (Revolt) Circular," a defense of political murder occasioned by the attempted assassination of Viceroy Hardinge in Delhi, December 1912.

10th of May, 1911. n.i. 4pp. IOL.
Review of revolutionary history, call for violent overthrow of the British.

Vatan Ka Rag (U). Aksir Sialkoti. Lahore: Saghal and Sons: Nashtar Steam Press, c. 1931. 40pp. NAI; PIB 29; GIPOL 1932, 114.
Appeals to history, poetry on revolutionary martyrs: "O Lenin, Mazzini, Washington and Napoleon, come and see the funeral of India's heroes."

Vidrohini (H). Prahlad Pandey ("Shashi"). Ujjain: Yugpravartak Granthmala Karalaya, Universal Directory Printing

and Publishing House (Bombay), 1942. 132pp. IOL B 29; NAI 69; PIB 210.
Revolutionary poems.

Yuvak Aur Svadhinta (H). Rahunath Prasad, pub. Bombay: Bombay Vabhav Press, 1934. 79pp. NAI 76; PIB 11; CRL.
Discussion of young men in politics, surveys past revolutionary efforts.

Abhan. n.i. 1p. English. PIB 7.
Call for a "festival of blood," poster.

An Appeal: The Youths of India from the Hindusthan Socialistic Republican Army and the Communist Party (Bengal Branch). Calcutta: 1931. 2pp. IOL .
Call for revolution (with Communist overtones), also commentary on the Lahore Conspiracy Trial of Bhagat Singh.

Are We Dogs? Mg. Po Sein. Rangoon: Republican Society, Burma, c. 1931. 1p. IOL; PIB 9.
Call for revolution in Burma.

Bande Mataram. n.i., c. 1911. 1p. IOL.
Postcard with a picture of V. D. Savarkar, the slogan "Bande Mataram," and a revolutionary pledge on the back (the oath of the Abhinava Bharat, a revolutionary society).

Bande Mataram. "President in Council, Red Bengal." Calcutta: c. 1923. English. 1p. PIB 162; CRL; J&P 1924, 3021.
Revolutionary war cry, attacks bureaucracy: "Out of the few revolvers and bombs and police murders, or a little white man's blood spilt here and there, we do not expect immediate independence. Today we mean to be no more than a standing menace to irresponsible tyranny, an abiding retaliation of flagrant misrule, and we mean to stay and work till these lawless laws are in fact wiped out, till government becomes responsible to the will of the people for all intents and purposes. If we fail in this, we may have to go on till we wake up the sleeping leviathan of potentiality of India, and our comrades of tomorrow will have to swim across an ocean of blood to get at the altar of Mother Freedom. If that be thy will, O Mother of Holy Blood, so be it. Om, Kali, Kali, Kali."

Ca Ira. Edward Hilton James. London: c. 1909. 3pp. English. GIPOL April 1910, 19–35A.
Background on international revolution, a handbill.

Freedom First. Burmese Republican Association, n.i., c. 1931. 2pp. IOL; PIB 7.

Poster calling for independence, the killing of British.

Gaurang Gunanuvad (H). "Muktajiv." 1p. IOL F 88; PIB 70.

Series of rhetorical questions such as "Who hanged Nand Kumar? Who sent Ranjit Singh's son to Europe? Who opened fire at Jallianwala Bagh? Who fired without cause at Peshawar? Who hanged Sukh Dev?" Ends with a call for blood and revenge.

Hindustan Men Angrezon Se Jang Karne Ka Yahi Vakt Hai (U). San Francisco: Hindustan Ghadar, c. 1914. 2pp. IOL 12.

Poster, *Now is the Time for Making War with the British in India.*

Hindustan Nal Sab Ton Vada Dhokha: Hindustani Naujavan Da Jagan De Vela A Giya (G). Amritsar: Nau Javan Bharati Dal, Sri Candar Press, c. 1934. 2pp. GIPOL 1935, 37/1.

Revolutionary handbill, *Biggest Fraud with India: Time for Indian Youth To Wake Up.*

Inkilabi Nara (U). n.i., c. 1935. 1p. GIPOL 1935, 37/2.

"Labourers and peasants of the world, unite yourselves and overthrow Imperialism. Government, which plays holi with the blood of the masses and its henchmen—Hindu, Sikh and Muslim capitalists, seeing the peace of the country being consumed with flames of fire set by them, feel pleased just as Nero felt happy on seeing Rome burn. These capitalists have looked with fright at the Hindu, Muslim and Sikh Alliance. Down with Hindu–Muslim boycott. Down with the capitalists. Down with the government which thirsts for Indian blood."

Inkilab Zindabad. n.i., c. 1931. 1p. IOL.

Broadside on Bengal and Punjab revolutionaries; calls for armed uprising.

Khun Ka Badla Khun (H). Panjab Intikaumi Party. n.i. 1p. IOL F 109; PIB 27; GIPOL 1932, 12/IVA.

Poster calls for revolution and criticizes Congress leadership. "If Sikhs and Muslims had not dishonored Punjab in the days of the mutiny, then we would have been free. If the youths of the Punjab do not discharge their duty in time some other party will come in the field and outstrip them, on account of which the head of the Punjab will hang down in shame for centuries." Also circulated in an Urdu version.

Khuni Karname Ya Angrezo Ki Nicata (H). "Republic Soldier." Calcutta: 1930. 2pp. GIPOL 1930, 171; J&P 1929, 4580.

Bloody Deeds or the Meanness of the British. Revolutionary poster calling for political assassination.

Madama Cama. n.i., c. 1912. 1p. IOL.
Picture of a revolutionary, Madama Cama, with the slogan "Resistance to Tyranny is Obedience to God."

Oh Martyrs. London: c. 1909. 3pp. CRL; GIPOL March 1909, 148–50A.
Published from India House, London, a poster containing historical references to the 1857 Mutiny and a call to revolt.

Pardeshi Hindustanion Ki Bharat Nivasion Ke Nam Par Khuli Chitthi (U). San Francisco: Hindustan Ghadar, c. 1920. 2pp. PIB 153; CRL.
Public letter to Indians, calls for revolution.

Shake to Earth Your Chains. Burma: n.d. 2pp. IOL; PIB 7.
On control of Burma by "white vermin." Requests terror such as existed during the French revolution, draws parallels between nationalist–revolutionary activities in Burma, those in Ireland and China.

Svadesh Bhimaniyon Ka Sandesh (H). All India Revolutionary Committee. n.i. IOL F 2; PIB 48.
Poster on revolution.

Vanguard. Mg. Ba Thaw. Rangoon: Burma Republican Army, c. 1931. 2pp. IOL.
Revolutionary statement.

Rowlatt Agitation, First Non-Cooperation Campaign[16]

Aphat Ki Holi Ya Rashtriya Phag (H). "Vinod." Lucknow: Hindi Pustak Mandar, Anglo-Arabic Press, 1922. 16pp. IOL B 276; NAI 43; PIB 168; CRL.
The Holi of Calamities, poetry primarily on Gandhi and his campaigns.

Bage Jaliyan (H). Ram Svarup Gupta, pub. Jullundur: Surdarshan Press, 1923. 40pp. IOL B 105; PIB 177; CRL.
Poems on Jallianwala Bagh and the 1919 Punjab disturbances.

16. Ravindar Kumar, ed. *Essays on Gandhian Politics: The Rowlatt Satyagraha of 1919.*

Bharat Durdasha Darshan: Panjab Ke Hatyakaro (H). Raghunath Prasad Shukla. Benares: Kanhaiya Lal, Bharat Press, c. 1921. 6pp. IOL B 137; PIB 51; R&R 1922, 1110.

Commentary on the sufferings of the Punjab during the 1919 disturbances.

Jaliyan Ki Krur Katha (H). Raghunath Prasad Shukla, pub. Benares: Shambhu Printing Works, n.d. 4pp. IOL B 70; PIB 51.

Poems on Punjab, Jallianwala Bagh.

Jalianvala Bagh, pt. 1 (H). Bihari Lal Agarval, pub. Cawnpur: Rajhans Press, n.d. 58pp. IOL B 160; PIB 56; R&R 1930, 720.

Poetic drama on the 1919 Punjab disturbances.

Jalianvala Bagh Ka Mahatma (H). Jagannath Prasad Gupta, ed. Benares: Lakshmi Narayan Press, n.d. 16pp. IOL B 370; PIB 37.

Poetry on Jallianwala Bagh and Gandhi's activities.

Mitra Monoj (H). Naga Narayan Sharma ("Mitra"). Manipur: J. L. Dvivedi, Walker Press, 1921. 28pp. PIB 153; CRL.

Discussion of the Rowlatt Act and the resulting unrest in Punjab.

One Year of Non-Cooperation from Ahmedabad to Gaya. M. N. Roy. Calcutta: Communist Party of India, 1923. 184pp. NAI; PIB 162.

Examines the reasons for the failure of the non-cooperation movement; is critical of Gandhi as utopian and politically impotent. The Congress is pictured as having a reactionary philosophy, masquerading "in the bewitching garb of spirituality," and basing action on fallacious economic theories and tactical blunders. Concludes that a Marxian approach alone will help India.

Panjab Ka Katyakand, Yani Bekason Ki Ah (H, U). Ratan Lal Zamarrud, pub. Bulandshahr: Bandri Printing Works, 1921. 11pp. H. IOL 128; PIB 56. U: PIB 183.

Poetry on the Punjab disturbances of 1919, Rowlatt agitation.

Panjab Ka Khun (H). "Das." Jabbalpur: Phul Cand Jain, n.d. 32pp. IOL B 237; PIB 56.

Poems on non-cooperation, Punjab sufferings.

Panjab Ka Khun (H). Ram Autar Shukla, ed. Cawnpur: Bharatiya Press, 1920. 28pp. CRL.

Poetry and prose on the 1919 disturbances, the tone of which is indicated by this comment on the title page: "The Punjab is weeping on the actions of the coward Dyer. The soil of Jallian is still wet with the blood of our babies."

Rowlatt Act Ka Asli Mansha (U). Delhi: Delhi Printing Works, 1919. 16pp. CRL.
Attack on British laws and legal maneuvers, very sarcastic.

Sangit O'Dwyer Shahid Yani Mazlum Panjab (U). Suraj Bhan, Bhivani. Amritsar: Arya Press, n.d. 44pp. CRL.
Song of the O'Dwyer Martyrs or the Oppression of the Punjab. Poetry and prose on the 1919 disturbances, British oppression.

Tark-i-Muvalat (U). Alfred Nundy. Lahore: Khad Multalin Steam Press, 1920. 85pp. PIB 52; CRL.
Treatise on non-cooperation and the 1919 unrest; plays up British insensitivity to legitimate Indian expectations.

Vakia-i-Panjab (U). Haji Ahmad, Aligarh, pub. Delhi: Fateh Printing Works, c. 1920. 16pp. IOL 123; R&R 1922, 1110.
Poetry on Jallianwala Bagh, the *khilafate* movement.

Zakhmi Panjabi (H). Kishan Cand. Calcutta: Durga Press, 1922. 128pp. NAI; PIB 63; CRL.
Fictitious account, poetry and prose, based on the Congress fight for freedom. Setting is the Punjab during 1919.

Asahyog (H). Revati Sharan Gupta. Benares: Brahmin Press, 1921. 1p. IOL F 112; PIB 51.
Poster on non-cooperation.

Asahyog Ki Tan (H). Ram Narayan Mastana, ed., pub. Urai: Utsah Press, c. 1921. IOL F 40; R&R 1922, 1110.
Appeal on many subjects, including poetry relating to nonpayment of taxes, aman sabhas, Hindu–Muslim problems, education, and boycott of government service.

Second Non-Cooperation Campaign[17]

Adalat Men Mister Vishnu Candar Ka Biyan, Ya Zila Muzaffarnagar Ki Pur Dard Dastan (U). Delhi: Agarval Book Depot, Congress Press, 1931. 94pp. PIB 6; CRL.
Summary of British activities in Muzaffarnagar district during the 1930–31 campaign. In the form of a court statement; highly critical of "imperialist" justice.

17. Background in *The Civil Disobedience Movement, 1930–34*; Pattabhai Sitaramayya, *The History of the Indian National Congress.*

Agra Satyagraha Sangram (H). Mahendra. Agra: Agra Congress Committee, Adarsh Press, 1931. 118+50pp. IOL B 33; NAI 92; PIB 27.

History of Congress activities in Agra district, 1930–1931, with financial reports, background. Biographical sketches of leaders.

Azadi Ka Jauhar Yani Namak Ki Puja (H). Svami Harishankar, pub. Dehra Dun: Abhai Press, 1930. 8pp. IOL B 273; NAI 52; PIB 29; CRL.

Self-Sacrifice for Freedom or the Worship of Salt. Poems on Gandhi's march to the sea and the salt satyagraha.

Azadi Ke Tarane Aur Kaumi Jhanda (H). Suryabali Singh, ed. Benares: Kashi Pustak Mandar, 1930. 16pp. IOL B 228; NAI 50; PIB 29; CRL.

Poetry on non-cooperation, patriotism, and national symbols.

Bam Ke Gole (H). Bal Bhadra Prasad Gupta ("Rasik"). Allahabad: Mahabir Prasad Shukla, Misra Printing Works, c. 1930. 16pp. IOL B 123; NAI; PIB 21; CRL.

Poems on swadeshi and patriotism. The author especially attacks the policies of Lord Hailey, Governor of the U.P., charging that he had become so frightened of Gandhi's movement that specters of the 1857 Mutiny arose in his "monkey-like brain," and he moved to stamp out all legal opposition to government.

Bhagvan Gandhi (H, U). Gokul Prasad Dvivedi Vaidya. Lucknow: Munshi Singh, Vidyal Bhandar Press, Lucknow: 1930. 3 pts. Hindi, 1 pt. Urdu. 4pp. each. H: IOL F 28; PIB 29. U: IOL 28; PIB 29.

Poems appealing for non-cooperation and also for patriots to go to jail. Typical of non-cooperation literature.

Bharat Ka Durbhagya (H). Nihal Datt Sharma, pub. Bhivani: Dinbandu Press, 1930. 8pp. IOL B 283.

Description and commentary on the salt march.

The Black Regime at Dharasana. Ahmedabad: Gujarat Congress Committee, Navjivan Mudranalaya, 1930. 107pp. IOL; NAI; PIB 29; CRL.

Background on the nationalist raid on the Dharasana salt works, with pictures and account of resulting official oppression.

Ek Aham Elan (U). Rajendra Prasad. n.i., c. 1933. 8pp. IOL 111; PIB 9.

An Important Declaration. A call for non-cooperation, references to British alleged atrocities. Also, extracts from newspapers and Congress communiqués.

Gandhi Ki Larai Urf Satyagraha Itihas (H). P. S. Varma, Prayag Singh. Bulandshahar: Ram Richpal, B. L. Brahmachari, Svadhin Press (Delhi), 1930. 16pp. IOL B 247; NAI 81; PIB 8.

Poetry on satyagraha, attempts to win freedom for India.

Gandhi Sangram (H). Svami Svarupanand, ed., pub. Delhi: Svadeshi Shreni Press, 1931 (various reprints). 3 pts., each 15pp. Pt. 1: CRL. Pt. 2: IOL B 174; PIB 173; CRL. Pt. 3: PIB 55; CRL.

Poems on coercive ordinances and British policy.

I Tell Everything: The Brown Man's Burden. Edward Holton James, pub. Geneva: Kundig Press, 1931. 229pp. R.A.

Survey of Indian politics, with chapters on Peshawar disturbances, "the Meerut Martyrs," and "Chambers of the Great Are Jails."

In the Wake of the Indian Ordinances. S. Venkatapathaiya. Bangalore: Indian Press, 1932. 2+134+15pp. CRL.

Documents and newspaper clippings collected for use by the Indian League of London. Primarily related to political developments in the Karnatak.

Karachi Ki Congress (H). Jitmal Luniya, ed. Ajmer: Hindi Sahitya Mandir, 1932. 174pp. NAI 111; PIB 9.

Survey of the 1931 Congress session, only six days after the execution of Bhagat Singh.

Lavana Lila Va Namak Satyagraha Natak (H). Budhinath Jha ("Kairav"), pub. Patna: Searchlight Machine Press, c. 1932. 65pp. IOL B 60.

Drama on the salt satyagraha.

Law and Order in Midnapore, 1930, As Contained in the Reports of the Non-Official Enquiry Committee. Calcutta: Dinesh Candra Lodh, Prabasi Press, 1930. 27pp. PIB 9; CRL.

Pictures, narrative on civil disobedience activities in Bengal.

Muzaffarpur Zila Aur Svadhinata Sangram (H). Jagdish Prasad Sharmik, ed. Muzaffarpur: District Congress Committee, Ratnagar Press (Hazipur), 1935. 8pp. IOL B 20; PIB 103; GIPOL 1936, 31/1.

Details on Congress efforts in Muzaffarpur district, 1932. Attention to alleged British mistreatment of protestors.

Navan Zila Rajnaitik Sammelan Ki Svagatadhyaksha Shrimati Ganga Devi Ka Bhashan (H). Ganga Devi. Cawnpur: n.d. 2pp. IOL F 25; PIB 9; *Navan Zila . . . Sabhapati Professor Raja Ram Shastri Ka Bhasan* (H). Raja Ram Shastri. Cawnpur: n.d. 2pp. PIB 9.

Speeches of the president, reception committee chairman, Ninth District political conference, Cawnpur (c. 1932).

The No-tax Campaign in Karnatak. Andanappa Dodmeti, Dictator, Karnatak Pro-Congress Committee. n.p., 1933. 19pp. NAI; GIPOL 1933, 48/3.

Background on the campaign in North Kanara, discussion of official recriminations. Pictures interspersed.

A Note on Government Excesses in Bihar. n.p., Bihar Provincial Congress Committee, c. 1932. 10pp. CRL.

On police activities during the 1931 civil disobedience campaign, Bihar.

Pandit M. N. Malaviya's Statement on Repression in India Up to April 20, 1932. M. N. Malaviya. Benares: Pandit Govind Malaviya, 1932. 13pp. IOL; NAI; PIB 1.

Background on Congress activities, British response.

Police Raj under Emergency Ordinance. Madura: Tamilnad Congress Committee, Satyagraha Press, 1932. 54pp. PIB 9; CRL.

Report on civil disobedience, April–June 1932, and alleged police brutality.

Puran Svadhinata Ka Mahatvapurna Divas (H). Agra: Dictator of Mainpuri Congress Committee, Adarsh Press, n.d. 4pp. IOL F 110; PIB 21.

Important Day of Total Freedom. Manifestoes, announcements.

Rajasthan Ki Pukar (H). Nar Sinha Das. Ajmer: Rajasthan Publishing House, n.d. 128pp. IOL B 12; PIB 60.

Description of Congress activities in Rajasthan.

Rashtriya Gan (H). Allahabad: Satyagraha Committee, 1930. 13pp. CRL.

Poems on the Allahabad satyagraha efforts and their place within the over-all nationalist movement.

Salt Par Kaisi Biti? Ciranji Lal, Har Govind Pant. Ranikhet: Congress Committee, Desh Bhakt Press (Almora), 1931. 32pp. IOL B 126.

Essay on salt policy and the Gandhi salt campaign.

Satyagraha Kand (H). Shalig Ram Singh, ed. Patna: Sri Raj Krishna Bhavan, Bihar Printing Press, c. 1931. 40pp. IOL B 348; PIB 6.

Poems on alleged British atrocities in the Central and United Provinces, aimed at uplifting the morale of Congress workers.

Satyagraha Yudh (H). Ahmedabad: Naujivan Prakashan Mandir, Naujivan Press, c. 1930. 64pp. IOL B 125; NAI 110; PIB 70; CRL.

Background on Gandhian satyagraha tactics, documents on various campaigns.

To the Delegates of the 44th Session of the Indian National Congress; Declaration of Independence. Sailendra Nath Ghosh and Ramlal Bajpai. Khustia: Sj. Shyamapada Bhattacharya, Jagaran Press, n.d. 6pp. IOL; PIB; CRL (Xerox).

Appeal from the American branch of the Congress to Congress delegates. Claims that British rule has become not only the greatest menace to India but also to modern civilization.

The Truth About Tarapore. Calcutta: Bihar Provincial Congress Committee, 1932. 47pp. CRL.

Report on police firing at Tarapore, Monghyr District. Also, sections on Kisan activities in Bihar.

Yudh Vir (H). Prabhu Datt, ed. Jhansi: 1930. 3 pts., each pt. 4pp. Pt. 1: IOL F 53; Pts. 1–3: PIB 67.

Commentary on satyagraha efforts.

Bande Mataram (H). Benares: Rup Cand Panjabi, Panchan Press, 1931. 1p. IOL F 91; PIB 74.

Poster containing an appeal for patriotism.

Congress Declaration of Complete Independence (various eds., English and vernaculars). 1p. GIPOL 1937/1.

Declaration first read at a Congress session in January 1930.[18]

Ganva Valon Ka Kartavya (H). Benares: Congress District, n.d. 1p. IOL F 114; PIB 65.

Political announcements, related to non-cooperation measures.

Kaidi Divas (H). n.p., Hartal Julus Sabha, c. 1932. 2pp. IOL F 6; PIB 1.

Broadside on hartal and jail life.

Mahatma Gandhi Ki Phauj Men Bharti Ho (H). Lucknow: Satyagraha Committee, Dayal Printing Works, 1930. 2pp. PIB.

Poster calling for participation in non-cooperation activities.

18. The history of the resolution is discussed briefly in Chapter 3 of this volume.

Pratigya Patra (H). Allahabad: Svaraja Press, n.d. 2pp. IOL F 38; PIB 38.

Pledge to be signed by non-cooperators. The material notes that participants should not expect financial aid if arrested.

Rajagopalachari Statement. n.i. 2pp. PIB 42.

Appeal and comments on the 1930–1931 non-cooperation campaign.

Ram Nimantran (H). Gaya Prasad Bhartiya. Cawnpur: Premier Press, n.d. 1p. IOL F 26; PIB 29.

Message to Congressmen on non-cooperation.

Rashtra Ko Rashtrapati Ka Sandesh (H). n.i. 2pp. IOL F 116; PIB 65.

Poster on the Congress.

Rashtrapati Sri Rajendra Prasad Ka Vaktavya (H). Rajendra Prasad. n.i., c. 1933. 1p. IOL F 80; PIB 47.

Declaration for nationalist struggle at any cost.

Sachar Virand (H). Mirzapur: c. 1932. 2pp. PIB 9.

Presidential speech at a district Congress meeting, Mirzapur, reprinted as a poster. Non-cooperation theme, discusses jailing of Nehru.

To the Warring People of India. Calcutta: 1930. J&P 1929, 4580.

Manifesto calling for firm nonviolent action against the British. Although very fiery and militant, supports Gandhi and peaceful techniques.

Second World War, "Quit India"[19]

The Anniversary of the Provisional Government of Azad Hind. n.p., Indian National Army, 1944. 8pp. CRL.

Background on I.N.A. activities, 1943–1944.

The Fifty Facts About India: Political and Economic Hell in India. J. P. Gupta, ed. Bombay: Hamara Hindustan Pubs., Bombay Vaibhav Press, 1943. vi+57pp. NAI; CRL.

Alleged exposure of British propaganda in America. Attempts to counter a pamphlet titled *Fifty Facts about India: Political and Economic Paradise in India*, distributed in America by British information agencies.

19. For background on events, see Francis G. Hutchins, *Spontaneous Revolution: The Quit India Movement.*

52 Larai Ka Sikshma Congress Alha (H). Pandit Chedi Lal Pandey, pub. Fatehpur: Arjun Press (Benares), c. 1940. 16pp. PIB 211; CRL.

Poetry of a Congress meeting.

India Ravaged. "Free India." Delhi: Hindustan Times Press. 1943. 163pp. CRL.

An "unvarnished, objective picture of the horrors practised by the British Government in India under the Guise of Crushing the Uprising . . . on the 19th of August, 1942." Chapters on alleged atrocities in the C.P., Bihar and Orissa, Bengal. Appended are letters and speeches. Judged by the British to contain "most poisonous documents" (background in GIPOL 1943, 37/1).

India Speaks. Mulraj Mehta, ed. Bombay: Kutub-Minar Publications, 1943. 100pp. NAI 29.

Addressing the book to "democrats of the Allied nations," the editor brings together statements of nationalist leaders as well as resolutions of the Congress, Muslim League. Generally on the Quit India movement.

Is This Communism? Freda Utley. Bombay: S. B. Chavan, Advocate of India Press, n.d. 24pp. NAI 34; CRL.

Extracts from an autobiography, questioning whether U.S.S.R. is really free and progressive. Author also explores whether England and India should be a part of a war between totalitarian imperialist countries.

Jai Hind (H). Satya Dev Vidyalankar. Delhi: Prabhat Karyalaya, Rajhans Press, 1945. 130pp. PIB 196; CRL.

Description of India's Freedom Struggle, 1857–1945. Attention paid to the I.N.A. and Subhas Chandra Bose.

Nehru Flings a Challenge. Bombay: Hamara Hindustan Publishers, 1943. 143pp. NAI.

Collection of Nehru's speeches and writings, primarily on the Second World War and Quit India.

The Ordeal Begins. Bombay: Hamara Hindustan Publishers, Vidyala Press, 1943. 37pp. NAI; PIB 5.

Criticism of government and discussion of nonviolence as a political weapon. Reprints Gandhi correspondence with the Viceroy.

A Phase of the Indian Struggle. Syama Prasad Mookerjee. Nadia: Monjendra N. Bhowmik, Modern Indian Press, 1942. 90pp. NAI; PIB 188; CRL.

Letters from the author, a Bengal nationalist, written during his tenure as Minister and addressed to the Viceroy and Bengal Governor (March–November 1942). Critical of the Cripps Mission.

Rashtriya Diary, 1941 (H). Calcutta: General Printing Works, 1941. 300pp. IOL B 185; NAI 174; PIB 128, 211.

Review of nationalist activities, then a diary with some English inscriptions.

Sattarah Din Ki Cahal-Pahal (H). Sri Ram Jalote. Bareilly: Mitra Press, 1942. 61pp. IOL B 306; NAI 131; PIB 204; CRL.

The Sensational 17 Days. On the Cripps Mission and Congress–British maneuvering.

Tarikh-i-Azad Hind Phauj (U). Imdad Sabari. 2d ed. Delhi: Ali Press, 1945. 200pp. IOL 179; PIB 215.

History of the I.N.A., strongly critical of British rule.

Why Cripps Failed. M. Subrahmanyan, ed. New Delhi: Hindustan Times, 1942. 48+58pp. NAI; PIB 6A; CRL.

Description of the Cripps Mission and the Congress position, prepared by the *Hindustan Times* staff during the voluntary closure of the paper in response to press restrictions. Appendices include documents.

Yuddha Aur Janata (H). Narendra Dev. Lucknow: U.P. Congress Socialist Party, Kalka Press (Patna), n.d. 40pp. PIB 209.

Analysis of Western motives and involvement in the Second World War. Calls for continued non-cooperation.

Europe Ki Larai Aur Bharat Varsh (H). Muzaffarpur: Zilla Samyavadi Dal, 1940. 1p. IOL F 75.

Mimeographed poster commenting on the Second World War.

INA Calendar (H, English). 1p. Lahore: Victory Stationery, 1946. CRL.

Pictures of Nehru, Bose, Abul Kalam Azad, and other nationalists surrounding a red-white-and-blue calendar.

Our Liberator: Subhas Babu Zindabad. n.i. 1p. CRL.

Picture of Bose centered in a green-red-and-blue poster, with people at his feet.

Students, Youth

Desh Ke Naujavan Kya Karen? (H). Tulsi Prasad Shrivastava. Cawnpur: c. 1936. 6pp. IOL F 122; PIB 75A.

What Can the Country's Youth Do? An appeal to students to join the Congress and fight British rule.

An Appeal to the Student. Committee of Action for Independence. n.p., c. 1932. GIPOL 1932, 207.

A poster asking that youth join the nationalist cause.

An Appeal to the Students of Bengal. K. M. Ahmad, President, Bengal Provincial Students Federation. Calcutta, Sri Bharati Press, c. 1940. 2pp. PIB 129, 135.

Poster. Socialist call for students to demand cultural, political, and academic rights.

An Appeal to the Young. Raj Kumar, President, Young Socialist Republican Association. Calcutta: n.d. GIPOL 1929, 27/1.

Call for "young comrades" to initiate revolution. Stresses armed revolt, attacks passive resistance. Sketches out a plan for violent attacks, including procurement of poison, arms, and bombs.

Arise, Awake. Moradabad: Jagdish and K. Shashi, S. M. Printing Press, c. 1930. 2pp. PIB 29.

Poster filled with references to rebellion, "the tri-color," and student revolt.

Call to Youth. n.p.: Swatantra Bharat Samiti, United Provinces, n.d., c. 1932. 1p. IOL.

Broadside calling for youth to revolt.

Naini Tal Ki Sarad Paharion Par Phirangion Ke Agenton Ke Nadir Shahi Hukum (U). Bareilly: Comrade Youth League, Qadiri Press, n.d. 1p. IOL 3; PIB 29.

Appeal for boycott of schools and colleges.

Vidharthiyo (H). Shabhu Narayan Dikshit, ed. Cawnpur: Agarval Press, 1930. 1p. IOL F 120; PIB 29.

Poster on why students should join the satyagraha campaign, the Congress.

A Word to College and University Students. Sampurna Nand. n.p., Hind Provincial Congress Committee, c. 1932. 2pp. PIB 65.

Short review of Indian history; calls for students to aid the Congress.

Workers, Farmers[20]

All India Kisan Sabha, 3rd Session Address of the Chairman of the Reception Committee. Kamini Kumar Dutt. *Presidential*

20. A number of organizations, Socialist and Communist, arose in

Address. Swami Sahajanand. n.i., c. 1938. 20, 23pp. CRL.
Addresses at the Comilla conference, May 14–15, 1938.

Annual Report of All India Kisan Sabha, 1939–40. Ahmedabad: All India Kisan Sabha, Sri Naryanan Printing Press, c. 1940. 48pp. NAI; PIB 128; CRL.
Criticizes government repression of the peasant movement. Resolutions include homage to dead comrades, support of tenantry legislation, resistance to the European war, and advocacy of Indian freedom.

Bismal Ki Tarap Aur Kisanon Ki Durdasha (U). Ram Prasad Bismil. Lucknow: Ram Svarup Caman, Lucknow, 1931. 8pp. IOL 116; PIB 21.
Bismal's Pain and the Wretched Condition of Farmers. Revolutionary poetry.

Dukhi Dunian, 1. Kartar Singh, pub. Meerut: Azad Press, c. 1937. 40pp. PIB 116; CRL.
Poems addressed to farmers.

Kaun Kaise Jita Hai? (U). Jai Bukhari. Bombay: Mazdur Party, Rahimi Press, c. 1933. 77pp. PIB 10; CRL.
Who Survives How? A Communist tract on labor problems and the plight of the working class.

Kisan Bhaiyon Ke Prati (H). Cawnpur: Cawnpur District Committee, n.i., c. 1931. 6pp. IOL F 118; PIB 65.
Call for non-cooperation, nonpayment of taxes.

Kisanon Ka Bugle (H). Ulphat Singh "'Nirbhaya." Ajmer: Jitmal Luniya, Sasta Sahitya Press, 1930. 48pp. IOL B 403; PIB 70.
Poetry addressed to farmers.

Kisanon Ke Sath Zulam (H). Vedkatsh Narayan Tivari, ed. Allahabad: All India Congress Committee, 1931. 74pp. PIB 6; CRL.
Study of rural conditions, reference to farmer unions. Statistical tables, Gandhi statements appended.

Kisanon Ki Kasht Kahani (H). Harisharad Tivari. Cawnpur: Cawnpur Printing Press, n.d. 15pp. PIB 78.
On the activities, conditions of farmers.

Kisanon Ki Pukar (H). Ram Candra, ed., pub. Aligarh: Shivaji Press, 1930. 8pp. IOL B 382; PIB 8.
Poetry on rural conditions.

North India during the 1920s and attempted to mobilize both the rural and urban lower classes. Background in Nanda, *Socialism in India.*

Kisanon Se Prarthana (H). "Ek Dukhi Kisan." n.i. 4pp. IOL B 395; PIB 21.

Call to farmers in simple Hindi. Urges political participation, non-cooperation with the British.

Mazdur Kisan (H). Prayag Narayan Srivastava. 2 eds. Bombay: Congress Socialist Publishing House, 1935. 16pp. NAI; CRL. Benares: Sarasvati Press, n.d. 16pp. PIB 106.

Short history of the Congress, with appeal to farmers and workers.

Navayuvakon Se Do Baten (H). Prince Kropotkin. n.p., n.d. 60pp. IOL B 148.

Edited translation relating to worker/peasant conditions.

Suraji Rasiya (H). Thakur Harnandan Singh, Muttra, pub. Agra: Adarsh Press, c. 1929. 8pp. IOL B 312; PIB 64.

Poetry on kisan activities, nationalism.

Zamindaron Di Pukar (P). Sialkot: Nau Javan Bharat Sabha, Mahbub-i-Am Press (Amritsar), c. 1932. 8pp. PIB 9; CRL.

Poetry and prose on rural conditions in India. Call for revolution.

Ab Kab Tak. n.p., Bihar Congress Party, n.d. 2pp. IOL F 127; PIB 212.

Mimeographed circular. Calls for unity of working class and describes alleged British exploitations.

Avahan (H). Cawnpur: Surya Prasad Avasthi, Chief Secretary, Cawnpur Mazdur Sabha. Agarval Press, c. 1930. 1p. IOL B 176.

Poster with messages addressed to workers.

Congress Committee Ka Elan (H). Ram Candra Sharma. Bulandshahr: c. 1930. 2pp. IOL F 73.

Poster with appeal to kisans, on non-cooperation theme.

Dvitiya Doaba Kisan Sammelan Sabhapati Ka Bhashan (H). n.i. 2pp. IOL F 24; PIB 9.

Presidential speech delivered at a U.P. meeting of kisans, September 1932. Appeal for non-cooperation, refusal to pay revenue.

Kisan Bhaiyo (H, U). Rafi Ahmad Kidvai. Allahabad: 1931. 1p. H: IOL F 92; PIB 74. U: IOL 182.

Poster on kisans, taxes, and nonpayment of revenue.

Kisan Shreni Sajag Ho (H). Onkar Nath, et al. Allahabad: Abhudaya Press, c. 1934. 2pp. IOL B 196; PIB 108.

Handbill calling for nonpayment of taxes.

Kisan Bhaiya (H). Brahmanand. Benares: Bharat Press, c. 1920. 1p. IOL F 1; PIB 51.
Poetry on non-cooperation.

Kisan Mazdur Bhuke Kyon Marte Hain? (H). Ladli Prasad Srivastava. Jhansi: Kisan Mazdur Sangh, Svadhin Press, 1930. 1p. PIB 29.
Poster on conditions of farmers.

Kisanon Ceto (H). n.i. 1p. IOL F 76.
Poster with poetic appeal to farmers.

Kisanon Ka Kartavya (H). Vaijnath Kapur. Allahabad: Misra Printing Works, 1930. 2pp. IOL F 74; PIB 47.
Appeal to farmers.

Kisanon Ko Sandesh (H). Pandit Moti Lal Nehru. Allahabad: Allahabad Law Printing Press, n.d. 2pp. PIB 153.
Handbill urging kisan–Congress cooperation.

Lagan Band Kar Do (H). Benares: Congress Committee, c. 1931. 1p. IOL F 117; PIB 65.
Statement addressed to farmers, on nonpayment of taxes.

Lagan Ka Ek Paisa Bhi Dena Pap Hai (H). Unao: Congress Committee, n.d. 1p. IOL F 115.
Addressed to farmers, an appeal on non-cooperation, in which it is claimed that giving the British a pice is a sin.

Mazdur Jhand Ki Prarthana (H). Cawnpur: Surya Prasad Avasthi, Agarval Press, n.d. 2pp. PIB 29.
Poster (poetry) calling for workers to revolt.

Prantiya Congress Committee Ka Kisanon Ka: Lagan Ka Ek Paisa Na Do (H). n.i., United Provinces Congress Committee. 1p. PIB 65.
Appeal for farmers to pay no land tax, rent.

Miscellaneous

Bande Mataram. Poona: Hari Ragunath Bhagvat, 1909. 93+100+108pp. 3 vols. PIB (vols. 2–3); NAI (vols. 1–3).
Articles reprinted from a controversial Calcutta journal. On Tilak, the bureaucracy.

The Burmese Situation, 1930–31. U. Saw. Rangoon: Burma Guardian Press, 1931. 15+xx pp. NAI; PIB 50; CRL; GIPOL 1932, 117.
The author, an elected member of the Burmese Legislative

Council, describes an uprising against the British (December 1930). Pictures, evidence appended.

Cand: Phansi Ank (H). Chatur Sen Shastri, ed. Allahabad: 1928. 323pp. IOL F 33/1; NAI 172; CRL.
Special number on capital punishment. The last section deals with Indians killed in the 1857 Mutiny, and since 1900 in the freedom struggle.

Char Aham Masail Par Tabsara (U). Lahore: Fazal Husain, Hazara Press, c. 1937. 16pp. PIB 145; CRL.
Commentary on four issues—cow slaughter, the Ahmadiya movement, Congress politics, and contemporary journalism.

Coolie Pratha (H). Lakshman. Cawnpur: Pratap Press, 1916. 46pp. IOL B 159; PIB 205A.
Criticism of social conditions, problems of coolies in India.

Forecast Book: Establishment of a New Government in the Year 1945: India Will Rule the World. Dattatraya Puranik. n.p., 1941. 35pp. NAI; CRL.
A former railway employee foretells that the British will leave India in 1945. He asserts that only his mantras (spells) and religious ceremonies can bring world peace. Supposedly Brahmans will rule the world after 1945.

Glimpses of the East for 1940–41. T. Kawata, ed. Tokyo: Nippon Yusen Kaisya Official Guide, 1941. 600pp. NAI; PIB 213.
Yearbook with facts on Asian nations. Three pages on India suggest that the country is a dumping ground for English goods.

India and Her People. Swami Abhedananda. Calcutta: Ramakrishna Vedanta Math, 1940. 2d ed. (1st pub. in 1905). 285pp. RA.
Survey of Indian civilization, slightly pro-Hindu but very mild in tone. It is unclear why this item was banned.

India and Her Peoples. A. Deavilla Walker. London: Wesleyan Methodist Missionary Society, 1922. 2d ed. (Livingstone Press, 1930) banned. 144pp. R&R 1938, 2129; R.A.
Written at the request of the United Council for Missionary Education, this survey apparently was too sympathetic to the Congress and Gandhi. Also, contains criticism of Muslims and comments on communal tension.

Jat Jati Ka Mukamal Halat Yani Jat Darpan (U). M. L. Gupta. Shaharanpur: Candi Prasad, 1934. 129pp. NAI; PIB 106; CRL.

Anti-Jat tract. Claims that Jats are foreigners, not Ksyhatrias (warrior class).

Krishna Janmasthan Ka Alha Arthat Jailon Ki Pol (H). Cawnpur: Vansh Gopal, New Order Press, c. 1936. 15pp. IOL B 409; PIB 32.

On condition of political prisoners in jails.

The New Magna Carta. Kanhaiya Lal Gauba. Lahore: c. 1941. 152pp. NAI; R&R 1938, 2129.

Criticism of the integrity of Chief Justice Douglas Young, Lahore High Court.

Shiva or the Future of India. Rubeigh James Minney. London: Kegan Paul, n.d. 96pp. CRL; R.A.

Survey of Indian life, emphasizing sexual practices. Very critical of social and religious ideas.

Tisri Pothi, Chauthi, Panchvi, Chathi Pothi (H). Ram Das Gaur, ed. Calcutta: c. 1930. 104+152+240+271pp. PIB 22.

Four works containing short stories and poems on history, religion, and Gandhi.

Ulate Cor Kotvale Dante (H). Sant Prasad Sharma, ed., pub. Benares: Hitcintak Press, n.d. 18pp. IOL B 278.

Condemnation of Brahman-non-Brahman marriages. Cites cases, calls for ostracism and other reprisals. Apparently controversial.

Zulami Sarkar (H). "Ek Jail Pravasi." Peshawar: c. 1934. 6pp. IOL B 435; NAI; PIB 144; CRL.

Poems on aman sabhas (peasant organizations) and Punjab history. Pro-Hindu, supports cow protection.

Azadi De Ashik Maut De Munh Vich (G). Amritsar: Rajsi Kaidi Committee, Sudharak Press, c. 1932. GIPOL 1933, 48/3.

Poster on jail conditions of those jailed in 1914–1915. "It is illegal for Punjabis to eat, drink and live because the national moths of 1914–15 rot in jails for our sake and fall into the jaws of death."

Future of India from July 1931 to June 1933. Shriut Tivri Tapasvi. Hyderabad (Sind): Hindustan Electric Press, n.d. 2pp. PIB 20.

Predicts communal riots followed by Hindu–Muslim cooperation, revolution, and a victory for the Congress and Gandhi.

Tracts for Rangoon, 1: Welcome to the Territorials. John Carmen. Rangoon: Y.M.C.A., c. 1914. 4pp. IOL.

Tracts for Rangoon, 2: 29th Street by Night. John Carmen. Rangoon: Y.M.C.A., 1914. 8pp. IOL.

Tracts for Rangoon, 3: There Be Your Gods. John Carmen. Rangoon: Y.M.C.A., 1914. 8pp. IOL.

Tracts for Rangoon, 5: Rangoon's Scarlet Sin. John Carmen. Rangoon: Y.M.C.A., 1914. 8pp. IOL.

Tracts for Rangoon, 9: Into the Deep. John Carmen. Rangoon: Y.M.C.A., 1915. 7pp. IOL.

Series of tracts on prostitution in Rangoon. Probably banned because of poor image portrayed of both Burmese and British (military) society.

Section 4

PATRIOTIC POETRY, SONGS

Indian nationalism fostered an outpouring of patriotic poetry and songs, probably the largest single category of printed matter confiscated by the British. The collections relate to a variety of subjects. For example, *Garam Ghazlen* contains six poems on topics such as non-cooperation, prophecies about India, Gandhi, the spinning wheel, patriotism, and "an appeal to the Viceroy." Because many works tend to be repetitive or deal with the same themes, annotation has been minimized.[1] The following translation from one collection, *Rashtriya Phag*, however, should provide the reader with the flavor of the material:

Poem 4. "Non-Co-operation is being preached."
Do not pollute yourselves by learning English. Preserve the reputation of Hindi. Do not be slaves of the English but be a true worker for your country.
Establish panchayats (local councils) as the entrances to justice. Boycott foreign goods and only use swadeshi (Indian goods) ones. The British courts suck your blood, and you become intoxicated as one who smokes hashish. False witnesses and pleaders eat delicious and fresh food at your expense.
The Hindus and Muslims should unite like brothers and do each others' work. They shall break the head of "disunity" and introduce swaraj (independence) into every family. "Give up practising in law courts and start national organizations" is the cry, like the roar of the lion, of Mahatma Gandhi.

Poem 5. Please listen to my song. While on tours, the British officials do not pay the least regard for the ryot. They exact begar (forced labor) and beat and thrash the poor. These men are hopelessly untrue to their salt. They try to pluck out the moustaches of respected people. These officials cannot be corrected as the tails of the dogs cannot be made straight. Injustice pervades their veins.

Poem 7. Do not touch polluted goods. In purifying sugar, the British use bullock's blood and bones. Through this you will be polluted and your sin doubled. The foreign saffron contains beef,

1. A detailed study and translation of some banned literature is in Dharam Paul Sarin, *Influence of Political Movements on Hindi Literature, 1906–1947*.

and camphor is mixed with fat. By lighting the imported camphor, you pollute your own faith. The English medicines contain wine. It is a sin to drink them. Your country has been robbed of its wealth by English "quacks."

Poem 11. The zamindars and the police always oppress the peasant. Petty officials indulge in a luxurious style of life. They send for prostitutes and opium while the kisans (peasants) lead a miserable life. The barristers and lawyers amass fortunes by creating disunion among us. These are the most irresponsible and dishonest (they make falsehood appear truth and are the origin of sin). Do not get into their hands. In spite of the fact that cows are being butchered continually and are in great suffering, yet rich men indulge in ease and comfort. All government servants from the high to the low accept bribes. It is folly to expect justice from the British *raj.*

The arrangement of bibliographic information follows the pattern in the preceding sections (where poetry on specific topics may also be found). In addition, translations of catchy or representative titles have been provided. A few words of caution are in order. First, the titles frequently do not accurately reflect the content of a work. A picture of Gandhi on the cover or mention of his name on the title page, for example, does not mean that all or even one poem in the collection deal with the Mahatma. Similarly, poetry with titles such as "revolution" or "blood" as often as not relate to nonviolence. Secondly, the poetry was reprinted on so many occasions (with title changes or slight alteration to throw off the police) that some titles in the section may duplicate each other. This also may have led to occasional misinformation or confusion as to publisher, compiler, and press.

Glossary of Frequently Used Words

alha—ballad in a traditional meter

carkha—spinning wheel

gan, *gayan*, *gitanjali*—song, poetry

kaum—nation, community

kranti—revolution

lahar—wave, movement

larai—fight, war

phag—typical song sung during *Holi* festival

rashtra, *rashtriya*—nation, national

sandesh—message

sangit—song

sangram—war, combat

shahid—martyr

singhnad—roaring of a lion, war cry

svaraj—independence, self-rule

svatantra—freedom

tarang—wave, movement

updesh—sermon, preaching

vatan—nation

Adarsh Pushpanjali (H). Delhi: Lakshman Pathik, Rajendra Press, n.d. 32pp. IOL B 144; PIB 70.

Adhunik Bharat (H). Pyare Lal Ganga Rade. Calcutta: Hindi Pustak Agency, 1923. 114pp. IOL B 108; GIPOL 1932, 209.

Ah-i-Bekas Urf Azadi Ki Lahar (U). *Sigh of the Helpless or the Freedom Movement.* Jagadhari: Bhai Sheo Prasad Sangal, Krishna Press, c. 1930. 56pp. IOL 161; PIB 45.

Ahimsa Ka Jhanda (H). *The Flag of Nonviolence.* Vishvanath Sharma, ed., pub. Benares: Sarasvati Press, c. 1930. 15pp. IOL B 292; PIB 70.

Ahimsa Ki Samshir (H). *The Sword of Nonviolence.* Thakur Prasad, ed., pub. Mirzapur: Khicri Samacar Press, 1930. 7pp. IOL B 245; NAI 48; PIB 64; CRL.

Ahimsa Sangram (H). *The Nonviolent War.* Benares: Pandit Ram Sammukh Shukla, 1922. 8pp. IOL B 353; PIB 56.

Ahimsatmak Mahatma Gandhi Ghor Sangram (H). Jagdish Prasad Tivari. Cawnpur: Jagdish Granthmala, Fancy Press, c. 1921. 13pp. IOL B 356; PIB 37, 67.

Allahabad Satyagrahi Svayam Sevakon Ke Rashtriya Gan (H). Allahabad: Satyagraha Committee, Rajpali Press, 1930. 13pp. IOL B 323; PIB 29.

Angrezon Ki Akar Phun Nika Gai (H, U). *The Removal of English Boastfulness.* Agra: Babu Ram Dunerya, Bharat Book Depot, n.d. 16pp. H: IOL B 397. U: IOL 117; NAI 59; PIB 21; CRL.

Angrezon Ki Tayen Tayen Phis (H, U). *The English Crowing Is Stopped.* Delhi: Pandit Babu Ram Sharma, Martand

Press, c. 1930. 16pp. H: IOL B 314; NAI 184; PIB 64; CRL. U: IOL 99, 102.

Asahyog (H). Bindeshvari Prasad Malaviya, ed., pub. Mirzapur: Jarj Printing Works (Benares), 1921. 2d ed. (another ed., Shambhu Printing Works, Benares). 15pp. IOL B 164, 190; PIB 52; R&R 1922, 1110.

Asahyog Anand (H). Nilakanth Gupta, ed., pub. Jhansi: Utsah Press, 1921. 28pp. IOL B 377.

Asahyog Bahar (H). Ram Narayan Mastana, pub. Cawnpur: Catcah Press (also, Utsah Press), 1921. 15pp. IOL B 141; PIB 51; R&R 1922, 1110.

Asahyog Cana (H). Nirbhayanand Etawah: Ganesh Anand Yatri (Adarsh Press), 1920. 10pp. IOL F 9; PIB 153.

Asahyog Ka Agrabomb (H). Cawnpur: Ramkrishan Lal, Rajhans Press (Khatri Press), n.d. 6pp. IOL B 357; PIB 37.

Asahyog Kajali (H). Mirzapur: Bindeshvari Prasad Malaviya, Myatin Press (Aligarh), 1921. 16pp. IOL B 369.

Asahyog Phag (H). Dvarka Prasad, pub. Allahabad: Krishna Press, 1921. 18pp. IOL B 138; PIB 51; R&R 1922, 1110.

Asahyog Tarang (H). "Ek Desh Premi." Cawnpur: Madhav Nandan Misra, Rajhans Press, 1920. 16pp. IOL B 372; PIB 37.

Asahyogi Divane Ki Tarang (H). Allahabad: Sangam Lal Agarval, Misra Printing Works, n.d. 16pp. IOL B 449.

Asahyogi Vir Bharat (H). Surendra Sharma, ed. Cawnpur: Cunni Lal Gaur, Rajhans Press, n.d. 16pp. IOL B 262; PIB 51; R&R 1922, 1110.

Asli Rashtriya Alha (H). Prag Datt Pande. rev.ed., Farukhabad: Ram Ratna Tivari and Ram Rakshpal, Cintamini Press, 1922. 10pp. IOL F 36; PIB 56.

Atal Raj Ki Kunji Arthat Mahatmaji Ki Pukar (H). Allahabad: Saryu Lal, Raja Press, n.d. 8pp. IOL B 86; PIB 47.

Azad Bharat Ke Gane (H). Pandit Ram Gopal Shukla ("Prakash"), ed. Benares: Azad Sainik Desh Bandhu Samarak Bhandar, Sarasvati Press, 1930. 16pp. IOL B 208; PIB 29; CRL.

Azad Bharat Varsh (H). Prabhu Narayan Misra, ed., pub. Benares: Shri Press, 1931. 16pp. IOL B 389; NAI 40; PIB 29; CRL.

Azad Gitanjali (H). N. M. Upadhyaya, ed. Kandva: Karmavari Press, 1931. 32pp. IOL B 445; PIB 6; CRL.

Azad Hind Urf Mubarakbadi (H). Pandit Ram Gopal Shukla ("Prakash"), ed. Cawnpur: Unshi Singh ("Ratna"), Vishnu Prayag Press, 1930. 6pp. IOL F 107; PIB 29.

Azad-i-Hind Urf Svaraj Ki Devi (U). Hadi Hussain. Moradabad: Shamas Press, n.d. 8pp. IOL 154.

Azade Hind Urf Daman Ka Divala, pt. 1 (H). Indra Prasad Gupta. Benares: Pramed Samaj, Shri Press, 1931. 16pp. IOL B 156.

Azadi De Git (U). Dev Raj Dev. Lahore: Am Ditta Mal, 1931. 16pp. CRL.

Azadi Ka Bigul (H). Allahabad: Uma Shankar Dikshit, Raja Press, 1930. 16pp. IOL B 91.

Azadi Ka Bigul (H). Kshama Candra Rastogi, ed., pub. Benares: Sarasvati Press, 1930. 15pp. IOL B 116; PIB 29; CRL.

Azadi Ka Bomb (H). Jagannath Prasad Arora, ed., pub. Benares: Lakshmi Press, 1930. 15pp. IOL B 152; NAI 2.

Azadi Ka Danka (H). Vishvanath Sharma, ed., pub. Benares: Sarasvati Press, c. 1930. 13pp. IOL B 240, 277; PIB 64.

Azadi Ka Danka (H). Allahabad: Beni Madho Gupta, Union Job Press, 1930. 19pp. PIB 215A.

Azadi Ka Jhanda (H). Agra: Hindi Sahitya Book Depot, A. B. Press, 1930. 8pp. IOL B 311; PIB 64.

Azadi Ke Nushke (H). Yamuna Singh, ed., pub. Calcutta: Lakshmi Vilas Press, c. 1930. 16pp. IOL B 304; PIB 70.

Azadi Ke Tarane (U). Comrade Amritsari. Amritsar: Hamid-ul-Hak, 1931. 32pp. PIB 36.

Azadi Ki Bansuri (H). Jogeshvar Prasad ("Khalish"), ed. Gaya: Vijay Kumar Sinha, Citra Gupta Press, n.d. 20pp. PIB 6.

Azadi Ki Camak (H). Shiva Ram Parivrajak, ed., pub. Benares: Sarasvati Press, c. 1930. 15pp. IOL B 184.

Azadi Ki Devi Lakhsmi Bai (U). Delhi: Pandit Babu Ram Sharma, J. M. Press, c. 1930. 15pp. PIB 57.

Azadi Ki Garjana (H). Ganga Prasad, pub. Cawnpur: Prem Printing Press, 1930. 8pp. IOL B 425.

Azadi Ki Gunj (H). Pandit Vishvanath Sharma, ed., pub. Benares: Sarasvati Press, 1930. 15pp. PIB 29.

Azadi Ki Hunkar (H). *The Roar of Freedom.* Pandit Ram Gopal Shukla ("Prakash"). Chapra, Sri Tribhuvanath Azad, Sarasvati Press (Benares), 1930. 16pp. IOL B 275.

Azadi Ki Larai (H). Candra Bhan Gupta, pub. Meerut: c. 1939. 8pp. CRL.

Azadi Ki Tan (H). Ramanandan Sah. Chapra: Jagdish Press, 1931. 16pp. PIB 1; CRL.

Azadi Ki Tarang (H). Sonepat: Kale Singh, Sarla Hindi Pustakalaya, Rajendra Printing Press (Delhi), c. 1932. 16pp. IOL B 309; PIB 42; GIPOL 1932, 117.

Azadi Ki Top (H). Bhola Nath ("Bedhab"), ed., pub. Benares: Lakshmi Press, 1930. 15pp. IOL B 423.

Azadi Ki Umang Athva Rashtriya Gan (H). Ganesh Shankar Vidyarthi, Kanhai Lal Dikshit, eds. Lucknow: Indra Pustakalaya, Bharat Bhushan Press, 1930. 16pp. IOL B 437; NAI 170; PIB 21.

Azadi Ya Maut (H). *Freedom or Death.* Ram Svarup Gupta, ed., pub. Muttra: H. D. Printing Works, 1931. 12pp. IOL B 62; PIB 27.

Bahan Satyavati Devi Ka Jail Sandesh (H, U). Babu Ram Sharma, ed., pub. Delhi: J. M. Press, n.d. 16pp. H: IOL B 146; PIB 70. U: IOL 98.

Bahare Hind (H). Lala Rattan Lal ("Zamarrud"), pub. Bulandsahar: Badri Printing Works, 1921. 8pp. IOL B 139; PIB 51; R&R 1922, 1110.

Baharon Ko Cetvani (H). *A Warning to Foreigners.* "Ek Becain." Cawnpur: c. 1930. 16pp. IOL B 96; PIB 64.

Bande Mataram (U). Siraj-ul-Daula. Lahore: Narayan Datt Saighal, c. 1931. 40pp. CRL.

Bas Cal Vase (H). Lakshmi Shankar Sharma. Agra: Arya Bhaskar Press, 1922. 8pp. IOL B 127.

Bedar-i-Hind (U). Jagdish Prakash Sharma, pub. 2 pts. Bedayon: Victoria Press, c. 1921. 8+8pp. Pt. 1: IOL 149. Pt. 2: IOL 150; PIB 37.

Bediyon Ki Jhankar (H). Jagannath Prasad Arora, ed., pub. Benares: Lakshmi Press, 1930. 16pp. IOL B 298.

Bekason Ke Ansu (H). *Tears of the Helpless*. Tribhuvanath ("Azad"), ed. Benares: Shivanandan Prasad Varma, Lakshmi Press, 1930. 15pp. IOL B 95; PIB 64.

Bhagvan Gandhi Athva Svatantra Bharat Ka Bigul (H). Thakur Munshi Singh, ed., pub. Lucknow: Jagdish Press, 1930. 16pp. IOL B 448.

Bhajan Carkha Va Jhanda (H). Siryaram Sharma Misra. Gorakhpur: Changur Tripathi, Gorakhpur Printing Press, 1930. 8pp. IOL B 84; NAI 105; PIB 47; CRL.

Bhanda Phor (H). Eta: Raghubar Dayal, Adarsh Press (Agra), 1931. 8pp. IOL B 50; PIB 27.

Bharat Ka Carkha (H). Jagat Narayan Sharma ("Mitra"), pub. Farukhabad: Cintamani Press, n.d. 8pp. IOL B 367; PIB 37.

Bharat Ka Mahabharat (H). Janki Prasad ("Bedhdak"), pub. Fatehpur: Rangeshvar Press (Benares), 1931. 16pp. IOL B 51; PIB 27.

Bharat Ki Lahar (H). Manda State: Pandit Gaurishankar Shukla, Sundar Bandhu Press (Jubbulpur), 1931. 8pp. IOL B 104; PIB 38.

Bharat Ki Rashtriya Alha (H). Babu Ram Pengoriya, pub. Agra: Jain Press, 1930. 32pp. IOL B 81; PIB 29.

Bharat Mata Ke Zakhmi Lal Arthat Azadi Ki Bhent (H). *The Wounds of Mother India or Freedom's Offering*. R. N. Sharma, ed. 2d ed. Delhi: Ram Richpal, Martand Press (also, Svadhin Press), 1930. 15pp. IOL B 420; PIB 70.

Bharat Mata Ki Latar (H). *The Degradation of Mother India*. Agra: Babu Ram Sharma, Svadhin Press (also Svatantra Press, Delhi), n.d. 16pp. IOL B 263; NAI 99; PIB 47; CRL.

Bharat Mata Ki Pukar (H). Pandit Lakshmi Candra ("Strotriya"). Jhansi: Pandit Ram Nath Trivedi, Anand Press, 1930. 13pp. IOL B 412.

Bharat Mata Ki Pukar (H). 4th ed. Bijnaur: Manni Lal Sharma, 1930. 8pp. IOL B 242; PIB 64.

Bharat Men Daman Carkha (H). Madan Mohan Malaviya. Benares: Pandit Govind Malaviya, 1932. 14pp. IOL B 132; PIB 1 (trans., PIB 35).

Bharat Picketing Bhajan (H). Markande Shayar. Benares: Meva Lal, Sri Bageshvar Press, 1930. 8pp. IOL B 320.

Bharat Rashtriya Ghazal (H). Kanhaiya Lal, ed. Benares: Mitra and Co., 1931. 8pp. IOL B 175.

Bharatiya Tarane (H). 2 eds. Lucknow: Bharat Bhushan Press, n.d. Delhi: Rajendra Press, n.d. 16pp. IOL B 220; PIB 42.

Bharatiya Tarang (U). Hulas Varma ("Premi"). Dehra Dun: Bharatiya Press, n.d. 48pp. IOL 167; CRL.

Bharatiya Vir (H). Delhi: Khaim Cand, Rajendra Press, c. 1932. 15pp. IOL B 221.

Bijli (H). "Cakar." Gorakhpur: Ram Das Jaisval, Kumar Press, 1930. 24pp. IOL B 322; PIB 8.

Caumasa Barsar (U). Fakir Cand. Cawnpur: Aziz Press, 1922. 8pp. IOL 158; PIB 56.

Caumasa Va Kajali (H). Benares: Bachu Lal, Raja Press, c. 1930. 8pp. PIB 67.

Camakta Svarajya (H). Ranchor Das, ed., pub. Benares: Gokul Press, 1930. 14pp. IOL B 114; PIB 67.

Carkhe Ka Tar (H). Gorakhpur: Ram Das Pandey, Hindu Mitra Press, 1931. 8pp. IOL B 49; PIB 27.

Chanik Sandhi Athva Mahatma Gandhi Ki Sujh (H). Lucknow: Vimal Granthmala, Oriental Press, n.d. 16pp. PIB 2.

Congress Bigul (H). Cawnpur: Pyare Lal Agarval and Ganesh Jog, heads, Satyagraha Committee, Agarval Press, c. 1930. 16pp. IOL B 233; PIB 29.

Congress Ka Bigul (H). 4th ed. Delhi: Thakur Devi Singh, Svadhin Press, 1930. 16pp. IOL B 48; PIB 64.

Congress Ki Dhum (H). Lucknow: Thakur Gangadhar, Bharat Bhushan Press, 1931. 8pp. IOL B 254; PIB 27.

Congress Ki Lalkar (H). Indore: Ramcaran Misra, Sri Lakshmi Vilas Press, n.d. 16pp. IOL B 271; PIB 6.

Congress Pushpanjali (U). Tek Cand ("Bharati"). Saharanpur: Faruki Press, 1930. 32pp. IOL 160; NAI; PIB 45.

Cunar Ka Rashtriya Jhanda (H). Cunar: Janardan Misra, Khicri Samachar Press (Mirzapur), n.d. 7pp. IOL B 428; NAI 32; PIB 21; CRL.

Cuncun Ka Murabba (H). Bhaggu Lal Rathor ("Mitra"), pub. Cawnpur: c. 1931. 16pp. IOL B 177; PIB 55.

Daivi Shakti (H). Shiva Shankar Dvivedi. Benares: Hitaishi Printing Works, c. 1930. 16pp. IOL B 251; PIB 64.

Dard Vatan (H). Lala Ratan Lal ("Zamarrud"). Sikandrabad: Kuncar Bhupal Krishna, Bandri Printing Works, 1921. 7pp. IOL B 340; PIB 51; R&R 1922, 1110.

Desh Ka Rag (H). Ciranji Lal Vidyarthi, ed., pub. Delhi: Pathik Co., c. 1932. 16pp. IOL B 44; PIB 29.

Desh Ki Tan (H). Jagannath Prasad Gupta, ed. Benares: Ganga Prasad Gupta, Sri Lakshmi Narayan Press, c. 1920. 16pp. IOL B 451; PIB 37.

Deshbhakton Ke Git (H). Satyendra Nath. Lahore: Sarasvati Ashram, Fine Art Printing Works, 1932. 16pp. PIB 6; GIPOL 1932, 149.

Deshbhakton Ki Lahar (H). Visvambhar Dayal Misra, ed., pub. Etavah: Sudharak Press, 1931. 14pp. IOL B 341.

Deshbhakti Ki Pukar (H). Mohan Lal ("Arman"), pub. Cawnpur: Shankar Press, c. 1931. 8pp. IOL B 364; NAI 35; PIB 1; CRL.

Din Ke Ansu (H). Natthulal Mahaur. Jhansi: Sri Bhagvan Das Joshi, Balvant Press, 1931. 6pp. IOL B 339; PIB 8.

Dukhi Dil Ki Pukar (U, G). "Panchi." Delhi: Svadhin Press, 1930. 16pp. G: IOL; PIB 70. U: PIB 70.

Dukhi Ya Hindi Ki Pukar (U). Muhammad Abad Allah, pub. Lahore: Roshan Steam Press, n.d. 8pp. PIB 87.

Dukhiya Bharat (H). Pyare Lal, Vaisya, ed., pub. Sahajahapur: Singhal Printing Works, c. 1931. 16pp. IOL B 380; NAI 24; PIB 8; CRL.

Gandhi Bigul (H). Cawnpur: Satyagraha Committee, Agarval Press, n.d. 16pp. IOL B 102; PIB 64.

Gandhi Gaurav (H). Lal Mahabali Singh, ed., pub. Rewah State: Bhagvan Press (Allahabad), 1930. 37pp. IOL B 415.

Gandhi Gaurav Gan (H). Ram Narayan Varma, ed., pub. Bareilly: Singhal Printing Works, n.d. 16pp. IOL B 328; PIB 64.

Gandhi Ghor Sangram (H). Jagdish Prasad Tivari. Cawnpur: n.d. 16pp. IOL B 356.

Gandhi Gitanjali (H). Prabhat Kumar Vidyarthi, ed. Cawnpur: Panna Lal Sharma, Sudarshan Press, 1930. 14pp. IOL B 260.

Gandhi Gitanjali (H). Ghasi Ram Sharma, ed., pub. Moradabad: Sharma Machine Press, 1930. 30pp. IOL B 230; PIB 67.

Gandhi Gitsagar (H). Lala Babu Lal, ed., pub. Cawnpur: Sursari Press, 1930. 16pp. IOL B 291; PIB 70.

Gandhi Ka Danka (H). Prayag Singh Varma, ed., pub. Benares: Bharat Press, c. 1921. 13pp. PIB 37.

Gandhi Ka Sudarshana Carkha (U). Mohar Cand ("Mast"), ed., pub. Gurgaon, Sreni Press, Ikbar Press (Delhi), n.d. 15pp. IOL 104; PIB 67.

Gandhi Ka Tir (H). Svami Ramanand Sarasvati. Aligarh: Pandit Ram Prasad Gaur, Rameshvar Press, 1930. 8pp. IOL B 317; PIB 64.

Gandhi Ka Topkhana (H). B. R. Sharma, ed., pub. Delhi: Martand Press, n.d. 16pp. IOL B 250.

Gandhi Ki Andhi (H). Candra Bhan Gupta, ed., pub. Agra: Model Printing Works, c. 1930. 8pp. IOL B 295; PIB 29; CRL (all copies galley proof).

Gandhi Ki Dhum (H). Pyare Lal, Vaisya, ed., pub. Shahajahapur: Singhal Printing Works, c. 1931. 16pp. IOL B 315; NAI 23; PIB 64; CRL.

Gandhi Ki Nangi Talvar (H). Pyare Lal Sharma, ed., pub. Eta: Cintamani Yantralaya, 1922. 8pp. IOL B 405; PIB 56.

Gandhi Ki Top (H). Ram Candra. Aligarh: Shivaji Press, 1930. 8pp. IOL B 302.

Gandhi Pratap, pts. 1–2 (H). Jagannath Pandey, ed., pub. Benares: Congress Committee, Adarsh Press, n.d. 15+12pp. IOL B 136; PIB 51; R&R 1922, 1110.

Gandhi Sandesh (H). Calcutta: Sarasvati Pustak Agency, Vedic Press, Calcutta: n.d. 16pp. IOL B 117; PIB 1.

Gandhi Topivalon Ka Jauhar (H). Ram Singh Varma, ed., pub. 2d ed. Agra: Kesari Press, 1930. 8pp. IOL B 293; NAI 64; PIB 70; CRL.

Gandhi Vijaya (H). Vishvanath Sharma, ed., pub. Barbanki: Deshbandhu Press, 1930. 15pp. IOL B 431; PIB 21.

Gandhiji Ka Carkha (H). Munshi Ram Nand Bihari Lal, ed. Allahabad: Panna Lal Varma, Raja Press, c. 1930. 8pp. IOL B 85.

Garam Ghazlen (H). Saryu Narayan Shukla. Cawnpur: Azad Granthmala, Sudhasancarak Press, 1923. 8pp. CRL.

Garib-ul-Vatan (U). Cawnpur: Pandit Uman Caran Dikshit, Aziz Press, n.d. 8pp. PIB 78.

Garibon Ke Nale (H). Shital Prasad Bishnoi. Cawnpur: Adarsh Press, c. 1922. 16pp. IOL B 168; NAI 126; PIB 76A; CRL.

Garibon Ki Ah (H). *Sigh of the Poor.* Bareilly: Ganga Ram Singh, Singhal Printing Works, c. 1935. 16pp. IOL B 194.

Ghadar Ke Git (H). Balbhadra Prasad Gupta ("Rasik"). Allahabad: Ram Sundar Sharma, Misra Printing Works, c. 1930. 16pp. IOL B 406.

Ghazab Ki Holi (H). Cawnpur: Bharati Bhandar, Anglo-Arabic Press (Lucknow), 1922. 16pp. PIB 37.

Hakumat Ki Pol (U). Bareilly: Arya Granth Ratnakar, Kaum Prast Tracts, #5, n.d. 8pp. IOL 147.

Hind Da Sitara (Panjabi in Nagri). M. S. Panchi. Lahore: Ram Ditta Mal, Virjanand Press, n.d. 8pp. PIB 8; CRL.

Hind Ka Sitara (U). Badayon Press: Muhammad Ghulam Nabi, Amir-ul Ikbal Press, 1922. 8pp. IOL 146; PIB 37.

Hind Ke Lutere (H). Masuria Din Tivari, pub. Allahabad: Union Job Printing Press (Katra), c. 1930. 7pp. PIB 67.

Hridaya Ki Ag (H). *The Fire of the Heart.* Kalyan Kumar Jain ("Shashi"). Moradabad: Kishore Dal, Jain Press, c. 1930. 1p. PIB 99.

Inkilab Ki Lahar, #1 (also printed as *Tuphan-i-Hind*) (U). Ram Prasad Bismil. Saharanpur: Faruki Press, 1929. 16pp. IOL 121; PIB 45.

Inkilab Ki Lahar, #2 (also printed as *Sarojini Sandesh*) (H). Shankar Das. Delhi: Martand Press, n.d. 16pp. CRL.

Inkilab Ki Lahar, #3 (also printed as *Shahidan Ka Sandesh*) (H). Govind Ram Gupta "Rahbar" ed., pub. Delhi: Martand Press, c. 1930. 16pp. IOL B 217; PIB 67.

Inkilab Ki Lahar, #4 (H, U). Govind Ram Gupta, ed. Delhi: Pandit Dvarka Prasad, Martand Press, n.d. 16pp. H: IOL B 337; PIB 67; CRL. U: PIB 29.

Inkilab-i-Hind (U). Hirde Prakash Bhardvaj. Meerut: Reformer Book Depot, Shanti Press, 1921. IOL 143; PIB 62; R&R 1922, 1110.

Inkilab Zindabad Ki Lahar (U). Saharanpur: Shiv Prasad Seth, Faruki Press, n.d. 16pp. IOL 128.

Itihasik Pushpanjali (H). Kunvar Sukhlal. Delhi: Lakshman Pathik, Pathik Pustakalya, c. 1932. 226pp. IOL B 43.

Jailor Ka Divala (U). Shyam Lal Khanna. Lucknow: Avadh Press, 1922. 8pp. IOL 155; PIB 56.

Jang Azadi, pt. 1 (H). Mahashya Moti Ram Varma, ed., pub. Delhi: J. M. Press, 1930. 8pp. IOL B 440; PIB 47.

Javahar Digvijaya (H). Shyamji Parashar. Delhi: Rashtra Nirman Granthmala, 1938. 336pp. NAI 75.

Javahir Ki Jhalak (H). Allahabad: Ganga Prasad Jaisval, 1930. 8pp. IOL B 100.

Javahir Sandesh (H). Gorakhpur: Pandit Ramdas Pandey, Gorakhpur Printing Press, 1931. 14pp. IOL B 257; PIB 21.

Javahrat Ke Tukre (H). Bhagvat Parshad ("Banpati"), pub. Allahabad: Union Job Press, c. 1930. 9pp. IOL B 88; PIB 47.

Jayi Bharat Ya Nutan Bharat (H). Rameshvar Nath Malaviya, ed., pub. Allahabad: Rangeshvar Press, 1931. 8pp. IOL B 342.

Jhankar (H). Candra Datt ("Arya"), ed. Agra: Adarsh Press, c. 1930. 15pp. IOL B 231; PIB 67.

Jigar Ke Tukre (H). *Pieces of Heart.* Vishvanath Prasad Gupta. Houri: Shiv Shambhu Prasad Misra, 1931. 14pp. PIB 1; CRL.

Kalam Ka Jauhar Yani Svarajya Devi (H). Svami Harishankar, pub. Dehra Dun: Tilak Pustak Bhandar, Abyha Press, 1930. 6pp. IOL B 429; PIB 21; CRL.

Kangal Bharat (H). *Pauper India.* Babu Ram Sharma, pub. Bareilly: Singhal Printing Works, 1930. 14pp. IOL B 216; NAI 216; PIB 67; CRL.

Karachi Congress (H). Prabhu Narayan Misra, ed., pub. Benares: Shri Press, n.d. 16pp. IOL B 301; PIB 8.

Kashganj Ka Khvab (U). Lal Bahadur Varma. Bareilly: Arya Granth Ratnakar, Sadat Press, n.d. 8pp. IOL 141; PIB 52; R&R 1922, 1110.

Kaumi Baiton Ka Potha Panjabi Men Te Nali Bismil Ki Tarap (U). Multan: Asha Nand Pracarak, Aman Sarhad Electric Press, n.d. 6pp. CRL.

Kaumi Parvana (H). Calcutta: Panna Lal Gujarati, 1931. 16pp. IOL B 130; PIB 1; GIPOL 1932, 116.

Kaumi Shahid (P). Ram Prasad Bismil, ed., pub. Lahore: Sanatan Dharm Press, n.d. 7pp. IOL; PIB 162.

Kaumi Tarana (H). Phaiyazhind. Badayun: Amil-ul-Ikbal Press, n.d. 8pp. IOL B 72.

Khun Ka Ansu (H). Benares: Ram Candra Candradev, Sri Yantralaya, 1931. 16pp. IOL B 210.

Khun Ke Ansu (H). Bhola Nath ("Dardi"). 2 eds. Calcutta: Kumar Press, n.d. 14pp. PIB 1; CRL. Calcutta: Sarasvati Pustak Agency, n.d. 16pp. IOL B 236.

Khun Ke Chinte (H). *Sprinkling of Blood.* Balbhadra Prasad Gupta ("Rasik"). Allahabad: Shiva Shankar Candra Bharatiya, Union Job Press, c. 1931. 92pp. IOL B 13; NAI 177; PIB 67.

Khuni Ghazlen (H). Sidh Gopal Shukla, ed. Cawnpur: Rashtriya Sarasvati Sadan, Rama Press, 1923. 2 pts. 14, 16pp. Pt. 1: IOL B 150; NAI 26; PIB 177. Pt. 2: IOL B 169; NAI 70; PIB 177.

Khuni Nazara (H). *Bloody View.* Pandit Shivshankar Lal Deviprasad, ed., pub. Cawnpur: Bharat Printing Press, c. 1930. 16pp. IOL B 249; NAI; PIB 64; CRL.

Khvab Parishan (U). Muhammad Hussain, pub. Moradabad: Moradabad Printing Press, c. 1921. 8pp. PIB 56.

Kranti Bhajnavali (H). Nand Lal ("Arya"). Gazipur: Prabhu Dayal, Yureka Printing Works (Benares), n.d. 16pp. IOL B 274; NAI 123; PIB 77; CRL.

Kranti Gitanjali, 2d pt. (H). Ram Prasad Bismil. Lahore: Lakshman Pathik, A. P. Press, c. 1931. 32pp. IOL B 57; NAI 107; PIB 29, 45; CRL. Apparently reprinted at least five times.

Kranti Ka Pujari (H). *Devotees of Revolt.* Mohan Lal ("Arman"), pub. Cawnpur: Shankar Press, n.d. 8pp. IOL B 330, 398; PIB 27.

Kranti Ka Sandesh (H). Babu Ram Sharma, ed. Cawnpur: Rashtriya Pustak Bhandar, Arjun Press (Benares), 1930. 15pp. IOL B 267; NAI 17; PIB 29; CRL.

Kranti Ka Shankhnad (H). "Azad." Cawnpur: Rashtriya Pustak Bhandar, Shukla Printing Press, 1930. 16pp. IOL B 332; PIB 8.

Kranti Ka Singhnad (H). Vihari Lal Sharma, ed. (Hindu Social Reform Series, no. 14). Lucknow: Vimal Granthmala, 1930. 16pp. IOL B 218; PIB 67. Other editions published (for example, Delhi: n.d. 16pp. IOL B 244).

Kranti Ka Singhnad (H). Cawnpur: Ganga Sahai Chauve, Rashtriya Sahitya Pracarak Mandal, Brahman Press, c. 1930. 24pp. NAI 188; PIB 22; CRL.

Kranti Ki Gitanjali (H). Mohan Candra ("Masta"), ed. Delhi: Svadesh Shreni Press, n.d. 15pp. IOL B 170; NAI 39; PIB 70; CRL.

Kranti Ki Jhalak (H). K. L. Gupta, ed., pub. Agra: Lakshmi Printing Press, 1930. 16pp. IOL B 201; PIB 74.

Kranti Pushpanjali (H). Pandit Banshidhar Sharma, ed. Cawnpur: Rashtriya Pustak Bhandar, V. P. Press, 1930. 16pp. IOL B 421.

Kranti Pushpanjali (H). Somendra Mukherji, ed., pub. Moradabad: Sharma Machine Printing Press, c. 1931. 34pp. IOL B 402; PIB 27; CRL.

Lahore Ka Congress Ka Elan (U). Sadhu Ram Das. Delhi: J. M. Press, 1931. 16pp. IOL 122; PIB 29; CRL.

Mahatma Gandhi (U). Cawnpur: Madad Ali, Azizi Press, n.d. 8pp. IOL 107; PIB 56.

Mahatma Gandhi Aur Asahyog (H). Aligarh: Yudram Gupta, Surendra Press, n.d. 16+14pp. IOL B 69; PIB 51.

Mahatma Gandhi Aur Carkha (H). Farukhabad: Prasad Maheshvari, Cintamani Press, n.d. 16pp. IOL F 18; PIB 153.

Mahatma Gandhi Ka Carkha (H). Girraj Kishore, Vaishya, ed., pub. Agra: Kesari Press, Arya Bhashar Press, 1930. 16pp. IOL B 78, 269; PIB 29, 67.

Mahatma Gandhi Ka Rashtriya Bigul (H). Cawnpur: Munshi Singh ("Ratna"), Bharat Press, c. 1930. 16pp. NAI; PIB 29.

Mahatma Gandhi Ka Risala (H). Agra: Pandit Babu Ram Dauneria, J. M. Press, n.d. 15pp. IOL B 432.

Mahatma Gandhi Ka Sandesh (H). Umacaran Dikshit ("Umesh"), pub. Cawnpur: Brahman Press, 1930. 16pp. IOL B 101, 433; NAI; PIB 21; CRL.

Mahatma Gandhi Ka Sandesh (H). Girraj Kishore, Agarval, ed., pub. Agra: Kesari Press, n.d. 8pp. PIB 20.

Mahatma Gandhi Ka Svatantra Alha (H). Mitthan Lal Purva. Cawnpur: Lala Babu Lal, Govind Press, 1930. 16pp. IOL B 155; NAI; PIB 64; CRL.

Mahatma Gandhi Ki Andhi (H). Delhi: Agarval Book Depot, Shreni Press, n.d. 15pp. PIB 29.

Mahatma Gandhi Ki Divyavani (H). Mathura: Vidyarthi Radhavallabh Sharma, Agarval Machine Press, n.d. 16pp. IOL B 284.

Mahatma Gandhi Ki Gazalen (H). Benares: Varanasi Company, 1921. 8pp. IOL B 374.

Mahatma Gandhi Ki Gazalen (H). Agra: Sandaya Press, n.d. 8pp. PIB 37.

Mahatma Gandhi Ki Gyarah Sharten (H). R. N. Sharma, ed. Delhi: Agarval Book Depot, Shreni Press, 1930. 15pp. IOL B 268; PIB 29.

Mahatma Gandhi Ki Jai, Pt. 1 (H). Benares: Varanasi Company, Sambhu Printing Works, n.d. 14pp. PIB 51; R&R 1922, 1110.

Mahatma Gandhi Ki Larai (H, U). Numerous editions. H: Ram Candra Sharma, Dvarka Prasad Sharma, eds., pubs. Delhi:

n.d. 16pp. IOL B 417; NAI; PIB 70; CRL. U: Dvarka Prasad Sharma, ed. Delhi: Svadhin Press, Delhi. 16pp. IOL 101; PIB 21; CRL.

Mahatma Gandhi Ki Sujh (H). Lucknow: Vimal Granthmala, Allahabad Oriental Printers, n.d. 16pp. IOL B 122; PIB 27.

Mahatma Gandhi Yash Holi (H). Vishveshvar Prasad, ed., pub. Benares: Adarsh Press, n.d. 14pp. IOL B 71; PIB 51.

Mahila Gitanjali (H). Sushila Devi, ed. Moradabad: Vaidraj Ban Ram Misra, Sarasvati Press, 1930. 13pp. IOL B 89.

Manharan Shyam (H). Manoharlal Shukla. 2 pts. Pt. 1: Allahabad: Misra Printing Works, n.d. 16pp. IOL B 419; NAI; PIB 70; CRL. Pt. 2: Allahabad: Raja Press, n.d. 16pp. IOL B 419; PIB 70.

Marvari Rashtra Git (H). Sarvai Ram Sharma, ed., pub. Malkapur (Berar): Sri Isvar Printing Press, n.d. 8pp. PIB 1, 343.

Masti Ke Tarane (H, U). Pralayankar: Yadunandan Sharma, ed., pub. Laheriyasarai, n.d. 11pp. H: IOL B 305. U: PIB 117.

Mata Ke Pujari (H). Puran Cand Jain, ed., pub. Benares: Sri Shiv Press, c. 1931. 16pp. IOL B 54.

Matvala Gayan (H). Mata Prasad Shukla. Benares: Raghunath Prasad Gupta, Sri Press, 1931. 16pp. IOL B 63; NAI; PIB 27; CRL.

Mausim Vahar (H). Rajendra Prasad, ed. Muzaffarpur: Bihar Standard Press, n.d. 12pp. IOL F 106; PIB 42.

Mazlumon Ki Ah Yani Dukhi Hindustan (H). Dvarka Prasad Sharma, ed. Delhi: Ram Richpal, Martand Press, c. 1931. 16pp. IOL B 92; PIB 64; CRL.

Muhib-i-Vatan (U). Guru Prasad. Allahabad: Desh Sevak Press, c. 1915. 50pp. IOL 140.

Mukt Sangit (H). Abhi Ram Sharma. Cawnpur: Vishnu Prayag Press, 1933. 77pp. NAI 182; PIB 65; CRL.

Musafir Ke Bhajan (H). Kumar Sukhlal Singh. Delhi: Lakshman Pathik, c. 1937. 32pp. NAI 173.

Namak Ka Gola (H). Ram Candra, pub. Delhi: n.d. 15pp. IOL B 399; PIB 8; CRL.

Namkin Jang (H). *Salt War.* Natha Ram Bihar. Cawnpur: Babu Ram, Prem Printing Press, c. 1930. 8pp. IOL B 45; PIB 29.

Nari Ratna Singar (H). Kapur Cand, ed., pub. Lucknow: Sri Sudharak Press (Pt. 1, Patna), Sri Bhagvata Press (Pt. 3, Bhagalpur). Pts. 1, 3. 8+8pp. IOL B 349, 350; PIB 27.

Nashebaji Ka Natija (H). *The Result of Addiction.* Jvala Prasad Varma, ed., pub. Agra: Arya Bhaskar Press, 1930. 8pp. IOL B 289.

Nauh-i-Ram (U). Svami Ramanand Sarasvati. Aligarh: Ladle Mohan Mathur, Hewett Press, 1921. 32pp. IOL 144; R&R 1922, 1110.

Naukarshahi Ki Tabahi (H). *The Ruin of the Bureaucracy.* Shyam Bihari Srivastava. Allahabad: Rashtriya Sadan Pustakalaya, c. 1921. 14pp. IOL B 149.

Naurang Garjana (H). Uma Shankar Dikshit, pub. Allahabad: Sarju Lal Raja Press, n.d. 8pp. IOL B 48; PIB 27.

Navin Rashtriya Gayan, Pt. 2 (H). Janki Prasad, ed., pub. Calcutta: c. 1923. 15pp. IOL B 181; PIB 38.

Nirbhaya Bhajnavali, Pt. 1 (H). *Fearless Devotional Songs.* Nemi Candra ("Arya"), ed., pub. Agra: Vadendra Sharma, Adarsh Press, n.d. 8pp. IOL B 347; PIB 6.

Panjab Ka Hatyakand (U). Bareilly: Arya Granth Ratnakar, Kaumprasta Press, n.d. 8pp. IOL 127; PIB 183.

Pap Ka Ghara (H). *A Pot of Sin.* Gyan Singh Varma, pub. Aligarh: Jagdish Press, 1923. 8pp. IOL B 359.

Phansi Ke Shahid (H). Raja Ram Nagar, ed., pub. Allahabad: Union Job Press, c. 1931. 12pp. IOL B 331; NAI; CRL.

Pharyad Jigar (H). Nihal Cand Saksena, pub. Bulandshahar: Saksena Medical Press, n.d. 16pp. IOL B 172.

Phirangia (H). Manoranjan Prasad. Farukhabad: Cintamani Press, c. 1920. 8pp. IOL F 17; PIB 153.

Political Holion Ka Guldasta (U). Lal Bahadur Varma. Bareilly: Arya Granth Ratnakar, Nami Press, c. 1920. 8pp. IOL 45; PIB 153.

Political Panjabi Bhajan (U). Gita Ram. Ambala: Duli Ram, Bharat Mata Press, n.d. 8pp. NAI; CRL.

Prabhat Pheri (H). Dadabhai Naik, ed. Bhivani: 1939. 15pp. IOL B 234; NAI 38; PIB 211.

Prabhat Pheri (H). "Vijaya." n.i. 10+22pp. IOL B 256; PIB 21.

Prabhati Bahar (H). P. V. Pathak, pub. Bombay: Sri Pandurang Vaibhav Press, n.d. 8pp. PIB 1.

Rana Garjana (H). Ranga Lal Baba. Burhanpur: Tapti Vijai Press, c. 1930. 14pp. IOL B 265.

Rashtra Ka Singhnad (H). Pandit Radhe Shyam Misra. Cawnpur: Pandit Nand Lal, Vishnu Prayag Press, 1930. 16pp. IOL B 329. Another ed., edited by Bhaggulal Rathore (Cawnpur: Devi Dayal, 1931). 16 pp. PIB 1; CRL.

Rashtra Vina (H). Brahmacari Ramanand, ed., pub. Benares: Sarasvati Press, 1930. 15pp. IOL B 79; PIB 29.

Rashtriya Alha (H). Pitambar Lal Singhal, pub. Cawnpur: Prem Printing Press, c. 1930. 8pp. IOL B 243; NAI 16; PIB 64.

Rashtriya Alha (H). Pokhpal Singh Varma. Lucknow: A. W. Press, 1930. 16pp. IOL B 426.

Rashtriya Alha (H). Rajbali Varma, pub. Bareilly: Rambadan Singh (printer, Azamgarh), 1931. 32pp. IOL B 391; PIB 27; CRL.

Rashtriya Avaz (H). Shiva Ram Paribrajak, pub. Benares: Lakshmi Press, 1930. 15pp. IOL B 238; NAI; PIB 64; CRL.

Rashtriya Bahar Urf Bharat Ki Pukar (H). Attan Kavi, ed., pub. Mirzapur: Khicari Samacar Press, 1930. 8pp. IOL B 87. The British citation (GIPOL 1930, 28) indicates that the editor was Thakur Prasad Sarju Prasad.

Rashtriya Bigul (H). Pyare Lal Agarval, ed., pub. Cawnpur: n.d. 16pp. CRL.

Rashtriya Bigul (H). Dvarka Prasad, pub. Kankhal: Gurukul Press, 1930. 15pp. PIB 67.

Rashtriya Camak (H). Ram Candra Saraph, pub. Benares: Sarasvati Press, 1930. 15pp. IOL B 319; PIB 47.

Rashtriya Cingari (H). Prabhu Narain Misra, ed., pub. Benares: Shri Press, 1931. 7pp. PIB 8.

Rashtriya Danka Athva Svadeshi Khadi (H). Candra Prasad Jigyasu. Lucknow: Hindu Samaj Sudhar Karalaya, Ganga Fine Art Press, 1930. 16 pp. IOL B 272.

Rashtriya Gan (H). Lahore: Rashtriya Pustak Bhandar, Ravi Fine Art Works, n.d. 30pp. PIB 282.

Rashtriya Gan (H). Calcutta: Sarasvati Pustak Agency, Vedic Press, c. 1930. 16pp. Various places of publication; some copies have no publication information. IOL B 404; PIB 1; R&R 1922, 1110.

Rashtriya Gan (H). Channumal Gupta, ed., pub. Delhi: Sreni Press, 1931. 16pp. IOL B 219; PIB 42.

Rashtriya Gan (H). Lal Bihari Tandan, pub. Lucknow: Sri Damodar Press, n.d. 16pp. IOL B 64; PIB 51.

Rashtriya Gayan (H). Ramdas Gaur. Calcutta: Mahavir Prasad Podar, Mastmatavala Press, n.d. 80pp. IOL B 188; PIB 1.

Rashtriya Gayan Athva Ubalta Khun (H). *Boiling Blood.* Hazari Lal, ed., pub. Allahabad: Rajpali Press, 1930. 14pp. IOL B 232; NAI 112; PIB 67; CRL.

Rashtriya Git (H). Allahabad: Narayan Press, 1930. 13pp. IOL B 198; PIB 74; CRL. Another ed., edited by Beni Madho Gupta. Fatehpur: Anand Press, 1930. 13pp. IOL B 115; PIB 67.

Rashtriya Git (H). Mirzapur: Matvala Mandal, Bisvin Sadi Printing Press, n.d. 12pp. IOL B 98; NAI 135; PIB 64.

Rashtriya Git (H). Svami Vicaranand Sarasvati, pub. Dehra Dun: Garhvali Press, 1921. 13pp. IOL B 163; PIB 51; R&R 1922, 1110.

Rashtriya Git Sangrah, Pt. 1 (H). Kashi Prasad Varma, ed. Patna: Babu Kanhaiya Lal, Jaganath Printing Press (Benares), c. 1921. 20pp. PIB 124. Pt. 2. Sayyad Mohammad Husain, ed. Patna: Babu Kanhaiya Lal, Jaganth Printing Press, c. 1921. 25pp. PIB 124.

Rashtriya Gitanjali (H). Hulas Varma ("Premi"). Dehra Dun: Ranvir Varma Prabhakar, Imperial Press, 1938. 44pp. PIB 200, CRL.

Rashtriya Gitsagar, Pt. 2 (H). Kavi Sumdaya. Benares: Indra Varma, Adarsh Press, c. 1931. 21pp. IOL B 444; PIB 51; R&R 1922, 1110.

Rashtriya Guldasta (H). Agra: H. L. Gupta, Jain Press, 1930. 15pp. IOL B 80; PIB 29.

Rashtriya Holi (H). Beni Madho Sharma, pub. Allahabad: Ganga Press, 1922. 8pp. IOL B 354; PIB 56.

Rashtriya Jhanda (H). R. N. Sharma, ed. Delhi: Agarval Book Depot, Sreni Press, n.d. 15pp. IOL B 224.

Rashtriya Kirtan Gan, Pt. 1 (U). Dharm Vir Varma, ed. Dehra Dun: Bharatiya Press, c. 1921. 30pp. IOL 105; PIB 37.

Rashtriya Lahar (H). Uma Caran Lal, ed., pub. Gorakhpur: Gorakhpur Printing Press, 1931. 16pp. IOL B 55; PIB 27.

Rashtriya Lahar (H). Purushottam Lal, pub. Jaunpur: Seva Press, n.d. 15pp. IOL B 287.

Rashtriya Malharen Athva Zakhmi Bharat (H). R. N. Sharma, ed., pub. Delhi: Svadesh Sreni Press, 1930. 16pp. IOL B 266; PIB 29.

Rashtriya Murli (H). Manoranjan Prasad. Benares: Ram Vinod Singh, George Printing Works, 1925. 8pp. PIB 90.

Rashtriya Padya Manjari (H). Hari Sharma, ed. Patna: Central Printing Press, c. 1922. 7pp. IOL B 387; PIB 42.

Rashtriya Padyavli (H). Bhikhu Tathe. n.p., n.d. 28pp. NAI 84; CRL.

Rashtriya Phag (H). Nand Kishore Shukla. Cawnpur: Vidyadhar Sharma Caturvedi, Rajhans Press, 1920. 12pp. IOL B 140; PIB 51.

Rashtriya Pukar (H). Babu Gauri Shankar Prasad, ed., pub. Benares: Sri Bageshvari Press, c. 1930. 8pp. IOL B 452; PIB 70.

Rashtriya Saman Har (H). Sita Ram Pathak, ed., pub. Ghazipur: S. V. V. Press, 1931. 16pp. IOL B 393; NAI; CRL.

Rashtriya Samar (H). K. L. Barman, ed., pub. Benares: Sri Yantralaya, 1930. 15pp. IOL B 310.

Rashtriya Sandesh (H). Gaya: R. P. Kandhva and Co., n.d. 16pp. CRL.

Rashtriya Sangit Mala (H). Kunvar Narendra Singh ("Arya"), ed. Satyarth Sharma, Kankhal: 1923. 60pp. IOL B 191; PIB 168; CRL.

Rashtriya Savan Bahar (H). Prasiddh Narayan Sinha. Jaunpur: Svadhi Sahitya Mandal, Seva Press (Mirzapur), 1930. 6pp. IOL B 90; NAI 20; PIB 47; CRL.

Rashtriya Shankhnad (H). Yati Yatan Lal, ed., pub. Cawnpur: Rajnaitik Sahitya Pracarak Mandal, Kesari Press (Agra), n.d. 16pp. IOL B 414; PIB 70.

Rashtriya Singhnad (H). Visvanath Sharma, pub. Benares: Sarasvati Press, n.d. 15pp. IOL B 75; PIB 29.

Rashtriya Tan (H). Lucknow: Hindi Pustak Bhandar, Rama Printing Press, 1933, 16pp. IOL B 151; PIB 78.

Rashtriya Tansain (H). n.p., n.d. 20pp. PIB 37.

Rashtriya Tarang (H). Buddhu Ram. Allahabad: Mohan Lal, Shishu Press, 1930. 16pp. IOL B 321; PIB 47.

Rashtriya Tuphan (H). K. L. Barman, ed., pub. Benares: Lakshmi Press, 1930. 15pp. IOL B 410; PIB 70.

Rashtriya Umang (H). Uma Caran Lal, ed., pub. Gorakhpur: Gorakhpur Printing Press, 1931. 16pp. IOL B 47; NAI 29; PIB 27; CRL.

Rashtriya Vina (H). Gaya: Prabhu Narayan Misra, Srivageshvari Press (Benares), n.d. 16pp. IOL B 381; PIB 8.

Reading Shahi Holi (H). M. P. Gupta, ed. Cawnpur: Ramdulare Sharma, c. 1921. 8pp. PIB 37.

Sangit Sarovar (H). Vishvanath Lal Srivastava ("Visharad"). Benares: Sarasvati Press, c. 1931. 128pp. Pp. 1–119, Hindi; 120–128, English. IOL B 187; PIB 1.

Sarojini Sandesh (H). Inkilab series, no. 2. Delhi: Govind Ram Gupta Rahbar, Martand Press, n.d. 16pp. IOL B 215; NAI 158; PIB 67; CRL.

Satyagraha Gitavali (H). Svarna Singh Varma ("Anand"). Agra: Sri Mukund Mandir, Kesari Press, 1930. IOL B 207; NAI 121; PIB 29; CRL.

Satyagraha Ka Bigul (H). Gyan Singh Varma, pub. Aligarh: Jagdish Press, 1923. 8pp. IOL B 358.

Satyagraha Ki Lahar (H). Gokarna Nath Shukla, pub. Cawnpur: National Press, c. 1937. 8pp. IOL B 259; PIB 21.

Satyagraha Sangram (H). Allahabad: Panna Lal Varma, Raja Press, n.d. 25pp. IOL B 441; NAI 61; PIB 64; CRL.

Satyagraha Sangram, Pt. 1 (H). Ram Candra Sharma. Delhi: Tula Ram Gupta, Sreni Press, n.d. 16pp. IOL B 118.

Satyagraha Sangram Ka Bigul (H). Raghuvar Dayal Vidyarthi, ed., pub. Agra: Adarsh Press, c. 1930. 15pp. IOL B 313; PIB 64.

Satyagrahi (H). Mahavir Singh Varma. Cawnpur: Ram Svarup Gupta, Prem Printing Press, n.d. 8pp. IOL B 73; PIB 29.

Satyagrahi Jhankar (H). Gorakhpur: Bhaskar, 1930. 8pp. IOL B 213; PIB 67.

Satyavati Ka Sandesh (U). Govind Ram Gupta, ed. Delhi: S. D. Gupta, Svadhin Press, 1930. 16pp. IOL 103; PIB 67.

Savan Ka Satyagraha (H). Gopal Lal Gupta. Benares: Meva Lal, George Press, n.d. 16pp. IOL B 246; PIB 64.

Savan Ka Senapati (H). Gopal Lal Gupta. Benares: Meva Lal and Co., Sri Bageshvari Press, n.d. 16pp. IOL B 294; NAI 86; CRL.

Savan Ka Singh (H). Gopal Lal Gupta. Benares: Gauri Shankar Prasad, Arjun Press, c. 1931. 16pp. IOL B 158; PIB 27.

Savan Svarajya (H). Pandit Bhairab Prasad Sharma. Benares: Bindeshvari Prasad, Sri Bageshvari Press, 1930. 7pp. IOL B 371.

Shahid Garjana (H). Allahabad: Beni Madho Gupta, Union Job Press, 1930. 15pp. IOL B 408.

Shahide Nau Ratan (H). Vimal Sharma. Cawnpur: Raijnath Bajpei, N. K. Press, 1931. 16pp. CRL.

Shahidi Naz (H). Canda Lal Dikshit. Delhi: Rajendra Press, 1931. 32pp. NAI 89; PIB 42; CRL.

Shahidon Ka Sandesh (H). Mohar Candra ("Mast"), ed., pub. Delhi: Svadesh Sreni Press, n.d. 16pp. IOL B 226; NAI 79; PIB 29.

Shahidon Ke Tarane (H). Bhola Nath Dardi. Calcutta: Sarasvati Pustak Agency, Kumar Press, n.d. 16pp. PIB 1; CRL.

Shahidon Ki Garjana (H). Thakur Devi Singh, ed., pub. Delhi: Agarval Book Depot, Svadhina Press, 1931. 8pp. IOL B 346; PIB 64.

Shahidon Ki Yadgari, Pt. 2 (H). Allahabad: Satya Narayan Lal Dhauria; Abhyudaya Press, 1931. 8pp. IOL B 422; PIB 8.

Shanti Ka Sangram (H). Girja Dvivedi, ed. Lucknow: Pandit Shiva Dayal Misra, Bharat Bhushan Press, 1930. 8pp. IOL B 297.

Shasan Ki Pol (H). Deva Datt Pathak, ed., pub. Sagar: Vishvanath Printing Works (Benares), c. 1922. 16pp. IOL B 129.

Sri Azadi Ka Cirag (H). Babu Ram Candra Dev. Gaya: Satyanam Press, n.d. 8pp. PIB 9.

Sudhar Ki Sirhi (H). Jagannath Prasad Gupta, ed. Laheriyasarai: Ganga Prasad Gupta, Lakshmi Narayan Press, n.d. 13pp. IOL B 368; PIB 37.

Sudharak Tract (H). Shad Malihabadi, pub. Lucknow: Fine Press, n.d. 16pp. IOL B 324.

Sulah Aur Rashtra Pukar (H). Ram Bilas Avasthi, ed., pub. Lucknow: Dayal Printing Works, 1931; 16pp. IOL B 56; PIB 27.

Svadesh Anurag Gitavali Arthat Bharat Odaya Bhajnavali (H). Murlidhar Gupta, pub. Aligarh: Surendra Press, n.d. 48pp. IOL B 143; PIB 51; R&R 1922, 1110.

Svadesh Gitanjali, Pt. 1 (H). Hari Datt Sharma, ed., pub. Aligarh: Bharat Bandhu Press, c. 1920. 70pp. IOL B 147; PIB 37.

Svadesh Ka Sandesh (H). Pandit Avadh Bihari Lal Sharma. Lucknow: Pandit Kanhaiya Lal Dikshit, Shukla Printing Press, 1930. 16pp. IOL B 227; PIB 29.

Svadesh Mangalcar (H). Ram Svarup Sharma, pub. Hathras: Sudarshan Press, n.d. 15pp. IOL B 167; PIB 76A.

Svadesh Satsai (H). Mahesh Candra Prasad, pub. Arrah: Desh Sevak Printing Works, 1930. 82pp. IOL B 205; PIB 70.

Svadeshi Gan (H). Allahabad: Uma Shankar Dikshit, Vijay Press, 1930. 8pp. IOL B 255; PIB 21.

Svadeshi Gandhiji Ka Phauji Elan, #2 (H). Mohar Candra ("Mast"), ed., pub. Delhi: Shreni Press, n.d. 16pp. PIB 27.

Svadeshi Gayan Ratna (H). Munshi Singh ("Ratna"), pub. Lucknow: Shukla Printing Press, 1930. 16pp. IOL B 124; PIB 21.

Svadeshi Khadi (U). Chadrika Prasad Jigyasu. Lucknow: Hindu Samaj Sudhar Karalaya, Bande Mataram Press, n.d. 16pp. PIB 74.

Svadeshi Pracar Mala (H). Balkrishan Vidyarthi, pub. Bijnour: Caitanya Printing Press, 1930. 8pp. IOL B 318, 430; NAI 62; PIB 4, 21; CRL.

Svadhinta Ka Bigul, Pt. 2 (H). Rameshvar Nath Malaviya, pub. Allahabad: Raja Press, c. 1930. 8pp. IOL B 182.

Svadhinta Yuddha Men Janata Ka Viplav (H). *In the Freedom Struggle the People's Revolt.* Narayan Candra Lahiri. Calcutta: 1940. 69pp. IOL B 9; PIB 212.

Svaraj Git Gunjan (H). Muzaffarpur: Kali Prasad, Central Printing Press (Patna), c. 1924. 8pp. IOL B 110; NAI 11; PIB 42; CRL.

Svaraj Ka Danka (H). Hari Bhagat Vaidya. Gaya: Lok Sevak Press, 1922. 18pp. PIB 124.

Svaraj Ki Devi (H). Saharanpur: Gordhan Das, Shanti Printing Press, 1921. 8pp. IOL B 411; NAI 13; PIB 70.

Svarajya Alha (H). Larali Prasad Srivastava, ed., pub. Jhansi: Jhansi Mazdur Sangh, 1931. 12pp. IOL B 392; PIB 27; CRL.

Svarajya Alha (H). Lala Bhagvan Das, ed., pub. Etawah: Hindu Press, 1930. 15pp. IOL B 316; NAI 100; PIB 47; CRL.

Svarajya Aur Jail (H). Benares: Goraksham Karyalaya, n.d. 15pp. IOL B 366.

Svarajya Git (U). Hukam Cand. Amritsar: Sri Ganga Press, 1931. 8pp. CRL.

Svarajya Ka Bigul (H). Nityanand Pandeya. Dehra Dun: Hari Datt Upadhyaya, Ubhay Press, c. 1931. 32pp. IOL B 252.

Svarajya Ka Jhanda (H). Babu Ram Sharma, ed., pub. Bareilly: Singhal Printing Works, 1930. 15pp. IOL B 285.

Svarajya Ka Terahmasa (H). Kanhaiya Lal Dikshit ("Indra"), ed. Lucknow: Bharat Bhusan Press, 1930. 8pp. IOL B 67.

Svarajya Ka Tuphan (H). R. N. Sharma, ed. Delhi: Agarval Depot, Shreni Press, 1930. 15pp. IOL B 223; PIB 29.

Svarajya Ki Banshi (H). Gyan Singh Varma. Aligarh: Sita Ram, Jagdish Press, 1922. 15pp. IOL B 280; PIB 168.

Svarajya Ki Dhum (H). Basant Chitari. Aligarh: Sita Ram, Jagdish Press, 1922. 15pp. IOL B 360; PIB 76.

Svarajya Ki Gunj (H). Aksir Sialkoti, ed. Lahore: Anglo-Oriental Press, 1930. 30pp. NAI 96; PIB 29; CRL.

Svarajya Ki Hai (H, U). Ram Lal Chedi, pub. Cawnpur: Prem Printing Press, 1930. 8pp. H: IOL B 434; PIB 67. U: IOL 149; PIB 64.

Svarajya Ki Kunji (H). Sita Ram Gupta, ed., pub. Moradabad: Sharma Machine Printing Press, 1930. 32pp. IOL B 134; NAI 77; CRL.

Svarajya Pratijya (H). Cawnpur: Ganpat Ram Gaur, Sri Lakshmi Press, n.d. 16pp. IOL B 365; PIB 56.

Svarajya Pukar Athva Desh Ko Cetavani (H). Kanhaiya Lal Dikshit ("Indra"), ed. Lucknow: Gaya Prasad Avadh Bihari, Bharat Bhushan Press, 1930. 12pp. IOL B 67, 120; NAI 155.

Svarajya Sangram Ka Bigul (H). K. L. Gupta, ed., pub. Agra: Lakshmi Printing Press, 1930. 16pp. IOL B 200; NAI 10; PIB 74.

Svarna Vihan (H). Hari Krishna ("Premi"). Ajmer: Sasta Sahitya Mandal, Sasta Sahitya Printing Press, c. 1930. 102pp. IOL B 42, 186; PIB 70.

Svatantra Bharat Alha (H). Cawnpur: Mitthan Lal Agarval, Prem Printing Press, n.d. 20pp. IOL B 303; PIB 47, 64.

Svatantra Bharat Ka Shankhnad (H). Avadh Bihari Lal Sharma, ed. Lucknow: Vimal Granthmala, Bharat Bhusan Press, 1930. 16pp. IOL B 344.

Svatantra Bharat Ka Singhnad (H). Candrika Prasad Jigjasu, ed. Benares: Tribhuvan Nath Azad Sainik, Arjun Press, 1932. 16pp. IOL B 77; PIB 67.

Svatantra Gitanjali (U). Ganga Ram, trans. Delhi: Martand Press, c. 1930. 16pp. IOL 100; PIB 47; CRL.

Svatantra Ka Bigul (H). Gorakhpur: Bhasakr Press, 1930. 8pp. IOL B 212; NAI 12; PIB 29; CRL.

Svatantra Ka Bigul (H). Pandey Punyatma. Benares: Arya Sahitya Mandir, Arjun Press, 1930. 16pp. IOL B 74; PIB 1.

Svatantra Ki Bhet (H). Ram Svarup Gupta, ed., pub. Mathura: Hindustan Davakhana Printing Works, 1931. 12pp. IOL B 53; PIB 27.

Svatantra Ki Devi (H). Girraj Kishor Agarval, ed., pub. Agra: Kesari Press, c. 1931. 16pp. IOL B 66; PIB 29.

Svatantra Ki Talvar (H). Jagannath Prasad Arora, ed., pub. Benares: Lakshmi Press, 1930. 15pp. IOL B 153; NAI 9.

Svatantra Ki Top (H). Jagannath Prasad Arora, ed., pub. Benares: Lakshmi Press, 1930. 15pp. IOL B 154.

Tarana-i-Azad (H, U). Kanvar Pratap Candra ("Azad"), ed., pub. Bareilly: Anand Press, n.d. 16pp. H: IOL B 439. U: IOL 96.

Tarana-i-Kaum, Pt. 2 (U). Bareilly: Birendra Gupta, Nadri Press, n.d. 15pp. IOL 48; PIB 52; R&R 1922, 1110.

Tarana-i-Mazlum (U). Master Nand Lal Kamar, pub. Lyallpur: Narendra Steam Press, 1930. 16pp. NAI; PIB 62; CRL.

Tarana-i-Svarajya (U). Shankar Dayal Avasthi. Cawnpur: Intazami Press, 1921. 16pp. IOL 89; PIB 37.

Taranye Azad (H). Sarayu Narayan Shukla. Cawnpur: Ganga Prasad Shukla, 1923. 8pp. IOL B 279; NAI 34; CRL.

Taranye Kaphas Arthva Agra Jail Ka Mushaira (H). Krishna Kant Malaviya, ed. Allahabad: Abhyudaya Press, 1922. 123pp. IOL B 23; PIB 56.

Teri Jai (P). Hans Raj Safari, pub. Amritsar: Arjun Press, c. 1930. 8pp. PIB 8.

Tikvala Gandhi (H). Dev Raj Dev. Lahore: n.d. 8pp. NAI.

Todi Baccha (H). Lala Saval Das. Delhi: n.d. 16pp. CRL.

Tuphan (H). Prahlad Pandey ("Shashi"). Ujjain: Yug Pravartak Granthmal Karalaya, Sri Umed Press (Kota, Rajasthan), 1943. 59pp. IOL B 308; PIB 210.

Uttam Bhajnavali (H). Sultanpur: Mahadev Prasad, Bajrang Press, 1930. 23pp. IOL B 94.

Varlap (U). Comrade Amar Nath Ahluwalia. Lahore: Sanatan Dharm Printing Press, 1931. 8pp. CRL.

Vicar Tarang (H). Svami Vicaranand Sarasvati, pub. Dehra Dun: Abhay Press, 1931. 48pp. IOL B 121; PIB 27.

Vicitra Deshbhakta (H). Raja Ram Nagar, ed., pub. Allahabad: Rangesvar Press, 1931. 8pp. IOL B 46; PIB 27.

Vijay Dundubhi (H). Ram Sahay Sharma, ed. Agra: Congress Committee, Jain Press, c. 1930. 15pp. IOL B 296; PIB 29.

Vijay Sundari (H). Ram Lagan Ray, ed., pub. Muzaffarpur: Bandhu Press, 1924. 12pp. IOL B 388; PIB 42.

Vijayi Bharat (H). Pars Nath Divedi. n.p., Sri Gopi Lal Gupta, 1931. 12pp. PIB 6; CRL.

Vir Bharati (H). Shital Prasad Bishnoi, ed. Cawnpur: Cunni Lal Gaur, Rajhans Press, c. 1920. 16pp. IOL B 59; PIB 153.

Viron Ka Jhula, Pt. 1 (H). Pandit Lakshman Lal Joshi, pub. Benares: Sri Yantralaya, 1931. 7pp. IOL B 157.

Viron Ki Garjana (H). Narayan Prasad. Agra: Phul Cand Jain, Kesari Press, 1930. 8pp. PIB 29.

Viron Ki Hunkar (H). Ram Candra Singhal Jain, ed. Sonepat: Sarla Hindi Pustakalya, Rajendra Printing Press (Delhi), 1931. 15pp. IOL B 222.

Vishva Prem (U). Svami Vishvendra, ed., pub. Dera Ghazi Khan: Narayan Steam Press, c. 1932. 39pp. IOL 169; PIB 115; GIPOL 1933, 48/3.

Vyagra Bamgole (H). Pandey Hiralal ("Vyagra"), pub. Benares: Hitaishi Printing Works, 1929. 8pp. NAI 33; J&P 1929, 4580.

Vyakul Bharat (H). Ramkrishna Tripathi, ed., pub. Unnav: Rangeshvar Press (Benares), 1931. 7pp. IOL B 52; PIB 27.

Yuvak Garjana (H). Kashi Ram Tivari, ed., pub. Allahabad: Union Job Press, c. 1931. 11pp. IOL B 401; NAI; PIB 27; CRL.

Yuvak Utsah (H). Amarnath Asi, pub. Kashipur: Jagdish Press, n.d. 7pp. IOL B 361; PIB 1.

Zakhmi Jigar (H). n.p., Rashtriya Mandal, n.d. 16pp. IOL B 300; PIB 8.

Zakhmi Lucknow (U). Mansa Ram, ed., pub. Lucknow: Vidya Bhandar Press, 1930. 8pp. IOL 184; PIB 74.

Zalimon Ka Nash (H). Cawnpur: Ram Govind Misra, Narayan Press, 1922. 8pp. PIB 37.

Zalimon Ki Cal (H). Dvarka Prasad Sharma, ed., pub. Delhi: Martand Press, c. 1930. 8pp. IOL B 93; PIB 64.

Zinda Bano (H). Dattatreya Bal Krishna Kalelkar. Calcutta: Sita Ram Seksaria, Shuddhi Khadi Bhandar, Pravasi, 1930. 1p. IOL B 214; PIB 67.

Asayhog (H). "Krishna." Benares: Candar Prabha Press, c. 1930. 1p. IOL F 16; PIB 153. Poster.

Bande Mataram Sucana (H). Hanuman. Benares: n.d. 1p. IOL F 20.

Bharatiyon Ko Cetavani (H). Kanhaiya Lal. Benares: Bharat Press, n.d. 2pp. IOL F 15; PIB 153.

Bhari Pol, Asahyogi Phag (H). Ram Lal ("Hakim"). Cawnpur: Lakshmi Press, c. 1922. 1p. IOL F 30.

Gore Kutton Ka Haramipan (H). Vaicain Yuvak. n.p., Utsahi Press, 1931. 1p. IOL F 93; PIB 74.

Mahatma Gandhi Ka Hukam (H). n.p., c. 1930. 1p. PIB 64.

Phirangiya (H). Baliya: Ram Dahin Ojha, Harittar Press, 1921. 1p. IOL F 11; PIB 153.

Rashtriya Sangram (H). Cawnpur: Sundar Lal Sharma, George Press, 1930. 1p. IOL F 86; PIB 70.

Sadhu Sandesh (H). Benares: Chatradhari Singh, Hitcintak Press, n.d. 1p. IOL B 173.

Savan Ka Svadhinta (H). Benares: Ram Candra Saraph, Sri Bageshvari Press, c. 1930. 1p. IOL F 27; PIB 29.

Svarajya Bhajnavali. Faizabad: Pandit Tribhuvan Datt Trivedi, Hari Singh Press, n.d. 1p. IOL F 39; PIB 51; R&R 1922, 1110.

Svarajaya Ke Liye Bhaiyon Se Vinay (H). Abhay Sinha. Baliya: n.d. 1p. IOL F 19; PIB 153.

Svatantra Ki Lahar (H). Thakur Prasad, ed., pub. Mirzapur: Kamla Art Press, 1930. 1p. IOL F 70; PIB 64.

BIBLIOGRAPHY

Private Papers

Chelmsford Papers (Frederic John Napier Thesiger, 1st Viscount). IOL MSS Eur E 264

Hailey Papers (William Malcolm, 1st Baron). IOL MSS Eur E 220

Halifax Papers (Edward Frederick Lindley Wood, 1st Earl). IOL MSS Eur C 152

Hirtzel Diaries (Sir Frederic Arthur). IOL Home Misc. 864

Morley Papers (John, 1st Viscount). IOL MSS Eur D 573

Minto Papers. National Library of Scotland M 825–2100

Montagu Papers (Hon. Edwin Samuel). IOL MSS Eur E 523

Reading Papers (Rufus Daniel Isaacs, 1st Marquis). IOL MSS Eur E 238

Thompson Papers (Sir John Perronet). IOL MSS Eur F 137

Willingdon Papers (Freeman-Thomas, 1st Marquis). IOL MSS Eur F 93

Government Publications

Bamford, P. C. *Histories of the Non-Co-operation and Khilafat Movements.* Delhi: Government of India, 1925 (confidential C.I.D. handbook).

Ewart, J. M. *Terrorism in India, 1917–1936.* Simla: Government of India, 1937 (confidential C.I.D. handbook).

India. *Britain Against Hitlerism.* Delhi: Bureau of Public Information, c. 1940.

———. *The Civil Disobedience Movement, 1930–34.* New Delhi: Central Intelligence Bureau, 1934.

———. *General Rules and Orders Made Under Enactments in Force in British India.* 11 vols. Calcutta: Government of India, 1927.

———. *India in 1917–1935.* 19 vols. Calcutta, Delhi: Government of India, 1918–1936.

———. *Legislation and Orders Relating to the War.* 3 vols. 3d rev. ed. Delhi: Government of India, 1942.

———. Legislative Assembly Debates, 1920–1947.

———. Legislative Council Debates, 1907–1919.
———. *Publicity Campaign in India.* Delhi: Government of India, 1918.
———. *Report of the Administration of Lord Reading, Viceroy and Governor-General of India, 1921–26.* Delhi: Government of India, 1928 (confidential).
———. *Report of the Press Commission.* 3 vols. Delhi: Government of India, 1954.
———. *Reports on the Working of the Reformed Constitution, 1927.* Calcutta: Government of India, 1928.
———. *Reports of the Local Governments on the Reformed Constitution.* Delhi: Government of India, 1925.
———. *Review of the Administration of Lord Chelmsford, 1916–1921.* Calcutta: Government of India, 1922 (confidential).
———. *The Unrepealed Central Acts.* 14 vols. Delhi: Government of India, 1935–1945.
Isemonger, F. C., and J. Slattery. *An Account of the Ghadr Conspiracy.* Lahore: Government of India, 1916.
Ker, James Campbell. *Political Troubles in India, 1907–1917.* Calcutta: Government of India, 1917.
Pakistan. *A Collection of Acts Relating to Press in Pakistan, As Modified Up to 31st March, 1954.* Lahore: Government of Pakistan, 1955.
———. *The Report of the Pakistan Press Committee.* Lahore: Government of Pakistan, 1959.
Petrie, D. *Communism in India, 1924–27.* Calcutta: Government of India, 1927 (confidential C.I.D. handbook).
Punjab. *Five Years of Provincial Autonomy in the Punjab, 1937–42.* Lahore: Punjab Government, 1944.
Vincent, W. H., ed. *Publicity Work in India, From 1st June 1918–31st March 1919.* Delhi: Government of India, 1919.
Williamson, H. *India and Communism.* Calcutta: Government of India, 1933 (confidential C.I.D. handbook).

Unpublished Government Records

India Office Library/Records
Crown Representative Papers, 1908–1945
Judicial and Public Department Proceedings, 1905–1945
Political and Secret Department Proceedings, 1905–1920
Record and Library Department Proceedings, 1905–1912
Registry and Record Department Proceedings, 1912–1945
National Archives of India

Home/Political Department Proceedings, 1907–1945
Home Department Proceedings, 1899–1907
Archives of the United States
Immigration Department Records, 1910–1921
Justice Department Records, 1912–1920

Monographs, Biographical Works

Adhikari, G., ed. *Documents of the History of the Communist Party of India*. Vol. I (1917–1922). Delhi: People's Publishing House, 1971.

Agrawal, Sushhila. *Press, Public Opinion and Government in India*. Jaipur: Asha Publishing House, 1970.

Ahmad, Muzaffar. *The Communist Party of India and Its Formation Abroad*. Calcutta: National Book Agency, 1962.

———. *Myself and the Communist Party of India, 1920–1929*. Calcutta: National Book Agency, 1970.

Ali, Muhammad. *My Life: A Fragment*. Edited by Afzal Iqbal. 2d ed., reprint. Lahore: Ashraf, 1966.

———. *Select Writings and Speeches of Maulana Mohamed Ali*. Edited by Afzal Iqbal. 2d ed. 2 vols. Lahore: Ashraf, 1969.

All India Congress Committee. *Congress Ministries at Work, 1946 April–1947 April*. Congress Economic and Political Series, No. 2. Allahabad: All-India Congress Committee, 1947.

All India Congress Committee. *Report of the Civil Disobedience Enquiry Committee, Appointed by the All India Congress Committee, 1922*. Allahabad: H. M. Hayat, 1922.

Argov, Daniel. *Moderates and Extremists in the Indian Nationalist Movement, 1882–1920*. Bombay: Asia, 1967.

Arya Satyagraha and Arya Requirements. Hyderabad: Hyderabad Government, 1948.

Barrier, Norman Gerald. *The Punjab Alienation of Land Bill of 1900*. Duke University Commonwealth Center Occasional Paper and Monograph Series, Monograph 2. Durham: Duke University, 1966.

———. *The Sikhs and Their Literature*. Delhi: Manohar Book Service, 1970.

———, and Paul Wallace. *The Punjab Press, 1880–1905*. Michigan State University Asian Studies Center Occasional Paper No. 14. East Lansing: Michigan State University, 1970.

Bazaz, Prem Nath. *The History of Struggle for Freedom in Kashmir*. New Delhi: Kashmir Publishing Company, 1954.

Bhattacharjee, Arun. *The Indian Press: Profession or Industry*. Delhi: Vikas, 1972.

Birkenhead, Earl of. *Halifax*. London: Hamish Hamilton, 1965.

Bonarjee, N. B. *Under Two Masters*. Bombay: Oxford Press, 1970.

Bose, Arun Coomer. *Indian Revolutionaries Abroad, 1905–1922*. Patna: Bharati Bhawan, 1971.

Bose, Mrinal Kanti. *The Press and Its Problems*. Calcutta: S. C. Sarkar, 1945.

Brown, Judith M. *Gandhi's Rise to Power: Indian Politics, 1915–1922*. Cambridge: Cambridge University Press, 1972.

Bruntz, George C. *Allied Propaganda and the Collapse of the German Empire in 1918*. Stanford: Stanford University Press, 1938.

Chatterji, Jogesh Chandra. *In Search of Freedom*. Calcutta: Paresh Chandra Chatterji, 1967.

Chattopadhyaya, Gautam. *Communism and Bengal's Freedom Movement*. Delhi: People's Publishing House, 1970.

Chopra, Pran Nath. *Rafi Ahmad Kidwai*. Agra: Shiva Lal Agarwals, 1960.

Chopra, P. N., ed. *Who's Who of Indian Martyrs*. 2 vols. New Delhi: Government of India, 1969–1972.

Choudhary, Sukhbir. *Indian People Fight for National Liberation, 1920–1922*. New Delhi: Srijanee Prakashan, 1972.

Communists Challenge: Imperialism From the Dock. Calcutta: National Book Agency, 1967.

Coupland, Reginald. *The Constitutional Problem in India*. London: Humphrey Milford, Oxford University Press, 1944.

Cumming, John, ed. *Political India, 1832–1932*. London: Oxford University Press, 1932.

Daily Pratap, 1919–1969. Delhi: Daily Pratap, 1969.

Das, M. N. *India Under Morley and Minto*. London: George Allen & Unwin, 1964.

Datta, K. K. *History of the Freedom Movement in Bihar*. 3 vols. Patna: Government of Bihar, 1957.

Datta, V. N. *Jallianwala Bagh*. Ludhiana: Lyall Book Depot, 1969.

Deol, Gurdev Singh. *Shaheed Bhagat Singh: A Biography*. Patiala: Punjabi University, 1969.

Dharmavira. *Lala Har Dayal and Revolutionary Movements of His Times*. Delhi: Indian Book Company, 1970.

Dignan, Don K. *New Perspectives on British Far Eastern Policy, 1913–1919*. University of Queensland Papers, Vol. I, No. 5. St. Lucia: 1969.

Dilks, David. *Curzon in India.* 2 vols. London: Rupert Hart Davis, 1969.

Dutta, Kalpana. *Chittagong Armoury Raid Reminiscences.* Bombay: People's Publishing House, 1945.

Easton, David. *A Framework for Political Analysis.* Englewood, N. J.: Prentice-Hall, Inc., 1965.

Farquhar, J. N. *Modern Religious Movements in India.* 2d rev. ed. Delhi: Munshiram Manoharlal, 1967.

Feroze, S. M. A. *Press in Pakistan.* Rev. ed. Lahore: National Publications, 1957.

Gabriel, Almond, and G. Bingham Powell. *Comparative Politics.* Boston: Little, Brown and Company, 1966.

Gallagher, John, Gordon Johnson, and Anil Seal, eds. *Locality, Province and Nation: Essays on Indian Politics, 1870–1940.* Cambridge: Cambridge University Press, 1973.

Gauba, K. L. *Inside Pakistan.* Delhi: Rajkamal, 1948.

Ghose, Akshaya K. *Laws Affecting the Rights and Liberties of the Indian People.* Calcutta: Mohun Brothers, 1921.

Ghose, Hemendra Prasad. *Press and Press Laws in India.* Calcutta: D. K. Mitra, 1930.

Ghosh, K. C. *The Roll of Honour.* Calcutta: Vidya Bharati, 1965.

Ghosh, K. K. *The Indian National Army.* Meerut: Meenakshi Prahashan, 1969.

Gilbert, Martin. *Servant of India.* London: Longmans, Green and Co., Ltd., 1966.

Gopal, S. *The Viceroyalty of Lord Irwin, 1926–1931.* London: Oxford University Press, 1957.

Guha, Arun Chandra. *First Spark of Revolution.* Bombay: Orient Longmans, 1971.

Gupta, Chitra. *Life of Barrister Savarkar.* Madras: B. G. Paul, 1926.

Gupta, Manmathnath. *They Lived Dangerously.* Delhi: People's Publishing House, 1969.

Gwyer, Maurice, and A. Appadorai, eds. *Speeches and Documents on the Indian Constitution, 1921–1947.* 2 vols. Oxford University Press, 1957.

Haithcox, John Patrick. *Communism and Nationalism in India.* Princeton: Princeton University Press, 1971.

Handa, Rajendra Lal. *History of Freedom Struggle in Princely States.* Delhi: Central News Agency, 1968.

Handa, Rajendralal. *Leaves From a Diary.* Bombay: Indian Publishing House, 1968.

Hardikar, N. S. *Lala Lajpat Rai in America.* New Delhi: Servants of the People Society, n.d.

Hardinge, Lord, of Pendhurst. *My Indian Years, 1910–1916*. London: John Murray (Publishers), Ltd., 1948.
The History of Freedom Movement in Madhya Pradesh. Nagpur: Government of Madhya Pradesh, 1950.
Hutchins, Francis G. *Spontaneous Revolution: The Quit India Movement*. Delhi: Manohar Book Service, 1971.
Hyde, H. Montgomery. *Lord Reading*. London: Heinemann, 1967.
India Ravaged. Madras: Indian Press, 1943.
Irshick, Eugene F. *Politics and Social Conflict in South India*. Berkeley: University of California Press, 1969.
Iyer, Vishwanath. *The Indian Press*. Bombay: Padma, 1945.
Jas, Jaswant Singh. *Baba Gurditt Singh*. Panjabi. Jullundur: New Books Company, 1965.
Jha, Manoranjan. *Katherine Mayo and India*. Delhi: People's Publishing House, 1971.
Katju, Kailash Nath. *The Days I Remember*. Calcutta: New Age Publishers, 1961.
Kaushik, Harish. *The Indian National Congress in England, 1885–1920*. Delhi: Research Publications, 1972.
Keer, Dhananjay. *Savarkar and His Times*. Bombay: A. V. Keer, 1950.
Khan, Badshah. *My Life and Struggle*. Delhi: Orient, 1969.
Khodwe, Achyut, ed. *The People's Movement in Hyderabad*. Bombay: c. 1948.
Koss, Stephen E. *John Morley at the India Office, 1905–1910*. New Haven: Yale University Press, 1969.
Krishnamurthy, Nadig. *Indian Journalism*. Prasaranga: University of Mysore, 1966.
Kumar, Ravindar, ed. *Essays on Gandhian Politics: The Rowlatt Satyagraha of 1919*. Oxford: Clarendon Press, 1971.
Lajpat Rai, Lala. *A History of the Arya Samaj*. 2d rev. ed. Bombay: Orient Longmans, 1967.
———. *Lajpat Rai Autobiographical Writings*. Edited by V. C. Joshi. Delhi: University Publishers, 1965.
———. *Lala Lajpat Rai, Writings and Speeches*. Edited by V. C. Joshi. 2 vols. Delhi: University Publishers, 1966.
———. *Young India*. Rev. ed. Delhi: Government of India, 1966.
Lal, Chaman. *British Propaganda in America*. Allahabad: Kitab Mahal, 1945.
Lasswell, Harold Dwight. *Propaganda Technique*. New York: Alfred Knopf & Co., Inc., 1927.
Low, D. A., ed. *Soundings in Modern South Asian History*. Berkeley: University of California, 1968.

Malhotra, S. L. *Gandhi and the Punjab*. Chandigarh: Punjab University, 1970.

Mathur, L. P. *Indian Revolutionary Movement in the United States of America*. New Delhi: S. Chand, 1970.

Mathur, Y. B. *Muslims and Changing India*. New Delhi: Trimurthi Publications, 1972.

Meherally, Yusuf. *The Price of Liberty*. Bombay: National Information and Publications, 1948.

Mehrotra, S. R. *India and the Commonwealth, 1885–1929*. London: George Allen & Unwin, 1965.

Menon, K. B. *The Press Laws of India*. Bombay: 1937.

Minto, Mary, Countess of. *India, Minto and Morley, 1905–1910*. London: Macmillan and Co., Ltd., 1934.

Mishra, Bharat. *Civil Liberty and the Indian National Congress*. Calcutta: Mukhopadhyay, 1969.

Moitra, Mohit. *A History of Indian Journalism*. Calcutta: National Book Agency, 1969.

Molesworth, G. N. *Curfew on Olympics*. Bombay: Asia, 1965.

Mukherjee, Haridas, and Uma Mukherjee. *Bande Mataram and Indian Nationalism, 1906–1908*. Calcutta: K. L. Mukhopadhyay, 1957.

Nanda, B. R., ed. *Socialism in India*. Delhi: Vikas, 1972.

Narain, Prem. *Press and Politics in India, 1885–1905*. Delhi: Munshiram Manoharlal, 1970.

Natarajan, J. *History of Indian Journalism*. New Delhi: Government of India, 1955.

Niblett, R. H. *The Congress Rebellion in Azamgarh, August 1942*. Edited by S. A. Rizvi. Allahabad: Government of Uttar Pradesh, 1957.

Nigam, S. R. *Scotland Yard and the Indian Police*. Allahabad: Kitab Mahal, 1963.

Nizami, Majid. *The Press in Pakistan*. Lahore: Punjab University, 1958.

Noorani, A. G., ed. *Freedom of the Press in India*. Bombay: Nachiketa, 1971.

O'Dwyer, Michael. *India As I Knew It*. London: Constable and Company, Ltd., 1925.

Overstreet, Gene D., and Marshall Windmiller. *Communism in India*. Bombay: Perennial Press, 1960.

Peace, M. L. *Sardar Kartar Singh Jhabbar*. Jullundur: M. L. Peace, n.d.

Phadnis, Urmila. *Towards the Integration of Indian States, 1919–1947*. Bombay: Asia, 1968.

Philips, C. H., ed. *The Evolution of India and Pakistan, 1858–1947*. London: Oxford University Press, 1962.

———, ed. *Politics and Society in India.* London: Allen & Unwin, 1963.

Prakasa, Sri. *Annie Besant As Woman and As Leader.* Bombay: Bharatiya Vidya Bhavan, 1962.

Pyarelal. *A Pilgrimage for Peace: Gandhi and Frontier Gandhi Among N.W.F. Pathans.* Ahmedabad: Navajivan Publishing House, 1950.

Ramesan, N., ed. *The Freedom Struggle in Hyderabad.* 4 vols. Hyderabad: Government of Andhra Pradesh, 1960–1965.

Rao, K. Rama. *The Pen As My Sword.* Bombay: Bharatiya Vidya Bhavan, 1965.

Rao, M. V. Ramana. *A Short History of the Indian National Congress.* Delhi: S. Chand, 1959.

Rau, M. Chalapathi. *The Press in India.* Bombay: Allied Publishers, 1968.

Read, James Morgan. *Atrocity Propaganda, 1914–1919, in the World War.* New Haven, Conn.: Yale University Press, 1941.

Resolutions of the All-India Newspaper Editors' Conference from 1940–1967. Delhi: All-India N.E.C., 1967.

Roy, Bijoy Prasad Singh. *Parliamentary Government in India.* Calcutta: Thacker, Spink and Company, 1943.

Roy, G. K. *Law Relating to Press and Sedition.* Simla: 1915.

———. *Law Relating to Press and Sedition.* 2d ed. Calcutta: Hare Press, 1922.

Roy, M. N. *M. N. Roy's Memoirs.* Bombay: Allied Publishers, 1964.

Sahni, Ruchi Ram. *The Gurdwara Reform Movement and the Sikh Awakening.* Jullundur: Desh Sewak Book Agency, 1922.

Samanta, Satish Chandra, et al. *August Revolution in Midnapore, 1942–44, Pt. 1.* Calcutta: Orient Book Company, 1946.

Saraf, Mulk Raj. *Fifty Years as a Journalist.* Jammu: Raj Mahal Publishers, 1967.

Sarin, Dharam Paul. *Influence of Political Movements on Hindi Literature, 1906–1947.* Chandigarh: Punjab University, 1967.

Sarkar, S. C. *Notable Indian Trials.* 2d ed. Calcutta: M. C. Sarkar and Sons, 1948.

Sen, S. P., ed. *Dictionary of National Biography.* 4 vols. Calcutta: Institute of Historical Research, 1972–1974.

———, ed. *The Indian Press.* Calcutta: Institute of Historical Studies, 1967.

Sen, Sunil. *Agrarian Struggle in Bengal, 1946–1947.* New Delhi: People's Publishing House, 1972.

Shakir, Moin. *Khilafat to Partition.* New Delhi: Kalamkar Prakashan, 1970.

Sharma, Sri Ram. *Punjab in Ferment.* New Delhi: S. Chand and Company, 1971.

Sharma, Jagdish. *Encyclopaedia of India's Struggle for Freedom.* Delhi: S. Chand, 1971.

Sharma, Jagdish Saran. *The National Biographical Dictionary of India.* New Delhi: Sterling Publishers, 1972.

Singh, Ganda. *History of the Gurdwara Shahidganj, Lahore, From Its Origin to November 1935.* Lahore: 1935.

———, ed. *Some Confidential Papers of the Akali Movement.* Amritsar: Shromani Gurdwara Parbandak Committee, 1965.

Singh, Gulab. *Under the Shadow of Gallows: Story of a Revolutionary.* 2d ed. New Delhi: Rup Chand, 1964.

Singh, Jagjit. *Ghadar Parti Lahir* (Panjabi). Amritsar: Sudarshan Press, 1955.

Singh, Khushwant. *Ghadar, 1915.* New Delhi: R and K Publishing House, 1966.

Singh, Sangat. *Freedom Movement in Delhi.* New Delhi: Associated Publishing House, 1972.

Singh, Sohan ("Josh"). *Baba Sohan Singh Bhakna: Life of the Founder of the Ghadar Party.* New Delhi: People's Publishing House, 1970.

Sitaramayya, Pattabhai. *The History of the Indian National Congress.* 2 vols. Bombay: Padmai Publishers, 1935–1947.

Smith, Wilfred Cantwell. *Modern Islam in India.* 2d rev. ed. Lahore: Ashraf, 1969.

Sperry, Earl E. *German Plots and Intrigues.* Washington, D.C.: Committee on Public Information, n.d.

Spratt, Phillip. *Blowing Up India.* Calcutta: Prachi Prakashan, 1955.

Suri, Vidya Sagar. *A Brief Biographical Sketch of Sohan Lal Pathak.* Patiala: Punjabi University, 1968.

Syngal, Munnalal. *The Patriot Prince.* Ludhiana: Doaba House, 1961.

Templewood, Viscount. *Nine Troubled Years.* London: William Collins Sons & Co., Ltd., 1954.

The Trial of Bal Gangadhar Tilak: The Kesari Prosecution, 1908. Madras: Ganesh and Company, n.d.

Tunney, Thomas J. *Throttled: The Detection of the German and Anarchist Bomb Plotters.* Boston: Small, Maynard and Company, 1919.

Venkatarangaiya, M., ed. *The Freedom Struggle in Andhra*

Pradesh. 3 vols. Hyderabad: Andhra Pradesh State Committee, 1962–1965.

"Victor Trench." *Lord Willingdon in India*. Bombay: Samuel A. Ezekiel, 1934.

Viereck, George Sylvester. *Spreading Germs of Hate*. New York: Horace Liveright, 1930.

Waley, S. D. *Edwin Montagu*. Bombay: Asia, 1964.

Walter, H. A. *The Ahmadiya Movement*. Calcutta: Association Press, 1918.

Wasti, Syed Razi. *Lord Minto and the Indian Nationalist Movement, 1905–1910*. Oxford: Clarendon Press, 1964.

Wolpert, Stanley A. *Morley and India, 1906–1910*. Berkeley: University of California Press, 1970.

———. *Tilak and Gokhale*. Berkeley: University of California Press, 1967.

Yajnik, Indulal. *Shyamaji Krishnavarma*. Bombay: Lakshmi Publications, 1950.

Yunus, Mohammad. *Frontier Speaks*. Lahore: Minerva Book Shop, 1942.

Yusufi, Allah Bakhsh. *Life of Maulana Mohamed Ali Jauhar*. Karachi: Mohamed Ali Education Society, 1970.

Zutshi, G. L. *Frontier Gandhi*. Delhi: National, 1970.

Articles

Banerjee, Kalyann Kumar. "East Indian Immigration into America." *Modern Review*, 116 (1964), 356–61.

———. "The Indo-German Conspiracy—Declining Phase." *Modern Review*, 119 (1966), 26–30.

———. "The U.S.A. and Indian Revolutionary Activity." *Modern Review*, 117 (1965), 97–101.

Barrier, Norman Gerald. "The Arya Samaj and Congress Politics." *The Journal of Asian Studies*, 28 (1968–1969), 339–56.

———. "How to Rule India." *Panjab Past and Present*, 5 (1971), 276–96.

———. "The Punjab Disturbances of 1907." *Modern Asian Studies*, 1 (1967), 353–83.

———. "The Punjab Government and Communal Politics, 1870–1908." *The Journal of Asian Studies*, 27 (1967–1968), 523–39.

———. "The Sikh Resurgence, 1849–1947." *The Indian Archives*, 18 (1969), 46–63.

———. "South Asia in Vernacular Publications." *The Journal of Asian Studies*, 28 (1968–1969), 803–10.

———, and G. R. Thursby. "South Asian Proscribed Publications, 1907–1947." *The Indian Archives*, 18 (1969), 24–53.

Belgaumi, Mahmud. "The Razakar Movement." *Journal of the Panjab University Historical Society*, 14 (December 1962), 1–15.

Cumpston, Mary. "Some Early Indian Nationalists and Their Allies in The British Parliament." *The English Historical Review*, 76 (1961).

Dignan, Don K. "The Hindu Conspiracy in Anglo-American Relations During World War I." *Pacific Historical Review*, 40 (1971), 57–76.

Ellinwood, Dewitt. "The Round Table Movement and India, 1909–1920." *Journal of Commonwealth Political Studies*, 9 (1971), 183–209.

Jones, Kenneth W. "Communalism in the Punjab." *The Journal of Asian Studies*, 28 (1968–1969), 39–54.

———. "Sources for Arya Samaj History." *The Indian Archives*, 18 (1969), 20–36.

Low, D. A. "The Government of India and the First Non-Cooperation Movement." *The Journal of Asian Studies*, 25 (1965–1966), 241–60.

Naidis, Mark. "Propaganda of the Gadar Party." *Pacific Historical Review*, 20 (1951), 251–60.

Reeves, P. D. "The Politics of Order." *The Journal of Asian Studies*, 25 (1965–1966).

Sarkar, Sumit. "Hindu-Muslim Relations in Swadeshi Bengal." *The Indian Economic and Social History Review*, 9 (1972), 161–216.

Singh, Ganda, ed. "The Akali Dal and Shiromani Gurdwara Parbandak Committee, 1921–1922." *Panjab Past and Present*, 1 (1967), 252–310.

Tucker, Richard. "The Proper Limits of Politics." *The Journal of Asian Studies*, 28 (1968–1969), 339–56.

Manuscripts, Unpublished Essays

Barrier, Norman Gerald. "The Punjab Disturbances of 1907." Ph.D. diss., Duke University, 1966.

Cashman, Richard Ian. "The Politics of Mass Recruitment." Ph.D. diss., Duke University, 1969.

Coghlan, Heather T. "The Role of the Council of India, 1898–1910." Ph.D. diss., Duke University, 1971.

Graham, Gail Minault. "The Khilafat Movement." Ph.D. diss., University of Pennsylvania, 1972.

———. "Urdu Political Poetry During the Khilafat Movement." Paper presented at the Western Regional Conference of the Association for Asian Studies, November 1972.

Lavan, Spencer. "The Ahmadiyah Movement." Ph.D. diss., McGill University, 1970.

Ramusack, Barbara Neil. "Exotic Imports or Homegrown Riots: The Kashmir Disturbances of the Early 1930's." Paper presented at the Punjab Conference, 1971.

———. "Indian Princes as Imperial Politicians, 1914–1939." Ph.D. diss., University of Michigan, 1969.

Singh, Diwakar Prasad. "American Official Attitudes Toward the Indian Nationalist Movement, 1905–1929." Ph.D. diss., University of Hawaii, 1964.

Spangenburg, Bradford. "Status and Policy: The Character of the Covenanted Civil Service of India and Its Ramifications for British Administration and Policy in the Late Nineteenth Century." Ph.D. diss., Duke University, 1967.

Stanwood, Frederick Jullian. "Britain in Central Asia, 1917–1919." Ph.D. diss., University of California, San Diego, 1971.

Thursby, Gene. "Aspects of Hindu–Muslim Relations in British India." Ph.D. diss., Duke University, 1972.

AUTHOR INDEX

SUBJECT INDEX